AF352123

Welfare State Transformations

Also by Martin Seeleib-Kaiser:

AMERIKANISCHE SOZIALPOLITIK

GLOBALISIERUNG UND SOZIALPOLITIK

SOZIAL- UND WIRTSCHAFTSPOLITIK UNTER ROT-GRÜN (ed. with A. Gohr)

THE DUAL TRANSFORMATION OF THE GERMAN WELFARE STATE (with P. Bleses)

PARTY POLITICS AND SOCIAL WELFARE : Comparing Christian and Social Democracy in Austria, Germany and the Netherlands (with S. van Dyk and M. Roggenkamp)

Welfare State Transformations

Comparative Perspectives

Edited by

Martin Seeleib-Kaiser
University of Oxford, UK

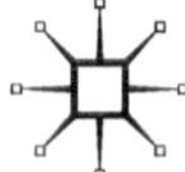

First published 2008 by
PALGRAVE MACMILLAN
Houndmills, Basingstoke, Hampshire RG21 6XS and
175 Fifth Avenue, New York, N.Y. 10010
Companies and representatives throughout the world

PALGRAVE MACMILLAN is the global academic imprint of the Palgrave
Macmillan division of St. Martin's Press, LLC and of Palgrave Macmillan Ltd.
Macmillan® is a registered trademark in the United States, United Kingdom
and other countries. Palgrave is a registered trademark in the European
Union and other countries.

ISBN-13: 978–0–230–20578–9   hardback
ISBN-10 HB: 0–230–20578–X   hardback

This book is printed on paper suitable for recycling and made from fully managed
and sustained forest sources. Logging, pulping and manufacturing processes are
expected to conform to the environmental regulations of the country of origin.

A catalogue record for this book is available from the British Library.

A catalog record for this book is available from the Library of Congress.

10   9   8   7   6   5   4   3   2   1
17   16   15   14   13   12   11   10   09   08

Printed and bound in Great Britain by
CPI Antony Rowe, Chippenham and Eastbourne

Contents

List of Figures

List of Tables

Acknowledgements

Contributions to this book were first presented in a seminar series at the Department of Social Policy and Social Work, University of Oxford, during Winter/Spring 2006. Revised versions and additional contributions were discussed at a workshop in Green College, University of Oxford, in Autumn 2006. The graduate students and colleagues who participated in the seminar series and the workshop have greatly enriched many contributions and have contributed significantly to this project – thank you to all of you. As always collaborative work such as this would not be feasible without institutional and financial support, for which I want to thank Green College and the British Academy. Many thanks to two of my DPhil students, Pavel Ovseiko and Marek Naczyk – without their research support and organizational talent this project would not have been possible. Last not least, I thank the authors for their great collaborative spirit.

List of Contributors

Jørgen Goul Andersen is Professor of Political Sociology and Director of the Centre for Comparative Welfare Studies (CCWS) at Aalborg University, Denmark. His main research areas are comparative welfare studies, electoral behaviour, and political participation. Among his recent publications in English are authored and co-edited volumes, such as *The Changing Face of Welfare: Consequences and Outcomes from a Citizenship Perspective* (Policy Press, 2005), *Europe's New State of Welfare: Unemployment, Employment Policies and Citizenship* (Policy Press, 2002); *Changing Labour Markets, Welfare Policies and Citizenship* (Policy Press, 2002); and *Democracy and Citizenship in Scandinavia* (Palgrave, 2001).

Dalia Ben-Galim is a DPhil candidate in the Department of Social Policy and Social Work at the University of Oxford. Her DPhil is focused on work–life balance policies and connects to wider debates about work, families, children and equality. She is co-author of: 'Equality and Diversity: A New Approach to Gender Equality Policy in the UK', *International Journal of Law in Context*, (2007) 3(1): 19–33.

Paul Bridgen is a Senior Lecturer in social policy at the University of Southampton. He was the joint academic coordinator (with T. Meyer) of the EU fifth framework project on private pensions and social inclusion, on which the chapter in this volume is based. On the basis of this project, he has also recently edited and contributed to *Private Pensions versus Social Inclusion?* (Edward Elgar, 2007), an assessment of the social inclusiveness of six public private pension regimes in Europe (with T. Meyer and B. Riedmüller). He is currently working (with T. Meyer) on a project on occupational pension in Britain and Germany as part of the Anglo-German Foundation's 'Creating Sustainable Growth in Europe' research initiative. He has also published widely on developments in British social policy from the end of the Second World War to the present day.

Mirella Cacace is a Research Fellow and PhD candidate at the Collaborative Research Center 597 'Transformations of the State' at the University of Bremen. Areas of her expertise include: international comparison of health-care systems, health-care economics and new institutional economics. Her most recent publications are: 'The Coexistence of Market and Hierarchy in the US Healthcare System', in H. Rothgang, M. Cacace, S. Grimmeisen and C. Wendt (eds), *The Changing Role of the State in OECD Health Care Systems. From Heterogeneity to Homogeneity?* (Palgrave Macmillan, forthcoming 2008); and with H. Rothgang, S. Grimmeisen and C. Wendt, 'The Changing Role of the State in OECD Health Care Systems', in Stephan Leibfried and Michael Zürn (eds), *Transformations of the State?* (Cambridge University Press, 2005).

John Clarke is Professor of Social Policy at the Open University where his research and teaching interests remain focused on struggles over the future of welfare states. Recent publications include *Changing Welfare, Changing States* (Sage, 2004) and *Creating Citizen-Consumers* (with J. Newman, N. Smith, E. Vidler and L. Westmarland) (Sage, 2007). He has also guest-edited a special issue of the journal *Cultural Studies* (November 2007) on the theme of 'Governing the Social'.

Daniel Clegg is a Lecturer in Social Policy at the University of Edinburgh. His research is focused on labour market policy and welfare state reform in comparative perspective. Recent publications include 'Beyond activation: reforming unemployment protection systems in post-industrial labour markets', *European Societies,* Volume 8(4), 2006 (with Jochen Clasen) and 'Continental Drift: On unemployment policy change in Bismarckian welfare states', in *Social Policy & Administration*, Volume 41(6), 2007.

Lorraine Frisina is a Research Associate at the Collaborative Research Institute 597 'Transformations of the State' at the University of Bremen. Her main research areas concern comparative health-care policy, particularly the cases of Great Britain and Italy. Selected recent works are: 'The Problem of Classification in the Social Sciences', with Richard Freeman, in *Journal of Comparative Policy and Analysis* (forthcoming 2008); 'Identifying Value Change in the Healthcare Systems of Great Britain, Germany and the US', with Klaus Albrecht in Heinz Rothgang et al., *The Changing Role of the State in OECD Healthcare Systems* (Palgrave Macmillan, forthcoming 2008); *Understanding Regional Development: Absorption Institutions, and Socio-economic Growth in the European Union: A Case Study on the Italian Regions* (Peter Lang, forthcoming 2008).

Richenda Gambles is a Departmental Lecturer in the Department of Social Policy and Social Work, University of Oxford. Her research interests focus on gendered dynamics of family, informal care and paid employment. She has published a number of journal articles and book chapters in this area and has recently co-authored with Suzan Lewis and Rhona Rapoport *The Myth of Work–Life Balance: The Challenge of Our Time for Men, Women and Societies* (London: Wiley).

Roger Goodman is Nissan Professor of Modern Japanese Studies at the University of Oxford, attached to both the Institute of Social and Cultural Anthropology and the Nissan Institute of Japanese Studies. He is also Head of the Social Sciences Division at Oxford University. His main research interests are in Japanese education and social policy, especially child welfare. He has also done comparative research in South Korea and the UK and his current research topics include: higher education reform, international education, child abuse and child protection. He is the author of *Japan's 'International Youth': The Emergence of a New Class of Schoolchildren* (Oxford University Press, 1990; Japanese version published by Iwanami Shoten in 1992) and *Children of the Japanese State: The Changing Role of Child Protection Institutions in Contemporary Japan* (Oxford University Press, 2000; Japanese version published by Akashi Shoten, 2004), and the editor or co-editor of numerous volumes including, most recently: *Ageing in Asia* (Routledge, 2007), *2004 and the 'Big Bang' in Japanese Higher Education* (Transpacific Press, 2005); *Global Japan: The Experience of Japan's New Minorities and Overseas Communities* (RoutledgeCurzon, 2003); *Can the Japanese Reform Their Education System?* (Symposium Books, 2002); *Family and Social Policy in Japan: Anthropological Approaches* (Cambridge University Press, 2002); and *The East Asian Welfare Model: Welfare Orientalism and the State* (Routledge, 1998).

Ana M. Guillén is Professor of Sociology at the University of Oviedo, where she teaches comparative social policy. She has written extensively on welfare state development, health policy and comparative social policy (published in English, Spanish, French, German, Italian, Greek, Portuguese, Turkish and Korean). Recently, she has written the report on Spain for the Finnish Presidency of the EU (published as a book chapter in *The Europeanisation of Social Protection*, (eds) J. Kvist and J. Saari, Policy Press, 2007). She has co-edited the special issue of the *Journal of European Social Policy* entitled *EU Enlargement, Europeanization and Social Policy*, Volume 14(3), 2007. In 1998–99 she was a participant in the European University Institute's 'European Forum: Recasting the European Welfare State'. She has acted as a consultant to the European Commission and the International Labour Organization. She is a member of the executive boards of ESPAnet and Research Committee 19 of the ISA. Currently she is doing research on the working poor, the reform of Bismarckian welfare states, and participating as coordinator within the Network of Excellence 'Reconciling work and welfare in the EU', RECWOWE.

Peter A. Kemp is the Barnett Professor of Social Policy in the Department of Social Policy and Social Work and a professorial fellow of St Cross College, University of Oxford. His research interests include housing, social security and income maintenance. Recent publications include *Private Renting in Transition* (2004); *Sick Societies? Trends in Disability Benefits in Post-industrial Societies* (2006); *Cash and Care: Policy Challenges in the Welfare State* (2006); and *Housing Allowances in Comparative Perspective* (2007).

Traute Meyer is Professorial Fellow in Social Policy at the University of Southampton. She has participated in international research projects in the area of pensions, informal and care work, and has published widely in these fields. She is one of the editors of the *European Journal of Social Policy*. Most recently she has edited *Private Pensions versus Social Inclusion?*, an assessment of the social inclusiveness of six public private pension regimes in Europe (with P. Bridgen and B. Riedmüller).

Maria Petmesidou is Professor of Social Policy at Democritus University of Thrace. Her former position was Head of the Department of Sociology at the University of Crete. From 2002 to 2006 she was Vice-Chair of CROP (Comparative Research on Poverty, a programme of the International Social Science Council). Her research interests focus on comparative analysis of social inequalities, poverty and social welfare in Southern Europe (as well as in the countries around the Mediterranean Sea). Her book publications include: *Social Classes and Processes of Social Reproduction* (Exandas, 1987, in Greek); *Planning Technological Change and Economic Development in Greece* (with L. Tsoulouvis) (Pergamon Press/Progress in Planning Series, Volume 33, 1990); *Social Inequalities and Social Policy* (Exandas, 1991, in Greek); *Modern Sociological Theory* (ed., Volumes I & II, Crete University Press, in Greek); *Poverty and Social Exclusion* (ed. with C. Papatheodorou, Exandas, 1997/98, in Greek); *Social Policy Developments in Greece* (ed. with E. Mossialos, Ashgate, 2006); *Poverty and Social Deprivation in the Mediterranean Area: Trends, Policies and Welfare Prospects in the New Millennium* (ed. with C. Papatheodorou, Zed Books, 2006).

Martin Potůček is Professor of Public and Social Policy and Head of the Center for Social and Economic Strategies at Charles University Prague, Faculty of Social Sciences and Permanent Guest Professor, University of Constance, Germany. He concentrates on the research of processes of forming and implementing public and social policy, and particularly on the regulatory functions of the market, government and civic sector, as well as on the European context and global dimension of public and social policy. He is, among others, the author, editor and co-author of the following books: *Not Only the Market; Public Policy in Central and Eastern Europe: Theories, Methods, Approaches, Capacities to Govern in Central and Eastern Europe; Strategic Governance and the Czech Republic.* He coordinates the comprehensive forecasting projects at the national level and the Excellence Sub-programme of the EU's 6th FP 'Civil Society and New Forms of Governance in Europe – the Making of European Citizenship'. He has been active as an adviser to the Prime Minister and two Ministers of Labour and Social Affairs in the Czech Republic since 1998.

Martin Powell is Professor of Health and Social Policy at the Health Services Management Centre, University of Birmingham. His research interests include the theory and history of welfare states, and the mixed economy of welfare. He is the editor of *New Labour, New Welfare State?* (Policy Press, 1999) and *Understanding the Mixed Economy of Welfare* (Policy Press, 2007).

Heinz Rothgang is Professor of Health Economics at the University of Bremen and Director of the Division for Health Economics, Health Policy and Outcomes Research, Centre for Social Policy Research, Bremen. His research interests are in the fields of health economics, health-care systems, long-term care insurance, and welfare economics in general. He has been a member of the core team of the EUROFAMCARE project on family carers, funded by the EU. At the Collaborative Research Center 'Transformations of the State' (CRC/Sfb 597) he is heading a project dealing with the transformation of OECD health-care systems since the 1970s. He also acts as a policy consultant. He has published widely in social policy and health journals. Selected recent book publications include: *Governance of Welfare State Reform. A Cross National and Cross Sectoral Comparison of Health, Pension, Labour Market and Educational Policies* (co-edited with Irene Dingeldey, Edward Elgar, forthcoming); *The Changing Role of the State in OECD Healthcare Systems. From Heterogeneity to Homogeneity?* (co-authored with Mirella Cacace, Simone Grimmeisen, Uwe Helmert and Claus Wendt, Palgrave Macmillan, forthcoming); *Financing, Service Provision and Regulation in OECD Health Care Systems. A Comparison of 12 OECD Countries* (co-edited with Mirella Cacace, Simone Grimmeisen and Claus Wendt, Open University Press, forthcoming).

Achim Schmid is Research Fellow and PhD candidate at the Collaborative Research Center 597 'Transformations of the State' at the University of Bremen. His main areas of research include comparative social policy and the comparison of health-care systems. Recent publications are, with Mirella Cacace and Heinz Rothgang (forthcoming 2008) 'The Changing Role of the State in Health Care Financing', in Heinz Rothgang et al. *The Changing Role of the State in OECD Healthcare Systems*; with Claus Wendt and Uwe Helmert 'The Changing Role of the State in Health Care Service Provision', in Heinz Rothgang et al. *The Changing Role of the State in OECD Healthcare Systems* (Palgrave Macmillan, forthcoming); with Richard Freeman 'Health Care Systems of Western Europe,' in Kris Heggenhougen (ed.) *International Encyclopedia of Public Health* (Elsevier).

Martin Seeleib-Kaiser is Reader in Comparative Social Policy and Politics at the University of Oxford and Fellow of Green College. Prior to his appointment at Oxford in 2004, he held appointments at the universities of Bremen and Bielefeld (Germany) as well as Duke University (North Carolina, USA). His research focuses on comparative welfare state analysis, with a special focus on the role of political parties and ideas, the relationship between globalization and welfare systems, as well as more recently on the interplay between 'public' and 'private' social policies. English language book publications include: *The Dual Transformation of the German Welfare State* (co-authored with Peter Bleses, Palgrave Macmillan 2004) and *Party Politics and Social Welfare: Comparing Christian and Social Democracy in Austria, Germany and the Netherlands* (co-authored with Silke van Dyk and Martin Roggenkamp, Edward Elgar, 2008). His journal articles have been published in among others *American Sociological Review, Politische Vierteljahresschrift, Social Policy and Administration, West European Politics,* and *Zeitschrift für Soziologie.*

1
Welfare State Transformations in Comparative Perspective: Shifting Boundaries of 'Public' and 'Private' Social Policy?

Martin Seeleib-Kaiser

Introduction

The dividing line between the 'public' and the 'private' is not fixed, but usually contested and constantly renegotiated (cf. Shonfield, 1965). During the so-called golden era of welfare state capitalism, direct *public* provision of social policy was perceived as the core element for the realization of 'social citizenship' (Marshall, 1950), social integration or the reduction of poverty by a majority of political actors and social scientists in Western Europe. Although the family, voluntary organizations and the market had been identified in addition to the state as constituent parts of the mixed economy of welfare very early on, the attention within public debates and academic analyses has been on the nation *state* as a financier and provider of social policy (Titmuss, 1958). Over the past two decades, however, public debates in many countries and international organizations have shifted, calling for a greater emphasis on private arrangements, said to be mainly resulting from a combination of three socio-economic developments: globalization, rapidly ageing societies and individualization.

In this context globalization is often perceived as restraining the state's autonomy to tax and thus limit the financial resources for public social policy provision. Although social policy is still *mainly* determined by domestic factors and globalization can affect welfare states in very different ways (Brady et al., 2005), globalization has figured prominently in many political discourses as a justification for 'unavoidable' welfare state adjustments, including an increased emphasis on private arrangements (Seeleib-Kaiser, 2001; Schmidt, 2002). Significant demographic changes, i.e. increases in average life expectancies and decreasing fertility rates, have been identified as major factors contributing to increased levels of public social expenditure, especially in the areas of old-age pensions and health care, while at the same time reducing the percentage of the economically 'active' population. In the light of these processes some observers have argued that public pension systems in a number of countries have become unsustainable and thus expanding complementary private pension provisions was identified as a necessity (World Bank, 1994). The process of individualization – partly the result of successful welfare state intervention – across post-industrial countries has allegedly turned (universal) public provision of benefits and services (largely based on a typical male life course) into an approach not fit for purpose, as the needs of people have diversified and their desire for choice has increased. In order to meet the needs and preferences of the people, more choices, including private arrangements, need to be made available (Giddens, 1998). Finally, the classic liberal argument, whereby private solutions are economically superior to public intervention, gained considerable political strength in many countries for an ever larger proportion of policies during the 1980s and 1990s (for a critical assessment see Jordan, 2006).

Despite years of debate, most research on the shifting boundaries between 'public' and 'private' social policy has centred around normative or functional perspectives and has stayed at a rather theoretical level (cf. Pearson and Martin, 2005; Gilbert, 2005). Consequently, we do not know empirically how far the pendulum has swung from 'public' to 'private' or to put it differently, whether we can speak of an increased privatization of social risks that has led to a transformation of welfare states. Thus, the aim of this book is not to add further to the literature focusing on whether we *should* or *should not* extend the role of private provision and responsibility for social protection, but to empirically analyse the development of social policies from a comparative perspective with special attention given to the redefinition of the mixed economy of welfare.

Public and private social policies from a comparative perspective

Although titles such as 'Decline of the Public' (Marquand, 2004) or the 'Silent Surrender of Public Responsibility' (Gilbert, 2002) suggest that, nation states have undergone a profound reconfiguration of the public sphere and public responsibility, path dependence and incrementalism were identified by comparative welfare state scholars as characterizing welfare state developments up to the early 2000s (cf. Pierson, 2001a). Overall a notion of 'frozen welfare state landscapes' (Esping-Andersen, 1996b, p. 24) and regime stability (Esping-Andersen, 1999; Esping-Andersen et al., 2002) has dominated academic debates in comparative social policy for years; however, more recent evidence from a variety of countries as well as policy areas seems to question the status quo findings of earlier studies (cf. Bleses and Seeleib-Kaiser, 2004; Taylor-Gooby, 2004a; Clasen, 2005; Streeck and Thelen, 2005a). To some extent the differing assessments of policy changes and continuities result from different theoretical conceptualizations as well as different ways of measuring the dependent variable (Clasen and Siegel, 2007).

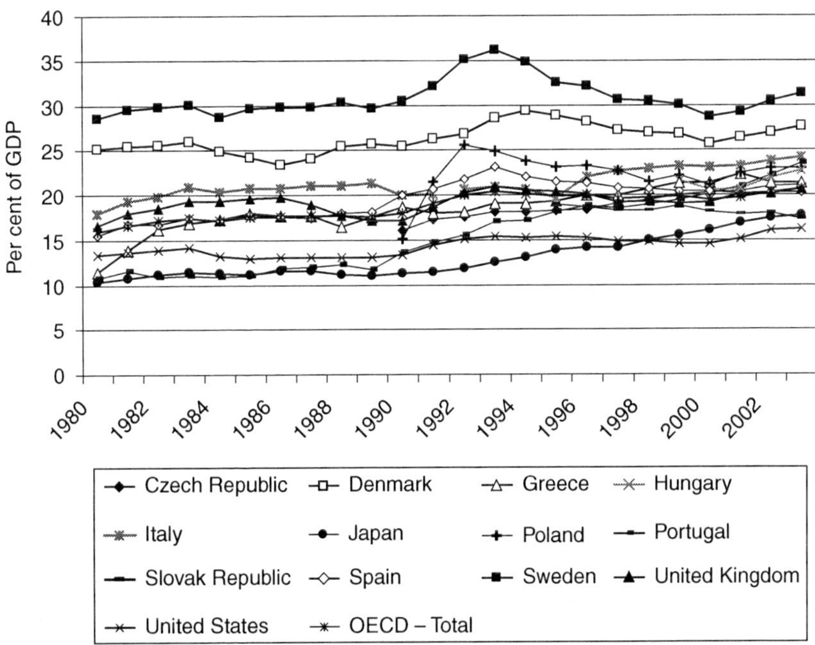

Figure 1.1　Public social expenditure of selected OECD countries as a percentage of GDP (1980–2003)
Source: OECD (2007b).

For some time *public* social spending and provision have been treated as the gold standard of comparative social policy analysis (cf. Kittel and Obinger, 2003). Building on this approach and taking public social expenditure as the dependent variable, one could argue that overall the public social policy effort in the OECD world has not declined during the past two decades; moreover, we are witnessing a convergence of spending efforts. While Scandinavian as well as comprehensive Continental European welfare states seem to have grown to their limits (Flora, 1986) and encountered some 'minor' spending reductions in the latter part of the 1990s,[1] Southern European countries and Japan have clearly increased their public spending efforts for social policies. And only a little more than a decade after the demise of Communism some of the Central European countries, such as the Czech Republic, Hungary and Poland spend more than the OECD average (see Figure 1.1).

This picture is complicated, however, by the fact that recent policy changes, differences in economic growth, and increased social needs are not sufficiently taken into account by an isolated analysis of public social spending data (cf. Clayton and Pontusson, 1998; Siegel, 2002). The effect economic growth can have on public social policy expenditure as a proportion of GDP is highlighted in a recent study on Japan by Kasza (2006, pp. 61 ff.), showing that, despite its seemingly low level of public social spending in a comparative perspective from the 1960s to the 1980s, the average growth rate in real social expenditure far outstripped the high growth rate of real GDP. *Ceteris paribus*, had Japan witnessed an economic growth more in line with other industrialized countries in Europe and North America during this period, the OECD would have recorded much higher public social policy efforts. In a similar vein, the comparatively high economic growth in the two most prominent liberal market economies, the United Kingdom and the United States of America, since the second half of the 1990s, will most likely have had a 'negative' effect on the reported social policy spending data for these countries. Finally, within the realm of pension policies, recent policy changes will most likely not be reflected in the current spending data, as these are usually to be phased in over longer periods of time.

To cope with the limitations of using spending data as a proxy for the comprehensiveness of the welfare state Offe (1984) suggested the concept of decommodification. Esping-Andersen (1990) has developed the concept further based on the notion of social citizenship, i.e. taking into account eligibility rules and replacement rates within social transfer programmes. According to Esping-Andersen (ibid., pp. 21–2) decommodification refers to the ability of a person 'to maintain a livelihood without the reliance on the market'. Subsequent comparative research picked-up on the criticism and primarily relied on three dimensions of welfare state change: retrenchment, recommodification, and recalibration (Pierson, 2001a; cf. Korpi, 2003; Korpi and Palme, 2003). Retrenchment is largely about, but not limited to, spending reductions, as it also aims at changing the conditions of future policy making that enhance the probability of a residual welfare state model, and is said to become a defining element of policy in an 'era of austerity'. Recommodification can be understood as the flip side of decommodification. Obviously, even in Scandinavian countries citizens were never fully decommodified, especially since these countries relied on a very strong tradition with regard to the duty to work. Nevertheless, recommodification can be characterized as a process leading to a greater reliance on the market, which may include reductions in benefit levels and/or restrictions of eligibility criteria. However, the process of recommodification is not limited to reducing state intervention; moreover, it can also entail new social policy programmes. For instance, to increase (low-wage) workers' and/or welfare recipients' participation in the labour market the process of recommodification might also entail new instruments, such as tax incentives and workfare or activation schemes (cf. Neyer and Seeleib-Kaiser, 1995). Recalibration is usually understood as an approach that 'updates' or 'rationalizes' social policy programmes to conform more closely to changed goals and demands for social policy provision.

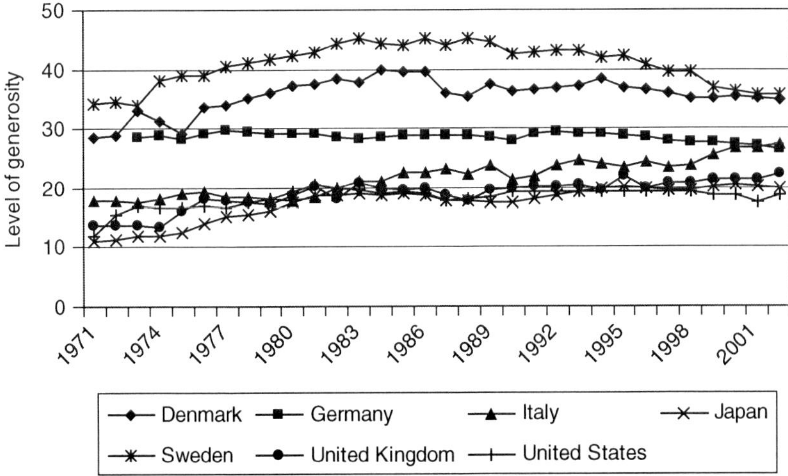

Figure 1.2 Welfare state generosity
Source: Scruggs (2004).

Recently, Scruggs (2004) has constructed a generosity index, very similar to Esping-Andersen's decommodification concept, based on unemployment, sickness, and pension programmes, reflecting such issues as replacement rates, coverage, waiting days, etc. for the time period since the early 1970s (see Figure 1.2). His data portrays a similar development as the public expenditure data, that is, we see an expansion in generosity within countries that in the past had rather restrictive approaches to public social policy and retrenchment in Scandinavian countries, which seems especially strong in Sweden, thus demonstrating convergence, rather than clear retrenchment of *public* social policies or processes or recommodification across the board.[2] Based on these aggregate, comparative data the increased emphasis in policy debates on the need to scale back public provision was not very effective. Moreover, to some extent we are even able to talk of an upward convergence (Obinger and Starke, 2007), implicitly demonstrating the attractiveness of the European Social Model (Kaelble and Schmid, 2004). However, it has to be emphasized that this data is limited to *current* cash transfer benefits and does not take into account any developments in the important dimensions of health care or social services. Overall, it is argued that 'left parties' in countries with comprehensive welfare states are limited in further expanding welfare states due to economic constraints, while 'right parties' cannot significantly curtail public social policies, due to popular support for social programmes among the electorate (Huber and Stephens, 2001).

Taking the notion of a Keynesian welfare state, with public responsibility for full employment at its core, we should also take the unemployment rate

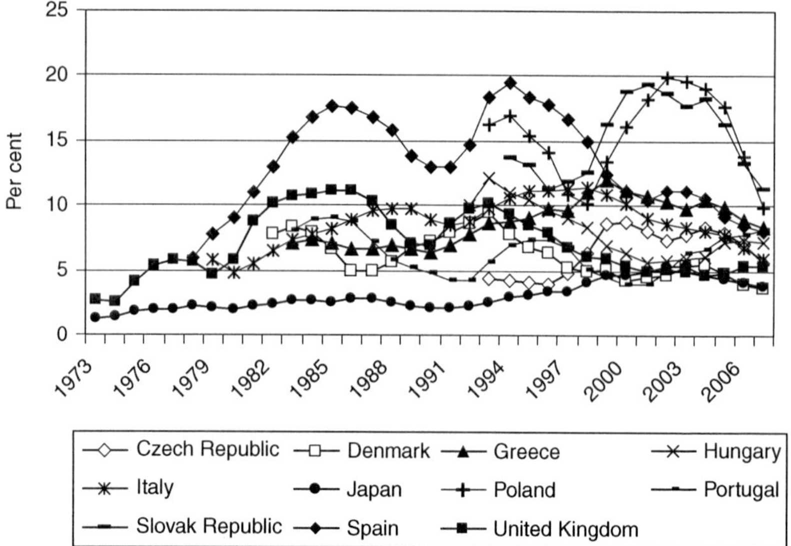

Figure 1.3   Standardized unemployment rates in selected OECD countries
Note: Data for 2007, second quarter.
Source: OECD data extracted on 2007/11/14 10:46 from OECD Stat.

into account within our analysis. Persistent mass unemployment would have
to be interpreted as retrenchment of public welfare state provision (Korpi,
2003; Korpi and Palme, 2003). The data of the selected OECD countries shows
that overall unemployment has declined significantly in recent years, but for
most countries it continues to be at levels well above those reached in the
'golden welfare state era' (see Figure 1.3).

Governments in many OECD countries increasingly perceive the various compensatory approaches to unemployment pursued in the 1980s and
1990s[3] as detrimental to the sustainability of welfare states and have introduced 'activation' measures (limiting eligibility criteria, enforcing stricter
conditionality rules, as well as changing the regulatory framework and offering more services), with the aim of reducing the dependency ratio, that
is, the percentage of people receiving income transfers, while simultaneously increasing the employment ratio (OECD, 2005a). To some extent one
might categorize 'activation' as constituting a process of recommodification,
i.e. increasing the reliance on income from employment, and thus as an
increased emphasis on the market or the 'private' domain. Such an evaluation would largely rely on the decommodificaton potential of (previously
existing) social policy programmes as the reference point.

However, 'enabling' citizens to work can also be understood as in accordance with the concept of social citizenship, which not only entails rights for

individuals to receive benefits, but also duties, including the duty to work (Marshall, 1992, pp. 88 f.; for a critical review see White, 2003, p. 139). Within the paradigms of activation and enabling, the specific mix of 'carrots' and 'sticks' becomes crucial for determining whether we witness a tendency towards 'privatization' of the risk of unemployment. Is the state relying on coercive recommodification measures, forcing people into any kind of work, or does it also provide 'support' in form of specific services or 'innovative' labour market regulations to achieve the aim of higher employment rates, perceived as crucial for the viability of welfare states? If the removal of dis-incentives or even discriminatory practices, that have marginalized certain groups of society, is at the heart of regulatory labour market measures, one might even argue that public responsibility has increased e.g. by enforcing tougher regulation upon employers. The most important policies within this realm have been policies relating to an improved reconciliation of employ-ment and family responsibilities, including parental leave or emergency leave during the sickness of a child.

Social regulation, however, is not limited to the labour market, but crucial to most social policy areas. For instance, any health-care system, inde-pendently of whether it is provided or financed publicly, without a set of (publicly) regulated standards is largely unthinkable in any advanced democ-racy. Assuming a state ends public provision, mandates private insurance and highly regulates contributions as well as benefits, similar to those found in statutory social insurance schemes, would such a change constitute a privati-zation? One certainly would have to acknowledge that such a system would differ substantially from an 'outright' privatization, where the system only relies on a general public regulatory framework. Even voluntary social poli-cies are often highly regulated by the state. Despite social regulation playing an important role in many aspects of social policy this dimension has been largely neglected in the social policy literature until recently (cf. Nivola, 1997; Leisering, 2003). Social regulation can be differentiated along two dimen-sions: extensity and intensity. The concept of extensity in regards to social policy regulation is concerned with the scope of regulatory measures and the concept of intensity relates to the 'depth of interference with private provision by regulatory measures' (Leisering, 2003, p. 9).

In addition to social regulation, tax incentives are core to many labour market activation measures and private social policies; although tax expen-ditures have been around for decades in most OECD countries in some form or another, they have not been at the centre of scientific scrutiny. Already five decades ago, the grand doyen of social policy research in the United Kingdom, Richard Titmuss (1958, p. 44), acknowledged the significance of – as he called it – fiscal welfare and criticized the fact that this aspect was not sufficiently reflected in public accounts: 'Allowances and reliefs from income tax, though providing similar benefits and expressing a similar social purpose in the recognition of dependencies, are not, however, treated as social service expenditure.' In effect Christopher Howard (1997) has unveiled that the US-American welfare state, instead of being based on weak state intervention, relies in large parts on the 'hidden welfare' of the tax code that provides substantial incentives for private social policy provisions. Individuals, voluntary associations and employers may benefit from such arrangements. Hence, in order to have a more comprehensive picture and to investigate change and continuity in the overall welfare effort as it relates to the mixed economy of welfare, we need to take tax incentives as well as private social policy provisions into account. This seems even more important if the observation proves to be correct that private social arrangements have increased in OECD countries during recent years (cf. Gilbert, 2002; 2005). Moreover, such an approach would be more in tune with T.H. Marshall's (1975, p. 15) classic definition of social policy as the use of 'political power to supersede, supplement or modify operations of the economic system in order to achieve results which the economic system would not achieve on its own'.

Despite the magnitude of tax expenditures for social purposes as well as private social provision these have usually not been taken into account in comparative analyses based on social spending data. Although not ideal, the OECD has quite recently developed a comparative dataset based on net social expenditure, to capture the overall social policy efforts, i.e. public expenditure, tax expenditure and private social policies. Based on this data the differences between countries almost seem to whither away;[4] indeed, in 2003, Liberal Britain or the Mediterranean welfare state of Italy spent more than Social-Democratic Denmark (see Figure 1.4).[5]

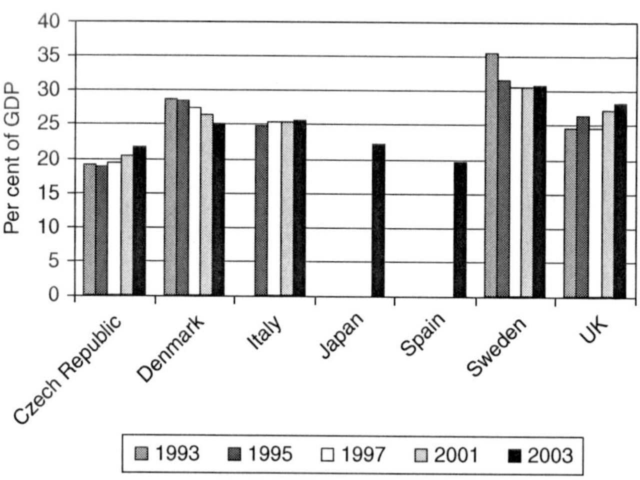

Figure 1.4   Net social expenditure of selected OECD countries as a percentage of GDP
Source: Adema (2001); Adema and Ladaique (2005); OECD (2007b).

Stressing the need to include private social policy and fiscal welfare is not to say that the kind of social provision does not matter in 'real' life. At the outcome level, fiscal and private welfare provisions are said to intensify 'divisions of welfare', as has already been noted by Titmuss (1958) decades ago, and now empirically demonstrated in a recent study by Castles and Obinger (2006, p. 21). They have shown 'it is gross spending – and the tax incidence that shapes it – that is central to the redistributive purposes of the welfare state'. So why should we care about the total welfare effort, knowing that the usual suspects in Scandinavia (and to a lesser degree in Continental Europe), which primarily rely on public programmes, indeed produce lower inequality and lower poverty?

First, the welfare state in many countries was not designed for redistributive purposes between classes. As Baldwin (1990) has shown, historically insurance against social risks was a core aim. In a sense one could argue that those, who perceive the key purpose of the welfare state to be primarily about redistributing income between classes, base their assessment on quite a narrow normative concept. Furthermore, it is questionable from a theoretical point of view that private social provision in combination with a universal or a generous means-tested scheme per definition has to lead to a higher degree of poverty.

Secondly, the net social expenditure data demonstrates that a greater reliance on private social provision does not necessarily come on the cheap. It thus questions arguments about the need to curtail *public* welfare provision and financing and to partially substitute it by private arrangements in an era of austerity, driven by increased globalization and rapid demographic change. This is not to say that there might be no other normative reasons, such as minimizing the control of the state and fostering more civil society engagement, that could normatively justify more 'private' social policy arrangements, as put forward by some *Communitarians* (cf. Etzioni, 1993).

Thirdly, and perhaps most importantly, an assessment of recent developments is academically warranted, as most comparative social policy research relies on regime categories, introduced by Esping-Andersen (1990) and based on data gathered around 1980. Longitudinal data on private social policy as well as fiscal welfare, which at this point is far from being comprehensive or systematic, seem to indicate that even states that in the past have primarily depended on *public* policies, increasingly rely on private arrangements, often supported through various tax measures or regulatory arrangements. As Peters (2005, p. 177) rightly observes 'although most European citizens and their governments might not want to acknowledge its existence, there is already a significant amount of private-sector involvement in the provision of social benefits in their countries'. It is time for comparative social policy analysis to acknowledge this.[6] Hence those interested in longitudinal, comparative public policy analysis should take systematic account of these developments, as they will most likely not only affect citizens, but also governance structures and the mode of government interventions. To understand the meaning of shifts between public and private, we need to go beyond (quantitative) analyses based on expenditure data and generosity indices of *public* social policies.

Methodological issues

The arguments presented so far demonstrate the need to look beyond conventional conceptualization of *public* social policy. Direct state provision might not only be complemented, but substituted by publicly financed and/or regulated 'private' social benefit or service provision, leading to a blurring of the boundaries between 'public' and 'private'. This seems to be especially the case if we do not primarily focus on transfer programmes, but systematically include social services into our analysis. As Wilensky (2002, p. 257) has put it so eloquently in regards to arrangements found in a number of Continental European welfare states:

> Several countries with strong Catholic party power ... lavishly subsidize 'private' nonprofit associations as major suppliers of personal social services ... Unless we wish to argue that the nearly total government financing of these religious and other nonprofits is not public provision, we must be careful in the claim that Catholic power blocks public services in favour of cash transfers.

This example makes obvious that *public services* do not necessarily have to be identical with *state* services. Furthermore, observing debates about the 'privatization' or 'marketization' of the National Health Service in the United Kingdom at the beginning of the twenty-first century and comparing those, for example, to the 'public' health-care sector based in large parts on 'private' provision and limited competition in Germany, it becomes apparent that 'private' and 'public' can have very different meanings in different national settings. In this context, it has to be stressed that competition among providers *can* indeed lead to improved outcomes, depending on the specific institutional design (Propper et al., 2006).

   Is it thus impossible to address the shifting boundaries between 'public' and 'private' in any meaningful comparative way? In past research I have emphasized the need to include arrangements that are functionally equivalent to state intervention to deal with the issue of comparability and suggested the concept of *welfare systems* (cf. Seeleib-Kaiser, 2001). Welfare systems can be related to an ideal understanding of welfare, defined as a political exercise 'to establish or guarantee societal situations in which the individual benefit and the common benefit do not diverge, but reinforce each other in the sense of synergic effects' (Kaufmann, 1994, pp. 357 f.; translation msk). Based on this definition of welfare, a welfare system could be imagined as a social arrangement, which insures against social risks in a collective, highly regulated, and/or redistributive manner with a relatively high degree of certainty for future claims [*Erwartungssicherheit*]. To some extent the meaning of such a welfare system overlaps with Marquand's (2004, pp. 26 ff.) concept of 'public domain'. Governance within this domain primarily relies on democratic, legal, and professional peer accountability.[7] Within a welfare system thus defined, *social* policy can ideally be provided by 'public' and/or 'private' actors without necessarily violating the boundaries of the 'public domain', because of a subordination of profit motives. Prime examples of 'private' provision within the public domain are the Ghent system of unemployment insurance[8] or earnings-related occupational pension systems in a number of European countries that are neither provided by the state nor through purely profit-oriented enterprises, but are governed by complex corporatist arrangements. Whiteside (2006) stresses that in the UK such governance structures are largely absent, leading to a more deep-rooted division between private and public.

In contrast, the private domain is based on individual private, family, community and purely market relationships, relying primarily on the logics of reciprocity, voluntarism, and philanthropy as well as market and reputational accountability. Thus policy in this domain is not functionally equivalent to public social policy, as it cannot provide the same degree of certainty and actors can only be held politically accountable in a very limited way.[9] Furthermore, the logics applying to the various relationships are not always clearly discernable and overlap – 'non-profit' actors especially seem increasingly to incorporate elements of market accountability.[10] This is not to argue that there are no differences between 'private' policy arrangements provided by families, non-profit organizations or for-profit enterprises; however, the overarching focus here is whether we are witnessing shifts from the 'public' towards the 'private' domain.

Based on this conceptualization we can differentiate analytically between the 'private' and 'public' domain, which, however, does not a priori tell us whether the actors are indeed public or private entities. Furthermore, the proposed conceptualization is not easily operationalized, as it is most likely to be dependent on specific policy and national contexts; in real life we will presumably be confronted with a layering of the two domains according to the different modes of social policy intervention. In order to capture the various possible shifts in the public–private mix it is therefore suggested that we analyse three different modes of policy intervention, that is, financing (spending and taxation), provision and regulation (cf. Barr, 1998; 2001),[11] as shifts between the 'public' and 'private' can differ depending on the mode of intervention. For example, as governments reduce direct public provision, they may at the same time introduce mandatory private provision arrangements or contract them out to a private provider, governed by a strict public regulatory framework. Hence it might be worthwhile imagining the modes/dimensions

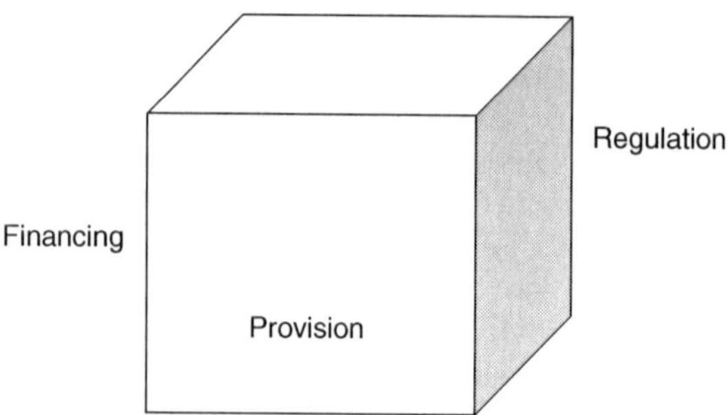

Figure 1.5   Modes of social policy intervention

of policy intervention as interacting within a three-dimensional space (see Figure 1.5).

In addition to differentiating between these three dimensions of social policy intervention, we suggest differentiating between three analytical levels: discourse, institutions and outcomes. Depending on the level of analysis we could arrive at very different conclusions. In other words, while we might witness quite significant changes of the social policy discourse, these may have not yet triggered institutional changes; or significant changes at the institutional level may have not yet affected policy outcomes. Finally, policy outcomes might change without a change in the social policy discourse or institutional arrangements. When evaluating the various possibilities of change the dimension of time is of utmost importance, especially as change at the outcome level often lags institutional changes at the policy level for a number of years, if not even decades as in the case of comprehensive pension reforms. Differentiating along the various dimensions of analysis will substantially improve our understanding of the nature of welfare state transformations.

Structure of the book

This book sets out to scrutinize welfare state change and continuity from multiple perspectives with a clear focus on the public–private mix. Part I analyses developments in 'mature' welfare states, in transition economies of Southern as well as Central and Eastern Europe and Japan. We have included as 'mature' welfare states both Denmark, usually characterized as a Social-Democratic welfare state, and the United Kingdom as *the* example of a Liberal welfare state in Europe, which is often said to have gone furthest in regards to 'market-oriented welfare state reform' (Taylor-Gooby et al., 2004, p. 573). Comparative chapters of the Southern European countries as well as Central and Eastern European countries are included, as they have undergone significant political transformations and are often neglected in comparative analyses. Finally, Japan is included in our study in order to analyse whether we witness similar social policy developments in an advanced industrial country with very different cultural and historical legacies. Ideally the country comparisons and case studies will focus on changes and continuities in the overall structure of the welfare state as well as address significant changes in the following key policy areas: employment, income security, family and care, and health.

In Part II, the country comparisons are complemented by cross-sectional analyses. Such an approach enables us to identify more clearly potentially common or diverse policy responses in specific policy domains. As previous research has shown certain social policy domains can deviate significantly from the welfare state regime framework (cf. Seeleib-Kaiser, 1995; Kasza, 2002)[12] and thus conceptually change in these domains might follow different trajectories having discrete effects on the specific public–private mix as well as provide us with a more nuanced understanding of welfare state change and continuity. The selection of policy domains for our cross-sectional analyses mainly draws on the 'classic' social risks of unemployment, old age, sickness and disability, which is complemented by more recent conceptualizations of 'new' social risks (cf. Bonoli, 2006), especially those resulting from the 'need' to balance paid work and family responsibilities.

Part III of the book consists of a conceptual chapter addressing welfare state change and a concluding chapter summarizing the findings. Ideally the contributions will answer the following questions:

- Are we witnessing a silent surrender or withering away of the public domain and thus finally the triumph of 'neo-liberalism' in times of increasing globalization and Europeanization? Or should we rather conceptualize the changes as a transformation of the state (cf. Leibfried and Zürn, 2005)?
- Does the scope of the changes differ among various policy areas and across countries? Can we identify country or programme specific patterns of change and continuity?

Part I
State Perspectives

2
Welfare State Reforms in the United Kingdom

Martin Powell

Introduction

There has been much debate about welfare state reforms in the UK under Conservative (1979–1997) and New Labour (1997–) governments. Accounts of welfare change are marked by large disagreements about terminology and chronology, reflecting a wider debate about whether the welfare state has been in crisis, under threat, in transition, resilient or robust, reshaped, refashioned, restructured, residualized, rolled back, recast, recalibrated, transformed, and even dismantled (Powell and Hewitt, 2002, p. 2). However, relatively few accounts tend to draw on the mixed economy of welfare and social division of welfare literature (Powell, 2007) and focus on the shifting boundaries of 'public' and 'private' social policy (Chapter 1). Accounts have often tended to be 'one dimensional' and thus paint partial and misleading pictures of change. Many studies concentrate on direct public provision or the 'pure public' sector (state finance and provision) (Burchardt, 1997; cf. IPPR, 2001; Powell, 2007), stressing the 'dependent variable' of the conventional 'gold standard' of public expenditure (Chapter 1).

This chapter examines changes in the mixed economy of welfare (MEW) and the social division of welfare (Powell, 2007; see Chapter 1). It explores the discourse, institutions and outcomes of welfare reform associated with the changing public/private mix. One major problem is that the discourse of political language tends not to be sufficiently precise to identify relevant trends. For example, both supporters and critics of 'privatization' tend not to differentiate between its many forms. It is difficult to assess the link between changing discourse and institutions and even more difficult to examine the changing public/private mix in terms of outcomes. Even data on inputs is rare (but see Burchardt, 1997; Smithies, 2005; Chapter 1). It is generally held that greater 'privatization' leads to greater inequality, but evidence of attribution is scarce.

The Mixed Economy of Welfare (MEW) and the public/private mix

In the UK the term welfare tends to be synonymous with state provision. However, the 'welfare state' has always contained a mix of state, private, voluntary and informal elements. Moreover, it is necessary to look beyond direct state provision to the more hidden mechanisms of fiscal and occupational welfare (see Powell, 2007). The mix between these elements has varied over time (and between countries) but an *etatiste* view of welfare gives only a partial picture. In short, 'social policy' is wider than the 'welfare state'. Even studies that recognize the MEW often are confined to a 'one dimensional account' of provision, and tend not also to recognize wider issues of finance and regulation. In addition to owning and providing facilities (e.g. NHS, state education), the state can finance private or voluntary provision (e.g. paying for care in residential homes) or regulate provision in terms of standards or prices (e.g. legislation on houses in multiple occupation; rent control).

Much recent writing has focused on moves from state to market such as privatization, marketization, or commodification (for example: Drakeford, 2000; Leys, 2001; Pollock, 2004). However, privatization is an overloaded term, with limited analytical power (Drakeford, 2000). Some studies examine 'privatization' in 'one-dimensional' terms, in that it refers to the changed MEW or changed mix without specifying roles or dimensions. However, a one-dimensional 'rolling back the state' or a move 'from state to market' does not differentiate between the dimensions of production, finance and regulation. A move from state to market fails to distinguish between very different strategies such as charging, contracting out, quasi-markets, vouchers, and so on. A one-dimensional account focuses on the single issue of provision and neglects the dimension of finance. The assumption here appears to be that ownership matters: a place in a private residential home is different to a place in a public residential home (whoever finances it).

Two-dimensional accounts examine provision and finance. The Institute for Public Policy Research (IPPR, 2001) reasserts the case for publicly-funded universal services, but distinguishes clearly between the funding and provision of public services. It differentiates means and ends: the case for public services needs to be made in terms of values and outcomes rather than particular forms of delivery. The founding principles of the NHS were that it should be free, universal and comprehensive, not that it should be provided through a particular structure, process, or set of employees. It rejects the blind alleys of the 'privatizers' – private good, public bad – and the 'monopolists' – public good, private bad. It sets out four models of public management: command and control; networks and trust; purchase and provide; privatize and regulate.

Three-dimensional accounts examine provision, finance and regulation. Unlike other disciplines (e.g. Hood et al., 1999; Moran, 2003), the social

Finance \ Provision	State	Market	Voluntary	Informal
State	1a (high reg) 1b (low reg)	2a 2b	3a 3b	4a 4b
Market	5a 5b	6a 6b	7a 7b	8a 8b
Voluntary	9a 9b	10a 10b	11a 11b	12a 12b
Informal	13a 13b	14a 14b	15a 15b	16a 16b

Figure 2.1 Dimensions of the mixed economy of welfare

policy literature has tended to ignore regulation (but see Bolderson, 1986; Powell and Hewitt, 2002). This is despite the long history of inspection and regulation in sectors such as health, education and housing. The recent rise in importance of regulation/inspection has made a two-dimensional view untenable, with commentators claiming that we live in an 'Audit Society' (Power, 1997) and a 'regulatory State' (Hood et al., 1999; Moran, 2003).

Figure 2.1 presents a way of examining change in the MEW as movements from origin to destination cells. The most far-reaching moves would involve all three dimensions (e.g. from 1a to 6b); from the core or heartland of the welfare state public provision, finance and regulation to private finance and provision with limited or no public regulation. It follows that 'privatization' could involve the three-dimensional move described above (1a to 6b), but might also cover any move down from the top row (e.g. 1 to 5; 2 to 10 etc.), any shift to the right from the first column (e.g. 1 to 2; 5 to 7 etc.) or any shift from high to low regulation (any a to b). In some ways, it might be preferable to differentiate destinations such as privatization (towards column 2 or row 5), voluntarization (towards column 3 and row 9), and informalization (towards column 4 and row 13). This could be linked with dimensions such as deprovided, definanced, and deregulated, but 'deregulated voluntarization' or 'deprovided informalization' are ugly terms.

The public discourse and the changing boundaries between 'public' and 'private'

During the period of the 'classic welfare state', Labour was generally more satisfied with the welfare mix than the Conservatives. Very crudely, the instinct of Labour was that the state should 'do something' about a problem, while that of the Conservatives was that there was a greater role for individuals (Finlayson, 1994; Stewart, 2007). Some elements within the Conservative Party wished to reduce the role of the state (see Lowe, 2004) and, from the 1960s onwards, these elements were prodded by pro-market groups such as the Institute for Economic Affairs (IEA). For example, according to IEA (1967, p. 19):

> the doctrines of state paternalism, equal social benefits and the badge of citizenship teach that a man with a broken leg should be given larger and stronger crutches as society advances. The opposite view is that unless he is allowed and encouraged to put his leg to the ground, tentatively at first but with increasing strength, it will atrophy.

In the 1970s, Conservative cabinet minister (and proto-Thatcherite), Sir Keith Joseph realized that he had 'not really been a Conservative', and Margaret Thatcher considered that 'a new vital debate is beginning, or perhaps an old debate is being renewed, about the proper role of government, the welfare state and the attitudes on which it rests' (cit. in Timmins, 2001, pp. 354–5). While the early years of the 1979 Conservative government tended not to change social policy (with the major exception of public housing), as Thatcher considered that the first priority was to focus on the economy, Timmins (2001, p. 369) notes that the first sentence on Thatcher's first public spending White Paper of 1979 stated that, 'Public expenditure is at the heart of Britain's present economic difficulties'. Nevertheless, public expenditure continued to rise throughout much of the Conservative era (noting yet again the major exception of public housing), albeit not as fast as critics from the left would have liked, and with some of this due to the large rise in the number of unemployed people claiming unemployment benefit.

The Thatcher Diaries (1993, pp. 676–7) record two main themes associated with social policy. First, she argues that privatization is:

> one of the central means of reversing the corrosive and corrupting effects of socialism ... through privatization ... the state's power is reduced and the power of the people enhanced ... privatization is at the centre of any programme of reclaiming territory for freedom ... Now that almost universal lip service is paid to the case for privatization it is difficult to recall just how revolutionary – how all but unthinkable – it all seemed at the end of the 1970s.

Second, there is the stress on the purchaser/provider split, internal markets, and 'enabling not providing'. Thatcher (1993, p. 572) records that the 1987 manifesto was the 'best ever produced by the Conservative Party.... [and] went to the heart of my convictions'. Similarly, Conservative minister (and formerly of the Downing Street Policy Unit and head of the Centre for Policy Studies) David Willetts stated that 'for us 1988, with the Education Reform Act, the NHS Review, the Griffiths Report and the Housing Act, was the 'annus mirabilus' of social policy' (cit. in Timmins, 2001, p. 431). The favourite council of Nicholas Ridley, Secretary of State for the Environment, was said to be in the American mid-west which employed almost no one and met just once a year to award all its contracts to the private sector (Timmins, 2001, p. 472). This strategic theme is clearly shown in housing and social care documents. 'There will no longer be the same presumption that the local authority itself should take direct action to meet new or increasing demands. The future role of the local authorities will essentially be a strategic one...' (DoE, 1987, p. 14). Thatcher (1993, p. 618) continues that 'in education, housing and health the common themes of my policies were the extension of choice, the dispersal of power and the encouragement of responsibility'. However, as we will see below, excluding public housing, 'privatization' did not feature heavily in social policy (Powell, 1996; but see Ruane, 1997) and internal markets had little to do with choice, responsibility or the dispersal of power. 'Privatization' was rejected by Prime Minister John Major in 1991 (Timmins, 2001, p. 480).

After its landslide election victory in 1997, New Labour was initially cautious on public expenditure. In 1997 Tony Blair announced that 'we have reached the limit of the public's willingness simply to fund an unreformed welfare system through ever higher taxation and spending' (cit. in Timmins, 2001, p. 559). For the first few years in office, the government stuck to Conservative spending limits, stating that New Labour would be 'wise spenders not big spenders'. Gordon Brown challenged 'the myth that the solution to every problem was increased spending' (cit. in Powell, 1999, p. 22). If New Labour was pragmatic rather than ideological on public expenditure, this was also the case on the mixed economy of welfare (Powell, 1999, 2007). There were some signs of movement on this issue before New Labour took office, and even before Labour became 'New Labour'. A Labour Party document of 1989 stated that: 'it is no longer possible or as necessary as it used to be to draw strict dividing lines between "public" and "private".' It rejected the 'Conservative dogma that public must be bad, private good ...'. Similarly, the Commission on Social Justice Report of 1994 rejected an 'entirely privatized future', but cautiously welcomed public–private partnerships (both cit. in Burchardt and Hills, 1999, p. 41).

Anthony Giddens (1998) – one of the intellectual architects of New Labour – regards 'the new mixed economy' as a key feature of the Third Way. The term is not clearly defined, but appears to embrace both the private sector and civil society. Giddens (1998, p. 7) states that in classical social democracy (the old left) there was a 'pervasive state involvement in social and economic life' and the 'state dominates over civil society' with a 'confined role for markets'. The new mixed economy involves government acting in partnership with agencies in civil society (p. 69), and looking for a synergy between public and private sectors (pp. 99–100). The welfare state should be replaced by the welfare society, with a larger role for third sector agencies in providing welfare services (p. 117). In short, the distribution of welfare should not be wholly through the state but by the state working in combination with other agencies, including business (pp. 127–8). Giddens (2002) is broadly supportive of Public Private Partnerships/Private Finance Initiative. He argues that more extensive partnerships between state and non-state groups in key public services in general are inevitable if such services really are to be brought up to a better standard. 'The public realm is not to be equated with the state, and that therefore partnership is not the same as privatization' (p. 63). Frank Field, the Minister of Welfare Reform, wished to see a revival of mutual aid, but

> I want to make one point crystal clear: the re-drawing of the boundaries between state and individual responsibility is not simply an exercise in downsizing state responsibility [but] crucial to the recreation of a civil society based on a partnership between individuals, organizations and Government (cit. in Powell, 1999, p. 20).

The Green Paper on welfare reform (DSS, 1998, p. 19) viewed the Third Way as combining public and private provision in a new partnership for a new age, but rejected 'a privatized future' as the limitations of private provision carries 'the risk of market "cherry picking" of the best risks, leaving the taxpayer to pick up the tab for the rest' (p. 39). It set out a plan for welfare in 2020, with mutual and private providers delivering a substantial share of welfare provision, especially pensions (cf. Powell and Hewitt, 2002, pp. 183–5). However, this 'new partnership' did not contain the Conservatives' Assisted Places Scheme, nursery vouchers, and medical insurance for those aged over 60 as they were all abolished by New Labour, presumably on pragmatic ('what works') rather than ideological criteria (Burchardt and Hills, 1999; Powell, 1999).

New Labour has moved much further down the paths of a pluralist rather than statist, and enabling rather than providing welfare state (Powell and Hewitt, 2002, p. 185). It now rejected 'monolithic' services, and argued that ownership does not matter. For example, it does not matter if a NHS patient is treated in a private hospital, so long as the treatment is free at the point of use, and the hospital is part of the regulatory regime. Secretary of State for Health Alan Milburn once speculated that he could envisage all treatments taking place in non-state hospitals, leaving the 'NHS' as a commissioner of a 'virtual NHS', but his successor, John Reid, suggested a maximum of 15 per cent of all treatments in private hospitals (Toynbee and Walker, 2005, p. 324). The watchwords for New Labour – with permeations on many policy documents – were choice and diversity.

The discourse concerning fiscal and occupational welfare has been limited. In 1997 New Labour aimed to 'streamline and modernize' the tax and benefit systems 'so as to fulfil our objectives of promoting work incentives, reducing poverty and welfare dependency, and strengthening community and family life.' Tax credits would 'associate the payment in the recipient's mind with the fact of working, a potentially valuable psychological tool … a payment through the tax system, associated with the recipient's work is likely to prove more acceptable to society at large' (cit. in Sinfield, 2007, p. 133).

Changing the public/private mix – an institutional perspective[1]

With the benefit of hindsight, it does not appear that the early years of the 1979 Conservative government had a coherent plan for social policy. Although ideologically favouring private, voluntary and informal over state sources of welfare, at times appearing to be a crude 'public bad; private good' view, no major strategy resulted. With the major exception of public housing, they tended to reject outright privatization (i.e. the transfer of assets from public to private sectors – from column 1 to column 2 in Figure 2.1), although there were instances of increased and new charges (recommodification). In the following, I will first analyse the realm of social services, before addressing the changes in regards to old-age income and employment.

First, in terms of ownership/provision, the largest 'privatization' involved the transfer of public housing to private ownership (from cell 5 to cell 6: Figure 2.1). This was, according to Timmins (2001, p. 378), the 'biggest single privatisation of the Thatcher era, raising £28 billion over thirteen years – more than the sale of gas, electricity and British Telecom put together'. The Conservatives introduced the 'Right To Buy' legislation in 1980, giving local authority tenants the right to buy their houses with generous discounts, leading to the 'Sale of the Century' as many houses changed from the public to the private sector. In addition to this 'retail' or individual strategy, Large Scale Voluntary Transfer under both Conservative and Labour governments have moved local authority (or 'council') housing to social landlords (from cell 5 to cell 7). This amounted to nearly one million homes, leaving only 50 per cent of English local authorities with council housing (Mullins and Murie, 2006, p. 189). Turning to regulation, there was initially a period of deregulation in housing under the Conservatives. For example, due to the creation of shorthold and assured tenancies in the private rented sector, Mullins and Murie (2006, p. 119) report that the percentage of regulated compared to all tenancies declined from 59 per cent to under 6 per cent by 2004. Through Housing Acts in 1980 and 1988 the Conservatives attempted to revive the private rented sector by tilting the balance of power between landlord and tenant back to the former. This de-regulated private renting, by allowing rent increases and placing time limits on lets, allowed landlords to regain control of their property. The Conservatives reduced the value of tax relief on mortgages through 'Mortgage Interest Tax Relief' (MIRAS), and it was finally abolished by New Labour.

In health care there were few early major changes to the public/private mix under the Conservatives. A policy of 'compulsory competitive tendering' (CCT) or 'contracting out' in 1983 required Health Authorities to put their 'hotel services' of catering, cleaning and laundry out to tender. In 1986 the NHS stopped supplying spectacles, and gave poorer patients vouchers that they could use in the market. The 1980s saw a large increase in private medicine, which was due less to the 'hidden hand of the market' than to the 'visible hand of government'. Prescription charges continued to increase, with new and increased charges being introduced in the dental and optical spheres, resulting in a degree of 'recommodification'. The 'quasi-market' of the purchaser/provider split came into being in 1991, but it was largely an 'internal' rather than an 'external' market, with competition between providers being confined largely to NHS hospitals rather than opening up competition to the private sector (Powell, 2003). Some tax incentives were given to patients to purchase private health insurance.

New Labour stated initially in 1997 that it would 'abolish the internal market', but did not, and later from 2000 onwards, would not reinvent the internal market, but did. Indeed, it went further than the Conservatives in a number of ways. First, it ended Old Labour's 'class war' with private medicine, signing a 'concordat' which encouraged private hospitals to compete for NHS work. Under the later 'Choose and Book' scheme, NHS patients are allowed to choose to have treatment at private hospitals. Forcing NHS hospitals to compete for business with the private sector, the development of Independent Sector Treatment Centre (ISTCs), and encouraging 'Social Enterprise' providers, completes the journey from a 'monolithic' public sector through the Conservatives' internal market to New Labour's 'external market' (see Powell, 2003). New Labour has also promoted 'Foundation Trusts' which supporters argue represent 'mutualization' but critics regard as 'privatization'. Finally, New Labour has strengthened the regulatory regime of health care with a number of rapidly evolving (and re-named) regulatory bodies such as the Commission for Health Improvement (CHI).

In education the Conservatives introduced the Assisted Places Scheme (APS) in 1980 – a means-tested programme – which allows parents to send their child to a private school. An attempt to introduce vouchers was declared to be 'dead' by 1983. The Conservatives flirted with student loans in the 1980s, but rejected them because of the expected middle class electoral backlash. However, loans were introduced in 1990. The Major government, in one of its few 'last hurrahs' of Thatcherite radicalism, introduced a £1000 per year voucher for nursery education in 1995 that could be spent in either the public, private or voluntary sectors. One of New Labour's first moves was to abolish the APS and nursery vouchers, but later introduced fees and subsequently variable top-up fees for higher education. It also required universities to use part of the increased fee income to be put towards bursaries to ensure that poorer students could afford higher education, and introduced an Access Regulator, the Office for Fair Access (OFFA).

In opposition in the late 1970s, Margaret Thatcher spoke of 'Victorian values' or 'virtues', while Sir Keith Joseph excoriated the 'permissive society'. As Prime Minister, Mrs Thatcher made her famous statement, usually truncated to the first sentence that:

> There is no such thing as society. There are individual men and women, and there are families. And no government can do anything except through people, and people must look after themselves first. It is our duty to look after ourselves and then to look after our neighbours. (cit. in Timmins, 2001, p. 431)

The Conservatives regarded themselves as defenders of marriage and the 'traditional family', and a number of Ministers criticized the rise of lone parents. Although the Conservatives did not produce an explicit 'family policy' per se, a number of developments influenced 'informal care' which includes families, friends, neighbours and other informal networks. Their general position was that informal care should increase, as encapsulated by a White Paper of 1981 that stated that 'the primary sources of support and care are informal and voluntary .... Care in the community must increasingly mean care by the community' (DHSS, 1981, p. 3).

From about 1979 social security offices, based on local agreements, began to contribute towards fees for private and voluntary residential homes for elderly people. This was formalized into a national agreement by 1983, and residential care became the single fastest growth in public spending, with numbers and costs virtually doubled each year. As Timmins (2001, pp. 414–15) put it, 'Unwittingly, the Conservatives had created a new state-financed, if privately run, industry'. However, it gave financial incentives for elderly people to go into residential homes, rather than their generally preferred option of retaining independence in their own homes. Sir Roy Griffiths, the Managing Director of Sainsburys, was invited by government to produce a report on community care, which is generally termed 'Griffiths II', as opposed to his report on NHS management of 1983 – 'Griffiths I'. He stated that,

> The proposals are aimed at stimulating the further development of the 'mixed economy' of care. It is vital that social service authorities should see themselves as the arrangers and purchasers of care services – not as monopolistic providers. (DH, 1988, p. 5)

Griffiths argued that 'care managers' should assist customers in making choices in spending public money to buy the best package of care, with the government stipulating that 85 per cent of the budget had to be spent outside the public sector. However, the scheme was means-tested, and elderly people with financial assets were forced to pay fees from their own pockets, and in some cases being forced to sell their homes to pay the fees. The 1996 Community Care (Direct Payments Act) empowered social service departments to make cash payments to service users aged between 18 and 65 in lieu of direct service provision. The scope of the Act has subsequently widened through regulations and the 2000 Carers and Disabled Children Act to cover new groups such as people aged over 65 and carers. However, the number of people taking advantage of Direct Payments has remained fairly low (Glasby and Littlechild, 2002).

Blair in a conference speech of 1996 condemned a country where elderly people had to sell their homes to pay bills for residential care. New Labour appointed a Royal Commission on Long Term Care, which reported in 1999. The majority recommended that all personal care should be free, but a two person minority report considered this too expensive. In the words of (majority) commissioner, Robin Wendt: 'the majority recommended what they thought a Labour Government should do: the minority what they thought a Labour government would do' (cit. in Timmins, 2001, p. 588). After initially tending towards the minority view, the Scottish Parliament later made personal care free, indicating a clear policy divergence with England (Stewart, 2004).

New Labour's 1997 Election Manifesto pledge was to 'help build strong families and strong communities'. It produced a discussion document in 1998, *Supporting Families*, which claimed that it was the first time any British government had published a consultation paper on the family. New Labour has claimed to be 'family friendly' in a number of ways, especially in its policies of directing assistance towards children. It has produced three relevant innovative policy aims: to end child poverty within 20 years; to achieve a target of 70 per cent of lone parents in paid employment; and to provide good quality and affordable childcare for all children under 14 (cf. Lewis and Campbell, 2007). New Labour has passed some legislation supporting carers, and introduced a National Strategy for Carers in 1999. The 2000 Carers and Disabled Children Act gave local authorities the powers to provide carers with direct cash payments. Direct Payments enable individuals to purchase their own support, rather than receiving services arranged by the local authority, and offer increased choice, control and flexibility over when, how, and from whom services are received (Glasby and Littlechild, 2002).

The Private Finance Initiative (PFI) was developed by the Conservatives in the early 1990s, according to which a private supplier enters into a contract with a public body to build and/or operate a facility (for example, a school, hospital, prison, road, or rail). Supporters claim that it increases the returns on public money, and shares risks with the private sector, whereas critics argue that its most valuable feature was the ability for major capital investment not to show up as 'public expenditure' and that the costs are high. PFI allows the state to 'live now and pay later'. In opposition, Labour was opposed to the scheme as it was seen as 'privatization'. However, just before the 1997 election, Labour was converted, and in office embraced PFI, albeit sometimes with the alternative term of Public–Private Partnership (PPP). Labour has made major use of PFI, for example in the largest hospital building programme in the history of the NHS (DH, 2000, p. 96).

After having discussed some of the major changes in regards to social services, I will now turn to pension and employment policies. The Conservatives cut the (brief – since the 1970s) link between pensions and earnings, and wished to abolish the (similarly young) Second Earnings Related Pension Scheme (SERPS). In the end SERPS was reduced rather than abolished, and members were encouraged to opt out of the scheme and transfer into private pensions. By 1993 more than 5 million, rather than the expected 500 000, people – encouraged by some optimistic pension projections – had taken this option. In his first Budget as Chancellor Gordon Brown ('the pension snatcher') removed an estimated £5bn a year from pensions, prompting a comparison that Robert Maxwell[2] 'only took £400 m' (Powell, 1999, p. 17). New Labour wished to change the balance of pension funding from 40 per cent private and 60 per cent public to the reverse. The area of pensions has seen frantic activity under New Labour with the introduction of the Minimum Income Guarantee, stakeholder pensions, the second state pension and Pension Credit, not to mention a number of reports, inquiries and Government Papers. This has not been helped by a regulatory regime that seems to have slept through issues such as the collapse of the 'Equitable Life' company: 'you would not be wise to bet your mortgage or pension on the performance of financial regulation, although that is precisely what you are meant to do' (Powell and Hewitt, 2002, p. 137).

In regards to employment policy, there has been a great stress on 'activation' which can be seen in terms of 'recommodification' (Chapter 1). Both governments have emphasized increasing employment through the carrots and sticks of 'active labour market policy'. The late 1970s and early 1980s saw 'the end of full employment' with unemployment reaching an estimated 3 million under the Conservatives, who attempted to tackle the 'why work syndrome' through a mix of limiting benefits and exhorting unemployed people to price themselves into work by accepting lower wages, and by greater mobility by getting on their bikes and looking for work. The Job Seekers Allowance – 'a defining moment in welfare state history' (Timmins, 2001, p. 528) – was introduced in 1996. It halved the entitlement to non-means-tested unemployment benefit from twelve to six months, and increased the degree of 'conditionality' associated with benefit through demonstrating a more active job search. This trend continued under Gordon Brown's

'New Deals' or 'Welfare to Work' programme. If Blair's mantra was 'education, education, education', Brown's was 'work, work, work', or the adapted phrase, 'I have seen the future, and it is work'. Brown introduced a different balance of carrots ('making work pay' through the National Minimum Wage; education, employment and training options; personal advisors) and sticks (reduction of benefits) for different groups.[3]

Although the 'fiscal' or 'tax' welfare state has always been important, its profile has increased under New Labour with the introduction of 'tax credits' – such as Children's Tax Credit and the Pension Tax Credit. These have been introduced in a variety of changing terms, and their complexity has baffled both administrators and officials, resulting in significant 'readjustments', or over- and under-payments (cf. Sinfield, 2007).

Although occupational welfare has long been recognized (Brunsdon and May, 2007), it has recently become a major issue with a perceived difference between some private and public sector workers. While the regulatory framework for occupational pensions seems to be rather complex, it has not protected workers and pensioners well in the past. Many private sector companies have closed their final salary scheme, while the public sector, it is said, continues to offer generous (and in the case of MPs) extremely generous pensions. Moreover, with the collapse of some company pension schemes, workers who have paid pension contributions all of their working lives are left with minimal or no occupational pension. To provide (a limited) compensation to members of eligible defined benefit pension schemes in the future, in case of insolvency or insufficient assets in the pension scheme, a statutory Pension Protection Fund was established in 2004 (Brunsdon and May, 2007).[4]

Summarizing the developments in the various policy areas, we can argue that we have witnessed an overall increase of regulation in many areas, and moves towards 'market provision' and to a lesser degree towards 'voluntary provision'. It is generally claimed that the importance of regulation has increased to form a 'Regulatory State' or 'Audit Society', where governments 'steer rather than row', or indeed where government has moved to governance, with 'more control over less'.

Outcomes: a new public/private mix?

It can be argued that, in terms of input/expenditure, the welfare state is resilient or expanding. Generally welfare expenditure has increased, and increased significantly in sectors such as health care and education. As Castles (2004, p. 71) puts it, changes in welfare state expenditure have been 'relatively modest', and downsizing has been counterbalanced by upsizing in other areas. However, as argued above, analyses based on direct expenditure are only part of the picture. Burchardt (1997) suggested a framework for examining changes in the mixed economy of welfare, and found that changes since 1979 had been relatively small. Smithies (2005) has updated this analysis: in the period from 1979/80 to 1999/2000, the pure public category fell from 52 per cent to 49 per cent while the entirely private category increased from 24 per cent to 29 per cent. However, these figures were heavily influenced by housing, where the figures changed from 18 per cent to 15 per cent and 58 per cent to 63 per cent respectively. This can be contrasted by the pure public category for social security which increased from 57 per cent to 64 per cent, and for personal social services which fell from 71 per cent to 42 per cent. Excluding the housing category, the total figures vary little with moves from 62 per cent to 61 per cent for pure public and 15 per cent to 17 per cent for pure private. Smithies (2005) concludes that shifts in the composition of welfare activity have been relatively small and gradual.

However, there are four caveats to this conclusion. First, as shown by Smithies (2005), some policy domains have seen more significant changes than others. Timmins (2001, p. 476) claims that the Conservative reforms rolled back the welfare state only in pensions and housing. With the trend towards 'workfare' through the Conservatives' Job Seekers Allowance and New Labour's Welfare to Work/New Deals, Ellison (2006, p. 94) claims that the changes in labour market policy in the UK over the past 20 years have been among the most marked in the mature welfare democracies. Similarly, he asserts that old-age pensions have been 'virtually privatized' (Ellison, 2006, p. 74). On the other hand, health care and education have expanded, albeit with greater emphasis on state finance of private provision.

Second, Smithies' (2005) data ends in 2000, and it is possible that significant changes may have occurred since then. In particular, in this period, the Labour government has been increasingly converted to the advantages of choice, competition, diversity, and pluralism, and it is likely that there has been a decline in the 'pure public' category. Moreover, the results of policy changes may take some time to 'kick in', and so there may be some time lag before policy changes are reflected in changes in expenditure categories.

Third, the analyses of Burchardt (1997) and Smithies (2005) do not consider regulation, or fiscal or occupational welfare, and so their analyses leave out significant changes in these categories. In terms of Figure 2.1, there have been broad moves from b (low regulation) to a (high regulation). However, there are many instances of regulatory failure (see Powell and Hewitt, 2002), or what Moran (2003, p. 171) terms 'the age of fiasco'. As Sinfield (2007) notes, the introduction of tax credits has the potential to move the tax welfare state from regressive to progressive, but 'most elements of tax welfare continue to widen inequalities' (p. 142). Similarly, as occupational welfare largely consists of discretionary rewards linked to labour market position, it is unlikely to deliver the equities expected of state benefits and services (Brunsdon and May, 2007, p. 171).

Fourth, while the 'size' of the welfare state may not have reduced, its 'texture' or 'character' may have changed (Powell and Hewitt, 2002). This may be seen in terms of mechanisms or policy domains. There have been moves towards selectivity or means-testing (especially in terms of fiscal welfare or tax credits) (see Sinfield, 2007). There is a greater emphasis on paid work, activation and conditionality and a greater readiness to blur the boundaries between market and state. All this suggests that welfare state reforms in the UK are multi-dimensional and defy easy classification. A three-dimensional account shows that it is misleading to look at one dimension such as provision in isolation. This means that a simple 'rolling back' (or 'rolling forward') of the state thesis fails to do justice to a complex situation. There have been moves backward and forward on all dimensions, and the overall balance may vary between sectors (cf. Burchardt, 1997; Smithies, 2005): perhaps two steps forward and one back in one sector, but vice versa in another.

Advocates of 'market socialism' such as Le Grand (2005) argue that choice systems can be progressive, giving examples such as differential vouchers and capitation formulas that favour poor people. The pessimistic argument is that like all DIY jobs, it can go disastrously wrong (Powell and Hewitt, 2002). Greater choice can easily result in the transfer and individualization of risk, resulting in inequality between good and bad choosers. However, it is not a question of choice disrupting a situation of existing perfect equity. It is likely that both choice and voice are linked with inequality, and it is an empirical question of the levels of inequality associated with both forms, and whether different people will be affected. Neither is it wise to put one's full trust in the state: there are many cases of women retiring with inadequate pensions, partly due to poor or no advice about pension decisions during their working lives. It follows that it remains difficult to come to any clear judgement about state control (direct ownership and finance against indirect regulation) and any effects on distributional impact.

Conclusions

The 'welfare state' in the UK has always been a mixed economy of welfare (Finlayson, 1994; Stewart, 2007). Although it would be fair to say that the state elements dominated the classic welfare state after 1945, private, voluntary and informal welfare never disappeared. There were clear differences between the largely state-provided health and education services and the greater pluralism found in housing and social care. Neither should it be forgotten that one of the most important parts of the classic welfare state was rooted in the regulation of employment levels through Keynesian demand management rather than by direct state employment, and that the 'architect' of the British welfare state, Lord Beveridge, always saw a limit to the role of the state (Powell and Hewitt, 2002). Similarly, the British welfare state has always been somewhat out of line compared with other welfare states, where there has been a larger role for non-state provision (e.g. Ascoli and Ranci, 2002; Bode, 2006; Hill, 2007; Shalev, 1996; Whiteside, 2006).

As we have seen, recent Conservative and New Labour governments have made major changes in the public/private mix of the welfare state in the UK, with significant moves in the dimensions of provision, finance and regulation, and in fiscal and occupational welfare. Adding these changes together is problematic. For example, there have been decreases in provision but increases in finance and regulation, but this cannot be simply represented as $F + R - P$. These changes are complex and cannot be captured by one-dimensional analyses and soundbite terms such as 'privatization'. Moreover, the pattern of change may vary by service and over time.

However, it is likely that the UK welfare state will see a different public/private mix in the future. Most commentators would probably agree that the degree of direct state *provision* will continue to decline. However, this does not necessarily mean that state *responsibility* will decline (depending on the roles for finance and regulation). The first scenario is that the preferred model will be the state as funder and regulator. This moves away from the traditional *etatiste* British version of the 'welfare state' towards other historical and comparative versions of the 'welfare state'. The second more radical scenario is based on reducing state responsibility within a 'welfare society' (e.g. IEA, 1967). This is a model linked largely, but not exclusively, with the political right (see Powell and Hewitt, 2002). For example, Freedland (1998, p. 219) regards welfare state users as 'passive recipients'. He argues that:

> we need to curb our instinct which makes us look to the state rather than to ourselves ('civil society') to solve our problems ... we have spent a century equating the state with compassion ... Any retreat from public provision is immediately condemned as a betrayal of a government's sacred obligation to protect the weak ... the goal is a smaller welfare state – embedded in a welfare nation.

Some, such as Frank Field, Paul Hirst, and David Blunkett point to the mutualism that provided 'socialism' before state welfare (Powell and Hewitt, 2002).

The current trends appear to be towards the first model. New Labour denies 'privatization', although many of its policies are remarkably similar to (or go beyond) Conservative policies that Labour in opposition termed 'privatization' (e.g. Choose and Book; ISTC; PFI; Foundation Trusts). As recommended by Think Tanks such as the IEA many years ago, and only partially implemented by the Conservatives, the promotion of individual choice from a range of public, private and voluntary sources paid for by state finance (moves towards cells 2 and 3 in Figure 2.1) now appears to be the preferred model. This is a de facto voucher scheme. In 1981 the Conservative Secretary of State for Education, Sir Keith Joseph, declared himself 'intellectually attracted' to the concept of vouchers. Despite being sidelined owing to operational problems, Margaret Thatcher remained attracted to a voucher scheme, but

Oliver Letwin (Mrs Thatcher's Policy Unit and later Conservative minister) stated in 1993 that it is 'something that by accident was invented by the right but it might well have been invented by the left' and 'it may be a Labour Government which introduces it' (cit. in Timmins, 2001, pp. 417–20). In the short term, Letwin was wrong. New Labour abolished the quasi-vouchers of nursery education and the Assisted Places Scheme (but kept Direct Payments). However, in the longer term, he may be correct: the British welfare state may be based on a similar vision of (to borrow the nicknames coined in 'Private Eye' magazine) the 'Mad Monk' (Joseph) and the 'parish vicar' (Blair).

3
Welfare State Transformations in an Affluent Scandinavian State: The Case of Denmark

Jørgen Goul Andersen

Introduction

Measuring welfare state change is controversial. Since Pierson's (1994) seminal book, most discussions about welfare state change have been phrased in the language of retrenchment, and Denmark is often listed among the countries with the most severe retrenchment (Korpi and Palme, 2003). However, another indicator reveals that public consumption expenditures increased by 35 per cent in fixed terms from 1992 to 2007. This is a reminder that it is essential to include welfare services and not only cash transfers. But it also indicates that 'retrenchment' is a highly problematical umbrella concept. As pointed out in Chapter 1, we need more adequate concepts to analyse welfare state change. In the Danish welfare state, we find substantial transformations with new mixes of collective responsibilities and new forms of public sector governance. We also find retrenchment – but not very much.

This problem goes beyond the 'dependent variable problem' (Pierson, 2001b, pp. 420–2) which is mostly about *indicators* of *state* retrenchment – for instance, micro-level indicators like compensation rates, aggregate level measures like social expenditures, or institutional change (Green-Pedersen, 2004). In the first place, we must analyse the complete mix of collective social responsibilities (see also Chapter 1 above), not just state welfare. Next, we must distinguish between several dimensions of change (Andersen, 2005; 2007a):

- *direction* of change: Retrenchment or something else?
- *level* of change: Change in paradigms, expenditures, institutions, or outcomes?
- *dynamic* of change: Abrupt or incremental? Conflict or consensual?
- *degree* of change: Transformative or non-transformative?

The following analysis of welfare state transformations in Denmark focuses on three broad policy fields: labour market and unemployment policy, pensions and retirement, and welfare services (health care, elderly care, child care and education). Before addressing these policy areas, however, we present a brief analysis of the overall development of expenditures. Owing to space limitations, we restrict ourselves to Scandinavian comparisons where the Danish pattern deviates significantly from other Nordic countries.

Expenditures

Unlike the other Nordic countries, Denmark was hit by mass unemployment immediately after the oil crisis of 1973–74, and Keynesian crisis policies only seemed to aggravate problems. By 1982 unemployment and inflation rates were close to 10 per cent, state deficits had reached 10 per cent of GDP, and foreign debts accumulated rapidly (Andersen, 1997). This paved the way for a Conservative–Liberal government (1982–93) which immediately liberalized capital markets and switched to harsh cost containment policies in the public sector. Alongside tough measures (from 1986) to cut private consumption, this served to cure structural imbalances in the economy, but at the expense of unemployment rates rising to 12.4 per cent in 1993. The Social Democratic–Radical Liberal governments of 1993–2001 empha- sized 'economic responsibility', but dropped short-term retrenchment and assigned priority to employment. This was largely continued by the Liberal– Conservative government which took over in 2001. Economic recovery from 1999 to 2007 was almost uninterrupted; unemployment declined to 5.7 per cent in 1999 and below 4 per cent in 2007.

From the figures on public expenditures (Figure 3.1), one could be tempted to infer that there had been a liberal revolution since 1993. After explosive growth in the 1970s and stagnation in the 1980s, total expenditures reached a peak of 60.6 per cent of GDP in 1993. By 2007, the figure was nearly 10 percentage points lower (see also OECD, 1999, p. 72; OECD, 2006a, p. 189; Ministry of Finance, 2007a, p. 156).[1] However, alongside declining interest payments on public debt, this reflects the extreme volatility of public finances in Scandinavia. When mass unemployment hit Finland and Sweden in the early 1990s, public expenditures sky-rocketed – in Finland from 44.8 per cent to 63.3 per cent of GDP in just four years (see Figure 3.2; OECD, 2006a, p. 189). But expenditures soon went back to normal, and all Nordic countries have moved from large budget deficits to large surpluses. In Denmark, the surplus averaged 4½ per cent of GDP in 2005–07 (Ministry of Finance, 2007a, p. 147; OECD, 2007a, p. 68).

The Danish figures conceal a marked improvement of social services. From 1982 to 1992, cumulative growth of public consumption was as low as 6.3 per cent at fixed prices. From 1992 to 2001, public consumption increased by 24.4 per cent at fixed prices.[2] And it is estimated to increase by addi- tional 8.8 per cent between 2001 and 2007 (Ministry of Finance, 2007b, p. 10). Altogether, public consumption has grown by 35 per cent at fixed

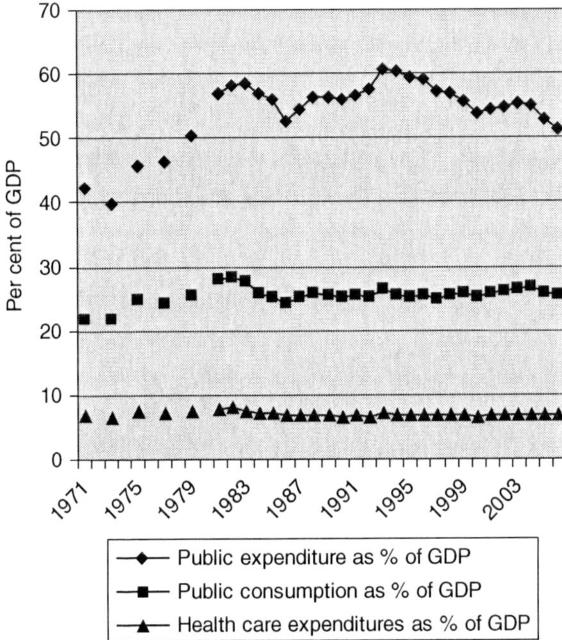

Figure 3.1 Public expenditures in Denmark as a percentage of GDP (1971–2007)
Source: Statistics Denmark (www.statistikbanken.dk/ OFF23, June 9, 2007). 2007 estimate: Ministry of Finance, 2007b. 1987/1988 change in GDP computation. 1993/1994: Change in payment of certain transfers (pensions, social assistance) into gross payments subject to tax ('artificial' increase of about 1.6 per cent of GDP – that is, there was a 'true' decline of about 1.7 per cent in public expenditures as per cent of GDP from 1993 to 1994).

prices from 1992 to 2007 – even though there has been no increase in the number of elderly people and only a moderate increase in the number of dependent children. These figures indicate that 'retrenchment' is not an adequate word to describe recent changes in the Danish welfare state. However, in contrast to austerity measures in the 1980s which contained few institutional changes – most of which were in fact towards universalism (in child benefits, student allowances and home help services) – economic prosperity has been accompanied by far-reaching institutional reforms since 1993 (Andersen, 2000, 2002a). Below we survey the main welfare policies.[3]

Unemployment and labour market policy

In the field of unemployment and labour market policy, changes in paradigms, expenditures, institutions and outcomes have not been synchronized. There was a substantial reduction of *compensation rates* in the

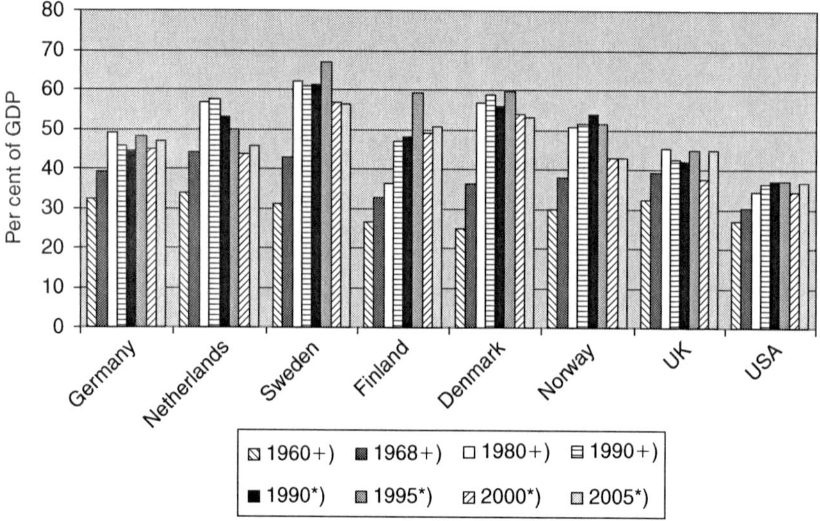

Figure 3.2 Total outlays as a percentage of GDP*

*Total outlays include both current disbursements, capital outlays and capital transfers. This involves some 'double counting'.

+) *Source*: OECD (1999); Andersen and Christensen (1991).

*) *Source*: OECD (2006a).

1980s, but *institutional* changes have been an effect of prosperity (Andersen, 2000, 2002a), including a silent revolution in financing unemployment insurance. A *paradigm shift* towards a supply-side perspective was introduced almost over night in 1989. It had little immediate impact but served to shape subsequent policies. The Social Democrats developed new policies in accordance with the new paradigm, but did not embark on a neoliberal incentive or workfare course. The bourgeois government has emphasized incentives but has embraced the notion of 'flexicurity' to legitimize a moderate course (except for immigrants). However, from an *outcome* perspective it seems that the full impact of tighter conditionality may have been realized through formal and informal changes in implementation since 2001.

Compensation rates

When mass unemployment hit Denmark in 1974–75, the benefit system had just been changed to one of the most generous in the world, with a compensation rate of 90 per cent of previous earnings (Andersen, 1996). This figure has remained, but indexation of the upper ceiling lagged critically behind in the 1980s. Even the wage indexation of benefits since 1991 has contained a small, hidden under-compensation (Andersen, 2004).[4]

Unemployment benefits have become almost a flat-rate benefit as nearly everybody receives the maximum (Clasen et al., 2001; Hansen, 2002). For higher-paid workers, Denmark has the lowest compensation rate in Northern Europe, with the exception of the UK (Hansen, 2002, pp. 34–5). If 1975 is taken as the reference year, compensation rates for an average production worker (APW) reveal radical retrenchment (Korpi, 2002; Korpi and Palme, 2003; Green-Pedersen, 2002a). Suspending indexation from 1983 to 1986 reduced the real value of maximum benefits by 15 per cent. Even by 2001 the maximum was 10 per cent below the 1982 level in real terms.[5] However, the Danish system has remained generous for the lowest income groups. With the exception of new immigrants after 2002, social assistance has also remained very generous by comparative standards (Hansen, 2006; Tranæs et al., 2006). Traditionally, poverty rates among unemployed in Denmark have been much lower – and life satisfaction higher – than in other Nordic and European countries (Whelan and McGinnity, 2000).

However, comparing compensation rates of unemployment benefits for an APW can be misleading. First, the typical unemployed worker earns less than an APW. Secondly, the most important change in many countries is the declining proportion receiving unemployment benefits. In Denmark, the proportion receiving unemployment benefits among those registered as unemployed has rather increased slightly and was about 85 per cent by 2005.[6]

Institutional and paradigmatic change: structural unemployment, conditionality and incentives

Whereas compensation rates have formally remained unchanged, duration of benefits has been shortened to four years. In the late 1970s and early 1980s, duration of unemployment benefits had been *de facto* extended from 2½ years to 8½ years. Formally, duration was 2½ years, but people could re-qualify twice by participating in a 6 months job offer or education programme. Re-qualification to a full 8½ year cycle required six months of ordinary employment. This system, which is about the closest any country has come to a 'citizen wage' system (Andersen, 1996), went on almost unmodified until 1993.

By and large, the bourgeois governments until 1989 were guided by the same economic paradigm as the Social Democrats: more demand for labour power was the key to full employment – only it should come from higher exports (Andersen, 2002a). An abrupt paradigm shift took place, however, in May 1989 when the government presented its '*White paper on the structural problems of the labour market*'. Unemployment was now defined as a 'structural' problem which even export-driven growth was unable to cure: because of mismatch, in particular between minimum wages and productivity, employers would start competing for the labour power of those already employed by bidding up wages long before full employment.

This corresponds with the NAWRU definition of structural unemployment as the 'Non-Accelerating Wage Increase Rate of Unemployment' – the lowest unemployment rate compatible with stable wage increases (Elmeskov and MacFarland, 1993).

Accelerating wage increases in 1987 were seen as evidence of the problem, and as an indication that the structural unemployment rate was around 8 per cent.[7] This helps explain why the new paradigm (contained in a somewhat more ambiguous discourse about 'structural problems at the labour market') was largely accepted by all major political actors. In a commission report (Udredningsudvalget, 1992) even the trade unions gave their consent (Andersen, 2002a; Torfing, 2004). In Hall's (1993) terms, this amounted to third order change, but until the Social Democrats took over in 1993, it had little practical impact. Further, some of the new government's first initiatives continued earlier paths: to break the unemployment curve as soon as possible, it not only stimulated aggregate demand but also extended parental and educational leave, introduced sabbatical leave, and extended a pre-early retirement scheme by enabling long-term unemployed to retire from the age of 50 (Andersen, 2002a).

Since 1993, focus was on mismatch, inflexibility and other supply-side problems. Pre-early retirement and leave arrangements (except maternity/parental leave) were terminated as soon as the employment situation improved (Andersen, 2002c). Still, solutions were mainly Social Democratic: wage inflexibility (minimum wages too high relative to productivity) was recognized as a problem, but instead of adjusting wages to productivity, productivity should be adjusted to wages by means of activation and education. Bottlenecks should be prevented by improved job placement guided by regional corporatist boards monitoring the employment situation and assigning priorities for the employment offices in the region (Andersen, 2002a; Jørgensen, 2000).

In compromises with bourgeois parties in 1995 and 1998 – later called the second and third stages of labour market reform – duration of unemployment benefits was shortened to four years, and conditionality was strengthened in terms of active job-seeking, commuting time, and willingness to take any job. Activation had been improved as a right in 1993, e.g. by elaboration of an 'individual action plan' for all unemployed. But owing to negative evaluations of impacts (Ministry of Labour, 2000), activation came to be seen more and more as a disciplinary device.

Movement along this path accelerated when the Liberal–Conservative government came into office in 2001. Duty to work, removal of disincentives and more efficient job placement were the main instruments. Two reforms stand out: *More people to work* (2002), adopted in agreement with the Social Democrats, and an integration package labelled *A new chance for all* (2005). The Social Democrats were also included in the political compromise over the latter, but withdrew support when the reform was to be implemented. The 2002 reform continued a strengthening of conditionality: Those unemployed were obliged to accept an 'appropriate job' from the first day of unemployment; activation became a duty (but not a right) throughout the unemployment period; 'individual plans of action' were relabelled 'job plans', and people below 25 were strongly pushed into education (Andersen and Pedersen, 2007).[8] More novel elements were a reduction of social assistance after 6 months for spouses (135 € per month for about 21 000 persons), and lower ceilings for social assistance to families with high expenses (cuts of up to 380 € per month for about 13 000 families) in order to remove any possible disincentive to work.

A dual welfare state?

In practice, even if *More people to work* was formally a package for the entire labour market, a large majority of those affected by the cutbacks were immigrants. In 2005 it was the other way around: general measures were included in an integration package for immigrants. The most significant new element was an obligation for couples receiving social assistance to have at least 300 hours of ordinary employment over two years in order to maintain their assistance; only a minority considered completely unable to work (the lowest among five 'matching groups') was exempted (Andersen, 2007d). When the new rules were put into force by 1 April 2007, only about 300 persons lost their social assistance, but because of delayed implementation and temporary loopholes, the effects will not become visible until 2008 (Christensen, 2007).

The most radical measure, however, was included in the 2002 'immigration package'. Here social assistance for (non-EU) immigrants[9] was replaced by a 'start assistance'/'introductory assistance' which was some 30–50 per cent lower (Andersen, 2007d). Whereas social assistance is comparatively generous, start/introductory assistance is among the lowest in Northern Europe (Hansen, 2006; Tranæs et al., 2006). This could indicate a move towards a dual welfare state with fewer social rights for immigrants. However, even though poverty among immigrants is more widespread in Denmark than in Sweden (Morrisens and Sainsbury, 2005), start assistance is the exception to the rule: In general, the universal Danish welfare state is relatively inclusive vis-à-vis immigrants (Andersen, 2007d).

Implementation

Formal rules of conditionality in Denmark became extremely tight in the 1990s and even more so after 2000, almost amounting to 'workfare' (Lødemel and Trickey, 2001a). But much depends on how the rules are administered. With a Social Democratic government, corporatist boards guiding implementation at the regional level, and a legacy from 20 years of mass unemployment where tight controls appeared meaningless, rules were not exploited to their limits. We also know that when duration of benefits was shortened to four years, some municipalities 'recirculated' people at risk of losing unemployment benefits. It is beyond doubt that since 2001, the administration of benefits has become much more restrictive. In Streeck and Thelen's (2005b) terms, one might speak of a *conversion* of the system to new goals, steered by explicit rules and informal signals from the government. Still, the most important driver of change is undoubtedly prosperity and the shortage of labour power.

Since the municipal reform in 2004–06, there has also been major change in the administration of active labour market policies (ALMP) (Madsen, 2006, 2007). State-run job offices for those registered as unemployed were formally merged with the municipal system for social assistance clients into municipal job centres. In most municipalities, administration so far remains divided, however, but the corporatist bodies of the new regions (reduced from 14 to 5) are given only advisory competence (Jørgensen, 2006). It remains to be seen whether the social partners will find new and less formal ways to influence. Further, the government has welcomed private providers and tried to generate quasi-markets, although on a smaller scale than in the Netherlands or in Australia. The public employment agency still has responsibility for two-thirds of all insured unemployed; and among 'private' providers, the labour movement is a key actor (Bredgaard et al., 2005; Bredgaard and Larsen, 2006, 2007). ALMP remains a battlefield between 'welfare' and 'workfare', but the pendulum has swung towards 'workfare' since 2001.

Change in financing: towards privatization of social risk?

In addition, there has been a silent revolution in the financing of the Danish unemployment benefit system. Similar to Finland and Sweden (until 2007), the unemployment system is a Ghent system, based on voluntary membership in unemployment insurance funds typically (but not *always*) controlled by the trade unions. Such 'voluntary state subsidized' institutions (Korpi and Palme, 1998) have been maintained for strategic reasons (Rothstein, 1992) as unemployment insurance provides a selective incentive for trade union membership.

Essentially, the voluntary state-subsidized insurance system represents a liberal legacy, built on the privatization of social risk. In a Social Democratic welfare state, however, financing is largely the responsibility of the state, while members' contributions are nearly symbolic. Thus, this variant of the Ghent model functions almost like a mandatory public insurance. Yet, this system can be reversed into a liberal institution if the burden of financing is shifted back to those insured by raising members' contributions. This was exactly what the bourgeois governments attempted to do in the 1980s. It illustrates how incremental modifications in settings (Hall's first-order change) can amount to transformative change. Contributions were raised in 1983, 1985, 1986 and 1987. In aggregate terms, contributions were raised from just below 10 per cent of expenditures on unemployment benefits in 1982 to 22 per cent in 1987, and due to lower unemployment, the figure had increased to 54 per cent by 2006 (Andersen and Kongshøj, 2007). With some justification, one can speak of a change from a Social Democratic to a liberal model of unemployment insurance. Needless to say, lower unemployment is part of the explanation, but arguably it is the *combination* of lower unemployment and a policy of *non-decision* to adjust members' contributions that is decisive.

Another explanation is the separation between contributions to unemployment insurance and to early retirement allowance. Until 1998, unemployment insurance contributions financed both schemes, but since 1999, a separate contribution for early retirement was introduced, and contributions to unemployment insurance were not lowered accordingly. From 1998, members' contributions to the early retirement allowance have been around 40 per cent of gross expenditures (Andersen and Kongshøj, 2007). Simultaneously, there were full tax deductions for contributions up to 73 per cent until 1986, as against some 33–35 per cent since 1999, because of a change of deductions in the tax reforms of 1993 and 1998 (lower tax rates – widening of the tax base).[10] By comparison, in Sweden members' contributions have remained negligible until 2006. Employees have paid a small amount for administration, plus about 80 € annually for insurance. In Denmark, payments for administration are about 6–7 times the Swedish level, and Danish wage earners paid about 440 € for insurance in 2006, about 5½ times the Swedish level.[11]

Conclusions

'Retrenchment' is inadequate to describe the *direction* of changes in Danish unemployment and labour market policies; since 1990, changes have not been primarily about saving money in times of alleged austerity. True, duration and compensation rates have been cut, and a strong emphasis on security has been replaced by an emphasis on inclusion through work. Still, cutbacks were from a very high point of departure in 1975, and a replacement rate of up to 90 per cent remains generous for low income groups. Unintentionally, unemployment benefits have become a flat-rate benefit, financed mainly by members' contributions (and with rather inadequate income replacement for higher earnings). To cope with incentive problems, there have been targeted efforts to remove disincentives, and to tighten *conditionality* (Ministry of Employment, 2005, pp. 23–4, pp. 70–1). Policies have come to include elements of workfare; activation has turned into a works test and a sanction. With the exception for some immigrant groups, the system has remained effective in protecting against poverty. Policies were shaped by a *paradigm shift* towards supply-side economics, but governments found alternatives to neoliberal solutions. The idea of *'flexicurity'* has served to legitimize the status quo, not as guidance to reform. From an *outcome* perspective, effective protection against poverty has largely been maintained, due to high minima, activation and long duration of benefits. Context is also important. Harsher policies were adopted exactly because of the improved employment situation, and in that context their effects have been less dramatic.

Finally, as to *processes* of change, there have been instances of rapid change as in 1982, 1993, and in 2002 – following shifts in governments. But most changes have been incremental and some went unnoticed like the change in the Ghent system. Policies have also been flexible: in 1993, new leave and retirement arrangements were introduced to reduce labour supply, but as the employment situation improved, these schemes were abandoned (Andersen, 2002c).

In assessing the potentials for the future, it would be tempting to extrapolate from the trends of change during the last decade. However, we would rather predict that the current paths of change are exhausted. It seems almost impossible to tighten conditionality further. The government has welcomed 'flexicurity' as a legitimation of a moderate course, and it has realized that incentives are not very efficient (Ministry of Employment, 2006) and cannot be driven much further without seriously increasing the risks of poverty (cf. Tranæs, 2007). The most interesting question is whether one can envisage a reversal of trends, should large-scale unemployment return. If not, the effects on poverty could be considerable.

Pensions and retirement

In pension and retirement policies, one also finds major transformations. Contrary to standard theories about double payment problems, the backbone of the Danish pension system has been switched from tax financed basic pensions to 'private', fully-funded labour market pensions within only 15 years. The state component is becoming a means-tested residual. This has happened without legislation and without substantial political controversy. As it stands, the system will remain one of the most redistributive in the world. More controversial have been the changes in 2006 of the age brackets of the generous early retirement allowance (currently from the age of 60) and old-age pension (currently 65). The full impact of the 2006 reform has gone largely unnoticed in public debates. At this point, distributional consequences are considerable as the weakest groups on the labour market (in particular women) will lose a generous voluntary early retirement opportunity.

Old-age pensions

After the Second World War all Nordic countries developed tax financed, universal, flat rate 'people's pensions' systems. Unlike the other countries, however, Denmark did not introduce an earnings-related second tier in the 1960s. The people's pension was more generous than in the other countries, voters preferred to continue along this path, and the Social Democrats were

Pillar 1 A. Tax-financed public pensions	People's Pension	a) Basic amount b) Pension supplement Supplementary pensions benefit	Tax-financed/ Pay As You Go
Pillar 1 B. Schemes targeted at old-age pensioners only	– Housing benefit for pensioners – Support for heating for pensioners Other individual supplements Tax exemptions and rebates		
Pillar 1 C. Fully funded public pensions	Supplementary pensions (contributions, funded)	ATP SP (suspended)	Funded: Financed by pensioners (but tax subsidy via deductions)
Pillar 2. Collective Contribution financed private pensions	Labour market pensions (collective agreements)		
Pillar 3. Individual voluntary private pensions	Other private pensions		

Figure 3.3   The Danish pension system 2007
Note: Gray-shaded = Means-tested schemes.

divided over the issue. Since then, the Nordic countries have moved institutionally in very different directions. In Sweden, Finland, and Norway, the second tier turned out to be the first step towards abolishing the people's pension system in favour of a defined contribution 'social insurance' system (Myles and Pierson, 2001; Bonoli, 2003), although with a guaranteed minimum. In Denmark, there has been no formal pension reform, and the people's pension is formally maintained. However, in reality, Denmark has developed a multipillar system which is becoming – in the formal sense – one of the most 'privatized' systems in the world. This developed through *layering* (Streeck and Thelen, 2005b) – by adding a fully-funded, 'private' scheme negotiated in collective agreements. This will partly crowd out the people's pension which has at the same time become more targeted.

The Danish system is continually changing and has not so far reached any 'deep equilibrium' (Pierson, 2004, p. 157). Figure 3.3 gives an overview of the system in 2007. The basic pillar is the people's pension which became universal in 1956 (Anderson, 2004; Green-Pedersen, 2007; Ploug, 2001; Andersen and Larsen, 2002) and completely flat rate in 1964 (finally implemented in 1970), except for a small, income-tested supplement which was in practice given to most pensioners. As a consequence of the 1993 tax reform pensions became fully taxable and were raised accordingly, but in a slightly tricky way as only the means-tested supplement was increased. By 2007, the means-tested supplement is of the same size as the basic amount (each about 8050 € for a single pensioner). The majority of pensioners still receive the full pension (16.100 € annually for a single pensioner), but in the future, more and more pensioners will experience deductions in the supplement; deductions for incomes above 7500 € constitute 30 per cent for singles and 15 per cent for couples (Andersen, 2007c).

1964 also witnessed the introduction of a supplementary contributory scheme (ATP). Unlike in the other Nordic countries, it is small, flat-rate, and fully funded. Since the mid-1990s, it has gradually been extended also to the unemployed so that virtually everybody will receive an ATP in the future. In 1998 yet another supplementary, funded scheme was introduced, called special pensions savings (SP). Contributions are 1 per cent of all incomes, about the same as ATP contributions for an average production worker. In 1999 SP was made strongly redistributive, with equal pensions to all. This would have secured an extremely high equality among pensioners, but it was reversed immediately in 2002 by the Liberal–Conservative government which eventually suspended the entire scheme from 2004 to 2007 in order to stimulate private consumption. At the time of writing, its future is uncertain. In 2003, a small supplementary means-tested pension benefit for the poorest pensioners (up to 1000 € annually) was introduced after pressure from the anti-immigration Danish People's Party.

However, the most important component – which is often overlooked – is a special housing benefit scheme for pensioners, and support for heating, which were introduced in 1978 and 1981, respectively. Although the housing benefits are income and wealth-tested most pensioners are currently eligible. Heating support, by contrast, is only for the poorest. This holds also for other individual supplements which are granted by municipalities on a more discretionary basis. Taken together, however, this means that effective minimum pensions are very high in Denmark. A single pensioner who has no income at all beyond a basic pension, is a tenant, and pays a rent of 675 € per month, has the same disposable annual income as a person receiving maximum unemployment benefits (23.850 €) and receives ordinary housing benefit (Andersen, 2007c). This should be taken into account when we consider the impact of the new element in the pension system: labour market pensions.

Labour market pensions are fully funded and are usually administered jointly by the social partners. They were introduced in collective agreements for white collar workers, mainly in the public sector, from the 1950s onwards. In the 1980s, the expansion had passed the point of no return; the only possibility of introducing collective earnings-related pensions was through labour market pensions negotiated as part of collective agreements (Myles and Pierson, 2001). By 1989 labour market pensions were included in collective agreements for all public employees, and in 1991–93 for nearly all employees in the private sector. In the 2007 collective agreements, the target of contributions was raised to 12 per cent (of which 4 per cent is paid by members, 8 per cent by employers). These pensions are fully funded and also cover risks of disability. When they are fully phased in, they will most probably constitute the backbone of the pension system.

Most actors originally thought of the labour market pensions mainly as a supplement, not as a replacement (Andersen and Larsen, 2004). But it is an instance of layering and differential growth (Streeck and Thelen, 2005b) which slowly transforms the entire system. As in the other Nordic countries, the backbone of the system is becoming a strict defined contribution pension. It is formally 'private', but almost equivalent to a public system, due to the high coverage of collective agreements. State old-age pensions remain generous but will increasingly become means-tested. Taken in isolation, it gradually becomes a residual system.

In the absence of further changes, the system will continue to provide high minima – and large tax incomes for the state to finance the costs of ageing. As the burden of financing has been shifted from the state to the social partners, public budgets will be less pressured in the long run. As compared to the new Swedish system, the Danish system seems equally sustainable, but it is likely to produce more egalitarian outcomes as it mixes actuarial equity with equality more than the Swedish system with a guaranteed (but low) minimum pension. In addition, the guaranteed minimum pensions in Sweden are indexed by price increases whereas the people's pension in Denmark is indexed by wages.

To summarize, the Danish pension system has undergone a major transformation – without legislation – towards mixed responsibilities. Labour market pensions have made the Danish welfare state robust to ageing, and by mixing a contributory scheme with a people's pension scheme, Denmark will avoid the full distributional impact of pure defined contribution schemes. The system satisfies all the economic concerns of World Bank (1994) recommendations (Ploug, 2001; Green-Pedersen, 2007), but it is much more egalitarian. As labour market pensions are formally private but almost functionally equivalent to state pensions, they involve an invisible increase in the proportion of GDP devoted to collective social purposes. But it is an institutionally vulnerable and unconsolidated system with an uncertain future. Because of gender segregation within the labour market, gender inequalities are extended into labour market pensions (Andersen, 2007c; see also Frericks et al., 2005).

Early retirement

In 1979, the Social Democratic–Liberal government introduced a voluntary early retirement scheme enabling people to withdraw from the labour market at the age of 60 with an allowance equal to unemployment benefits, in order to provide more jobs for young people. Eligibility was conditional on membership in a voluntary unemployment insurance fund. Although the qualifying contribution period was successively elevated to 20 years, an initial reduction of the benefit after two years was abolished at the same time. Until 1998 a large majority received the maximum unemployment benefit. Because the scheme became more and more expensive, it was reformed in 1998. The contribution requirement was raised to 25 years, and a separate early retirement contribution was introduced. People were given incentives to continue working until the age of 62. In parallel the pension age was lowered from 67 to 65 years, in order to save money as the old-age pension benefit is lower than the early retirement allowance. These changes had a 'positive' impact with regards to minimizing early retirement among men but less so among women. The proportion of women among those who receive the early retirement allowance has increased from 38 per cent in 1984 to 55 per cent in 2004.

The entire scheme has been criticized by employers and economists, not least in the context of discussions about ageing. Eventually a broad compromise was reached in the welfare reform of June 2006. The most important element was a change of the age brackets in the retirement system. The implementation is not to begin until 2019–22 at which time the age limit of early retirement allowance is gradually raised from 60 to 62 years. Correspondingly, the pension age will be increased from 65 to 67 years from 2024–27. However, these age brackets are subject to full indexation by life expectancy at the age of 60. This means that age brackets will be raised to 63/68 years from 2025/2030 and to 64/69 years from 2030/2035. Provided that Danes by 2025 have reached the same life expectancy at 60 as the French had by 2004, age brackets will be 65/70 years from 2035/2040 (Andersen, 2007c) – effective for people born after 1970. In addition, the contribution record was raised to 30 years and required to begin from the age of 30. Owing to the higher age brackets, the early retirement allowance will become unattainable for some of the core groups of industrial workers and female service workers for whom the scheme was originally designed. At the same time, access to disability pensions has become more restrictive since 1999.

In a nutshell, the changes in the pensions and early retirement system constitute large institutional transformations that will in most respects produce the same outcomes as previously. Adaptation to increasing life expectancy is secured partly by fully-funded pensions, partly through higher age brackets. But as far as the early retirement allowance is concerned, one can speak of a genuine decline of social citizenship for the lowest skilled workers who (until now, at least) have not fully benefited from general improvements of health and life expectancy.

Welfare services

Welfare services are often given too little attention in welfare research. In Denmark, services enjoy higher legitimacy than transfers (Andersen, 2007b), and costs for welfare services have come to exceed expenditures for transfers. In 2005, 256 billion DkK was spent on transfers to households; but public consumption expenditure totalled 400 billion DkK of which nearly three-quarters went to social, educational and health care-services (Statistics Denmark, 2006). Even though services in Denmark are more generous than in most other countries – unlike transfers to households – pressures for expansion are strongest on services which are backed by public employees and by middle-class users with rising expectations.

From cost containment to renewed expansion

When the bourgeois government came to power in 1982, it had one over-riding concern: cost containment. Apart from harsh budget requirements to municipalities, a main instrument was a new budgeting system with 'total frames' so that budgets were determined top-down, not bottom-up. The aim was to maintain zero growth in output, and with a calculated annual productivity gain, this would trigger a reduction in the number of public employees (Schlüter, 1982). Although the government did not manage to cut public consumption, it actually managed to maintain average growth rates as low as ½ per cent until 1992. These policies were highly unpopular, and subsequent governments aimed at small annual increases. However, pressures for increased spending increased even more, and as mentioned, the cumulative growth from 1992 to 2007 was as high as 35 per cent. Thus, welfare state change in Denmark has become a question about growth priorities, not about retrenchment.

Paradigmatic change

Institutionally, the most important changes in services have been shaped by the *New public management* paradigm (Hood, 1991; Greve and Ejersbo, 2005; Ejersbo and Greve, 2005; Greve 2007; Christiansen, 1998) which has been disseminated across modern welfare states, e.g. by the OECD.[12] In Denmark, the political keyword was 'modernization'. The first 'modernization' programme was presented by the bourgeois government in 1983 (Bentzon, 1988), and in 2002 the government launched a new programme that has subsequently been implemented, *inter alia*, in an elderly care reform (2002). It has also been underlying a municipal reform (2004–06) and a proposed quality reform (2007).

In government discourse, the term 'modernization' has served as an umbrella concept covering a number of more or less coherent ideas rooted in the application of a market perspective to public services. The underlying premise is that there is little difference between public and private service 'production'. This means that principles of management from the private sector can be transferred to the public sector, and that services wherever possible should be exposed to competition and consumer choice by generating quasi-markets. Competition requires, in turn, a separation of buyers and providers of welfare within the public sector – the latter should in principle function as private companies and be paid according to performance, as agreed upon in a contract. Consumer choice requires information about quality. Allocation according to customers' demands becomes easier if there is a price mechanism like user fees. Obtaining efficiency becomes easier if wages are more individualized and less compressed. And incentives or control is needed to avoid 'sharking' among public employees ('agents') vis-à-vis their employers ('principals'). In short: The new paradigm creates new challenges which require institutional adaptation.

In the 1980s modernization efforts were mainly focused on cost containment and better management (decentralization and stronger management, contracting, output controls) and less on marketization (competition, user fees and outsourcing). In addition, programmes also contained 'rule simplification', later called an 'action plan for de-bureaucratization' (Ejersbo and Greve, 2005). The latter was not very successful (Christensen, 1991), nor was the idea to increase user charges. Nevertheless, new public management ideas have continued to shape policies. The Social Democratic leadership accepted and developed many of the ideas. But they did not actively promote outsourcing or freedom of choice between private and public providers; owing to internal resistance, they largely tried to keep private providers out of core welfare tasks.

Interestingly, the modernization programme of the 1980s also came to include reforms to increase user influence through voice, by establishing elected user boards wherever possible in the public sector, first and foremost in schools. This builds on another paradigm of user influence or user democracy, which has been very strong in the 'activist' Scandinavian welfare states (Hernes, 1988; Andersen and Hoff, 2001). To the bourgeois government, this was welcomed as an instrument to limit the power of public employees. Since 2001 it is the market approach to welfare production that has been stressed, in particular free choice: emphasis has been on citizens as consumers and on 'exit' rather than 'voice'. However, it must be underlined that the two have worked together well: in the first place, 'exit' can be an alternative to 'voice' when users (such as hospital patients) are difficult to organize. In addition, 'exit' is complementary to 'voice' by making it possible to satisfy the preferences of minorities among users. And finally, 'exit' can be a resource for 'voice': users have larger influence if they can sanction by voting with their feet.

Changing the welfare mix in services

As mentioned, there were few institutional changes towards mixing state and market in the 1980s. Another global idea – that of mixing state and civil society – also had limited impact. A basic characteristic of the Nordic welfare states is the degree of de-familialization (Esping-Andersen, 1999) and state responsibility for care functions. This development seems irreversible.[13] In a full dual earner family model, money for family care must be generous but targeted to extraordinary situations (Andersen, 2002c). Unlike in Continental European welfare states (Naegele et al., 2003), switching between work and care over the life course is not really an option. There have been a few reforms enabling people to take leave from jobs to care for seriously ill family members, and parental leave has been extended to one year. It has also become possible to receive *cash for care* for own children and for providing home help for one year. But take up is low. Liberals and Conservatives have traditionally favoured cash for care, but lack of voter interest, society's need for women's labour power, and the risk that such arrangements would mainly be used among immigrants have cooled the parties' active interest quite a bit.

The role of *voluntary associations* is recognized by everybody, but nobody envisages that they could take over functions from the state; their role can be described as supplementary and highly specialized (Bundesen and Henriksen, 2001; Henriksen and Bundesen, 2004; see also Dahlberg, 2005). As to *social responsibility of firms*, this has increasingly been taken seriously as something more than just a euphemism for subsidized employment (Martin, 2004). Another trend is the explosion in firm-based health-care insurances which the government has made a tax-free fringe benefit. So far, these insurances are cheap due to low take up. It is impossible to assess what will happen if people learn to *use* the insurances, and if premiums increase accordingly – will employers' interests cool off, will the state take the opportunity to save money, and will there be a 'crowding out' where people become less willing to pay for public health care in addition to private insurance? So far, the idea of free public health care is so strongly rooted that 'crowding out' seems less likely than a 'push on' effect where private hospitals increase expectations for public health care.

There are as many far-reaching potentials in new mixes of state and markets as there are ways to combine regulation, financing and provision of welfare (Barr, 1998). Since the mid-1980s, there has been little discussion about full privatization, let alone mandatory private insurance. New or higher user fees were also given up as these were highly unpopular among voters (Andersen, 2007b). Ironically, it became the task of a bourgeois government to introduce free universal home help in 1992 and to reduce user fees for childcare after 2005.

Outsourcing/contracting out means that delivery is private (profit or non-profit), but financing and regulation remain public. Unlike user fees, this has no immediate distributional impact. Voter resistance is substantially lower, but resistance among public employees remains strong (Andersen, 2003, 2007b). Social Democrats have accepted outsourcing as a principle, but have been somewhat more reluctant to implement it than their Swedish sister party (Green-Pedersen, 2002b). Bourgeois governments, on the other hand, have worked hard to increase outsourcing – in the 2007 economic agreement with the municipalities it was agreed to increase outsourcing from

20 to 25 per cent before 2010. Because of the critical discussions about outsourcing in the 1980s, it has become important for governments to underline that outsourcing is not aimed at saving money, only at improving quality. Furthermore, outsourced services are often exposed to so much critical media coverage and government control that firms do not consider this market attractive. After negative experiences, firms have almost completely exited the market for childcare.

Vouchers allow users to choose between private and public providers (as in elderly care), or between public providers (as in health care – unless waiting lists are long). Vouchers have expanded 'from above', not as a result of demand 'from below'. Consumers have even had to 'learn' being consumers (Rostgaard, 2006). But they are very popular among voters who see it as an extension of social rights (Andersen, 2003).

Health care

Until the mid-2000s, Denmark was successful in containing costs for health care. In the 1970s health-care expenditures were growing very fast, even in relative terms, from 6.8 per cent of GDP in 1971 to 8.0 per cent in 1982. However, in spite of low economic growth and an ageing population, bourgeois governments managed to lower expenditures from 8.0 per cent of GDP in 1982 to 6.6 per cent of GDP in 1992 (Figure 3.3). This reflects that cost containment was really harsh. Seemingly it also had negative effects on quality and even on life expectancy (Andersen and Christiansen, 1991). Although expenditures have expanded at a faster rate than GDP (in spite of rapid economic growth) in subsequent years, there has been virtually no overall growth in health-care expenditures as per cent of GDP over the past 35 years (Andersen, 2002d).

This is not an effect of privatization of financing. Except for (comparatively large) co-financing of medicine and dental care, health care has remained completely free of charge, whereas there are small fees in the other Nordic countries.[14] Since 2002, patients have been granted the right to choose treatment wherever they want in the public system, and a right to treatment in a private hospital if treatment cannot be provided within two months – from 2007 one month. This has increased outsourcing to private hospitals. Health care used to be financed by the counties, but from 2007 counties were replaced by five regions without providing them with the right of taxation; like waiting list guarantees, this is likely to increase expenditures. The spread of private health insurance and the waiting list guarantee has led to an expansion of private hospitals. Initially, Danes were strongly opposed to the establishment of private hospitals, but since the late 1980s, they have largely been accepted. However, the principle of free universal health care has not been contested, and private hospitals are more likely to have a 'push on' effect than a crowding out effect on public health-care expenditures.

Elderly care

Unlike Sweden, which introduced user fees for elderly care as part of the crisis policies in the 1990s (and maintained them afterwards), Denmark abolished means-tested user fees in 1992. In Norway user fees are of a more symbolic nature (Szebehely, 2005). Compared with other countries, Denmark has an unusually large proportion of senior citizens (aged 65 and over) receiving elderly care – about 25 per cent. Only Norway and Iceland come close to these figures whereas the Swedish figures are around 15 per cent. In short, Denmark is currently the herald of Scandinavian universalism in elderly care.

From time to time, it has been debated whether user fees should be re-introduced, and about half the population supports such a proposal (unpublished findings from a 2000 survey). Meanwhile, municipalities have been rationing 'practical assistance' (help for cleaning, etc.) by one-third from 1997 to 2005 (Nielsen and Andersen, 2006). Often people are granted only one hour of cleaning each second week, because municipalities assign priority to those in need of personal care. Besides, rest homes are being abolished in favour of centres where people typically have their own, fully equipped two-room apartments and are offered the care they need. The apartments are rented on normal conditions (favourable due to the special housing benefit scheme for pensioners, see above), and seniors have to pay for meals and other services, but care is provided free of charge. These priorities run counter to rational choice theories of retrenchment. Even though universalism is formally maintained, the significant cuts in practical assistance mean that in real practice, the differences between the Danish and the Swedish situation are smaller than they might seem.

However, the most important change is the marketization of home help services. In 2002 municipalities were forced to calculate a unit price and invite private producers to deliver services at the same price, which effectively offered the elderly free choice between public and private providers. This necessitated an organizational division so that service providing units became separated from public authority functions. In principle the providing units are organized as private producers who sign a contract with the municipality. Private producers (typically 'for profit' producers) are gaining an increasing share of the market – some 20 per cent of the 'customers' by 2005 – but as they mainly provide practical assistance, their share of total number of hours worked was only three per cent (Nielsen and Andersen, 2006). User satisfaction is marginally higher among those using private providers who are considered to be more responsive and flexible: even though contracts are based on a minute-by-minute specification of what the home helper should do, the most important parameter on which private providers can compete is by neglecting such specifications and deliver what customers want. Finally, private providers can compete by offering additional service against payment – an opportunity which is much wanted among the municipalities.

But this is opposed by both private providers who fear competition, and welfare 'fundamentalists' who fear that municipalities would assign priority to additional services for the better off elderly.

It remains to be seen whether free choice will have any behavioural and ideological impact (as normative institutionalism would suggest), and whether private firms will become a new strong interest group in this policy area (as historical institutionalism would have it). In the short run, however, the main effect is an empowerment of users, and this is the main reason for the popularity of such reforms. In the long run, there may be institutional feedback effects, but 'systemic *retrenchment*' is not likely to be an adequate label.

Child care and family policy

Unlike in Sweden, private 'for profit' providers have failed in the field of child care in Denmark (Udliciteringsrådet, 2004, 2005). Public attention and controls have simply made it unattractive for producers. Nevertheless, the government has tried to promote freedom of choice in other ways. There has always been free choice between institutions (or public child carers) within the municipality, but since 2001, the government has sought to introduce free choice across municipalities (even though this has not always been fully implemented, due to waiting lists). Another change is the possibility of establishing private child care with public support. This has turned out as a flexible way to meet special needs, for instance regarding opening hours.

However, rather than increased choice possibilities, the most important change is the obligation for municipalities to provide public child care for anyone in need. Unlike in the 1980s, this also includes care for children of nonworking parents: unemployed and immigrants are strongly urged to let their children attend nurseries and kindergartens in order to learn the language better and in order to alleviate 'negative social heritage'. Furthermore, user charges have been reduced from a maximum of one-third of the costs to a maximum of one-quarter, with 50 per cent rebate for the second child and additional siblings (however, this followed a period of de facto user charge increases in the 1990s). Even though instances of retrenchment are discernible (they always generate loud protests) when municipalities cut back on personnel or introduce payments per hour, the entire policy field has been one of expansion, not retrenchment.

When it comes to cash payments, child allowances were made universal from 1985, justified as compensation for the losses of a tax reform that reduced deductions for interest payments (which were largest for young families). Curiously, this is the only instance where a significant proportion of voters want to reintroduce means-testing. However, government and opposition have been united in rejecting this proposal, mainly because of fear of adverse effects on work incentives.

Education

Like child care, education belongs to the 'social investment' part of the welfare state, and except for a few economists, even die-hard neoliberals have never challenged the stance that education at all levels should be free of payment. Not even the unusually generous student allowances that were introduced in the mid-1980s have been questioned. By 2007 students above 20 years old and not living at home receive 650 € per month regardless of parents' income (with the possibility of getting loans on favourable conditions on top of that). Moreover, new schemes for cheap transport and improved support for students with dependent children have been introduced. Like in the field of child care, it is difficult to find much retrenchment here, even though productivity gains are sometimes presupposed in budgets of the state-run parts of the education system.

By tradition, Denmark has been the country of user influence in schooling par excellence (OECD, 2004). In the first place, all schools are directed by user boards with a majority of parents. Secondly, there is free choice not only between public schools in the municipality (recently extended to go across municipality borders, but with some deficiencies regarding implementation), but also between public and private schools. Since the 1850s, Denmark has had a unique tradition of publicly supported 'free schools', which can be established for pedagogical, religious, political or ethnic reasons. The fees to be paid by parents constitute on average about 100 € per month (OECD, 2004). There are also a few boarding schools with upper-class recruitment, but these are the exception. Even though there are social biases in recruitment to private schools, they reflect differences in education, not in income (Jørgensen, 2007). Looking at outcomes, the positive side is a unique feeling of user influence among Danish parents – even in comparison with the other Nordic countries that have moved in the same direction (Andersen and Rossteutscher, 2007). However, on the negative side there have been tendencies towards segregation, mainly in neighbourhoods with high proportions of immigrants.

Summing up

In public services there has been little retrenchment since 1992. Moreover, with a cumulative growth of about one-third in a period with virtually no demographic pressures, the label of retrenchment is misleading. There is no questioning of universalism or state responsibility, and it is a field of credit claiming rather than blame avoidance. The major institutional change – especially since 2001 – is the effort to increase freedom of choice everywhere in the public sector, in accordance with the modernization programme of the Liberal–Conservative government. Although this is to some extent guided by *new public management* philosophies, it is not by any means about saving money or about minimizing the state; consumerism ('exit') is mixed with formal and informal user influence ('voice'); and finally, the choice revolution is in practice more about providing an outlet for dissatisfaction and individual preferences than it is about transforming the service sector into a marketplace. The latter would be far too demanding for consumers. Looking at outcomes, there is little doubt that we face an empowerment of the individual citizen. As to normative side effects (Blomqvist and Rothstein, 2000; Blomqvist, 2004), these do not currently seem to lead away from the welfare state; moreover, they seem to 'push on' in the sense of raising expectations further.

Conclusions

The Danish experiences strongly disconfirm notions about the 'stickiness' of the welfare state. Borrowing from another branch of literature, one could say that 'reform has become the routine' (Brunsson and Olsen, 1993). There have been a lot of reforms, quite a few of them even transformative, some abrupt, others incremental. With a few exceptions, reforms have been adopted in relatively broad compromises or subsequently accepted by the opposition. Whereas retrenchment and cost containment was a common denominator of the reforms in the 1980s, the reforms since then have been more of an institutional character, and they have seldom been driven by short-term cost containment concerns. Rather, they have been aimed at bringing more people to work, at securing long-term sustainability, or at improving efficiency or responsiveness.

As far as directions are concerned, we find paradigmatic and discursive changes in a somewhat more liberal direction (especially supply-side economics and new public management). But by and large governments have refrained from neoliberal solutions. With the partial exception of an obsession with incentives and competition from time to time under the Liberal–Conservative government, most solutions have been pragmatic and more or less in accordance with Social Democratic/social-liberal traditions. Institutional changes have been large, even transformative in some fields, notably pensions and labour market policy. Another feature is the continued prioritization of social investments in the young. There have been substantial modifications in the division of labour between the state and the social partners, and between the state and the market in provision of welfare. It is reasonable to speak of an 'activation of social protection' in the sense that there is much more emphasis on bringing people back to work. A related overriding change is the efforts to bring the welfare state to act more in conformity with the market.

However, there has been little questioning of the responsibility of the state for final outcomes. Thus, it is difficult to speak of a deterioration of citizenship, in spite of a few examples pointing in that direction. It is easier to discover instances of empowerment. This is also why we refrain from using the keyword 'recommodification' to describe market-oriented changes. True, there have been deteriorations for unemployed workers and in particular for immigrants living on social assistance as well as increased conditionality rules, stretching almost to workfare in some instances, but these changes should be seen in the context of the improved employment situation which is also an important driver of the tightening (although some economists might claim the reverse causal relationship).

There are clear indications of increasing inequality and poverty – the ultimate measures of outcomes – in the case of poverty directly related to policy change, i.e. the emphasis on incentives. Although increasing poverty is a serious self-inflicted challenge, the most critical questions should be addressed to the future: what will happen to (the administration of) social protection if and when the decline in unemployment is reversed? What will happen to those 60–65 years old in 2019 who are too worn out to work but not eligible for disability pension? What are the chances that the tax system will become substantially less redistributive? And will the state be able to maintain a relatively high level of equality if wage dispersion continues to increase? All of these questions are uncertain. But as to the last couple of decades, one feels tempted to conclude that there have been large institutional transformations of the welfare state – indeed systemic change – which however have the net effect of maintaining or even ensuring the status quo with regard to outcomes.

4
The Public–Private Mix in Southern Europe: What Changed in the Last Decade?

Ana M. Guillén and Maria Petmesidou

Introduction

Welfare states are undergoing a process of transformation that redraws the balance between the public–private welfare mix under the pressure of rapid socio-economic and political changes. Southern European (SE) countries experienced an expansionary phase of social welfare over much of the 1980s, but soon faced serious fiscal constraints that became even more pressing when these countries embarked on the project to join the European Monetary Union. This considerably stalled the welfare state expansion trends of the 1980s and called for comprehensive social reforms. In this endeavour a common language for institutional change and policy reform developed, embracing guidelines, strategic options, benchmarking and other performance criteria, in the various fields of co-ordinated European strategies (e.g. equal opportunities, employment policy and social inclusion, pensions and health), which deeply affected research and policy agendas. Nevertheless, different starting points, socio-cultural patterns, institutional structures and reform capacities account for a variety of responses. In Spain, Italy and, to a lesser extent, Portugal negotiated agreements have been important vehicles of structural reform. Furthermore, in Italy and Spain, enhancement of multilevel governance through decentralization and a wider distribution of power among institutions of various jurisdictions, national, regional and local, has significantly influenced policy innovation.[1] In Greece no major platform of social concertation for radical reform has emerged that could tackle inherent distributional imbalances and bring forth administrative and policy rationalization: decentralization in respect of social policies and programmes is proceeding very slowly, and the scope of multilevel governance is restricted. A tradition of statist-paternalistic forms of social organization,[2] closely linked with highly politicized and conflictual industrial relations in this country are starkly conducive to policy stalemates and reform impasses.

A detailed examination of policy reform in SE is outside our main concern here. Our aim is to review trends in financing, organization and governance of welfare systems. We primarily focus on Greece and Spain, but where appropriate also include comparative perspectives on Italy and Portugal. The first part of the chapter offers an overview of major reform challenges and interventions in the last few years; in the second and third parts we examine funding trends as well as modes of regulation and delivery in respect to four major social policy areas (social security, employment policy, health and social care). We are particularly interested in how far SE countries have responded to increasing pressures for new regulatory and financing structures in social welfare, which are prevalent across the EU.

Reform trends and milestones

In all four countries an expansion of social protection (in expenditure and institutional terms) occurred during the 1980s. In Spain, Portugal and Greece significant changes in the balance of social and political powers, following the restoration of political democracy in the mid- to late 1970s, largely contributed to this. Social protection in SE combines a corporatist-conservative configuration of income maintenance with social democratic principles in health care (and education) systems. National health services were introduced from the late 1970s in all four countries with varying degrees of success in the development of a universalist frame (Guillén, 2002). Initially, social insurance was plagued by a high degree of fragmentation and polarization (particularly in Italy and Greece). Over the last two decades, however, successive reforms in all four countries (varying in scope and effectiveness) attempted to tackle fragmentation and particularism and improve administrative efficiency in social security. Correcting serious imbalances in the face of an imminent financial crisis due to rapid demographic ageing has been an imperative goal of reform efforts for a long time.

Equally important has been the strategic issue of rationalizing funding and improving accounting transparency, for instance, through a clear distinction between contributory benefits and redistributive (tax-funded) measures embracing a range of social assistance cash benefits and services (mostly health care and education), in parallel with promoting equity and efficiency. Social care, on the other hand, is a less developed policy area. Some efforts to expand and improve service provision (e.g. to families and children, elderly people and specific groups in need) have substantially increased per capita expenditure on such functions in all four countries since the 1990s; yet the gap in respect of EU countries with well developed care provision systems is still considerable (Petmesidou, 2006b, pp. 325–9). As to labour market and employment policy there has been a clear trend towards liberalization and flexibilization measures, while a concern with flexicurity is varyingly incorporated in discourse and practice.

Greece's wavering responses to reform challenges

(a) Early 1990s: the neo-liberal turn

The fall of the socialist government under pressure from political and economic scandals at the end of the 1980s, and ensuing political instability during the early 1990s greatly affected social policy trends in Greece. *New Democracy*, which governed the country for a short spell in the early 1990s, used the fiscal crisis and the Maastricht requirements to leverage changes along neo-liberal lines. The EMU requirements prompted consideration of privatization (particularly of public utilities) as a primary financial tool for the public sector; a policy persistently followed to the present time. In other fields (e.g. industrial relations, employment and incomes policy) direct government intervention in collective bargaining (a policy pursued for many decades in Greece) was eliminated, the automatic inflation indexation system for wages was abandoned and new measures were introduced supporting part-time and fixed-term employment and allowing flexible working hours.

The deepening crisis of social security, reflected in the mounting deficit in the largest social insurance organization for private sector employees (IKA), the rapidly decreasing ratio of employed workers to pensioners, the large public debt and the fast increasing budget deficit made a reform of pensions imminent. Legislation passed in the early 1990s was targeted to these fiscal problems, yet drastic changes for overcoming social insurance fragmentation were postponed. Legal provisions increased the pensionable age for civil servants and lengthened the minimum requirements of years worked for retirement under the general scheme of IKA, raised contributions, discontinued the indexing of pensions to wages and introduced cuts in benefits for new entrants (after 1993) into the general scheme.[3] Further, eligibility criteria for invalidity benefits were tightened, without, however, the parallel strengthening of social assistance and rationalization of funding structures (so as to make transparent the boundaries and rules for contributory and tax-funded benefits). Most importantly, inequalities deepened and the number of pensioners living in poverty dramatically increased (Petmesidou, 2006a, pp. 41–5).

As to health care, less than a decade ago a major reform by the PASOK party founded a National Health System free at the point of delivery and aiming to improve equity and efficiency. Yet many provisions of the NHS, such as the prospect of unification of major health insurance funds,[4] the setting up of a primary health system, the decentralization of authority and crucial aspects concerning organizational efficiency were hardly implemented. A serious lack of support by major social actors, conflicting interests within the medical community and discretionary privileges and complex ties between the public and private sector account for this. The Act 2071 of 1992, passed by the conservative government, made significant amendments to the 1983 legislation in favour of private provision: it gave the right to hospital doctors to combine part-time employment in the public sector with private practice, introduced co-payments for drugs, allowed insurance funds to contract with private clinics and diagnostic centres, introduced tax deductions for private insurance premiums and also increased per diem hospital reimbursement rates.[5]

(b) The run up to the Euro and the reform agenda

The socialist party in power over the rest of the decade through to the early 2000s concentrated its effort to bring down inflation and achieve budget consolidation. An attempt to launch a social dialogue for strategic social reform (in spring 1997) did not bear results. Thus significant changes, in the direction of increasing labour market liberalization and employment flexibility, were introduced more or less unilaterally by the government. In parallel some provisions were made for regulating atypical forms of work (in a flexicurity vein) and offering incentives for the regularization of informal employment.[6] In addition, measures were set up to promote active labour market policies for the first time. The reorganization of the public manpower agency (OAED) was announced and new legislation permitted the establishment of private placement offices.

Wage restraint and liberalization measures were balanced with moderate benefit increases and provisions, particularly as the government confronted rapidly increasing unemployment during the 1990s, persistently high poverty rates and a serious deterioration of income levels for a large number of elderly people. In 1996 a social assistance benefit (EKAS) and co-payment reductions for low-income pensioners were introduced in parallel with health insurance subsidies for the young and the aged (long-term) unemployed.

In July 2000, PASOK announced a new, ambitious proposal for the overhaul of the NHS, to be achieved within a six-year period. Two subsequent laws led to the establishment of a health inspectorate and the administrative deconcentration of the NHS through the creation of 16 regional health administrations responsible for the supervision of hospital management and health service delivery; in parallel, hospital management and administration were to be reorganized. Other major reform issues, such as the development of an integrated system of primary health care in urban areas and the amalgamation of health insurance funds did not succeed in being incorporated into the legislative programme. As a result equity, efficiency and cost-containment have persistently been poor (see Davaki and Mossialos, 2006), making Greece's NHS highly deficient compared with health care in Spain and Italy. This has also been one of the reasons for the rapid increase in private health expenditure over the last decade.

Tackling the macroeconomic problems of social insurance has persistently been a pressing priority. Deteriorating demographic trends are expected to increase expenditure on pensions to a maximum level of 24.8 per cent of GDP by 2050 (twice the rate of the expected EU-25 average). As a consequence drastic measures of benefit reduction and an increase of retirement age were proposed in spring 2001. The plan met with strong trade union opposition and the government was forced to abandon it. One year later a watered-down version turned into law. Its main provisions were the unification of public utilities and bank employee funds into IKA (to be enforced in a five-year time period), the introduction of a clearly stated state subsidy to IKA set at one per cent of GDP annually, and some adjustments in the minimum pension conditions stipulated by the 1992 insurance legislation.[7] In addition, the law provided for the establishment of second pillar schemes through the creation of occupational funds that would operate on a funded basis under the control of the National Actuarial Authority.[8]

Enhancing activation and flexibilization was the aim of the legislation on employment promotion enacted in 2000. Wages for part-time workers increased by 7.5 per cent, and in-work benefits were introduced for previously long-term unemployed workers who took up part-time employment (for up to 12 months). The law relaxed dismissals conditions for small firms and redefined flexible working time arrangements along with provisions for cutting down overtime. In parallel OAED was extensively restructured. Subsequently, a network of newly established Employment Promotion Centres (of which there are about 80) and local OAED employment offices (about 40) were charged with the implementation of activation measures linked to 'pathway' approaches and 'individualized support' for jobseekers. Vocational training and labour market monitoring, however, were transferred to two newly established companies under private law.

(c) From 2004 to the present: the Conservatives' return to power

Immediately following the Conservatives' electoral victory, their main concern was tackling the major budgetary imbalances. In the realm of social insurance, the government limited its activity to implementing previous legislation and has been reluctant to introduce a new round of reform. In order to buy time and find a more propitious moment for reform, the government has recently commissioned a review of social insurance to ILO experts.[9] In health and social care, the Conservatives have been very active in new legislation, but the enacted changes only marginally affected the structure of the system. The emphasis is placed on administrative components of delivery.

An analysis of disaggregated social service expenditure demonstrates a static condition of a highly deficient, ex-post, reactive mode of public welfare service provision (Petmesidou, 2006b). A growing need for welfare service provision, in parallel with available EU funding, contributed to the creation of new programmes (e.g. home help, day care centres for elderly people, and centres for support to people with disabilities). Services focus on the most deprived and vulnerable groups, and scarcely face the challenge of opening up the debate for universal, holistic and user-focused services.

Systematic social services departments across first-tier local authorities have hardly developed. Equally absent is a regulatory framework for integrating public, private and voluntary provision. By far the most important reform in respect to the public–private mix concerns the introduction of a private finance initiative (PFI) by Law 3389 of 2005, according to which provisions are made for the private funding of construction and maintenance of social infrastructure (schools, hospitals and welfare centres).

In contrast to the other SE countries no major reform in the field of social assistance took place in Greece in the last decade. Overall cash transfers exhibit a strong 'pension bias' (equally pronounced in Italy, but less so in Spain and Portugal). The few non-contributory (some of them means-tested), categorical benefits are characterized by great gaps in coverage and high fragmentation, while a minimum income scheme is lacking. The social security system is the least effective in Greece and the country exhibited the highest poverty rate (together with Portugal) from the mid-1990s to the early 2000s.

In a nutshell, Greece had to meet specific wage-restraint and deficit-reduction targets in a short time period. Piecemeal changes have been introduced mostly in line with the need for Greece to approximate its legal and policy framework to a range of hard and soft EU requirements. Adjustments have, however, not added up to wholesale transformations that could substantially change the rules of the game (as was the case in Italy during the 1990s or in Spain) and tackle pronounced disequilibria in social welfare with roots in a tradition of paternalist and particularist allocative practices. Needless to say such conditions favour persistent (and even growing) formal and informal privatization (as is strongly evidenced in the field of health and social care).

Spain: a smooth, though not costless path of reform

(a) The 1990s: seeking enhanced efficiency

What is peculiar to the Spanish case are the early rationalizing reform (1985) of the pension system in comparison to the other SE countries and significant moves towards narrowing protection gaps in the realms of family and care policies, non-contributory pensions for the elderly and the disabled, and social assistance (minimum income schemes were introduced between 1989 and 1994 at the regional level). Finally, activation measures began to be introduced in the mid-1980s. The Maastricht Treaty initiated a significant change in public discourse, even though the Socialist party remained in office until 1996. Austerity challenges became even more acute because of the early 1990s economic recession and the public effort undertaken to finance the Universal Exhibition of Seville and the Olympic Games in Barcelona. It is hardly surprising that Spain did its homework properly and was able to put in place a smooth and well-organized process of convergence to access the EMU, especially after 1996. However, cost-control and austerity measures left a clear mark on social policy developments.

Unemployment protection policies were retrenched starting in 1992. The minimum contributory period was expanded from six to twelve months, payment duration was reduced and replacement rates cut. Coverage rates fell dramatically from 80.3 per cent in 1992 to 50.7 per cent in 1995 (Ministerio de Trabajo, 1996, p. 803). The introduction of fixed term contracts through the 1983–84 labour reform resulted in a significant increase of temporary employment, constituting more than 30 per cent of all contracts. Such a situation meant continuous entries to and exits from employment significantly affecting the costs of passive unemployment protection. As a consequence, the National Institute for Unemployment (INEM) went almost bankrupt and retrenchment was necessary. Expenditure growth on activation policies also slowed down for the rest of the decade (Gutiérrez and Guillén, 2000). In 2000, an active integration subsidy was created for older long-term unemployed workers. Two years later, a softened version of a controversial reform proposal aiming at enhancing geographic mobility and limiting the rejection of job offers was passed (CES, 2001 and 2003).

The 1990s witnessed two waves of labour market flexibilization. Part of the first wave (1993–94) included measures aimed at job creation through new tax and social contribution exemptions for employers hiring young people, long-term unemployed, people aged 45 and over, and disabled persons. The measures also included the fostering of work-experience and job-training contracts, and the reduction of barriers for dismissal. On this occasion, and in contrast to the 1984 reform, part-time contracts were more vigorously promoted through public subsidies (CES, 1994). The 1993 reform also included the legalization of non-profit private employment agencies, ending the monopoly of the National Institute of Employment with regards to job placement. The second wave of reform was introduced by the newly elected government of the Partido Popular (PP) in 1996, after 16 years of Socialist rule. It was the first consensual labour market reform and promoted the creation of open-ended contracts, modified part-time contracts and drastically reduced the cost of redundancies for the first time since the advent of democracy (Gutiérrez and Guillén, 2000).

By the mid 1990s worries about future sustainability of the public pension system in a context of austerity and rapid population ageing had grown so much that a parliamentary commission was appointed. After a year of consultation, the commission decided that the existing system should not be fundamentally changed and suggested recommendations for reform in order to secure future viability. This commission came to be known as the 1995 Toledo Pact, to which both the unions and employers' associations quickly adhered. In line with the Toledo Pact a new agreement on rationalizing social security was reached in 1996 (turned into law in 1997). Among many other measures, the rules to calculate contributory pensions were tightened (the first drastic reform in this direction was passed in 1985). To cushion the overall effects pensions for widows and orphans were increased (Chuliá, 2006) and measures benefiting workers with a high number of temporary contracts were agreed. In other words, a reduction of core workers' rights went along with a (modest) amelioration of the conditions for non-core workers. More recent pension legislation (of 1999, 2001 and 2006) proceeded along similar lines (CES, 2000, 2002; CES August–September 2006), while successive social pacts further improved protection of non-core workers (e.g. peasants in southern Spanish regions, part-time and temporal workers). In 1995 the average retirement pension surpassed the level of the minimum wage as result of successive reforms.[10] Furthermore, a reserve fund was created. As for the private sector, personal plans were introduced in 1989. They have grown substantially ever since, both in terms of coverage and accumulated capital. Conversely, second tier occupational pensions have not matured much (CES, 2006).

Health-care services have followed a totally different path. By the early 1990s the change from health insurance to universal coverage had been completed: the Spanish NHS had become a reality. Worries about increasing expenditure were present as early as the late 1980s, as health expenditure grew rapidly, and were conducive to the establishment of a parliamentary commission (Abril Committee, AC) in charge of producing recommendations for rationalization of health-care expenditure and the introduction of cost-control measures. The AC did produce a whole set of reform proposals, which, however, were rejected by the population; the proposal to expand the co-payment for drugs to pensioners, who are traditionally exempt from it, met fierce opposition. Thus rationalization had to be put in place in a low-visibility way. The Spanish NHS was reformed in subsequent years by introducing, for example, programme agreements and prospective funding in hospitals, broader choice of primary doctors and specialists, and some mild managed competition measures (Cabiedes and Guillén, 2001). Overall, attempted rationalizing measures have focused to date on supply-side factors, a condition that kept the level of equity unaffected. In fact, it has not been possible to introduce any co-payments up to the present, which is a very peculiar trait compared with other EU health-care systems.

(b) Recent developments: enhancing equity and protecting dependency

Still under Conservative rule, the process of health-care decentralization was completed in 2001. Today, all 17 autonomous regions enjoy their own health-care system. This was coupled with a new agreement on regional financing and a new statute for health professionals. In 2003 a law on Cohesion and Quality was passed aimed at securing territorial equity and quality levels in the provision of health care. In 2002 the private pillar of pensions was reinforced by increasing tax exemptions (CES, 2003). A new major reform of the labour market was agreed by the social partners in 2006. The main aim of the reform is to reduce temporary employment in the labour market (CES, June–July 2006). Last but not least, two other important laws have been passed. The law on gender equality was approved in 2007. It aims at establishing equality measures for women in employment and social security, as well as in access to goods and services, and closely follows EU recommendations. The most salient achievement of the recent phase of social dialogue has been the tripartite Agreement on Protection of Dependent People in 2005. The aim of the law on Dependency is the creation of a public National System of Dependency with universal coverage for all people in need of care. Implementation started in January 2007 and should be fully developed by 2014. If properly implemented, it may mean the overcoming of the resilient familialism of the Spanish welfare state.

All in all, the Spanish welfare state has undergone major change. This is clearly evident in the realm of health care, where a health insurance model was transformed into a national health service. The change may not be so apparent in the field of pensions, since reports issued by the OECD, the IMF or even the EU on the evolution of pensions in Spain talk about mere path dependency with cost-control adjustments. Nonetheless, the present Spanish pension system can hardly be compared to the one existing in the early 1980s. As shown above, changes aimed at reducing first tier pensions did take place. But reforms initiated since the 1980s show a clear commitment towards internal redistribution. Reforms in the mid-1990s enhanced the protection of non-core workers. Labour market policies have also experienced wide-ranging changes; the rigid labour market of Francoist times remains only a vague memory.

Bringing Portugal and Italy into the picture

Portugal and Italy have substantially benefited from social concertation processes in an attempt to confront the institutional (and financial) predicaments of and gaps in their welfare states and meet the challenges of joining the EMU. In Portugal the Strategic Agreement of 1996 (under a socialist government that came to power after ten years of centre-right rule) constitutes a crucial landmark. It included issues such as income policy, working-time regulation, tax reductions for low-income earners, expansion of unemployment protection and tailored employment policies targeted at different social groups (Guillén et al., 2003, pp. 258–61). Yet by far the most important measure was the introduction of a minimum income scheme at the national level in the late 1990s. It bears not only a strong symbolic role but also a paradigmatic one that enabled a path-shifting movement starting in the mid-1990s (Adào e Silva, 2003).

In the early 2000s reforms introduced voluntary private pension funds with fiscal incentives, and cost-control measures (stricter rules for pensionable earnings, tightening of indexation rules and pension regulations so as to eliminate privileges of public employees). The aim was to secure the fiscal balance of the system at least until 2015.[11] Even if positive in terms of rationalization, experts fear the impact of these reform measures on poverty rates among the elderly in Portugal, especially considering that the poverty rate in

2001 stood at 20.8 per cent,[12] a very high figure, if compared with the EU-15 average of 16 per cent. Similar to Greece, the Portuguese national health-care system (created in 1979) has not reached the state of a fully-fledged NHS. Despite intense public financial efforts (Portugal ranks very high in the EU regarding public expenditure on health over GDP), the private sector remains broad (particularly in primary care) and several occupational categories are entitled to different packages of services (Oliveira et al., 2005). Co-payments were introduced already in the 1980s and reinforced in 1993. Compared with Spain, the Portuguese NHS benefited neither from long periods of socialist rule nor from a process of decentralization.

In Italy the decade of the 1990s constitutes a landmark of reform both in procedural and substantive terms. For the first time, a tradition of conflict-ual industrial relations gave way to more consensual practices facilitating trade-offs between the social partners that considerably changed the rules of the game in policy practice.[13] Faced with the prospect of an increasing fiscal imbalance, radical transformations were introduced over the last ten years on the basis of wide social negotiations. The reforms manifest an important shift away from traditional incrementalist policy. They significantly transformed the pension arrangements by tackling extreme fragmentation and high inequalities in the generosity of the system. The PAYG character of the system is retained, but it is gradually moving to a (notional) defined contribution scheme (applied fully to all entrants into the labour market from 1996).

A means-tested social pension is available for the uninsured aged people, as well as top-ups for low-income pensioners. Furthermore, proposals by a number of expert committees in the last decade stressed the need for more comprehensive, universal-type measures. Along these lines an experimen-tal minimum insertion income scheme (RMI) was implemented in the late 1990s, but discontinued when the right-wing government took office in 2001, leaving any initiative in respect to social assistance entirely to local authorities (Saraceno, 2002).

Reform of the Italian NHS (created in 1978) has been a priority for succes-sive governments over the last decade. The goals are both to contain spending and improve the quality and efficiency of services. The course of action embraced provisions such as user charges; devolvement of powers to regional authorities; introduction of managerial criteria in the running of health-care facilities; and a 'governed competition' mode of steering behaviour of health-care organizations (Anessi-Pessina et al., 2004).

Although devolution of powers in welfare provision to the regions and municipalities was initially enacted in the late 1970s, a comprehensive regu-latory framework for decentralization was only developed at the turn of the century. Since then regional and municipal responsibilities in health, social assistance or even social insurance[14] have been rapidly expanding, with sig-nificant, challenging effects on nationally bounded and standardized social rights (Ferrera, 2003). As in Spain, the increasing importance of the regional and local levels adds more complexity to the Italian welfare system, particularly as multiple variations of institutions, regulations and experimentation practices have emerged in a process of transition for local governance, that is still in progress (Natali, 2006; Bifulco and Vitale, 2006).

Finance and expenditure trends

General trends

In all four SE countries social protection systems are financed largely from social contributions, although there are some differences in national trends. Taxes (as a main source of social protection funding), substantially increased in Portugal and Italy from the mid-1990s to the early 2000s covering over 40 per cent of social expenditure in 2003. In the same period, in Greece, general government funding remained stable at about 29 per cent (well below the EU-15 average, 37 per cent), while in Spain it slightly decreased (from 30 per cent to 28 per cent).

Moreover, Portugal and Greece have relatively high shares of indirect taxes in total tax revenues among EU-15 countries (in the mid-2000s the ratio of indirect to direct taxes was 3:1 in both of these countries; while Spain and Italy exhibited a more balanced distribution, with indirect taxes only slightly surpassing direct tax revenues). In Greece revenue from personal income taxes is the lowest among the EU-15, accounting for merely 4.8 per cent of GDP in 2004 (the corresponding rates for Spain, Italy and Portugal being 6.4, 10.4 and 5.5). Also, the Greek local government levies only 0.3 per cent of GDP in taxes; a feature that exhibited no marked change over the last decade and starkly contrasts Greece to Spain and Italy. Employers' contributions were well above the EU-15 average in Spain and Italy in 1993 and remained so in Spain in 2004. A significant reduction took place in Italy and to a lesser extent in Portugal. Conversely, workers' contributions have remained pretty stable, with the only exception of Greece, where they surpassed the EU-15 average in 2004.

Expenditure trends also differ among SE welfare states, measured both as a percentage over GDP and in per capita terms. As a percentage of GDP, Italian social protection expenditures largely mirror the development of the EU-15. In Portugal, growth is spectacular, with only a reversal of the trend during the second half of the 1990s. Greece also grows very significantly although departing from higher levels. Spain is the only case in which a pronounced decrease occurs and stays, so that the levels of expenditure of 1993 fail to be recovered in 2000s (see Figure 1.1 in this volume). In per capita terms, one can ascertain the pronounced impact of austerity in Italy and Greece and less so in Spain (see Figure 4.1). Conversely, such an impact is not visible in Portugal. By function, as a percentage over total social expenditure, SE welfare states concentrate expenditure on old age and health care, at the

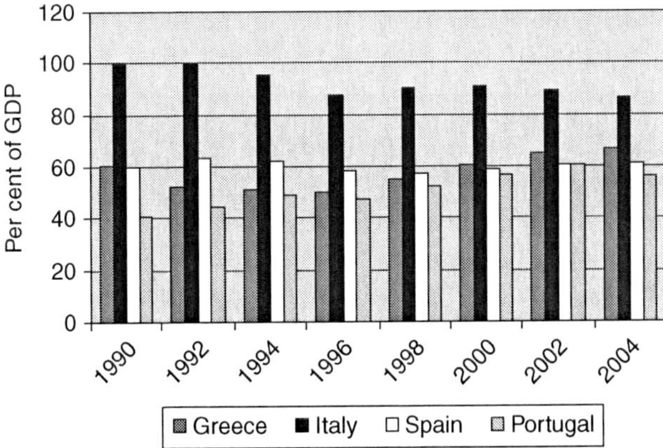

Figure 4.1   Total social expenditure per head in PPS as a percentage of EU-15 average
Source: ESSPROS data base of Eurostat (electronically accessed at http://europa.eu.int./comm/
eurostat/).

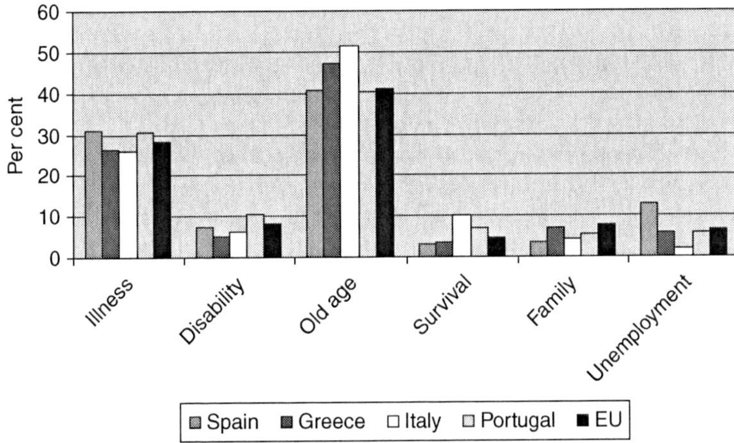

Figure 4.2   Social expenditure by function as a percentage of total social expenditure
(2004)
Source: Own elaboration, based on European Commission (2007).

expense of family policies and unemployment (with the exception of Spain
in this latter case) (see Figure 4.2).

Last but not least, it is important to note that SE welfare states tend to
under-spend in social protection in relation to their wealth. For example,
in 1997, GDP per capita in Spain amounted to 79.9 per cent of the EU-15
average, while per capita expenditure on social protection reached only

61.81 per cent of the respective EU-15 average. A similar gap characterizes the other three countries.

Social security

In SE countries, pensions are extensively based on the public pillar. Major problems arise in respect to the adequacy and sustainability of the Greek pension system. Particularly as it is the most fragmented system in SE, driven by extensive inequalities among the numerous schemes for main and auxiliary pensions, lump sums and assistance benefits, with different rules, contribution rates, level of provisions and state subsidies. Theoretically the system provides a very generous average gross replacement rate (to be reduced though for entrants after 1993). Yet this can barely be realized due to considerable evasion of contributions, resulting from strong disincentives built into the system and a tendency among the self-employed to under-report their income. Consequently a large number of pensioners receive very low pensions.[15]

In Spain, the reforms guided by the Toledo Pact of 1995, and its subsequent renewal in 2003, have had a positive impact on the sustainability of the first pillar. In addition, the separation of financial sources, that is, social contributions being used strictly for contributory benefits, and intense immigration, together with employment growth, played a prominent role in balancing the accounts of social security in Spain in the last six to eight years. The stabilization fund had accumulated a reserve of 40 334 million € by March 2007 (*El Mundo*, 1 March 2007, p. 45), allowing the system to run without deficits until 2020 (CES, 2006, pp. 591–2).

Adequacy of minimum pension benefits is low in Greece, given the high rate of poverty among pensioners and particularly among elderly women: in 2001 the poverty rate stood at 30.2 per cent for households headed by a pensioner, and 33.0 per cent for elderly women living alone, compared with a national average of 21.8 per cent (Papatheodorou and Petmesidou, 2006, pp. 70–2). Equally high is poverty among pensioners in Portugal: in 2001 the corresponding rates were 24.2 per cent for households headed by a retired person and 37.7 per cent for elderly women compared with the national average of 20.8 per cent. Due to substantial reforms in pensions and the broader field of social security in Italy and Spain during the 1990s, poverty rates among the elderly were considerably lower (13.4 per cent in Italy and 20.7 per cent in Spain (ibid.)).

Occupational pensions are scarcely developed in Greece. This second pillar currently amounts to a little less than 0.3 per cent of GDP. The same applies to Portugal and Spain. Conversely, the corresponding rate for Italy is 8 per cent of GDP.[16] It is rather difficult to assess the importance of individual retirement savings (third pillar) in SE countries as these take different forms. Life insurance is not much developed in any of the four countries, while other forms of saving instruments tend to be more important. Life insurance only accounts for 8 per cent of savings in Italy and 10 per cent in Spain, while mutual bonds and direct equity amount to 70 per cent and 49 per cent respectively (Association of British Insurers, 2004, p. 13). Moreover, personal pension products, e.g. funded pensions (based on the EET[17] model, as for instance this has developed in the UK) have only recently been introduced in Spain and Italy; they are absent in Greece and Portugal (ibid., p. 12). As to life-insurance schemes, lump sums are preferred to annuity benefits in all four SE countries.

The percentage of the working population contributing to personal pensions ranges from about 2 per cent or less in Italy, Portugal and Greece to about 22 per cent in Spain (ibid). In Greece total premiums stood at 2.17 per cent of GDP in 2005 (EU-25 average being 8.5 per cent in 2005; Association of Greek Insurance Companies, 2006, pp. 13–4). However, the life insurance industry is expanding rapidly in all four countries: between 2004 and 2005 total life premiums increased in real terms by 8.1 per cent in Greece and 9.7 per cent in Italy (well above the EU-25 average of 6.5 per cent), while Portugal exhibited an astonishing rate of 43.1 per cent (European Insurance and Reinsurance Federation, 2006, p. 29). It is most likely that demand for private pension savings in SE countries will grow further in the future. This, however, very much depends on prospective pension reforms in each country and the extent to which they may entail substantial cuts in the state-managed PAYG systems, the fiscal conditions concerning long-term and medium-term savings products and tax incentives.

Health

Both Greece and Portugal have seen steady increases in health expenditure reaching about 10 per cent of GDP in the early 2000s, whereas the expansion has been less pronounced in Italy and Spain, spending 8 per cent and 8.7 per cent respectively (see Table 4.1). In Greece much of this expansion is the result of an increase in private health expenditure, which rose from 2.9 per cent of GDP in 1980 to approximately 5 per cent in 2004, while in the other three countries private expenditure ranged between 2.2 per cent to 2.7 per cent of GDP.

As Table 4.1 shows, between 1990 and 2004, private health expenditure per head (in US$ Purchasing Power Parities) increased more rapidly than public health expenditure particularly in Spain, Italy and Greece, while in Portugal public expenditure per capita almost doubled. Private expenditure over total health expenditure (Figure 4.3) has grown in Italy during the 1990s to decrease in the 2000s. It has also grown in Spain, not dramatically, but the trend has not been reversed in the 2000s. By contrast, the proportion of private expenditure has fallen most significantly in Portugal.

In Greece, in 2004, a little over 20 per cent of total health expenditure was financed by taxation (with indirect taxes accounting for a large part of it). In the other three countries taxation covered more than two-thirds

Table 4.1   Health expenditure trends

	1990		1995		2000		2004	
	Health Expenditure as a Percentage of GDP							
	Total	*Private*	*Total*	*Private*	*Total*	*Private*	*Total*	*Private*
Greece	7.4	3.4	9.6	4.6	9.9	4.7	10.0	4.7
Italy	7.7	1.6	7.1	2.0	8.1	2.3	8.7	2.2
Spain	6.5	1.4	7.5	2.1	7.2	2.0	8.1	2.4
Portugal	6.2	2.1	8.2	3.1	9.4	2.6	10.1	2.7
	Health Expenditure per capita (PPP US$)							
	Public	*Private*	*Public*	*Private*	*Public*	*Private*	*Public*	*Private*
Greece	453	391	650	600	850	766	1141	1021
Italy	1097	290	1104	430	1521	562	1852	615
Spain	688	185	861	332	1055	465	1484	610
Portugal	442	232	686	410	1145	479	1335	489

Source: OECD (2006b).

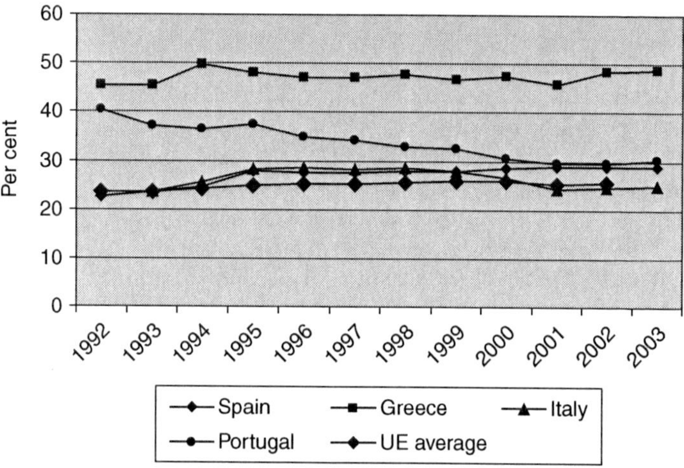

Figure 4.3   Private expenditure as a percentage of total health expenditure
Source: OECD (2005).

of health expenditure. Out-of-pocket payments account for 46 per cent of expenditure in Greece; the proportion is much lower in the other three countries. This extensive reliance on out-of-pocket payments and indirect taxes makes the system highly regressive. Social insurance contributions are an equally important source of funding (29.5 per cent) in Greece, but are negligible particularly in Italy and Portugal. In Spain, the separation of financing sources began to be implemented in 1998 with the aim of financing health-care services fully out of taxes – a process which is still ongoing, but near to completion.

Labour market policies (LMPs)

In Greece public expenditure on labour market policies as a percentage of GDP is the lowest among EU-15 countries (0.5 per cent in 2003).[18] Greece exhibits the highest share of passive measures in total LMP expenditure among the four countries.[19] Expenditure on active labour market policies (ALMP) in real terms (per capita) declined by an annual average of about 10 per cent from 1998 to 2003, while compensation/support of unemployed persons slightly increased in real terms (per capita) by a yearly average rate of 0.15 per cent. Over this period unemployment was persistently high and predominantly long-term. In the other SE countries, activation measures seem to have acquired a more prominent role: annual average growth in expenditure on such measures (in real terms per capita) amounted to 6 per cent in Spain and about 10 per cent in Italy and Portugal between 1998 and 2003. Among the four SE countries, Italy exhibited the highest share for ALMP in the early 2000s (52 per cent of total LMP expenditure).

As to the composition of ALMP expenditure, we observe the following trends since the late 1990s. Training measures in Greece declined in importance and accounted for 29 per cent in 2003, employment incentives stood at 16 per cent, integration of the disabled at 20 per cent, while a comparatively large share (35 per cent) concerned start-up incentives (due mostly to the high percentage of self-employed in the labour force, 25.5 per cent in 2006). In the other three countries employment incentives and training measures accounted for the largest share (63 per cent in Spain, 87 per cent in Italy and 82 per cent in Portugal). Undoubtedly, the resources for training courses and employment subsidies have increased in the last decade in all four countries, due to assistance from EU structural funds, while the European Employment Strategy guidelines have set specific priorities in these countries that lacked planning experience. Particularly in Greece, given the insufficient national resources for employment policy, the policy outcomes are disappointing.[20]

To summarize: fiscal reforms in SE countries have been persistently confronted with the difficult balancing task of implementing austerity measures while at the same time rationalizing and reconfiguring revenue and social expenditure structures, as well as securing resources for expansion of coverage, given the considerable unmet needs owing to serious gaps in the protection of old and new social risks.

Delivery and regulation

Over the last 15 years significant reforms to expand the scope, accessibility and universality of welfare services in SE countries were accompanied by attempts to reform delivery and regulation of services (among others, see Capano, 2003; Torres and Pina, 2004; Ongaro, 2006; Tavares and Alves, 2007; and Borghi and van Berkel, 2007). In Italy and Spain devolution and reforms in a 'federalist' orientation were designed to respond to a particular configuration of politico-historical demands by some regions, rather than being propelled primarily by efficiency and flexibility concerns as, for instance, in the UK and other Anglo-Saxon countries (Torres and Pina, 2004, pp. 452–3). In addition, in SE the involvement of non-state actors in welfare delivery is often sought as a solution to poor (or absent) public provision, rather than as a reaction to 'too much state involvement' in social welfare (Borghi and van Berkel, 2007, p. 99).

Furthermore, of crucial importance for the effective implementation of new governance techniques is the availability of institutional capacities and resources promoting bureaucratic entrepreneurship, managerial autonomy and accountability in policy processes. Reforms along these lines, however, have followed a slow and frequently cumbersome path in SE. The legalistic administrative tradition largely accounts for this, limiting considerably public sector capacities for implementing strategic management, evaluation and systems' control mechanisms; however, the devolution of welfare services, in Italy and Spain, has increased opportunities for innovative strategies. It must be emphasized that important elements of new governance, such as the separation of politics from administration/execution, accompanied by the proliferation of independent bodies overseeing and auditing service outcomes, have only partly been introduced in SE countries. Furthermore, as is especially highlighted by the Greek case, expanding private provision (e.g. in health and social care) may not be matched by increasing public regulation and control. Equally in Spain, nation-wide monitoring and evaluation procedures have not been developed systematically (Torres and Pina, 2004, pp. 454–5).[21]

Social security

In Spain devolution of welfare services to regional governments has gone furthest among SE countries, while the contributory income-maintenance system has remained in the hands of the central state.[22] The system is managed by a single institution (the National Institute of Social Security, INSS) whose Treasury is in charge of collecting all social contributions. The Spanish pension system has undergone a significant process of reduction in its complexity. Numerous new insurance funds ('special regimes') were amalgamated until the early 1980s with the aim of closing coverage gaps. Since then a trend towards convergence among funds together with a substantial reduction in the number of funds has been the norm. Presently, the Spanish Social Security is split between seven funds (general regime, autonomous workers, agrarian workers, miners, seamen, household service and labour accidents). Existing differentials in access rules and provisions for the self-employed are currently being ironed out. As noted above, both the second and third pillars have undergone substantial development for two reasons: the first is related to the enactment of the restrictive reforms of 1985 and 1997, both reducing the replacement rate. The second expanded tax incentives for personal pension schemes in the late 1990s and in 2003; tax incentives were initially introduced in the late 1980s.

By contrast, the Greek public pension system is made up of approximately 130 social insurance funds operating on the basis of labyrinthine rules and great differentials in provisions. They constitute self-governing bodies managed by representatives of employees, employers and the state, while the Ministry of Labour and Social Solidarity provides general supervision. On the basis of recent legislation only four (second pillar) occupational funds have been established. These are run by the social partners on the basis of capitalization and are monitored as well as regulated by the National Actuarial Body. As in the other SE countries, the expansion of funded occupational and personal pension schemes very much depends on the extent of generosity of the public system in the future.

Health and social care

Health care is organized along the lines of a national health service in Spain, decentralized however at the regional level. The system departs from the characteristics of a national health service from the point of view that coverage has become universal but it is not yet recognized as a citizenship right. In fact, insurance (or poverty) still constitutes the criterion for access. Furthermore, public servants may benefit either from public or private provision, at their own choice, in both cases publicly financed, while the rest of the population cannot make such a choice. Some 200 000 people belonging to the highest income bracket remain outside the system.

Devolution of health powers to regions began in 1981 and was completed in 2002. Devolution has entailed a very agile process of innovation. Most regions directly manage service delivery; while some others rely on indirect or 'contractual' management systems where service providers are allocated a package of resources in a way that resembles a capitation formula (in some regions, e.g. Catalonia, both models are in force). All doctors are state salaried employees and patients are referred to higher levels of care by primary doctors (gate-keeping). A positive list of services financed publicly was established in 1995, but regions may add services to the list. National health surveys are conducted on a regular basis for monitoring performance, and quality differentials are kept low. Still, some system imbalances may be ascertained. While Spain counts on one of the best transplant systems of the world, dental care (other than extractions and services for children under 14 and pregnant women) is not included among public health services and psychiatric care shows deficiencies in terms of access and co-ordination. The existence of long waiting lists constitutes another negative aspect and is most likely one of the main causes for the increase of private expenditure in the late 1990s.[23] Deceleration of public health expenditure growth since the 1990s may well cause problems in the near future because of its potentially negative impact on the incorporation of the latest technologies. Improvements in management, increased patients' choice, and cost-control measures on health-care services and drugs were introduced in the 1990s and 2000s, albeit with limited success in controlling expenditures for pharmaceuticals. However, as mentioned earlier, no new co-payment was created.

Greece stands in stark contrast to Spain. A noticeably mixed system of service delivery by public and private providers characterizes both primary and secondary health care. Primary care is largely provided by private physicians, most of which are specialists. There are very few GPs in the country and a gate-keeping system is absent. Within the public sector, IKA runs primary health centres (about one hundred) for its insured population. Physicians in IKA health centres are salaried staff but they can pursue private practice as well. Other social insurance funds contract physicians (on a fee-for-service basis) for primary health consultation. Primary care is also provided in the outpatient departments of hospitals, the 1000 rural health posts and the 200 semi-urban and rural health centres.

Successive reforms of the NHS hardly brought about any significant changes in delivery and regulation as the fragmentation among purchasers and the issue of effectively regulating transactions were not tackled. At the same time the private health market is steadily growing. Health insurance funds, the NHS and life insurance firms purchase a wide range of services from private providers either by fee-per-item or per diem. In addition, most non-core services (e.g. catering, laundry, maintenance and security) of the NHS are outsourced to private suppliers. Patients, under the social insurance schemes can choose a public or a contracted private hospital.

More importantly, however, the private sector controls the largest part of new medical technologies within the system (84.4 per cent of radiology laboratories and 74.7 per cent of nuclear medicine laboratories; Davaki and Mossialos, 2006, p. 297). High technology services required by NHS patients or the health insurance funds are largely purchased from private providers on a contractual basis. These transactions, however, are not systematically monitored or controlled and, most importantly, they foment discretionary privileges and complex ties between the two sectors. Consequently, waste of resources, inflated demand and low efficiency are the major predicaments of the system.

In respect to social care, universally available provision of first-stop systematic services has scarcely developed, both in Greece and in Spain, despite a clear expansion of services in both countries. However, similar to the other SE countries, provision departed from comparatively very low levels. Intervention when problems are compounded often leads to institutionalization with dubious results; not to mention serious deficiencies in institutional settings because of lack of resources. Particularly wanting is preventative work as well as prompt responses to crisis situations, supporting families, lone elderly people as well as persons with long-term disabilities in the community (Petmesidou, 2006b; Rodríguez Cabrero, 2004). One crucial difference between the two systems is, however, that social care in Spain is in the hands of regional (and also local) governments, which has enhanced expansion and innovation, while at the same time contributed to territorial heterogeneity.[24]

To the extent that care services have been expanding in the last few years, there is a great diversity of programmes (and modes of co-operation) across public and private for-profit and non-profit institutions, with most action depending on initiatives by local political personalities and councils, in parallel with the degree of activity of communities, NGOs and other local actors. Furthermore, EU-wide policy orientations, such as the reconciliation of family and work and encouraging women to work, have guided most recent policy measures, largely funded under the Community Support Framework (e.g. establishment of all-day schools and centres of creative activities for after-school care, day care centres for frail elderly people, as well as centres for early diagnosis, counselling, support, education and training of disabled people).

Long-term care provision is of a mixed type in both countries. Social insurance funds exhibit high inequalities as to the range and quality of services offered in Greece. For instance, IKA provides therapeutic care in contracted private clinics for the chronically ill. Yet, per diem cost is kept low and the quality of services deficient. Thus, extra care needs to be provided by the patient's family or by privately (often informally) paid nurses. The situation is not very different in Spain, with the exception of some regions where specific programmes have been developed.

Notwithstanding excessive strains, the family continues to be the main provider of care in SE, while at the same time the informal market is rapidly expanding in these countries. Increasing demand for care services, due to changing family patterns and growing female employment rates, combined with demographic ageing and a steadily increasing number of lone elderly people, is met by female migrant labour. Thus a mode of informal privatization in care arrangements is emerging where the family still plays a co-ordinating role but care tasks are undertaken by foreign minders. Particularly in Italy and Greece it is mostly female migrant workers from Albania, Bulgaria, Poland and Romania[25] that constitute a cheap care labour reserve (Bettio et al., 2006; Cavounidis, 2006). In Spain, foreign minders are mainly female migrants from Latin America. Equity concerns and the sustainability of such care arrangements raise serious questions. The more so as statutory care remains patchy and no major foci of specialized care development, regulation and coordination are formed.

Employment policy

EU influence on national structures in respect to employment policy is significant. Transformations have affected particularly the organization and delivery of employment services and vocational training, partially as a result of various EU directives and rules (as well as of actions by the European Court of Justice). Equally important is the issue of flexibilization that to one degree or another informs policy choices. In addition, the countries have adapted to the European Employment Strategy flagships of 'employability' and 'activation'.

The recasting of national employment service frameworks facilitated a mixed model of service delivery by public and private providers in all four countries. In Greece, the restructuring of the Public Manpower Organization in the early 2000s signalled a transformation (in the direction of liberalization) in service delivery, largely instigated by EU priorities and the need to manage EU funding for employment promotion and social inclusion in a more effective way. In parallel, the number of private employment agencies increased. Legislation passed in the early 2000s, eased conditions for companies to 'lease' workers for short periods from temporary employment agencies.[26]

In Spain, private non-profit temporary employment agencies (ETTs) were introduced in 1985, shortly after the first wave of labour market flexibilization. In 2004 ETTs managed 14.6 per cent of all fixed-term contracts. The success of ETTs is probably based on their capacity for rapid response, which the public system of intermediation tends to lack (CES, May 2005). The end of the public monopoly with regards to job placements in 1994 did not lead to a proliferation of private employment agencies in Spain. Overall, intermediation in job searches is still underdeveloped in both Spain and Greece. Legal-administrative limitations and deficiencies in public placement services and a not fully-fledged non-state sector account for this. As a result, informal contacts and relational capital remain basic assets, often limited to specific social groups.

In the field of training Greece's newly established OAED's subsidiary private firm is responsible for the management of a wide range of vocational education programmes (funded both by EU and national sources). These are delivered mostly by private bodies (i.e. accredited Centres for Vocational Training). In the early 2000s, for the first time, quality criteria of performance by private vocational centres were taken into account in the accreditation process, implemented by the National Accreditation Organization. However, so far regulation of the vocational training system is underdeveloped. A mechanism for systematic collection and elaboration of information on the programmes' effectiveness in respect to employment promotion is absent. Lacking also is information for evaluating the impact of in-firm training programmes and the links between the labour market and secondary as well as post-secondary vocational training schemes. Overall, a system for assessing needs in the vocational training sector is still at an incipient stage.[27]

Compared with Greece, the public vocational training system has advanced significantly in Spain. Its reorganization has resulted in increased flexibility and offers students an alternative route to build sensible career itineraries. Conversely, in-firm training (for the employed) and occupational training (for the unemployed) have shown less positive developments. The programmes are run by the social partners, are co-funded by the EU, and have been devolved to regions. Although medium and small size firms dominate the Spanish economy, they tend to benefit little from either in-firm or occupational training.

Conclusion

The public–private welfare mix in SE has undergone important changes since the early 1990s. Contrary to North European countries, where governments' withdrawal from direct responsibility in welfare provision (at times as a reaction to an 'over-expanded' welfare state) has for some time been at the forefront of concern, in SE countries we often witness trends running in opposite directions. On the one hand, extensive unmet need (reflected in comparatively high poverty levels) creates strong pressures for public intervention in certain welfare areas, and subsequently widens the scope of institutionalized rights (e.g. the right to a universal minimum income guarantee introduced in Portugal in the late 1990s; and the law recently passed in Spain for the protection of frail and dependent persons). Overall this process can be characterized as a catch-up process. On the other hand, however, supranational fiscal discipline measures, domestic austerity conditions and neoliberal ideological overtones impact negatively on public social expenditure trends and increasingly contribute to growing private expenditure and procurement as well as informal privatization, which can be particularly observed in social care. Here informal privatization results from increasing welfare needs under conditions of low public coverage and the weakening ability of the family to provide support.

In the first part of this chapter we briefly reviewed policy changes that have led to a diversified welfare mix in the four SE countries, while in the second we traced funding and expenditure trends. We called attention to the varying effectiveness of fiscal reforms, in each country, since the early 1990s, to tackle the historical hypertrophy, fragmentation and distributive distortions of social insurance; achieve a clear distinction between contributory and universal non-contributive benefits; and secure resources for social services and assistance benefits that have traditionally been an underdeveloped element of social protection in SE. We also emphasized the widening fiscal basis of subnational authorities, particularly in Spain and Italy. Concern about redefining the activities and purpose of government is evident in all four countries through strategies of outright privatization of public utilities, recasting of various public bodies such as, for instance, the National Employment Services and establishment of a range of more or less autonomous agencies for planning, research and inspection functions in various policy areas. Devolution trends have also been prominent mainly in Spain and Italy. In the third part we briefly examined policy developments encouraging a wide scope of mixtures of public–private providers and new governance strategies (quasi-markets, contracting-out, performance criteria, etc.). The extent to which such strategies trigger wide-range and systematic reforms in welfare arrangements and embed regulatory mechanisms into everyday routines greatly varies among SE countries and regional jurisdictions. Moreover, the 'legalistic' administrative culture (particularly strong in Greece) is not fit for purpose, as the regulatory requirements of the changing welfare mix are increasing.

SE countries are facing a daunting task: to tackle extensive inequalities and inefficiencies of their old regimes and at the same time enter into unchartered territories of more diversified yet highly regulated welfare mixes. How successful this attempt will be in the future remains to be seen. At the current stage, however, concern is growing about the overwhelming influence in these countries by a discourse (and practice) that largely frames aspects of social welfare – previously expressed in the language of need, vulnerability and redistribution – in terms of workfare and market competition. In the absence of well-developed safety nets and universal guarantees, there is a danger that such an orientation may pre-empt equity and redistribution criteria with detrimental effects on social cohesion.

5
Metamorphoses of Welfare States in Central and Eastern Europe[1]

Martin Potůček

Introduction

This chapter deals with the protracted processes of social policy transformations in Central and East European post-communist countries. Parallel processes of political democratization, institutionalization of the market economy, globalization and Europeanization form the relevant context of genuine domestic decision making and implementation. From a scholarly point of view, the processes of their societal transformations have been – and still are – a series of exciting natural experiments. As Esping-Andersen (1996a, p. 267) remarked: 'East and Central Europe is clearly the most under-defined region, a virtual laboratory of experimentation'.

In the first part of this chapter, eight post-communist Central and East European states (CEEs) that became European Union (EU) Member States (the Czech Republic, Estonia, Hungary, Latvia, Lithuania, Poland, Slovakia, and Slovenia) in May 2004 are analysed with regard to welfare state financing, regulation and provision. In addition I will scrutinize some social policy outcome variables with regard to the recent transformations. In the second part, the development of the Czech Welfare State is analysed in greater detail.

Central and Eastern European welfare states

The core contextual changes that have influenced social policy-making since the fall of Communism were the abrupt shifts from a centrally planned economy to a market economy, and from authoritarian to democratic and pluralistic political systems. Correspondingly, the regulatory power of the state has diminished and that of the market has sharply increased. In the first part of this section, I will discuss the institutional changes of welfare state policies, before addressing the dimension of outcomes.

Institutional dimensions

The actors of the market economy spilled over to welfare provision both in a regulated and unregulated way. The regulated channels of provision include public as well as partially privatized health and social care facilities and various social security schemes. In addition, all countries allow insurance contracts between individuals and private providers alongside the publicly financed provision. The unregulated channels of provision are typical for dual two-tier systems of social and health care, where formally universally accessible services suffer from insufficient public resources, thus forcing people to pay bribes to professionals in order to get a service in time and of sufficient quality. The role of the civic (nonprofit) sector remains, for a whole set of reasons, rather marginal, though with an appreciable rise of its influence and scope of operation (Kendall et al., 2000).

There have been strong external factors influencing the various national social and health policies. Initially the European Union did not developed strong, clear-cut requirements in the field of social policy-making towards the future candidate countries (Potůček, 2004; Horibayashi, 2006), even though Orenstein and Haas (2003) identified positive effects for those post-communist countries that have joined the EU compared with post-communist countries without an immediate perspective of joining the EU. This initially rather reluctant policy approach by the EU provided considerable policy space for other international actors, namely the World Bank and the International Monetary Fund (Potůček, 2004).

Since the beginning of the new millennium, however, the situation has been changing slowly as the European Union has contributed to the increasing salience of social policy issues on the political agenda, and has provided support for institution building through the transfer of skills and money. The Open Method of Coordination (OMC) has become the main instrument for the 'Europeanization' of social policies in the New Member States (NMS). Nevertheless, the standard of preparing and implementing national programmatic documents was not very advanced. Poorly defined goals and responsibilities, lacking programme evaluation, poor inter-departmental coordination, and missing links to budgetary resources provide plenty of room for further improvements (cf. Atkinson et al., 2005).

Taking a closer look at labour market developments, the general tendency in the region has been towards a steady decline in the number of employed people and rising unemployment. The centrally planned economies inflated the labour force by creating an artificial demand. Thus, unemployment was virtually an unknown phenomenon in the region prior to 1989. Transition brought about a sharp rise of unemployment – from close to zero to two-digit rates in some countries. The current unemployment rates have decreased below the average of Old Member States (OMS), with the important exceptions of Poland and Slovakia, which have significantly higher unemployment rates, and Hungary.

Table 5.1 Unemployment rates in New Member States

Country	2000	2007
Slovenia	6.7	4.8
Czech Republic	8.7	5.3
Slovakia	18.8	11.1
Hungary	6.4	7.4
Poland	16.1	9.6
Estonia	12.8	4.7
Lithuania	16.4	4.3
Latvia	13.7	6.0
OMS	*7.7*	*7.0*

Source: Eurostat, 2008.

Table 5.2 Public expenditure for labour market policies

Country	Public expenditure for labour market policy measures, % of GDP, 2004	Expenditure on active labour policies, % of all public labour market policies expenditures
Czech Republic	0.39	34.0
Slovakia	0.39	18.4
Hungary	0.59	35.3
Estonia	0.23	19.0
Lithuania	0.26	58.3
Latvia	0.46	18.3
OMS	*2.11*	*30.5*

Source: Eurostat, 2006.

Although labour market policies compatible with the market economy have been developed in the region, acute shortages of financial resources and available labour market services continue. Overall public expenditures on labour market policies remain very low compared with spending in OMS; with regards to active labour market policies we witness huge differences among the NMS.

The changes in the realm of pension policies have also been far reaching. The introduction of mandatory second tier old-age pension schemes run by for-profit private pension funds represents a clear trend towards recommodification. The move in this direction has been considerable: Hungary introduced a mandatory second tier in 1998, Poland in 1999, Latvia in 2001, Estonia in 2002, Slovakia in 2003, and Lithuania in 2004. At the same time, the purchasing power of the public old-age pension for current beneficiaries continues to be very low (see Table 5.3).

The changes in health care have largely been characterized by retrenchment, leading Ferge (2001) to argue: 'The public health funds operating now mostly as public insurance schemes severely limit the services they pay for.

Table 5.3   Average monthly old-age pension (in Euros)

Country	2003
Slovenia	420
Czech Republic	223
Slovakia	138
Hungary	176
Poland	222
Estonia	108
Lithuania	95
Latvia	94

Source: CANSTAT (2004).

Table 5.4   Comparison of the satisfaction with health-care system: Old versus New Member States (2003)

	Old Member States	All New Member States plus Turkey, Romania and Bulgaria
Very and fairly satisfied	56%	32%
Not at all and not very satisfied	42%	67%

Source: Alber, 2003, own calculations.

Many types of prevention, screening, and medical interventions, dentistry, and a long list of pharmaceuticals have been excluded from public funding.' Retrenchment within the realm of health care severely contributed to the high level of dissatisfaction with the performance of the (public) health-care system in the NMS.

The mediocre to poor quality of the formal, universally accessible health care has in some NMS contributed to an 'informal' or 'private' care system, financed through out-of-pocket co-payments to doctors (Leven, 2005; Bolanowski, 2007). Unfortunately, systematic data about the extent of these informal payments is not available. Nevertheless, despite these policy developments, the overall health status of the population in the NMS, measured by the life expectancy at birth, has improved since the beginning of the transformation.[2]

There is a considerable gap between the capacities and quality of institutionalized social care in OMS and NMS. Whereas only 4 per cent of adults in OMS report 'additional' family responsibilities, more than 28 per cent of respondents in NMS report such responsibilities (Alber, 2003, his own calculations). Partly this might be driven by the very low satisfaction rates with social services in NMS. This data reflects the extraordinary burden for

Table 5.5 Satisfaction with social services in Old and New Member States (2003)

	Old Member States	All New Member States plus Turkey, Romania and Bulgaria
Satisfied (values 6 to 10 on the 10 point scale)	52%	24%
Not satisfied (values 1 to 5 on the 10 point scale)	43%	74%

Source: Alber, 2003, own calculations.

Table 5.6 Family allowances as a percentage of total household income

Country	1991	1999
Slovenia	0.6	1.4
Czech Republic	4.7	1.6
Slovakia	6.4	4.3
Hungary	8.1	3.8
Poland	4.2	1.2

Source: UNICEF, 2001.

family caregivers. Insufficient institutional capacities create a form of dependency that burdens mostly women and in complex ways contributes to their normative preferences.

Traditional forms of public support for families with children significantly weakened during the transformation period: access to crèches and kindergartens was at least partially re-commodified as many of these previously public facilities were privatized and corresponding public subsidies were abolished. Family allowances declined in all countries with the exception of Slovenia, during the 1990s. This can be understood as privatization largely through the (re-)familialization of risk.

To sum up: compared with the former communist welfare systems, public responsibility for social risk coverage has obviously declined, and private financing has risen due to the recommodification of important welfare sectors. However, the transition to market economies has not made the public sector superfluous as it still dominates the financing of health and social care in the NMS. Compared with public social spending in OMS, public social expenditures – both in absolute and in relative terms – are more modest in the NMS (see Table 5.7).

Social policy outcomes

The general consequences of the political and economic changes after 1989 for the people in all NMS have been an *improvement* in the standard of living

Table 5.7   Total public social and health expenditures as a percentage of GDP in the New Member States (2005)

	Slovenia	Poland	Hungary	Czech Republic	Slovakia	Lithuania	Latvia	Estonia	EU-27
Total public social and health expenditures	23.4	19.6	21.9	19.1	16.9	13.2	12.4	12.5	27.2

Source: Eurostat, 2008.

for some and *stagnation or deterioration for many*. The differences between the lower and upper strata have rapidly increased. The inequalities have risen more rapidly in the Baltic States with Poland following suit. Income inequality in the region at the end of the communist period was low compared to most OECD countries. By the late 1990s, however, the average value of the Gini coefficient in Central and Eastern European and Baltic States had risen to about the average OECD level (UNICEF, 2001, p. 26). The transition has been accompanied by a serious increase in poverty (Orenstein and Haas, 2003). Although the official EU statistics show rates of relative poverty similar to those in OMS (see Table 13.1), the level of absolute poverty in some NMS is quite high: 7.3 per cent of Hungarians, 8.3 per cent of Latvians, 7.8 per cent of Lithuanians, and 5.2 per cent of Estonians are reported to live on less than 2 USD per day at the beginning of the 2000s (GVG, 2002, p. 27).[3] As in most other countries, children are more vulnerable than the rest of the population. There are only two countries in the region that do not show signs of extreme forms of child poverty: Slovenia and the Czech Republic. In the NMS, about 440 thousand children lived on less than 2.15 USD a day by the end of the millennium. With the exception of the Czech Republic and Slovakia, there has been no attempt to define and provide an adequate subsistence minimum.[4] In Poland the rules of eligibility are so strict as to exclude the majority of the poor (cf. Ferge, 2001).

Table 5.8 provides three different variables of social exclusion and deprivation. The first column provides the mean number of items lacking from a list of seven durable consumer goods (TV set, video recorder, telephone, dish washer, microwave, car (or van) and personal computer). The second and the third columns present the proportion of the adult population admitting either having had solvency problems or been unable to save money.

Commonalities and differences of welfare state transformations

Owing to the variable speed of the reform processes and the lack of appropriate data, it is very difficult to offer any consistent conclusions concerning

Table 5.8 Mean deprivation of the population in the New Member States

Country	Index	% with solvency problems	% not able to save
OMS	**0.64**	–	–
Slovenia	0.54	5.2	67.7
Czech Republic	0.80	4.0	63.2
Slovakia	1.29	7.3	72.9
Hungary	1.37	14.3	87.5
Poland	1.52	11.3	86.1
Estonia	1.54	18.8	85.5
Lithuania	1.79	21.7	84.0
Latvia	2.07	24.2	88.2

Source: Russell and Whelan, 2003.

the ideal-typical welfare taxonomy emerging in the NMS or to identify a clear emerging public/private mix. Nevertheless, let us dare to offer some cautious characteristics of the general tendencies, similarities and differences, which should be submitted to further scholarly scrutiny. Slovenia is the country that most closely resembles the traditional Western European Continental model. The Czech Republic follows suit with universal access to core social and health services and universal access to a minimum of subsistence, but with less generous social welfare benefits and more targeting in less vital areas. Hungary and Poland grapple with major difficulties and combine universal access in some fields with a residual restrictive approach in others. Slovakia has made access to social welfare very tough and conditional at the beginning of the twenty-first century, thereby moving from a continental model towards a liberal welfare state approach, which is dominant in all three Baltic States. At the same time, the Baltic States have been – contrary to Poland, Hungary and Slovakia – able to preserve relatively high employment rates and a more flexible labour market (comparable to the OMS average). This summary underlines that we have not been witnesses of a one-dimensional transformation of welfare states in Central and Eastern Europe, but that welfare state transformations are indeed very complex. To get a better understanding of such welfare state transformations in one NMS, we will analyse the welfare state developments in the Czech Republic in greater detail.

Czech welfare state transformations

Historically elements of the current institutional design of the Czech welfare state can be traced back to Bismarck; first corporatist, compulsory health and social insurance schemes evolved at the end of the nineteenth century. In the interwar period, democratic Czechoslovakia possessed a comparatively advanced social legislation that was emulated by other countries – namely Greece. Pre-1989 communist propaganda often showcased the well-organized Czechoslovakian health and social services. Hence, the reason for the final collapse of Communism was not so much related to the mediocre, technically outmoded quality and sometimes limited availability of social services as to the sorry state of the economy, and the loss of political legitimacy. A universal and uniform system of social security was to become the core of the state's social policy during the first turbulent years after the collapse of communism in 1989. Associated with the victory of neoliberal and conservative political parties in the 1992 elections, liberal and residual tendencies began to be asserted more forcefully in this field. This conception of social reform began to impose limitations on social security policy, which subsequently led to the conception of a three-tiered system: the first tier is based on compulsory public social insurance, reacting to foreseeable situations in a citizen's life, following the pay-as-you-go principle; the second tier consists of state social support, reacting to unforeseeable events, financed through general taxation; finally, the third tier relies on the social assistance principle of supporting citizens who find themselves in an emergency situation, co-financed by central and local authorities, nonprofit organizations and clients.

The subsequent development of social policies in the Czech Republic until present can be differentiated into three phases.

1st phase: Designing new institutions (December 1989–June 1992)

Social policy was developed and embodied in legislation on both the federal (Czechoslovak) level (Federal Ministry of Labour and Social Affairs) and national level (Ministry of Labour and Social Affairs of the Czech Republic). Although cooperation between the two ministries was not always ideal, from a political standpoint their position and those of the respective governments were always compatible. What they did is best described as an effort to systematically replace state paternalism by introducing more resilient and decentralized mechanisms that would be compatible with ongoing economic reform. These mechanisms were to be beholden to the regulative and executive powers of the state only where necessary. From the standpoint of the governments' prevailing political philosophy, this approach was a combination of socio-liberal and social-democratic philosophies.

The Czech social policy reform was based on three basic components: first, active employment policy; second, liberalization and pluralization of social welfare based on a Bismarck-inspired insurance system that has been deeply rooted in the country's modern history since the end of the nineteenth century; and third, the development of a social safety net for people in need. The 'Scenario of Social Reform', which was drafted and adopted by the federal government, became the core conceptual policy document guiding reform in the social sector; it was significantly influenced by social-democratic as well as social-liberal ideologies. A plan for a universal and unified system of social welfare was adopted, which would offer universal compulsory health and social insurance (complemented by voluntary supplementary insurance for individuals or groups), and means-tested state social assistance. The latter would only be provided in the event of a citizen's inability to provide for him or herself *and* if all alternate possibilities of welfare and assistance had been exhausted.

2nd phase: Retrenchment (July 1992–June 1998)

Owing to a change in government a neoliberal policy, emphasizing the priority of economic reform, dominated in the coming years. The government not only declared it would limit the role and spending powers of the state in the sphere of social security, but also enacted some legislation along these lines, specifically the targeted and means-tested child allowances. Many social policy institutions, originally designed as pluralistic and corporatist, remained firmly in the hands of the state (e.g. the system of social insurance), due to the distrust by the government in the intermediary role of civil society institutions. The Czech neoliberal and conservative governments neglected conceptual work and a practical orientation towards long-term goals, especially preventive social policies (Potůček, 1999). Finally, the government was not enthusiastic in joining the EU and subsequently lagged in the implementation of EU requirements, as was reflected in the annual reports by the European Commission.

3rd phase: Social policy back on the political agenda (July 1998–June 2006)

The core of the consecutive governments' policies, dominated by the Czech Social Democratic Party, was the idea of a socially and environmentally orientated market economy. This was in sharp contrast with the more or less residual social policy accents implemented by the previous governments. However, the implementation of such programmes was seriously threatened by budgetary constraints caused by the acute fiscal problems of the country, the legislative delays caused by the weak position of the governments, the insufficient implementation capacity of the state, and the long-drawn-out reform of public administration.

An important aspect of social policy regulation was represented by the EU-accession preparatory process, speeded up by a clearly pro-European governmental policy. The EU's Open Method of Coordination began to be applied with the annual elaboration and implementation of the National Employment Action Plans, guided by the European Employment Strategy at the end of the 1990s (Ministry of Labour and Social Affairs, 2004a). In 2002 the European Commission asked all candidate countries' governments to elaborate Joint Inclusion Memoranda in order to identify key problems and policy measures to fight poverty and social exclusion. A social inclusion

Table 5.9 Public social and health system expenditures as a percentage of GDP (1992–2006)

Year	1992	1997	1998	2006
Pension security benefits	7.6	8.0	8.1	8.3
Sickness and maternity benefits	1.2	1.1	0.9	1.0
Unemployment and employment policy expenditures	0.4	0.2	0.3	0.4
Family allowances (state social support system)	1.8	1.6	1.6	1.1
Social care benefits and social services system	0.8	0.7	0.8	0.9
Others	1.8	0.1	0.1	0.2
Administrative expenditures	0.2	0.3	0.3	0.3
Social security system expenditures – total	13.7	12.1	12.1	12.2
Health care system expenditures	5.4	6.7	6.6	6.8
Total Expenditure[5]	19.2	18.8	18.7	19.0

Source: Research Institute for Labour and Social Affairs, 2007.

agenda was formally set with the preparation and approval of this document by the representatives of the European Commission and the Czech government in 2004 (Ministry of Labour and Social Affairs, 2004b). The preparation and approval of a National Action Plan on Social Inclusion 2004–2006 followed suit (Ministry of Labour and Social Affairs, 2005a). Despite the progress achieved, the weak spot of the document is the lack of explicit goals, poorly defined responsibilities for implementation, and missing links to the budgetary process (Potůček, 2007).

Despite the shift from liberal-conservative governments (in power from 1992 until 1997) towards coalition governments led by Social Democrats (in power from 1998 until 2006) and their respective approaches to social policy, the overall trend in public social expenditure has been surprisingly stable (see Table 5.9).

The majority of these expenditures are financed through obligatory employees' and employers' contributions to the social and health insurance funds. The state pays contributions into these funds for children, pensioners, parents on maternity or paternity leave, the unemployed, the disabled, soldiers and prisoners (see Table 5.9).

Although the share of private funding for social and health care is still comparatively low, some fields have seen a slow and steady increase of the private share (e.g. through co-payments for prescription drugs).

Employment and unemployment policies

The attention paid to active and passive employment policy fluctuated significantly over the years according to the political orientation of the

Table 5.10 Compulsory social insurance contributions as a percentage of gross earnings

Czech Republic, 2007	Employee	Employer	Employed person, total	Self employed person – see note
Pension insurance	6.5	21.5	28	28
Health insurance	4.5	9.0	13.5	13.5
Sickness insurance	1.1	3.3	4.4	4.4 (or 0)
State employment policy contribution	0.4	1.2	1.6	1.6
Total	12.5	35	47.5	47.5 (or 43.1)

Note: Self-employed persons decide the basis for the contribution calculation by themselves, with minimum level of 50 per cent of income after deduction of expenses, but at least 25 per cent of average monthly salary, and with a maximum ceiling of 40 500 CZK, representing approximately 2 times the average monthly salary. The basis for their health insurance is calculated according to the formula of 50 per cent of average monthly salary. They may decide to opt out from sickness insurance and arrange it for themselves privately.

Table 5.11 Expenditure for ALMP as a percentage of all LMP expenditures (Czech Republic, 1991–2004)

Year	1991	1992	1993	1994	1995	1996	1997	1998	1999	2000	2001	2002	2003	2004
%	31	55	35	28	26	21	14	18	25	37	43	44	N/A	34

Sources: Ministry of Labour and Social Affairs, 2006; Eurostat, 2006.

various governments, with the right-wing orientation being more in favour of passive policies, and the left-wing orientation supporting active employment policies, which is also reflected in spending levels (see Table 5.11).

The share of expenses for active employment policy stabilized at the level of about one-third of total LMP expenditure. In 2006 European structural funds added approximately one-third to the amount allocated by the Czech state budget. Nevertheless, the share of ALMP expenditure as a percentage of GDP comprises only about one-third of the resources allocated to these policies in the OMS. Not surprisingly only 8 per cent of the unemployed participated in individual measures; the ratio of clients/case-workers fluctuates between 250–400/1 (Sirovátka, 2007a). The government launched (and Parliament accepted) the first National Programme of Employment in early 1999. The National Employment Action Plan 2004–2006 (Ministry of Labour and Social Affairs, 2004a) has been elaborated under the auspices of the European Commission and the Czech Ministry of Labour and Social Affairs.

Despite these improvements, the unemployment insurance system only provides very modest benefits. On average unemployment benefits provide a net replacement rate of 28.5 per cent of the estimated net average earnings in 2005. Unemployed workers under the age of 50 are entitled to receive benefits for a period of 6 months; unemployed workers between 50 and 55 for 9 months; and those above 55 for one year. About 4–6 per cent of households claim social assistance benefits, and most social assistance claimants (62–3 per cent) are unemployed (Sirovátka, 2007b).

Czech employment policy is executed overwhelmingly via assigned public institutions, i.e. labour offices. Through the implementation of the Employment Act in 1991 a network of public regional Labour Offices was created to administer state employment policy in the regions. In addition to offices in regional capitals, branch offices were established in the bigger regional towns. Their services are relatively easy to access for job-seekers throughout the country. Private firms focus their services nearly exclusively on finding good candidates for high executive positions in multinational companies. As there are scarce resources allocated for the active employment policy, the space for the engagement of private enterprises and civic associations in the provision of labour market services is very limited. Nonetheless, there is clearly a window of opportunity in the utilization of the European Social Fund.

Old-age pensions

Pension insurance covers old-age pensions, disability pensions, widow and orphan pensions, contributions for the treatment of a family member, and administration costs. 1995 saw a significant legislative change in the structure of compulsory social insurance with the passing of a new law on old-age pensions. According to this new law, the statutory retirement age for women was raised from a minimum of 53 to 57 years (the actual limit depends on the number of children), while for men the retirement age rose from 60 to 62. These reforms were to be implemented over a 12-year period. In 2003 the retirement age was further raised to 63 for men and for women without children. Again the age increase will be phased in over a longer period of time; the new pension age will be fully effective for men in 2016 and for women in 2019. The basic pension insurance law conceives the old-age pension as consisting of two components made up of a fixed amount paid to all senior citizens and one that is dependent on the number of years worked and the income earned; the law is based on the principle of substantial redistribution of accumulated finances towards persons with a lower level of earnings. Old-age pensions for persons with higher working incomes are affected by a regressive calculation formula. The average net replacement ratio of old-age pension benefits declined from 66 per cent (1990) to 52.7 per cent in 2006. The gross replacement rate dropped over the same time period from 52.7 per cent to 40.8 per cent and will further decline to 38 per cent by the year 2010 and to 35 per cent in 2015. The average, actual monthly public old-age pension benefit was 8173 CZK (approx. 290 €) in 2006. This decline is the result of various reforms enacted by the conservative-liberal governments. The low replacement rates reflect a very residual conception of old-age insurance that differs considerably from the Continental practice; furthermore, the future prospects do not rule out the possibility of average public pension benefits falling below the subsistence level. The collection of the contributions as well as the management of the pension fund is fully in the hands of the state, instead of the originally envisaged independent public corporation – a Social Insurance Fund.

Although the public compulsory social insurance still dominates the Czech system of old-age pension insurance, voluntary private pension insurance contracts, introduced in 1994, are attracting ever more customers. The employer may pay part or the whole contribution on behalf of the insured, providing the employee has agreed. The state supports participation in private pension schemes through the provision of state subsidies and income tax allowances. This scheme represents a popular and quite successful example of public–private mix of welfare provision. The attraction of these schemes among the middle and upper classes will further increase with the projected decline of the public pension. At the end of 2004 there were almost 3 million contracts of voluntary private pension insurance in the Czech Republic, covering about 37 per cent of the Czech population above the age of 18. It presents an increase in participation of 8.2 per cent since 2003 (Úřad státního dozoru v pojišťovnictví a penzijním připojištění, 2005, p. 25). Employers contribute to about 27 per cent of all voluntary private pension insurance contracts (ibid., 2005, p. 36). Many contractors, however, use this scheme as a profitable opportunity for short-term savings only.

Since 1995 there has been a public discussion under way on reforming the whole concept of the old-age pension system. It was initiated by experts from international financial institutions, especially the International Monetary Fund and the World Bank, who strongly recommended that the country opt for compulsory private co-insurance. This new type of old-age insurance would complement the pay-as-you-go public scheme that would gradually lose its importance. It was argued that this change would be inevitable owing to demographic trends (aging of the population) and the demand for investment in the national economy that would be satisfied by the newly established and privately run for-profit pension funds. In contrast to most of their neighbours among the CEE, the Czech Republic resisted this pressure. There were two main factors that explain this significant difference:

(1) The country was not in as deep a fiscal crisis as the other CEE countries and was less dependent on loans provided by international organizations.
(2) There was strong political opposition among the Social Democrats, who were the main party in government between 1998 and 2006, and trade unions. They emphasized the risks of such a reform referring to the fragility and volatility of financial markets. In addition they were sceptical about the huge demand for additional financial resources during first decades after the introduction of such a private pension system.

Although a comprehensive pension reform has not yet been introduced, the discussions are ongoing. Neoliberal theorists, right-wing politicians and representatives from financial institutions continue to support the idea of compulsory private co-insurance, whereas institutionalists, left-wing politicians and trade unions favour voluntary nonprofit co-insurance schemes (with financial contributions from both employees and employers). In 2005–06, a task force, with members from political parties, experts and civil servants, was established by the government to draft a policy document stating the principles for future pension reform. The task force suggested reforms of the statutory pension system, including the further increase of the retirement age, the creation of a reserve fund and support for the further development of voluntary private pensions. Although the document did not include the element of compulsory private insurance that had been discussed previously and despite its modest reform proposals, Parliament did not approve the document as the Communist Party of Bohemia and Moravia's deputies refused to support it, even though the party's representatives in the task force endorsed it.

Health services

The Bismarckian legacy shaped the reform of the Czech health services after 1989. Even though there were good reasons for the transformation of the over-institutionalized state-owned communist health care system into a more flexible National Health Service model financed through general taxation, older professionals and the general public overwhelmingly preferred the system of compulsory health insurance financed by employees, employers and the state. Subsequently, major changes were achieved: the decentralization of health care, the establishment of public Health Insurance Funds, the privatization of most primary health-care providers and some (smaller) hospitals, and the modernization as well as the improvement of care delivery. Consequently, the overwhelmingly public funding of health care is associated with an increasing share of private provision.

Paid work and family responsibilities

Until 1995 child allowances were paid to all families with dependent children, but through the introduction of the State Social Support Act this universal benefit was changed into a means-tested benefit. Although the Social Democrats proposed a return to the previous universal benefit, they were unsuccessful in re-introducing the scheme, because of political resistance among the coalition parties, the opposition parties, as well as fiscal constraints. The real purchasing value of child allowances and tax credits have declined between 1989 and 2002 by 27 to 45 per cent (the actual decline depends on family type) (Hiršl, 2003). This has contributed to a worsening of the situation for many families. In 2002 37.7 per cent of children lived in households with incomes in the lowest income quintile and 25.7 per cent

Table 5.12 Trend of public and private expenditure on health services in the Czech Republic

Year	Public (CZK, per inhabitant)	Private (CZK, per inhabitant)	Total (CZK, per inhabitant)	Public (%)	Private (%)
1995	9 032	905	9 938	91	9
2000	12 748	1 336	14 085	91	9
2001	14 298	1 612	15 909	90	10
2002	15 208	1 749	16 957	90	10
2003	16 499	2 057	18 556	89	11
2004	17 212	2 179	19 391	89	11
2005	18 149	2 668	20 818	87	13

Source: Institute of Health Information and Statistics of the Czech Republic, 2006, pp. 196–7.

in households with incomes in the second income quintile. 13 per cent of children are at risk of being poor, based on the EU threshold of less than 60 per cent of median income (Večerník, 2005).

The subsequent decline in the fertility rate to the lowest level (at about 1.2) in Europe was one of the decisive reasons – apart from ideological factors among the governing Christian and Social Democrats and the EU's programmatic and political influence – contributing to the articulation and approval of an explicit Czech family policy in 2005 (Ministry of Labour and Social Affairs 2005b). As a consequence, a maternity leave benefit at 69 per cent of the previous salary (with the upper ceiling of 694 CZK per day) is now paid for 28 weeks. Furthermore, the monthly parental leave benefit, which is paid for a maximum of four years, was increased from CZK 3696 (ca. 130 €) in 2006 to CZK 7582 (ca. 270 €) in 2007. In addition a dense network of (mostly public) kindergartens, with newly introduced free access for pre-school children (5–6 years old) is available to parents.

The status of the Czech welfare state

The situation of full employment, income levelling and relatively generous aid to families with children contributed to low levels of poverty during Communist rule. Although poverty has increased, various public social policies have effectively mediated the effects. The Czech Republic does exhibit typical features of strong adherence to the continental, or even more specifically, Central European, Bismarckian, corporatist, achievement-type welfare state. It stems from its modern history and has been revitalized even after more than four decades of etatist bureaucratic collectivism (Deacon, 1997). It is ideologically rooted in the social thinking of Albín Bráf, Tomáš Garrigue Masaryk, Karel Engliš, Josef Macek and others, in the long tradition of the Social Democratic movement,[6] and the strong support among the Czech public for policies based on the principles of achievement-remuneration and

Table 5.13 The status of the Czech welfare state as of 2006

		Policies			
		Employment and unemployment	*Old-age pensions*	*Health services*	*Paid work and family responsibilities*	*Summary*
Dimensions	*Financing*	national public, with the contribution of ESF	mostly public; increasing share of private co-investment	mostly public (below 90%)	mixed; disproportionally low share of public resources	public resources prevail; modest
	Regulation	national public, with EU intervention; collaboration with firms in an effort to increase employability and employment	public; collaboration with private funds in delivering voluntary co-insurance	public, weak	public and non-profit private	centralized at the national level; involvement of EU and civil society weak; corporatist institutions matter
	Provision	prevailingly public	prevailingly public	mixture of public and private	mixture of private and public	prevailingly public; share of private (non-profit and for-profit) providers increasing
	Outcomes	mediocre	modest, universal	good, universal	families with children and caring women in a disadvantaged position	in general satisfactory; important deficiencies and inefficiencies identified
	Summary	centralized, underdeveloped	reform necessary to sustain the system in the long run	underfinanced, better regulation needed	unsatisfactory, new public initiatives and provisions needed	coping with challenges – with difficulties and shortcomings

social justice.[7] It has much in common with the neighbouring German and Austrian welfare states (including the institutional and attitudinal resistance to change) – despite the increasing incidence of residual elements. The policies with regard to their specific public/private mix are summarized in Table 5.13.

As can be derived from Table 5.13, the various reforms until now have not comprehensively changed the post-communist welfare state established in the early 1990s. The public still plays a crucial role. Partially this is the result of the limited influence of external actors and the domestic political system. Because of the proportional electoral system, Czech governments are relatively weak in designing and enacting any 'radical' reform. The requirements as well as the institutional and financial support provided by the EU have been important, especially with regards to institution building.

Conclusion

The end of Communism was characterized by an underdeveloped and skewed market, ill-functioning and misused state, and a very weak civic sector. The years to come brought about the maturation of the market, still fragile, badly performing and politically fragile states, and a recovering, but not very influential civic sector. What ramifications did these developments have for welfare state transformations in NMS? Is there a newly emerging post-communist welfare state in Europe?[8] Our analysis shows that, a broad variety of approaches and institutional frameworks have evolved in the various NMS. Despite some similarities, each country has developed its own approach towards social welfare restructuring. With regard to the public/private mix it has to be emphasized that the Baltic countries seem to rely much more on private and market elements compared with the other five countries studied. Although the provision of welfare has been partially privatized in all these countries as an inevitable consequence of the introduction of a market economy, the Czech example shows that the public sector still dominates many policy areas. The transformations do not only differ between the various countries, but also between the various policy domains. For instance, although the provision of health care was largely privatized in the Czech Republic, it relies for about 90 per cent of its finances on public funding. Hence, overall it would be wrong to speak of a one-dimensional trend towards outright privatization and the surrender of public responsibility. Furthermore, political parties and power resources still seem to have a great influence on the design and the transformations of the welfare states in NMS. After nearly 20 years since the collapse of Communism and subsequent economic, political and social transformations it is not clear whether these have led to new social policy equilibria.

6

The State of Japanese Welfare, Welfare and the Japanese State[1]

Roger Goodman

Introduction

This chapter uses a detailed case study of the Japanese social care system as a means of highlighting some of the embedded assumptions in the development of, and literature on, the Anglo-Saxon and Scandinavian welfare models, in particular in relation to the public/private divide in the provision, financing and regulation of welfare services. In comparison with these western systems, the Japanese system has been characterized by: relatively low public spending; greater reliance on family, community and corporations; an emphasis on social policy as investment rather than as a safety net. The delivery of social care has been characterized by (i) reliance on unpaid local volunteers (*minseiiin*) under the direction of local government bureaucrats and (ii) the placement of those who come into the care of the state in privately-owned (*minkan*) institutions, which are regulated and almost completely funded by the state under what is known as the *sochi-seido* system. Both the *minseiiin* and *sochi-seido* systems have provided interesting challenges to the normative assumptions about 'rights', 'citizenship' and 'professionalization' of welfare delivery that are embedded in much of the western literature on social policy. In the 1980s these systems were also seen as part of the explanation for Japan's so-called 'economic miracle' in that high quality care could be provided at low cost to the tax-payer. The 1990s saw economic recession, dramatic demographic changes and a growing civil society in Japan, all of which led to the re-examination of some of the assumptions of the welfare model. The state invested heavily in programmes to increase fertility and provide for the needy elderly but reduced its extent of support for the less needy through reforms of pension and unemployment programmes. The 1990s also saw private welfare providers increasingly subject to market forces, evaluation and accreditation. What is still far from clear is what will be the long-term effects of these welfare reforms on the role of women and on social indicators such as longevity, social equality, health, education and the national economy.

The 'Japanese model' of social welfare

It is quite clear that scholars, both inside and outside the country, have had trouble in situating the Japanese welfare state in a comparative perspective. Even Esping-Andersen (1990) in *The Three Worlds of Welfare Capitalism* was unable to fit Japan into any of his three categories of social democratic, conservative-corporatist and liberal regimes. While at first gloss it seemed to him that it shared much with many of the Southern European 'familistic' forms of welfare systems, he decided in a later piece (Esping-Andersen, 1997) that because of, among other reasons, its greater public spending on family services and less use of unpaid women's work, it should not be included in the same category and he declared it a 'hybrid' model. Against Esping-Andersen, Kasza (2006) in his recent book on Japanese welfare argues against any exceptionalism in the development and structure of the Japanese welfare system. I intend to return at the end of this chapter to the question of how best to characterize the Japanese system, but first I want to describe how the system has operated over much of the postwar period, and how and why it has changed so much in the past decade.

John Campbell (see Campbell, 2002), the American doyen of Japanese social policy studies, has sought to set Japanese social policy in a broadly comparative perspective in which he sees three elements as characterizing the social welfare model: (a) low spending by the state; (b) high level of reliance on family, community and corporations for welfare functions that in the West would be undertaken by the state; and (c) an emphasis on social policy as investment in the economically productive element of the society – i.e. state spending on education or public health to maintain a productive work force rather than providing a safety net for those who cannot contribute to national wealth – leading to women ending up with carrying a large proportion of the care for the elderly and children, a role variously described as either marginalization or a gendered division of labour depending on individual commentators' prejudices. Elsewhere Gordon White and I (Goodman and White, 1998) have argued that these same features extend broadly to what we termed the East Asian Welfare Model. As Campbell points out, this model was perceived negatively (as welfare dumping) by most foreign commentators until the end of the 1970s, but then more positively as a 'Japanese-style welfare state' which could be directly associated with the growing economic strength of Japan. The East Asian economic crisis of 1997 and economic stagnation in Japan has again led to a more negative evaluation, but there has been very little disagreement with the model itself (see Goodman, 2001). The model has relied on a mixture of, on the one hand, public financing and regulation, especially in the areas of employment, health and education, to ensure a strong and productive workforce and, on the other, private provision, often through the family and the local community, to look after the less productive members of society.

A closer look at the support systems for children in need gives a good sense of how the Japanese welfare system works in practice. Such support has generally been provided via a mixture of locally-based quasi-volunteers, unqualified local government bureaucrats, and privately-run (often family-run) not-for-profit institutions. The quasi-volunteers are known in Japanese as *minseiiin* and are a direct carry-over from the pre-war system when they were known as *homeniin*. The *homeniin* system was set up in response to the 1918 rice riots in the Osaka area and was based on the Elberfeld system and the Charity Society of London model of local elite volunteers collecting information on local conditions and seeking community forms of relief. In the war-time period the *homeniin* became synonymous with the local community groups (*tonarigumi*), which played a major role in policing local communities but, despite this, the system was allowed to continue in the postwar period initially simply because there was no money to set up a 'professional' social work system (Goodman, 1998).

Today there are over 200 000 *minseiiin* in Japan, with an average age of over 60. Around ten per cent are over 70 and some are over 80 years old. Until the 1980s most of them, unusually for frontline welfare support workers, were male. *Minseiiin* pay visits to local community members (on average 120 such visits each per year) and report to city offices social welfare department workers (*shakai fukushi shuji*) about those they believe are in need of support. What is not clear, however, is whether *minseiiin* are more active in supporting or policing local communities; single mothers for example sometimes complain that elderly *minseiiin* lecture them on the morality of having children outside wedlock (illegitimacy in the postwar period never having been over 1 per cent of all births)[2] rather than making them aware of their rights to welfare benefits. On the other hand, those (most famously Vogel, 1980 but see also Ben-Ari, 1991) who support the role of the *minseiiin* point out that they are central members of their local communities, unlike professional social workers who in most industrial societies come in from outside. In this sense, their position might be considered closer to that of the Church in many of those societies. Like members of the Church elsewhere, they have no professional social work qualifications but are regarded as upright and experienced individuals who enjoy the respect of the community. Indeed it is this high status position that means few *minseiiin* retire at the end of their three-year terms and hence the average age continually increases. On one thing everyone is agreed; the *minseiiin* system is cheap to run – they are paid only their expenses and indeed some may well at times be out-of-pocket – but since they receive no salary it is not surprising also that the level of activity varies hugely from individual to individual.

The 200 000 *minseiiin* report to a mere 18 000 *shakai fukushi shuji*, local government bureaucrats charged with administering the state welfare system. Put another way, there are only 18 000 of the latter for a population of 124 million, and of these only 1200 are *jidōfukushishi*, bureaucrats who are charged specifically to deal with child-care cases. Statistically each of these bureaucrats carries a huge case load (often well over a hundred cases) and hence it is small wonder that in many cases they rely so heavily on the local voluntary *minseiiin*. Like the *minseiiin*, the local government bureaucrats enjoy high status and also like them they generally are not qualified in social work; indeed, the two facts are connected. As Ito (1995) has pointed out, while there are many Japanese universities offering courses in social policy, these are taught almost exclusively at lower level universities from which very few pass the difficult examinations to become part of the local government bureaucracy. Those who are qualified in social work therefore are rarely employed in generic social work posts and those who hold such posts in most areas of Japan (there are important exceptions such as in Kanagawa, Osaka and Niigata) do not have any social work qualifications. Indeed, they will generally only work in a local government social work office for three years or so before, in the normal rotation of local government officials, being transferred to another department. In general these representatives of the state have been very reluctant to intervene in family matters such as cases of child abuse and domestic violence – indeed several recent tragedies in these areas have been blamed on this tendency (see Goodman, 2006) – and if they do get involved they generally play the role only of regulators who pass on cases to be dealt with by social welfare institutions.

Social welfare institutions are, along with the volunteer *minseiiin* and the *shakaifukushishūji* bureaucrats, the third point in the triangle of Japanese social work provision. While such institutions are all not-for-profit, a very large proportion are privately run, especially after the 1970s since when local government institutions (which have historically had much higher levels of staffing and provision) have been closed down and private institutions have filled the gap in the market. In the case of Japan's 540 children's homes (*jidō yōgoshisetsu*) for example, over 90 per cent are private institutions. It is important to note, however, that around 95 per cent of their funds comes from the money they receive from the state for each child they accept. While many of the workers in such institutions have graduated from university courses in social welfare, many members of their management have not. This is because a high proportion of such homes are either religious foundations or else family businesses where management positions are reserved for those from the religious organization or the family of the founder. While it is not surprising that the business of providing homes for the elderly is flourishing in Japan (which is ageing faster than any other industrial society), it is somewhat more surprising that children's homes are also doing well – despite the collapse in Japan's fertility rate – due to Japan's discovery of child abuse in the 1990s (see Goodman, 2002). The above account of what happens to children in need raises a number of points that suggest the Japanese system operates on a rather different basis from Scandinavian (or what Esping-Andersen calls 'social democratic') welfare systems. First of all, and perhaps most conspicuously, it is probably not exaggerated to say that there is no self-defined social work *profession* in Japan: a high general level of intelligence, on-the-job training and all-round experience has tended to be more highly rated in the Japanese system than professional qualifications. Whether this is through historical accident, political expediency, budgetary constraint or cultural proclivity, however, is, as Campbell (2002) among others has pointed out, very difficult to answer.

Secondly, also in the light of the western literature on social policy, it is very conspicuous how muted the notions of rights and citizenship are in the Japanese model described above. In the case of child welfare, this mutedness was particularly noted in the debates in Japan in the early 1990s over ratification of the UN Convention on the Rights of the Child (see Goodman, 1996). Government officials argued that the UN Convention was based on western assumptions about not only the concept of rights (which has historically had low or even negative status in Japan) but also of the child as a being separate from its parents. Japanese 'cultural practices' such as *oyako shinjū* (family suicide) and the notion of *shinken* (which give fathers the constitutional right to use physical force to discipline unruly children) were seen by some as demonstrations of the belief in Japan that the child was a *mono* (a thing or an extension of a parent) as opposed to an independent being. Indeed, many in Japan in the early 1990s argued that giving rights to children had largely undermined the family in many western societies and was at the root of many of the problems of juvenile delinquency that those societies faced.

Similarly, there has until recently scarcely been a vocabulary with which to express the concept of citizenship in Japanese social welfare services. Most people in Japan have accepted that the state has the authority to act on behalf of its citizens; bureaucrats have been allowed to wield their authority because of what many believe is the meritocratic nature of the education system which had led them to be appointed in the first place (see Boling, 1998, pp. 185–6). The ancient expression *'kanson minpi'* (praise the bureaucrat, despise the people) has held considerable potency in Japan throughout the postwar period as the bureaucracy was credited with (and certainly took credit for) Japan's so-called 'economic miracle'.

Since there has been so little discussion about rights and citizenship and since there has been little investment in a social work profession to argue on behalf of marginalized groups in society, it is perhaps no surprise to learn that there has been little investment in public welfare institutions in Japan. There has been a long history, on the other hand, of private welfare agencies, which have long enjoyed high status within their local communities, even though almost all of their finances in the modern era have come from public coffers. Any history of Japanese welfare development tends to start from the premise that this has historically been down to the good deeds of Buddhist, Christian and Imperial individuals and agencies (see Goodman, 2000, chapter 2 for an overview of historical accounts of welfare development in Japan). Christianity indeed, in a country where less than 0.5 per cent of the population profess to be Christian, is largely associated with its welfare (and educational) institutions.

To summarize the above account of what Watanuki (1986, p. 265) has described as the 'Japanese model' of welfare provision during most of the postwar period (although its roots can be found in the pre-war period): the provision of welfare services has been very largely through private institutions and organizations, but financed out of public funds and overseen and regulated (though often at some remove) by public agencies.

The 'Japanese model' of welfare under attack

The 'Japanese model' of welfare described above – a description with which few commentators would disagree whether they approve of the system or not – has come under sustained attack during the past ten or so years. There are four main sources of this attack, most of which, it should be pointed out, are common to other industrial societies:

(a) Rising unemployment – in a society where full employment has been the main welfare policy through much of the postwar period – has led to: a shift away from the so-called 'three pillars' of the Japanese postwar employment system (life-time employment; seniority promotion; and company welfare); a dramatic decline in the reported sense of security that individuals say they enjoy; and apparent signs of rising social inequality. It is important to stress, however, that, by comparison with western welfare systems, employment practices still constitute a major element of welfare. While, under external pressures, the protection of sectors such as agriculture and retail have been greatly reduced in the past two decades, this has been replaced to a very considerable extent in the 1990s by a policy of deficit spending on public works projects that has kept unemployment at a much lower rate than pure economic conditions would predict. Large companies, while they have scaled back on the employment of life-time workers, still have on their books many workers who would have been made redundant by their western competitors as a result of which Japanese white collar productivity remains very low by international standards. According to Seeleib-Kaiser (2006, p. 713), without these government programmes and company policies, unemployment in Japan would probably be roughly double the official rate of 5 per cent maintained during the recession of the 1990s and early 2000s. The sense of insecurity among workers in Japan comes in part from the realization of this fact, but also in the cuts in the amount and duration of unemployment benefits instituted in the 1980s and 1990s and the tightening up of eligibility criteria for claiming them: the proportion of those unemployed receiving unemployment insurance benefits dropped from almost 60 per cent in 1980 to under 40 per cent in 1998. At the same time, eligibility criteria for livelihood assistance programmes were also tightened which added even further to people's sense of insecurity.

(b) The emergence of what some term 'civil society' (*shimin shakai*) – following the inability of the state to deal with the recession of the 1990s as well as catastrophes such as the Kobe earthquake of 1995 and the Tokyo underground gassing of the same year – has lead to a loss of confidence in the state and its bureaucrats and a much stronger sense that the latter work for the tax payer who has a right to know what happens with their tax money (Bestor, 2002). In the case of welfare policy, there has been a huge growth in locally-based citizens' groups, volunteer activity and NPOs largely due to the unintended consequences of a conservative regional decentralization (*chiiki fukushi*) welfare policy in the 1990s which had been designed to cut costs by throwing back responsibility for welfare provision on to local communities (see Peng, 2005, pp. 90–1).

(c) Both the community and the family – previously seen as the bedrocks of Japanese society – have come under increasing attack as 'feudalistic' institutions, for example, in the form of the increasingly loud discourse during the 1990s of Japan as a 'caring hell' with its legal requirement to care for lineal relations and the pressure of care falling on women. This attack, of course, was driven in part by changing patterns of gender relations during the bubble economy of the 1980s as more women were drawn into the labour force and by their refusal to return to the domestic sphere in the 1990s (leading to them being sometimes demonized by the state as 'parasite singles' who keep their earnings and live off their parents). One might also add – related to the 'discovery' of child abuse in the 1990s (Goodman, 2002) – that there has been a changing discourse about the 'person' in Japan, involving a shift from a belief that people are basically good (*seizensetsu*) to a sense that some, at least, may be basically bad (*seiakusetsu*), a shift that has somewhat changed the perception of parents, bureaucrats and those who work in welfare organization.

(d) Perhaps the most significant pressure on the welfare system in Japan, however, has come from Japan's dramatically changing demography, its rapidly ageing society and shrinking population allied with genuine fears about the lack of children being born, the dangers of open immigration, and the calamitous state of its pension system (cf. Harada, 1998).

The response of the 'Japanese model' of welfare to attack

How has the Japanese welfare state been affected by these external factors? Has the state taken a more active role in helping the vulnerable, or is it still relying on private agencies to do so? Has a more inclusive idea of welfare state been developed? What is the evidence for welfare expansion in terms of financing – despite the recession, which has even in 2007 not officially been declared over after 15 years? A look at some recent programmes in the areas of family policy and social care gives us some clues about the direction in which the welfare system has been developing.

(a) Probably best known is the development of a state programme through the 1990 *Gold Plan* and 1995 *New Gold Plan* for supporting the elderly; state expenditure on elderly care increased from ¥0.57 trillion in 1990 to ¥3.57 trillion in 2000, mainly in the form of home help support introduced under these plans (Peng, 2005, p. 82). The recently introduced Long Term Credit Insurance – introduced largely to avoid social hospitalization which was becoming a chronic problem in 1970s – means a 10 per cent patient co-payment with the remaining 90 per cent of the cost shared between social insurance and general taxation (Campbell and Ikegami, 2003); this system involves a major move from care by the family to care by the state in the sense not only that there is more money in the system as a whole, but also, as Peng (2005, p. 84) puts it, a move from means-tested care to rights-based care. As Webb (2002) points out, this process has gone a long way towards destigmatizing recipients by replacing the old language of welfare (*fukushi*) with a new language of care (*kaigo*).

(b) *1994 Angel Plan*: underlying this programme was a shift from blaming 'selfish women' for Japan's falling birth rate to blaming society for not providing support for women with young children (Roberts, 2002). The plan was the responsibility of three government ministries: the Ministry of Health and Welfare (charged with increasing state child care); Ministry of Labour (charged with encouraging companies to be more family-friendly); and the Ministry of Education (charged with providing more support for parents and grandparents). The plan led to a massive increase in day-care centres, places and subsidies: the child-care budget increased from ¥1.6 trillion in 1990 to ¥2.74 trillion in 2000 (Peng, 2005, p. 82); by 2000, 25 per cent of all children under school age were in licensed, subsidized centres, costing £300 per month at the very top of a steep scale with most families paying much less, if indeed anything at all. A large number of advice centres for parents were established and the government invested heavily in an (apparently unsuccessful) advertising campaign to get more fathers involved in child care.

(c) Following the ratification of the UN Convention on the Rights of the Child, the Japanese state has become much more proactive in developing programmes to establish and protect children's rights; it has also been involved in removing parental rights in certain cases, something which was unthinkable only a decade ago. Courts have become much more involved in child abuse and domestic violence cases; the police have found themselves statutorily obliged to undertake home visits where child abuse is suspected and doctors and teachers to report concerns in the case of patients and pupils (Goodman, 2006). The state has even begun to regulate foreign adoptions and there has been a noticeable (though by US and UK standards still very low level) increase in prosecutions of those working in social work fields for providing inadequate or inappropriate levels of care.

(d) One can also see a major change in the role that is being played by the private sector in welfare provision. As we have seen, in the past private agencies in Japan have been very similar to 'public' agencies in a number of 'conservative' welfare states in the West in the way that they operated under what was known as the *sochi itaku* or *sochi seido* system. Under this system the state had control over placing individuals in private institutions. It dictated terms and fees, and institutions had no right to refuse placements if they wished to continue to be registered and to be eligible for state funds. The *sochi seido* was a system left over from the immediate postwar period when there was no money to build state welfare institutions, and private institutions needed state support in order to survive as going financial concerns. The 1990s, however, saw a significant move from such a placement system to a contractual relationship being developed directly between individuals and service providers, introduced in large part to make service providers more responsive to consumer demand and the market. Although as yet the state is still not able to make payments to for-profit welfare institutions (though this is currently under consideration),[3] it has certainly been possible to see the emergence of competition in some, if not yet all, of the private welfare markets (Hiraoka, 2001). Value-for-money, transparency, competition, deregulation, accreditation and an emphasis on measuring outcomes are all becoming part of the new social welfare (and educational) discourse in Japan in a way that they have been in the UK and US for at least 20 years (Kono, 2005).

(e) Finally, there are the first signs of the emergence of new welfare-related professionals trained at the expense of, and accredited by, the state, in particular the statutory requirement to employ clinical psychologists in schools, and in children's homes with a certain proportion of children who have suffered abuse before they were admitted. Overall, one could thus argue that public responsibility in the realm of family policy has been clearly expanded.

What changes have taken place in the past decade in Japan outside the realm of family policy? The thrust of recent reforms have focused mostly on developing more of a partnership between the state and the individual in terms of financing their welfare.

(a) Unemployment Policy: As we have seen above, the rise in unemployment, combined with the tightening of eligibility for unemployment benefits, has been the source of increasing insecurity in Japan over the past decade. Not all commentators, however, are agreed that this sense of alarm is necessarily justified. While Rebick (2005, pp. 102–3), for example, clearly shows there has been a major shift in recent years in Japanese budget allocations for employment stabilization away from purely investing directly in employment maintenance (84 per cent of the total budget in 1978) towards investment in persons with special difficulties to find jobs, support for elderly workers and human resource development, especially skill development and retraining, more indirect forms of employment stabilization can be found in the Japanese government's reluctance to push for a rapid resolution of problems in the Japanese financial sector and its continuing reliance on public works. But perhaps more significantly, Rebick (2005) argues that the opportunity to work has been considered a basic right in Japan and hence the state has been under pressure to create jobs if none are available in the private sector. This notion contributed to the significant Keynesian deficit spending to finance traditional public works projects in the 1990s. In the late 1990s, the annual budget deficit had reached 10 per cent and the government debt had climbed to about 120 per cent of GDP, a strategy Chorney (1996) has described as 'Keynes in the Orient' (cf. Seeleib-Kaiser, 2006).

(b) Pension Policy: While during the boom years of the 1980s, the Japanese government introduced for the first time a genuinely universal national pension system, including those, such as housewives, who had not contributed direct payments into the programme, the recession of the 1990s saw a huge drop in tax revenue and this, combined with the ageing of the Japanese population, meant that within ten years of this new policy there was strong pressure to reduce pension benefit levels. The government announced that the age for qualification for the main part of the pension, the Employees' Pension (*Kōsei Nenkin*) will, from the year 2013, be increased gradually from 60 until it reaches 65 in 2025; in 2004, the government introduced further reforms that will see the level of benefits lowered by 15 per cent over the next 12 years (Rebick, 2005, pp. 129–30). Finally, the government has also moved to close a loop-hole whereby those who retired at 60 in order to take their pensions then became eligible for unemployment benefits which, in effect, constituted a 'second pension'. These three reforms help explain to a large degree why such a high proportion of elderly in Japan believe that they need to stay in the workforce in their late 60s.

(c) Health Policy: The third policy reform area which has increased anxiety in Japan has been in health. Here the level of co-payments expected from individuals drawing on health services has been increased during the 1990s as the system has struggled to meet rising demand, especially from an ageing population. However, the state has set maximum levels and continues to provide free medical care for the poor. In the case of the long-term care insurance system, individuals over 40 have been compelled to invest in their own insurance policies for old age.

Overall the picture in (un)employment, pension and health policies is rather mixed in regards to shifts in the public/private divide. While some developments point towards some form of privatization in terms of financing pensions and health care, the state has by-and-large continued to accept its 'public' responsibility for 'full employment'.

Conclusion

Is it yet possible to draw any conclusions about the effects of the new programmes, discourses and pressures on Japan's welfare system? In many ways the changes have been so dramatic – in contrast to the years of inactivity that preceded them – that few are yet prepared to predict what is likely to happen over the next few years. Tamai Kingo (2003, pp. 45–6), one of the leading historians of Japanese welfare developments, summarizes the recent trends thus:

> Since the 1990s... the functions of the families and companies, which make up the core of the Japanese model of welfare provisions, have significantly weakened. As for the family, the model based on the male family breadwinner and full-time housewife has been changing with increasing rates of labour participation among married women... Closure, bankruptcies and mergers of companies [have] weakened the provision of... company welfare schemes. Companies have started replacing full-time workers with part-time workers in order to reduce the cost of salaries and welfare payments. It has become increasingly difficult to sustain the Japanese model... [with] the newly emerged concept of a 'safety net'.

Even with this newly-emerging language about a state-provided 'safety net', it is too early to say with any confidence if women will be relieved of the burden of caring for the elderly and young (see Peng, 2002; Osawa, 2005). It is also too early to say if the marketization of private welfare institutions and agencies as well as the new pressure on individuals to invest in their own long-term futures, as a result of pension and health reforms, will lead to a more effective system or the development of greater social inequality in Japan. Some influential commentators (see, for example, Tachibanaki, 2005) are certainly concerned that greater social inequality could be the outcome. If so, it would be ironic in that the welfare mix that has existed in Japan during the postwar period has kept costs down well below those of all of Japan's industrial competitors while Japan's social indicators in areas such as health and education have consistently been among the best in the world. Despite 15 years of economic stagnation, Japan in 2007 still possesses the world's second largest economy with the world's highest figures for longevity, lowest rates of infant mortality, highest rates of general education and literacy and lowest rates of serious crime, drug use, illegitimacy and divorce. All of these indicators still point to very stable families and communities by global standards. As the Japanese state increasingly plays a regulatory role in trying to ensure best value-for-money in the welfare field, it will be interesting to see if there is any effect – direct or indirect – on these statistics and social patterns which those in Japan have come to take for granted.

To conclude, let us return to one of the questions with which we started this chapter: how should one characterize the Japanese welfare system? As we saw, Kasza (2006, p. 109) takes the firm position that one should not characterize the Japanese welfare system, either now or historically, as either 'unique' or indeed unusually reliant on the family. He argues that 'culture has minimal explanatory power in relation to Japan's welfare programs', in large part because the two pillars of its system, its health and pension policies were largely patterned after the policies of western welfare states (Kasza, 2006, p. 109). He admits that its employment system is distinctive but puts this down not to culture but to Japan's high-speed growth from the 1960s through to the 1980s; full employment in this period meant that a fully developed unemployment programme was never introduced. He concludes that: 'If there is a culture that has given rise to Japan's welfare state, it is mainly a global culture shared by welfare policy makers of the industrialized states, not anything peculiar to Japan' (Kasza, 2006, p. 112).

While it is difficult to disagree with most of Kasza's analysis of the development of welfare policy, his does not represent the mainstream view of the Japanese system today. There continues to be in the western literature a widespread view that Japan's pattern of public financing and regulation combined with private provision is not only distinctive but also somehow 'worse' than the normative 'Scandinavian model' which relies on public rather than private provision.[4]

The Japanese system has always involved a partnership between the public and the private: public hospitals, schools, and welfare institutions have always been supplemented by private institutions. In most cases, in opposition to the experience in most western societies, the public institutions have generally been better staffed, have had higher status and have been more expensive to run which is why there has been a trend in several sectors to close down public institutions and allow private ones to pick up the resultant demand created for services. The Japanese system has also always relied on the role of state-appointed, quasi-volunteers, such as the *minseiiin*, and there is no evidence that this system is disappearing; indeed, with the development of the new language of 'civil society' (*shimin shakai*) in Japan, it is being supplemented by the emergence of volunteer groups who are more independent from the state.

The state has also begun to play a greater role in regulating and evaluating welfare providers; these are no longer assumed to be 'naturally good' and their actions are put under much greater scrutiny than previously. Nevertheless, there has been little evidence that the state wishes to take over or compete with the services in Japan that have been provided through private agencies and institutions; if anything, the evidence from sectors such as old people's homes, children's homes, pensions policy, health policy, education policy, and even to some extent employment policy (in as much as there is still a social expectation that permanent workers will not be laid off) suggests that the state has stepped back from the limited provision it has previously offered in favour of private institutions filling the gap. What has perhaps changed most radically in this context, however, has been the increasing pressure that Japanese private institutions have been placed under to demonstrate how they have been using the funds they have received from the state and the quality of care they provide for their clients.

There is no doubt that the Japanese welfare system is at a crossroad. It is hard to see if it is converging with foreign models or moving away from them. To a large degree this is dependent on the direction of the Japanese economy and also other political decisions, in particular the extent to which labour policies will open up to allow the entry of immigrants into Japan to deal with the ageing of the Japanese work force. One can see signs of convergence with and divergence from other welfare models just as, indeed, other systems are themselves changing. This surely is the only conclusion that one can reach. Welfare systems are always in flux and many have become so complex that it is hard to talk about a homogeneous welfare policy or even design. Welfare policies reflect local demands, political expediencies and financial constraints as much as philosophical or ideological models. 'Tradition' and 'culture' have been useful terms for legitimating welfare practices in Japan as elsewhere, but probably have not played a very big role in determining them. The language in which a system has been legitimated, however, does affect the way that those who use it perceive it, and for this reason alone we need to have an emic understanding of how individuals in Japan conceive of the concept of public and private in the context of welfare and should not assume that these understandings are universal.

Part II
Policy Perspectives

7
Politically Dominant but Socially Flawed: Projected Pension Levels for Citizens at Risk in Six European Multi-Pillar Pension Systems

Paul Bridgen and Traute Meyer

Introduction: The political power of multi-pillarism

The development of pension policies in industrialized nations has in recent years been dominated by 'multi-pillarism' as a political goal. In perhaps no other area of social policy have policy-makers, economists and academics been in such strong agreement over the necessary course of action: highly industrialized, ageing societies cannot provide reliably for retirement solely by financing pay-as-you-go systems, controlled by the state; instead they must introduce pre-funded elements and strengthen private savings. In Europe the power of this 'pensions orthodoxy' is most clearly visible in countries whose Bismarckian or socialist legacy left little room for non-state, pre-funded pensions: Italy, France and Germany, Poland, the Czech Republic and Hungary. However, all of these have recently turned towards multi-pillar regimes which are believed to be financially more sustainable and robust.

Pensions are therefore a very suitable policy area to study the relationship between public and private from a comparative perspective, and to explore whether the shift towards more private regimes denotes the decline of collective provision or rather stands for a reorganization of means without substantially affecting the ends. Following the framework established in Chapter 1, this chapter will assess the extent to which typical public–private pension mixes in Europe are part of 'welfare systems', that is, whether private elements have been incorporated in the public domain in a way that is 'functionally equivalent to state intervention' (see Chapter 1) or whether protection against income loss after retirement more strongly rests on individual and market relationships (Bode, 2005; Leisering, 2007; Nullmeier, 2001).

One would expect that substantial research exists to answer this question. In fact despite the almost universal shift towards non-public forms of pensions it is not clear how successful the joint pillars of current regimes actually

111

are with regard to income maintenance or indeed social inclusion and there is also a lack of knowledge about what type of 'public–private mixes' best ensure not only financial sustainability but also a retirement free from social exclusion for the large majority of citizens.

Against this background this chapter will assess the degree to which six current European pension regimes meet the defining characteristics of a 'welfare system', that is, 'a social arrangement, which insures against social risks in a collective, highly regulated, and/or redistributive manner with a relatively high degree of certainty for future claims' (Chapter 1, p. 11). We begin by assessing the regulation of public and private pensions in relation to coverage, pooling of social risks and horizontal redistribution. This allows us to assess the rationales guiding state and private provision in each country and to see how each contributes to the welfare system. However, without sufficient income retired citizens will face social exclusion, no matter how fair the rules for the public or indeed the private system: they will be at risk of exclusion from the customary activities of the society in which they live (Townsend, 1979). Thus, in addition, our analysis also includes the microsimulation of projected pensioner income under public and private schemes for a range of hypothetical individuals with life-time incomes on or below average wages.

Empirically this chapter builds on the findings of collaborative research which explored the relationship between pension regimes and retirement income for citizens at risk in Britain, the Netherlands, Switzerland, Germany, Italy and Poland. The chapter draws on the work of all researchers who contributed to this study as well as on the comparative results generated on the basis of the country studies (Meyer et al., 2007). These countries can be grouped according to their 'Beveridgean' or 'Bismarckian' legacies. The former three developed multi-pillar systems fairly early during the second half of the twentieth century and recent reforms constitute adjustments but not structural changes. The latter three were dominated by one public programme until the 1990s (Bonoli, 2003), and since all have conducted structural reforms, reducing the role of public pensions and giving more support to non-state provision. We have thus chosen three public–private 'veterans' and three 'newcomers'. We show that public insurance itself is not consistent with the characteristics of a welfare system, that is, with universal coverage, redistribution and strict regulation and that therefore private provision has a crucial role in all of our countries. In some it plays this role successfully through various forms of compulsion, albeit even highly regulated private pensions are less broad in coverage, less redistributive and more variable in outcome than state provision. In others the state is more passive, leaving engagement in pensions to voluntarism. Here socially inclusive outcomes are still possible, but citizens at risk are subject to much arbitrary variation and for a significant number a sufficient income becomes a product of chance. Under such conditions a welfare system cannot develop. Overall, therefore, public–private pension regimes disappoint the confidence placed in them. In the final section we assess the prospect of improvement, especially for the less developed 'newcomers'.

Public and private pensions in welfare systems: regulation

Above we suggested that broad coverage, pooling of social risks and defined, socially-inclusive benefits are features of provision in the welfare system while income-dependent coverage, the exclusion of bad risks and market-dependent benefits are the hallmark of provision in the private domain. If we use such a definition to compare the public and private regulatory regimes of the six countries the following picture emerges.

Regulation of public pensions

The Swiss and Dutch public pensions are broadest in scope and the most redistributive (Table 7.1). In the Netherlands all residents of 50 years are entitled to a full flat rate pension for which they pay earnings-related contributions. This makes the system highly redistributive. Moreover, the public pension is set at the level of a poverty-preventing minimum (Bannink and de Vroom, 2007). The Swiss public pillar is universal, too; all citizens above the age of 21 have to pay contributions or are entitled to have their contributions paid by the state. Married couples share contributions. The system is redistributive: payments are entirely earnings-related while the level of benefits is limited to between 20 and 40 per cent of the average wage. Thus, contrary to the Netherlands, no poverty-avoiding minimum exists in the insurance system. Redistribution also occurs between spouses due to contribution sharing (Bertozzi and Bonoli, 2007).

The British and German public systems are more limited in scope because they are stricter in applying employment as condition for entitlement. The British full Basic State Pension, a flat rate benefit, is obtainable only for employees of 44 years, although limited periods spent caring are acknowledged as employment equivalent. Employees without full employment careers or carers' credits are entitled to a proportion of the Basic State Pension.

Table 7.1   Regulation of public pensions

	NL	CH	GB	D	It	Pol
Scope	Residents	Residents	Workers & Carers	Workers & Carers	Workers	Workers
Degree of redistribution	High	High	Medium	Medium	Low	Low
Poverty threshold as part of public insurance	Yes	No	No	No	No	No

This can be supplemented by the State Second Pension, under which bene-fits are related to earnings but relatively higher for those on lower incomes. The system has no minimum poverty threshold (Bridgen and Meyer, 2007a). The German system also has no minimum threshold and carers receive cred-its. However, the individual level of public pension entitlements depends more than in Britain on length of contribution time; thus, public pension levels are more strongly income-related, making the system less redistributive (Riedmüller and Willert, 2007).

The scope of the Italian and Polish public pension systems is the most limited with both structured according to notional defined contribution principles. Only formal employment counts towards a public pension and very few redistributive mechanisms acknowledge times spent outside the labour market. In Italy no minimum pension level exists and the many self-employed and atypical workers have to pay lower contributions and thus receive lower benefits. However, uniquely for the six countries employer con-tributions in Italy are, at 22 per cent of wages, twice that paid by employees (Raitano, 2007).

Polish public pensions are split. The first tier assigns all workers notional defined contribution accounts, while the second part of employees' and employers' mandatory contributions are paid into funded defined contri-bution accounts. The capital thus generated is paid into 16 Open Pension Funds and invested by managers who are state regulated, but otherwise inde-pendent. The final individual pension for this tier depends on contributions and pension fund performance. A minimum threshold of 28 per cent average wages is available but only after a minimum contribution period: 20 years for women and 25 for men (Benio and Ratajczak-Tuchołka, 2007).

Our overview illustrates the fairly encompassing nature of public pension provision in all countries and their significant variation. It is clearly the most consistent with a 'welfare system' in the Netherlands and Switzerland. Scope is broad and the degree of redistribution significant. Nevertheless, even here coverage is not total. Elsewhere public provision offers little to citizens who are not employed for longer periods of their lives, redistribution is less significant and benefits are allowed to fall below the poverty threshold.

Means-tested benefits designed specifically as a last resort for pensioners are in place in all countries but Poland, where only one social assistance system exists for all. However, we exclude them in our assessment because means-testing risks stigmatizing those it seeks to assist (Townsend, 1979) and it regularly encounters problems of take-up, such that significant pro-portions of those entitled to a benefit do not actually receive it (Evandrou and Falkingham, 2005).

Regulation of private pensions

In all the programmes discussed above non-state actors, businesses, trade unions or individual citizens have no influence on the governance of schemes; this is left entirely to the state, with the exception of a slight involvement of investment managers in Poland. In contrast non-state actors can influence pension benefits generated by all schemes included below.

Dutch and Swiss non-state actors are under the strongest obligation to offer benefits (Table 7.2; OECD, 2005b). In the Netherlands in 2005 more than 90 per cent of all workers had access to occupational pension schemes. Only the self-employed and those employed in the very few economic sectors where businesses did not offer occupational benefits were exempt (Bannink and de Vroom, 2007). This level of coverage is achieved through legislation passed in 1957 according to which after approval by the state all businesses in a sector must provide occupational provision once one employer in that sector makes a pension scheme available. Dutch social policy-makers have also used tax policies to extend coverage and to influence benefit levels (Anderson, 2007; Bannink and de Vroom, 2007). All employees with earnings above a set threshold must pay into the schemes; it is lowered considerably for part-time workers. Details such as age of entry, of retirement or level of benefit are open to negotiation between employers and trade unions within sectors (Clark, 2003a; van Riel et al., 2003). However, the state plays a powerful role, and during the 1990s threatened a withdrawal of fiscal benefits to enforce the abolition of expensive early retirement rules and impose a general transition from final salary to average salary schemes (Anderson, 2007). Dutch private savings schemes receive some tax incentives but enrolment is entirely voluntary and generally they are unimportant.

In Switzerland in the 1990s all male and 80 per cent of all female workers had access to occupational pension schemes. As in the Netherlands only the self-employed were excluded but a higher share of part-time female workers than in the Netherlands were not covered because of a higher Swiss entry threshold. This quasi-compulsion is accomplished because all employees earning at least 1.5 times the amount of the lowest public pension are legally obliged to pay minimum nominal contributions whose level are age- and income-related to employer-based occupational schemes. Employers pay at least half the contributions and they must ensure that a minimum occupational pension can be achieved. Its level is determined by the fixed minimum contributions, a legislated nominal interest rate and by a fixed conversion rate to calculate the annuity. As long as businesses observe these conditions, employers are free to determine how to invest the capital to generate the target pension, and they can and in the past often have offered more generous schemes to workers than legally necessary. Citizens paying into private savings schemes receive tax benefits which are higher for the self-employed; personal schemes have gained popularity in recent years, but still only play a small role for protection after retirement (Bertozzi and Bonoli, 2007).

Occupational provision in all remaining countries is entirely voluntary, but the state has aimed to involve employers and employees in the welfare system through fiscal incentives. Personal pension schemes receive some

Table 7.2   Regulation of private pension schemes

	NL	*CH*	*GB*
Scope	Obligation to cover most workers 90% coverage, 2005	Obligation to cover most workers 100% coverage of men, 80% of women, 1990s	No obligation to cover workers Coverage ca. 50% of private, 80% of public sector, 2003
Degree of redistribution	High	Medium	Low
Minimum threshold	No	Yes	Yes

	D	*It*	*Pol*
Scope	No obligation to cover workers Coverage ca 60% of all workers, 2006 Coverage low	No obligation to cover workers Auto-enrolment in occupational schemes	No obligation to cover workers Coverage negligible
Degree of redistribution	Low	None	None
Minimum threshold	No	No	No

public support in all countries, too, but play a minor role (Bridgen and Meyer, 2007b).

In the voluntarist group Italy comes closest to imposing contributions to occupational schemes on employees, despite being a newcomer to private pensions. Until 2007 very few occupational pension funds to which employers and employees pay contributions existed and coverage was very low. However, this situation could change because government hopes to turn an existing occupational benefit, the *trattamento di fine rapporto* (TFR) into an occupational pension. All employees except for the self-employed and atypical workers pay 6.9 per cent of their gross wage towards the TFR; employers are allowed to use the capital as cheap credit, but are obliged to grant 1.5 per cent plus three-quarters of the inflation rate as rate of return. The employee is entitled to receive the TFR as a lump sum when the work contract ends or when he or she requests the money for special expenses. So far generally the TFR has not been used as a retirement vehicle, on average workers have paid into it for no longer than ten years before claiming the money (Castellino and Fornero, 2000; Raitano, 2007). However, new legislation determines that from 2008 all TFR contributions will automatically go towards an occupational pension scheme unless the employee rules otherwise. Ferrera and

Jessoula (2007) believe that because of this law the TFR in Italy provides an '"institutional gate" for policy change' towards a multi-pillar system. However, Raitano (2007) is less optimistic and argues that workers, employers and trade unions have strong interests in maintaining the TFR and that a majority of employees may opt to pay into this vehicle rather than a pension scheme.

Voluntarism is more advanced in Britain where employers have provided occupational pension schemes since the early twentieth century. As a result in 2003 about half of private sector workers and around 80 per cent of public sector employees were members of occupational schemes (DWP, 2004; Pensions Commission, 2004). The businesses that run them have the opportunity to contract out of the state second pension, which means paying part of their social insurance contributions into their company scheme instead, and to receive tax benefits. In return they must guarantee benefits no lower than the state second pension, and they cannot exclude part-time workers with earnings above a lower earnings limit from occupational schemes. In the past this has made contracting out an attractive option for the majority of large and medium-sized employers, but most small businesses have been discouraged by cost considerations and in 2003 only 31 per cent of employees there had access to company pension schemes (Bridgen and Meyer, 2007a). More recently it has been argued that employers have lost interest in occupational schemes (see below).

In Germany for a long time occupational pensions did not play a significant role. However, since government made the effort to introduce a multi-pillar system in 2001 by supporting voluntarism through strong incentives its regime has moved closer to the British. Under the new law in principle all employees have the right to request their employers to pay up to 4 per cent of their payroll[1] into an occupational or personal pension scheme. Employees' choice is somewhat circumscribed favouring collective bargaining arrangements: if the employer runs an occupational scheme, this must be used. Also, in sectors covered by collective agreements employers and organized labour negotiate the conditions of the pension settlement and these are binding for the individual employee. Contributions to private pension arrangements are exempt from tax and social insurance contributions, making the schemes attractive (Bundesministerium für Arbeit und Soziales, 2007).[2] Since 2001 occupational pensions expanded and in 2004 about 80 per cent of all workers covered by collective agreements had access to such schemes (Bundesministerium für Wirtschaft und Arbeit, 2007). However, employers only pay substantial contributions in few sectors of the economy, including the public sector, construction, food and textiles; as a result no more than 60 per cent of all employees paid into occupational pension schemes in 2004 (tns Infratest, 2005; Riedmüller and Willert, 2007).

Like Italy and Germany, Poland enacted reforms in the 1990s aimed at decreasing public spending on pensions. However, even though some tax exemptions and regulations for investment of assets have been introduced to help the growth of occupational and personal schemes, these have been ineffective and coverage is negligible. In a tight labour market employers have the view that they can recruit and retain employees without investing in occupational benefits and individual citizens are still influenced by a socialist legacy where personal insurance payments were unnecessary (Benio and Ratajczak-Tuchołka, 2007).

The role of public and private regulation for the welfare system

So, to what extent does joint public and private sector regulation meet the standards of a welfare system, broad risk pooling, broad coverage and a minimum threshold?

We have seen that public pensions alone are insufficient and that only the Netherlands comes close to fulfilling the criteria. Swiss coverage is as broad and almost as redistributive as Dutch, but it lacks a minimum threshold as part of the insurance system. In Britain and Germany not all residents but only workers and carers have access to the redistributive public scheme. In Italy and Poland coverage only stretches to workers and redistributive elements to compensate for labour market detachment are very weak. In fact some core features of public pensions are typical for private insurance: benefits are largely calculated on actuarial principles, 'bad risks' are excluded and outcomes are market-dependent to a greater extent than elsewhere. From this it follows that to meet the criteria the private sector has a decisive role to play which could be even more significant in those countries where the public sector is weaker.

In reality the countries with strongest public provision also offer the most encompassing private coverage. In the Netherlands and Switzerland employers are bound by law, and by collective agreements in the Netherlands, to facilitate occupational schemes and they have to include almost all employees. Yet even though they play a similar role as public pensions it is not equivalent. Protection for periods of labour market detachment is weaker, they are less redistributive and there is less certainty with regard to the final level of provision, particularly in Switzerland where occupational provision is generally of a defined contribution type.

In all other countries the private sector most definitely does not play the strong role required if the regimes as a whole were to meet the criteria of a welfare system. Regulation of private pensions in Britain, Germany, Italy and Poland is much weaker than that of public schemes even if we take into account that the latter are less encompassing. Occupational coverage is patchy in Britain and Germany and schemes contain few redistributive elements. Italian and Polish private provision is extremely limited. However, in Italy increased coverage may be on the horizon because of the introduction of auto-enrolment in 2008.

Our presentation of the regulatory regimes and their scope alone has generated a clear indication of the best performers: in the Netherlands and

Switzerland public–private regulation meets the criteria of welfare systems. The other four countries do not match these criteria because of deficiencies in the regulation of public and/or private pensions. However, as we discussed above, an analysis of the potential of public–private regimes to constitute welfare systems must include an assessment of outcomes.

Public and private pension programmes as part of a welfare system: outcomes

An individual's overall pension is obviously decisive for their living standard, yet only very few pioneering comparative studies have evaluated the public *and* private pension benefits of individual citizens. These have focused strongly on the lifelong full-time worker and they did not use social inclusion thresholds (Social Protection Committee, 2006; OECD, 2005b; Zaidi et al., 2006). However, to assess pension regimes as welfare systems we need a clear sense of the role of public and private provision in securing benefits above the level of social exclusion for citizens with more complex lives that might put them at risk. Against this background our empirical evaluation considers the performance of the six public–private pension regimes in relation to a range of hypothetical individuals leading lives during which each faces a range of social risks illustrative of aspects of the main labour market and social trends in developed post-industrial societies.[3]

1. The mother and unqualified part-time worker in the retail sector (bio 1), allows us to explore the impact of a fairly low lifetime income, 39 per cent of average wages,[4] because of low qualifications and part-time work, as well as employment gaps related to care responsibilities. She is married to a worker in manufacturing (bio 4), but she divorces and remarries a partner in the same trade.
2. The risk profile of the mother and qualified part-time worker in the welfare sector (bio 2) also enables us to assess the role of an employment career that changes to meet the needs of children. She works in the public sector and owing to a higher level of qualification her wages are 42 per cent of the average. She is married to the middle-manager (bio 5), but divorces and remarries someone in the same trade.
3. The married carer and informal worker (bio 3) has an independent income of only 22 per cent of the average. Even though she works no less than the first two types, she does so mainly informally in a family business. She leaves the labour force at the age of 57 to care for her elderly mother. She is married to a small business entrepreneur (bio 6).

Our next three types are male. They too represent low and medium levels of qualification, and where the women experience care-related employment gaps, some of the men are temporarily out of paid work because of unemployment, illness or training. Notwithstanding this gendered ascription, the results for 'men' and 'women' are applicable to all individuals with similar features.

4. The unqualified worker in the car industry (bio 4) is a fordist worker and breadwinner. His level of qualification is low, yet he has a lifelong career as a manual worker in large companies, interrupted only by one year of unemployment at the age of 26 when between two employers. His lifetime wage amounts to 79 per cent of the average.
5. The middle manager in the financial services (bio 5) earns 131 per cent of average wages over his lifetime, and his employment career is uninterrupted. We included him to allow a comparison with the better off in the national regimes.
6. The small business entrepreneur (bio 6) illustrates the effect of atypical working lives. He has a medium level of qualification, yet his lifetime income is only 84 per cent of the average because for most of his life he runs his own small business.

Below we show the pension entitlements in public and occupational schemes of these individuals. These calculations were based on the assumption that each individual would be 18 years old in 2003 when those with a lower level of qualification (bios 1, 4 and 6) started employment; those with a higher level (bios 2, 3 and 5) started in 2005. Unless otherwise specified all individuals retire at 65 in 2050.

Individual entitlements for the public pillar were based on the conditions for rights accrual operating in 2003 (Table 7.A.1 of the appendix to the chapter). Decisions on non-state provision were more complicated because the degree of compulsion varies significantly. One approach would have been to include only the compulsory part of the pension regime, like the authors of the recent OECD study (2005b). Thus, second pillar pensions would only have been included for the Netherlands and Switzerland. However, because we want to assess the role of the private sector as part of welfare systems we decided instead to include second pillar schemes in those cases where our individuals would have a reasonable prospect of access to them (Table 7.A.2 of the appendix to the chapter). However, we also make clear what would happen if access was not secured. As a consequence we have included below simulations for second pillar coverage for Germany and Britain, but not for Italy and Poland.

Tables 7.3 and 7.4 show the comparative performance of the individuals in relation to a social inclusion threshold set at 40 per cent of average income, with the total pension of each biography divided into its public and private components. These results allow us to assess and compare the respective role of public and of occupational provision in the six regimes and evaluate the overall success of each in providing incomes above the social inclusion

Table 7.3 Projected state and non-state pensions of female biographies in 2050 as a percentage of the social inclusion line

	The mother and unqualified part-time worker in the retail sector (bio 1)			The mother and qualified part-time worker in the welfare sector (bio 2)			The married carer (bio 3)		
	State	*Occupational*	*Total*	*State*	*Occupational*	*Total*	*State*	*Occupational*	*Total*
Netherlands	48	25	73	48	47	95	48	8	56
Switzerland	53	18	70	53	26	78	62	0	62
Britain	31	38	69	27	80	107	8	0	8
Germany	41	3	44	52	28	80	22	0	22
Italy	67	0	67	74	0	74	26	0	26
Poland	50	0	50	61	0	61	27	0	27

Sources: Tables 3, 4: Bannink and de Vroom; Benio and Ratajczak-Tuchołka; Bertozzi and Bonoli; Bridgen and Meyer; Raitano; Riedmüller and Willert, all 2007.

Table 7.4 Projected state and non-state pensions of male biographies in 2050 as a percentage of the social inclusion

	The unqualified worker in the car industry (bio 4)			The middle manager in financial services (bio 5)			The small business entrepreneur (bio 6)		
	State	*Occupational*	*Total*	*State*	*Occupational*	*Total*	*State*	*Occupational*	*Total*
Netherlands	48	90	138	48	188	236	48	9	57
Switzerland	63	49	112	53	57	110	62	0	62
Britain	21	52	74	19	169	188	27	0	27
Germany	72	5	77	100	26	126	13	0	13
Italy	132	0	132	248	0	248	86	0	86
Poland	92	0	92	170	0	170	56	0	56

threshold. A threshold of 40 per cent of average wages was chosen, rather than the more customary 60 per cent median, because median income data from one dataset was not available for all countries. The 40 per cent average wage threshold was found to be closer to national 60 per cent median figures in most of our countries than 50 per cent of average wages.

With regard to public provision, the significantly redistributive nature and the good protection against labour market detachment in the Netherlands and Switzerland is illustrated well by Tables 7.3 and 7.4: Dutch and Swiss pension levels are fairly uniform between individuals, including the married carer (bio 3) whose income is very low. The situation in Switzerland is a little more varied given the slightly earnings-related basis for public provision, and because of the varied effect of contribution-sharing between marriage partners, but nevertheless there is only a 10 percentage point range between the highest and lowest public pension. However, public pensions remain below the social inclusion line for all. Thus, the extent to which we can consider even the regimes with the broadest and most redistributive public pensions as welfare systems rests on the role played by private provision.

In Germany, Italy and Poland the differences between our individuals' public pensions are much larger, reflecting the closer relationship between benefits and earnings and/or labour market detachment in state regulations. For example, the difference between the highest and the lowest Italian public pension is 222 percentage points, and it is 143 percentage points in Poland. This also means that some of the better paid have much higher public pensions than their Dutch or Swiss equivalents; this is true for the manager (bio 5) who in Italy, Germany and Poland has a public pension above the social inclusion line; this is also true for the car worker (bio 4) who in Italy is also above social inclusion. At the same time the lower paid retail and welfare workers (bio 1, 2) have at least similar pensions in relation to social inclusion as their Dutch and Swiss counterparts. In Italy the high level of employer contributions boosts the size of state benefits for all employees. Polish outcomes are dependent on assumptions about constant high returns from the pre-funded part of the first pillar (Rzeczpospolita, 2005; Gazeta Wyborcza, 2005). In Germany the gender-sensitive redistributive mechanisms compensate for labour market detachment. However, none of these mechanisms helps individuals with very low lifetime income and weak labour market attachment such as the married carer (bio 3). Because of the closer general tie between earnings and pensions in Germany, Italy and Poland her public pension in relation to the social inclusion threshold is less than half that received by the equivalent Dutch or Swiss biography.

The pattern of public pensions for British individuals is unique. Benefit levels are fairly uniform, but the public pension received by some of the lower paid (bio 1, 2) is higher than that received by the better paid (bio 4, 5). This is because British contracting-out arrangements exclude altogether from the State Second Pension employees above a certain level of income who have occupational provision. This and the credit system make the state system strongly redistributive, notwithstanding the fact that contracted-out employees generally pay slightly lower national insurance contributions. Even so, the comparatively low level of state benefits means that the public pension of the retail and welfare worker is lower than that received by the equivalent individual in the other countries. For the married carer the situation in Britain is particularly bad, because her level of labour market attachment is below the minimum required to qualify for the Basic State Pension.

In summary, none of the regimes included in this study can be classed as welfare systems purely on the basis of public provision. Dutch and Swiss public pensions are redistributive and broad in coverage, but they do not provide sufficient to lift citizens above the social inclusion line. The British system is also redistributive, but pension levels are much lower and affected to a greater extent by coverage limitations. Public pensions in Germany, Italy and Poland succeed in saving some better paid citizens from social exclusion, but levels of inequality are greater and the lowest paid are disadvantaged by the limited scale of redistribution.

Only on the basis of the combined effect of public and private provision, therefore, can any of our countries' pension regimes be classed as welfare systems. We would expect the Dutch and Swiss regime to come closest given that they came out on top in our assessment of the regulatory frameworks.

As Tables 7.3 and 7.4 show, the Dutch performance in particular confirms this expectation. Occupational provision makes a significant contribution to the final pension outcome of most of our employed biographies, even for the low paid retail worker (bio 1). The mix of inclusive redistributive public and compulsory private provision makes the Dutch the best of our six regimes. The median pension for our illustrative biographies is 84 per cent of the social inclusion line (Table 7.5; for a broader overview, Bridgen and Meyer, 2007b).

Nevertheless even in the Netherlands joint state and non-state provision is insufficient to lift all workers above the social inclusion threshold. This result is not surprising for the very low paid married carer (bio 3), but both other women and the self-employed entrepreneur also fail to exceed this standard. These results reveal differences in the functional role of the two sectors. Whereas the state system is inclusive and redistributive, occupational provision is less so: state regulation ensures broad access to occupational schemes but the entitlements of the two women, for example, is not protected when they are not working and given the earnings-related nature of occupational provision they are also disadvantaged by the lower wages they earn due to part-time work. The threshold arrangements detailed above ensure that many part-time workers are covered for occupational provision but they do not compensate in any other way for part-time workers' lower income. As a result, there is much more variation in the occupational pensions of our individuals compared with their state provision, and the occupational system fills the gaps left by the state more successfully for those higher up the income scale.

The situation in Switzerland is similar, but here the contribution made by the second pillar is smaller because of the differences in the governance

Table 7.5 Median projected total pension of biographies in 2050 as a percentage of the social inclusion line

	Median pension
Netherlands	84
Switzerland	74
Britain	72
Germany	50
Italy	79
Poland	60

of occupational provision in the two countries outlined above. Indeed, the greater susceptibility to retrenchment of occupational pensions in Switzerland means that overall its regime performs less well than Italy's in relation to the outcomes of the six biographies (Table 7.5; Bridgen and Meyer, 2007b).[5]

British occupational provision can be favourably compared with that in the Netherlands and Switzerland. Some British individuals such as the welfare worker (bio 2) and the middle manager (bio 5) are lifted above the social inclusion threshold by their non-state benefits, which dwarf their state provision. However, even the retail worker (bio 1) receives an occupational pension sufficient to lift her income in retirement to a level comparable with the same woman in the Netherlands and Switzerland, notwithstanding the much higher level of state provision in these countries.

Despite these strengths the British regime does not perform well as a welfare system because a greater proportion of the working population are excluded from occupational benefit due to more permissive regulation. Thus, for example, while most British citizens who work in the welfare sector are covered, like our illustrative biography, fewer than 40 per cent of British retail employees are as fortunate as our retail worker. If she had been employed by companies that did not provide occupational provision she would have received a pension 22 percentage points lower in relation to the social inclusion threshold. These variations in coverage are influenced to a significant extent by class and gender (Sinfield, 1978; Arber, 1989; Ginn and Arber, 1991, 1993), but they are also the product of chance. Thus, while occupational provision is more common among the professional classes and men, a significant minority of non-professionals are covered. This spread of occupational provision beyond the most privileged workers means that some vulnerable individuals will avoid poverty in retirement. However the main determinant of who escapes among this group and who does not is largely arbitrary: it is the result of accidents of opportunity rather than planning or intention (Meyer and Bridgen, forthcoming).

Of the other countries the influence of occupational provision on pension outcomes is only evident in Germany, but even here its contribution is much lower. With occupational provision granted on a voluntary basis and much less developed than in Britain, only the welfare worker (bio 2) and manager (bio 5) receive occupational pension income amounting to more than 25 per cent of the social inclusion threshold (Tables 7.3, 7.4).

In Italy and Poland occupational provision plays even less of a role, notwithstanding government attempts to encourage its development, particularly in Italy. An assessment of the pension regimes in these countries as welfare systems thus rests entirely on the performance of the public sector, and we showed above that, notwithstanding the quite strong performance of the Italian system especially for higher paid workers, this is deficient both in relation to regulation and outcome. Thus, while the median pension for the six individuals in Italy is higher than that in Switzerland, the pension of all the lower paid women is higher in the Swiss system than the Italian (Tables 7.3–7.5).

In summary, if we only classify pension regimes as welfare systems that succeed in lifting most citizens out of social exclusion in retirement, including those with below average lifetime income, only the Netherlands comes close to reaching this standard. Even here, the less redistributive and more work-focused nature of occupational provision in comparison with state pensions means that some lower paid individuals fall significantly short. Thus even where private provision has been incorporated most firmly into the public domain, it retains important dissimilarities from state provision with implications for the overall performance of the regime. In the other five countries a combination of the inadequacies of the state system and an even more limited incorporation of private provision in the public domain means that they perform even less well overall.

Are private the new public pensions?

Our analysis above has demonstrated that private provision can complement public pensions, and that both combined have the potential to form a welfare system which ensures social inclusion for most of the population. We identified the criteria that need to be met to achieve this aim, criteria which two countries, the Netherlands and Switzerland, come closest to fulfilling. In all other cases significant social exclusion risks exist for citizens on lifetime incomes below average wages. Given the political hegemony of multi-pillarism in all six countries studied this is not an encouraging result. However, it could be argued that it is too early to draw broad conclusions – are the newcomers in particular on the way to provision comparable to the most inclusive regimes? There is little evidence for such developments happening in the next decade. Employer voluntarism, on which Britain, Germany, Italy and Poland are depending, is too unreliable or in decline, yet states are reluctant to impose compulsion.

Historically employers had two main reasons to support voluntarily occupational pensions: first, they used them to manage their workforce, that is, to attract new staff, retain existing workers or to retire them early, and secondly companies with strong trade unions saw them as a tool to forge industrial peace. Yet even where these reasons gave employers a principal interest in occupational schemes, employer action depended on other structural constraints: on the availability of resources, on macro-economic conditions, on the incentives or disincentives created by the national regulatory framework, and on the age of the workforce (Clark, 2003b; Cutler and Waine, 2001; Mares, 2001; Whiteside, 2003). For small employers these constraints have always been prohibitive. In fact, not only did they opt out under conditions of voluntarism, but they were often exempt from the obligation to pay for retirement schemes even in compulsory regimes, such as the Swiss and the

Dutch (Bertozzi and Bonoli, 2007, Bannink and de Vroom, 2007). This left large employers as the prime providers of occupational welfare, even if the coverage they offered was also incomplete, as discussed above.

Over time these interests of large businesses in occupational pensions and the conditions under which they make decisions have changed. With regard to human resource management, the decline of large fordist organizations meant that the qualified workforce became more mobile, and companies have less interest in long-term pension schemes that tie valuable employees to one firm. Secondly, levels of unionization have dropped, easing the pressure on businesses to ensure stability through occupational welfare. In addition the availability of company resources for pension schemes has been affected by the rise of shareholder interests and the growth in international economic competition; the national regulatory frameworks have tightened as a result of corporate scandals, European legislation and the attempts of national governments to make businesses take over a substantial role as social policy players; finally, increased longevity makes occupational pension schemes more expensive for employers (Sass, 1997, 2006; Clark, 2006; Clark, G. et al., 2007; Cutler and Waine, 2001; Whiteside, 2003). For all these reasons businesses today are less interested in giving the broad and long-term pension guarantees private arrangements would need to play their full part in a welfare system and trade unions have less power to sway this position. As a consequence of such changed interest during the last decade we have seen retrenchment in occupational pensions in Britain, but also a reduction in the minimum level legally prescribed in Switzerland (Bridgen and Meyer, 2007a; Bertozzi and Bonoli, 2007).

This change in business preferences ran concurrently with the political rise of multi-pillarism. Thus governments are under pressure to facilitate the establishment of non-state provision at a time when companies' interest in occupational benefits is declining. In these circumstances the recent policy initiatives in voluntarist countries have been cautious at best. Indeed, in Poland, where companies show no inclination at all to engage in voluntary occupational provision and where public awareness of the future problems of the pension system is weak, governments have felt able to remain inactive (Benio and Ratajczak-Tuchołka, 2007). In Germany the trade unions' attempts to instate auto-enrolment in occupational schemes were opposed by employers and insurers and in 2007 there were no signs that government would side with labour (Riedmüller and Willert, 2007). In contrast Italian politicians have indeed introduced auto-enrolment of employees into occupational schemes from 2008. This was possible without increasing employer costs because the reform rests on the re-direction of resources from an existing compulsory occupational benefit towards pensions (Raitano, 2007; Ferrera and Jessoula, 2007). However, doubts have been raised about the likely success of the reform (Raitano, 2007), and the many atypical workers that exist in the Italian employment structure are exempt from auto-enrolment, while more encompassing legislation is not planned. The British government, a staunch supporter of employer voluntarism in the past has finally accepted the need for a greater level of compulsion. In 2007 a broad societal consensus, including employers and insurers favours an increase in the universal state provision, and a reform in 2007 began preparations for the introduction in 2012 of auto-enrolment in pension schemes for workers not sufficiently covered otherwise, including compulsory employer contributions (Bridgen and Meyer, 2007a). British employers remain opposed to compulsion (CBI, 2006), but appear to have accepted the reform in return for a proposed rise in the retirement age and the state's commitment to share more of the pensions burden. However, while more compulsion for employers amounts to a significant change in the British context, the level of compulsory contributions is likely to be low and projections suggest that the planned reform could still leave many without sufficient income in retirement (Meyer and Bridgen, 2008; PPI, 2006).

To conclude: our discussion has shown that in the field of pensions the gradual replacement of the welfare state by multi-pillar systems is not a problem in principle because state and employer involvement combined can reach high levels of social inclusion. However, in the current circumstances even those public–private regimes which come closest to matching the characteristics of welfare systems are under pressure and have experienced retrenchment. In countries where such systems do not exist, prospects for their emergence are not good. Citizens on incomes below the average are affected the most: they are being turned away by states which no longer accept full responsibility for their insurance against the social risk of ageing, only to find that businesses are taking a similar position.

128

Table 7.A.1 Details of assumptions used in simulations

Assumption	Details	Comments
Economic data		
Average Wages	Annual Gross Earnings in Industry and Services: Eurostat data for 2003. http://epp.eurostat.ec.europa.eu	Gross earnings are remuneration (wages and salaries) in cash paid directly to the employee, before any income tax and social security contributions paid by the employee. Data is presented for full-time employees in industry and services. We used average rather than median earnings because median earnings were not available for all countries.
Inflation	1.9% – based on EU assumptions (www.ecb.int/mopo/html/index.en.html).	1.9% is the European Central Bank's inflation target.
Gross Earnings	Annual rise 2% above inflation.	Gross disposable income rose in the Eurozone by an average of 3.9% in the five years up to 2003 (European Central Bank 2004).
Exchange Rate	As of 1.1.2003. For CH: 1 CHF = 0.68951 €; UK: 1 GBP = 1.53 €	
Pension system assumptions		
State Pension System	Rules and stipulations of public pension regime as valid in 2004.	
State Pension Age	In Poland the state pension age for women is 60. To allow comparison, the pensions of Polish women on retirement have been projected forward to 65 on the basis of the price index.	

Early Retirement	In circumstances where a biography retires early any pension they receive on retirement has been projected forward to 65 on the basis of the price index.	
Occupational Pension Scheme Stipulations	Rules and stipulations of selected occupation schemes as valid in 2004.	
Tax	Our simulations exclude tax and social insurance contributions or benefits. We use gross earnings to calculate pension entitlement and our pension outcomes are gross figures.	Tax and benefits are excluded as a means of simplifying an already complex comparative methodology. Recent research undertaken by the OECD suggests that the effect of tax on pension outcomes is similar across the six countries included in this study. It concluded that 'the differential between gross and net replacement rates for low earners is 17% on average', with little significant variation between countries OECD (2005b, p.17).
Threshold		
Social Exclusion	Social inclusion threshold: 40% of average wages.	Median income data from one dataset was not available for all countries, thus we could not use the standard EU threshold for social exclusion – 60 per cent of median income, but used average wage data instead. For social inclusion we chose a 40% average wage threshold rather than the more standard 50% threshold because of concerns that the latter was significantly higher than 60% median figures in some of our countries.

Table 7.A.2 Type of employer-supported pension coverage assumed in simulations

Type of coverage		*Model scheme basis for simulations*	*Scheme details*
1) The mother and unqualified part-time worker in the retail sector			
Britain	DC	Boots stakeholder	Contributions 3% from employer and employee Charges: 0.65 per cent/annum
Germany	DC	Retail pension fund. Tarifvertrag über tarifliche Altersvorsorge im Hamburger Einzelhandel 20 July 2001 (expanded to Germany), para. 2.	Flate-rate employer contribution of Euro 300 annually reduced in relation to working time
Netherlands	DB	Pension fund for retail sale food sector, Bedrijfstakpensioenfonds voor het Levensmiddelenbedrijf	Average wage, accrual rate 2.0%
Switzerland	DC	Obligatorium	Contributions range from 7 to 18 per cent of wages depending on age. Notional rate of return 2.25 %; annuity conversion rate 6.8%
2) The mother and qualified part-time worker in the welfare sector			
Britain	DB	NHS pension	Final salary, accrual rate 1.25%
Germany	DC	Public sector pension fund. Tarifvertrag über die betriebliche Altersversorgung für Bedienstete im Öffentlichen Dienst 12 March 2003	Employer contribution 8.5%, employee 1.4%
Netherlands	DB	Pension fund for the civil service, Algemeen Burgerlijk Pensioenfonds	Average wage, accrual rate 1.9%
Switzerland	DC	Obligatorium	Contributions range from 7 to 18 per cent of wages depending on age. Notional rate of return 2.25 %; annuity conversion rate 6.8%
3) The married carer and informal worker			
Britain, Germany, Switzerland	None		
Netherlands	DB	Pension fund for retail sale food sector, Bedrijfstakpensioenfonds voor het Levensmiddelenbedrijf	

4) The unqualified worker in the car industry

Britain	DB/DC	Rover/Peugeot pension	Rover: Final salary, accrual rate 1.42%; Peugeot, variable contributions, contributions of 5 per cent employer, 3.4% employees used.
Germany	DC	Volkswagen	Employer contribution 1%
Netherlands	DB	Pension fund for metal and electrics, Bedrijfstakpensioenfonds Metalektro	Average wage, accrual rate 2.2%
Switzerland	DC	Obligatorium	Contributions range from 7 to 18 per cent of wages depending on age. Notional rate of return 2.25 %; annuity conversion rate 6.8%

5) The middle manager in financial services

Britain	DB/DB	Lloyds and Nationwide	Lloyds: Final salary, accrual rate 1.7%; Nationwide: Average Salary, accrual rate 1.85%
Germany	DB	Pension fund in Banking. BVV Versicherungsverein des Bankgewerbes a.G.	
Netherlands	DB	Constructed final salary pension; based on traditional pension objective and franchise equal to single AOW	Final salary, accrual rate 1.75%
Switzerland	DC	Obligatorium	Contributions range from 7 to 18 per cent of wages depending on age. Notional rate of return 2.25 %; annuity conversion rate 6.8%

6) The small business entrepreneur

Britain, Germany, Switzerland	None		
Netherlands	DB	Pension fund for the retail sale food sector, Bedrijfstakpensioenfonds voor het Levensmiddelenbedrijf	Average salary, accrual rate 2.0%

Source: Bannink and de Vroom; Bertozzi and Bonoli; Bridgen and Meyer; Riedmüller and Willert, all 2007.

8
The Changing Public–Private Mix in OECD Health-care Systems

Heinz Rothgang, Mirella Cacace, Lorraine Frisina and Achim Schmid

Introduction

The economic recession following the oil price shocks of the 1970s triggered a broad range of cost containment measures in social polices throughout the OECD world. Health care was no exception. Globalization, demographic change and advancements in medical technology have strengthened the need for reforms that assure both the quality and efficiency of health-care systems while at the same time guaranteeing equal access to services (OECD, 1994). The pertinent question to be dealt with in this contribution is how the role of the state and the market in attaining these challenging and somewhat contradictory objectives, has changed over time. Evidence suggests that although common challenges are experienced, the responses to various socio-economic pressures have differed considerably across health-care systems (Tuohy, 1999; Rothgang et al., 2006). Starting in the 1990s, for example, we observe that in many predominately publicly financed health-care systems market-oriented health-care reforms have been implemented or proposed (van de Ven, 1996; Freeman and Schmid, forthcoming), whereas in countries with private insurance systems access to health care and the introduction of universal health insurance have gained political salience (Skocpol, 1994; Zweifel, 2000). This contribution focuses particularly on the 'hybridization' of health-care systems induced by the changing public–private mix. In order to capture these developments systematically, we differentiate between dimensions of health-care systems: financing, service provision and regulation.

Dimensions of health-care systems

For our analysis of health-care systems, we propose a slight modification of the multidimensional concept of financing, service provision, and regulation offered earlier in this volume (see Chapter 1). Using the analogy of a house that represents the health-care system in total (see Figure 8.1), we can depict

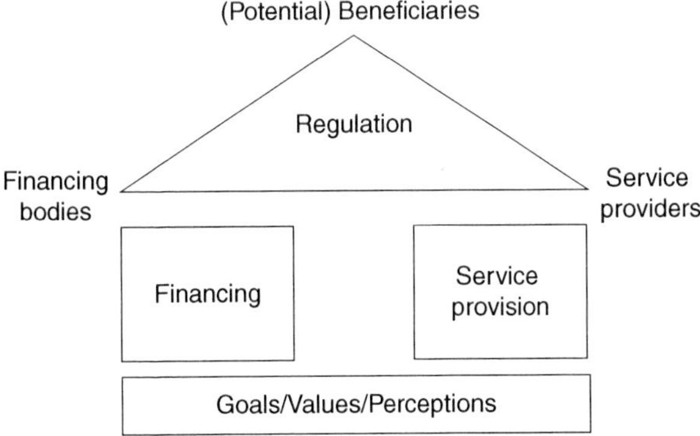

Figure 8.1   Financing, service provision, and regulation in health-care systems
Source: Rothgang et al., 2005.

financing and service provision as the major pillars. The regulation dimension builds the roof and therefore relates to the pillars by defining which aspect of the health-care system – financing or service provision – is regulated. Under the roof of regulation, the fundamental relationships between financing agencies, service providers and (potential) beneficiaries are subsumed, whereas at its base, goals, values, and perceptions form a normative foundation (Rothgang et al., 2005, 2006).[1]

Accordingly, for each of the three dimensions of interest here, a public, societal, and private modality can be distinguished. Starting with the financing dimension, a transfer of this trichotomous public–private division leads to a differentiation between tax-funding, social insurance contributions, and private (insurance) payments. Correspondingly, in service provision we distinguish between public, private for-profit and private non-profit providers. In the regulation dimension, either the state, corporate actors, or private market participants can regulate the major relationships in health-care systems.

It is with this schema in mind that we proceed to quantitatively explore 23 OECD countries in the financing dimension and 14 OECD countries in the service provision dimension. As the regulatory dimension can only be assessed qualitatively, we will select three cases that represent the closest approximations to ideal types of health-care systems – namely, the National Health Service (NHS) of Great Britain;[2] the social insurance system of Germany; and finally, the private insurance system of the US.[3]

The changing public–private mix in financing

How has the public–private mix in financing changed in the OECD world[4] as economic pressure put health-care systems under strain? To answer this

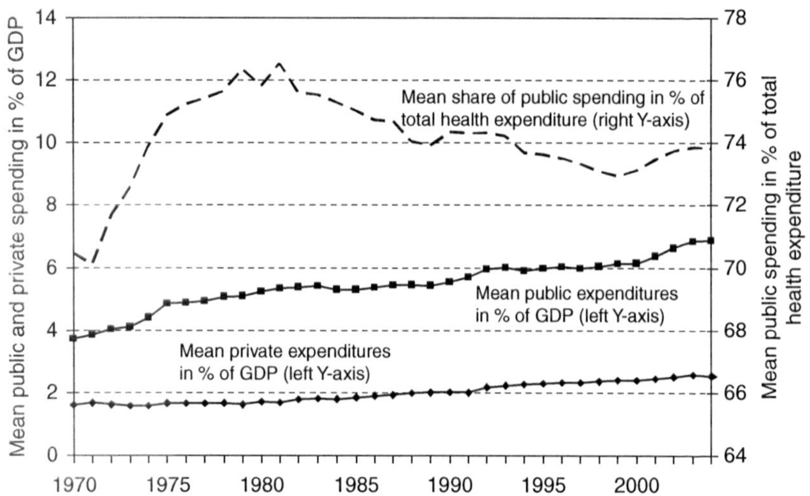

Figure 8.2   Average health-care spending as a percentage of GDP and share of public spending in 23 OECD countries

Source: OECD health data 2006b, 2nd version of October 2006, public expenditure data for Belgium only from 1995–2004.

question we describe the changes in public expenditure levels as a share of GDP and total health-care expenditure (see Figure 8.2). In deviating from our trichotomous concept, we subsume tax and social insurance financing under public funding sources (cf. OECD, 2004b), since data limitations do not allow for a separate consideration over time.

During our period of analysis, health care on average consumed ever increasing economic resources in the selected 23 OECD countries (OECD, 2006b). Considering the development of public financing measured in percentages of GDP, we find a most remarkable increase in the beginning of our period of analysis. On average, public expenditure rose from 3.7 per cent to 4.9 per cent between 1970 and 1975. As expected, public funding sources came under strain from 1975 on. Thus marked increases in the early 1970s were followed by decelerated growth from 1975 to about 1990. Within these 15 years, public spending on health increased only by 0.7 percentage points, reaching 5.5 per cent in 1990. After a sudden surge at the beginning of the 1990s, growth was rather sluggish again until about 2000. Public financing spurted from the beginning of this millennium, eventually reaching 6.9 per cent of GDP in 2004. Private financing grew continuously from 1.6 per cent of GDP in 1970 to 2.5 per cent of GDP in 2004.

While both funding sources grew on average, the structure of the public–private mix in health-care financing changed over time. When measuring public funding as a share of total health-care expenditure, as depicted in the broken line in Figure 8.2, we find that public spending increased from 70 per cent to 76 per cent between 1970 and 1980. From the 1980s onwards, private funding played an increasing role in financing health care, while the public share decreased respectively. Taking these observations together indicates that – considering the average over all countries – privatization and a retreat of the state in health-care financing is only a phenomenon of the 1980s until the mid-1990s. Further, as public spending per GDP escalates throughout the period of analysis, we can only speak of a *relative* retreat of the state in financing, which is set off between 1975 and the early 1980s. Of course the OECD-23 mean obfuscates distinct developments of the observed countries.[5] Most countries follow the 1980s and 1990s privatization trends, with the exception of Portugal, Japan, Switzerland and the US, where we observe a constant increase in public health-care funding from relatively low levels. What happens in the beginning of this millennium is that the privatization trend ends or pauses in most countries while in countries such as those named above, the public share continues to grow. A turning point at the beginning of the millennium, that is, the public share stops falling and begins to rise, as shown by the OECD-23 mean, is only witnessed in the UK and in Ireland.

Further analysis supports the finding that public financing became increasingly important in countries that started at low baselines (see Figure 8.3). When comparing the growth rates of public health-care expenditure

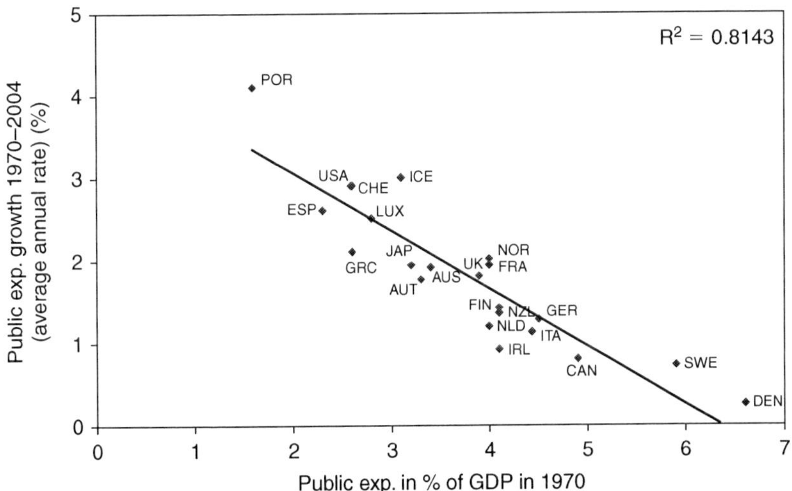

Figure 8.3   Correlation of public expenditure growth (1970–2004) and public financing in 1970

Source: OECD health data 2006b, 2nd Version of October 2006, OECD 22 (Belgium omitted), years with breaks in time series have been excluded, own calculation.

(1970–2002) with their corresponding levels in 1970, we find that countries with low public spending have eventually caught-up with the leaders.

To sum up, starting from the mid-1970s to the early 1980s the public–private mix has been altered in favour of private financing in most of the observed countries. At the same time, public financing as a percentage of the GDP has increased. Therefore we rather speak of *relative privatization*. Some countries, however, particularly those which primarily rely on private financing, experience a constant growth of public health-care financing, leading to a catch-up effect which can technically be described as beta-convergence (see Schmid et al., forthcoming).

The role of public funding in health care, however, is not comprehensively captured when considering OECD health data alone. Apart from direct public spending as reflected in the OECD health data set, the provision of tax exemptions is an alternative and more indirect way of channelling public funds towards health care (Hacker, 2002). In general, tax exemptions influence the public–private mix in health care either by directly reducing health-care expenditures for the consumers or by supporting certain health insurers, as for example the private non-profit insurers or voluntary mutual aid societies (Immergut, 2001). When tax exemptions are provided directly to the consumer, either the take-up of private insurance or medical out-of-pocket expenditures may become subsidized. Thus, in addition to their funding function, tax exemptions are a public policy instrument applied to influence the consumption and/or the provision of certain types of medical goods and services (Immergut, 2001; US OMB, 2006; Colombo and Tapay, 2004).

The quantitative importance of tax exemptions, however, has varied crucially between health-care systems. Adema and Ladaique (2005) have collected data on tax exemptions for at least some of our 23 OECD countries. The authors conclude that tax exemptions tend to be least important in countries with relatively high direct tax levies (Denmark, Finland, Norway and Sweden) and its value is also minimal in Austria, Iceland, New Zealand and Spain. Australia is a reverse case: a tax is imposed on private insurance benefits in order to prevent a duplication of the public scheme (Colombo and Tapay, 2004, p. 47). Tax breaks to support private health insurance are especially important in the US, projected to consume almost 1 per cent of the GDP by the end of 2007 (US OMB, 2006), but they also play a role in Germany, Ireland, and in the Canadian health-care system (Adema and Ladaique, 2005; Colombo and Tapay, 2004). When taking these results together, public tax policy is most important in the private US health-care system and least important in the tax-funded systems, indicating a considerable 'upwards move' of the private insurance funded US health-care system on the public–private scale in financing. Since internationally comparable figures on the role of tax exemptions in health care have only been estimated for single years, we cannot yet consider this element of public financing when we analyse *changes* in the public–private mix.

The changing public–private mix in service provision

Common knowledge about health-care system types suggests that public provision is the dominant form of health-care delivery in the NHS systems, which are most prominently represented by the Nordic countries (Denmark, Finland, Iceland, Norway), Australia, Great Britain and New Zealand. In social insurance systems, represented by Austria, France, Germany, Japan and the Netherlands, the state typically gives more leeway to societal actors, which points to a more mixed system of service provision. Finally, in market-based health-care systems – such as those in the US and Switzerland – we would expect that private provision is preferred to the delivery of health services by public institutions.

While internationally comparable time series data on health-care financing give a clear indication of the role of public relative to private financing, there is no such common standard for the service provision dimension. The absence of a simple and straightforward indicator to measure the public–private mix of health-care provision might be one reason why the role of the state in service provision has been only poorly scrutinized (Wendt et al., 2005a). In order to overcome this difficulty we attempt to construct a single indicator as a weighted mean of the public–private mix in all sectors, that is, the *inpatient, outpatient, dental,* and *pharmaceutical sectors.* To this end, we use the resource flows devoted to each sector as a weight. Within each sector then, the health employment status and the number of inpatient beds by ownership category are used to describe the public–private mix in each sector. As a formula for assessing the role of the state across all sectors we multiply the share of resources allocated to each sector with its respective public shares of service provision in percentages:[6]

$$\textit{Public Service Provision Index}: PPI = \sum_i a_i \cdot P_i$$

with a_i = share of total health spending on sector i; P_i = share of public service provision in sector i and i = inpatient sector, outpatient sector, dental sector, pharmaceutical sector.

In the following section we describe shifts in resource flows between the various health-care sectors. Then we examine developments along the public–private axis within healthcare sectors. In a final step, these data are then merged into a *public service provision index.*

Developments across health-care sectors

Looking at the resource flows to each of the four sectors, there are some common trends among the 14 OECD countries (cf. OECD, 2006b).We find that in all countries, apart from the US, the inpatient sector attracts most of the resources. Only in the US does the outpatient sector overtake the inpatient sector with respect to resources used. However, these data should be treated with caution as an institutional classification might show different results (cf. Cacace, 2007). Despite problems of comparability, the resource flows do reveal that most NHS systems allocate considerably larger shares of resources to inpatient care. Since the NHS concentrates specialist physician services in hospitals, this sector tends to consume more resources in NHS systems than in other health-care systems. In Germany, by contrast, specialist care is available in hospitals and in outpatient settings (Rosenbrock and Gerlinger, 2006). Apart from most NHS countries, Switzerland and Austria stand out with more than 50 per cent of resources spent on the inpatient sector. Since half of inpatient costs are covered by public funds while ambulatory care has to be financed completely by social insurance, there are important incentives for Swiss insurance funds to prefer inpatient care (Rosenbrock and Gerlinger, 2006). In addition, the Austrian health-care system includes incentives to maximize inpatient and minimize outpatient care (Stepan and Sommersguter-Reichmann, 2005, p. 21). However, a common trend is the relative reduction of resources spent on inpatient services. While in most cases there is only a moderate decline, the trend is more pronounced in Australia, Finland and the US (cf. OECD, 2006b).

Developments within health-care sectors

In order to evaluate changes within health-care sectors we have to categorize services along the public–private axis. For this purpose, we use the employment status of doctors, dentists and pharmacists in the outpatient, dental and pharmaceutical sectors. Self-employed professionals are classified as private, while the employment status 'public employee' stands for public provision. The inpatient sector is classified by ownership categories.[7] The degree of public penetration with respect to service provision is then approximated by the share of inpatient beds owned by public institutions.[8]

Starting with the sectors that offer the most consistent results on the public–private mix of service provision, we can classify the pharmaceutical sector and dental services as private in almost all of the 14 countries. In these countries pharmacies are privately owned businesses. Dental services are commonly delivered by self-employed dentists who either contract with public financing institutions or receive private payments. For example, in Great Britain about two-thirds of all dentists work under NHS contracts while one-third works exclusively for the private sector (Grimmeisen, forthcoming). In Norway, dental services are not covered by the NHS but are left to the private market (European Observatory on Health Systems and Policies, 2000). By contrast, in Finland the provision of dental services is overwhelmingly in public hands through the municipal health centres (OECD, 2005c).

Analogous to dental services in most countries outpatient physician care is provided by self-employed doctors who either work under public contracts or get paid on a private basis. This is also true within an NHS environment: 'Since the establishment of the NHS in 1948, GPs (General Practitioners) have been self-employed professionals who provide services to the NHS under contract' (European Observatory on Health Systems and Policies, 1999, p. 54; cf. also Øvretveit, 2003).[9] In Britain, only about 200 GPs compete in the private sector niche, most of them located in the city centres of southern England (cf. Grimmeisen, forthcoming).

In some countries, we find doctors in the outpatient sector employed by public institutions. In Austria a minor share of doctors is employed in outpatient clinics of social insurance organizations and therefore qualified as public employees (Stepan and Sommersguter-Reichmann, 2005). In Iceland we find private provision in medical clinics of specialists and diagnostic research centres, but GPs are predominantly public employees in public health-care centres (Sigurgeirsdóttir, forthcoming). In Norway, municipal councils which are responsible for outpatient care are free to employ GPs or to contract them as private professionals (Johnsen, 2006). While there is no information on the development of public GPs vis-à-vis private specialists in Iceland, there is evidence for privatization in Norway: the share of private contract GPs increased from 54 per cent in 1990 to 71 per cent 1998. By 2005 about 90 per cent of GPs were self-employed (Pedersen, 2005). In Finland the provision of outpatient services is organized through municipal health centres which employ GPs and specialists; only 8 per cent of all doctors practise full-time privately (Øvretveit, 2003). Thus, as opposed to the other countries, a considerable share of outpatient services is provided by government institutions in the Nordic countries.

Finally, the inpatient sector is characterized by a mix of service providers in all observed countries. Here, we estimate the public–private mix according to the share of inpatient beds provided by public agencies. 'Public ownership' refers to beds in hospitals owned by governmental institutions, while 'private ownership' includes private for-profit as well as non-profit hospitals. This practice will rather underestimate state involvement, because the state supports non-profit providers in several ways. In Germany, the US, Austria and Switzerland private ownership is dominated by non-profit providers that gain government support in many respects (Statistisches Bundesamt, various issues; Cacace, forthcoming; Österle, forthcoming; Filippini and Farsi, 2004). Governments grant tax-reductions or other subsidies to non-profit institutions. In Switzerland, some cantons guarantee to cover the deficits of private hospitals (Bundesamt für Statistik, 2001). In Japan and the Netherlands, the state even prohibits for-profit management of health services (Henke and Schreyögg, 2005); hence, the private hospital sector in these countries is completely 'non-profit'. However, in the Netherlands the government has begun to tolerate forms of organizations which give opportunities to for-profit providers to enter the market (Maarse and Okma, 2004). In France, for-profit providers dominate the provision of private hospitals. As expected, the public share of inpatient beds is traditionally high in the NHS countries. In the Nordic countries and Britain, the share exceeded 90 per cent in the early 1990s. In Iceland, the public share is even increasing in the observation period. Meanwhile, all inpatient beds are provided by public hospitals (Sigurgeirsdóttir, forthcoming).

Against this, we see a moderate decline of public provision in Britain and Denmark and no major changes in Finland and Norway (WHO, 2006; Statistik Norway, 2006). Australia and New Zealand, which also belong to the NHS category, have always had a larger proportion of private hospitals accounting for roughly 25 per cent of inpatient beds. Since the early 1990s, the private share increased moderately in Australia to about one-third and significantly in New Zealand to almost 50 per cent (AIHW, various issues; Statistics New Zealand, 2005). In the case of New Zealand the role of public hospitals in medical care is probably underestimated since the statistics do not exclude all long-term care beds, most of which are provided by private hospitals. Among the social insurance systems, Austria and France show a persistently high share of public hospital ownership compared with Germany and the Netherlands, underlining the strong public elements in the health-care systems of France and Austria (Ministère de la Santé et des Solidarités, 2005; Österle, forthcoming). In the US, public provision with inpatient beds is typically low and even declines over the past three decades (Cacace, forthcoming). Summing up this information and combining the information on resources across and within sectors, we can construct an index of public service provision (see Table 8.1).

Despite data limitations, we observe that public provision is declining in all countries apart from Iceland, the Netherlands[10] and Japan. Finland experiences an increase of the public service provision index until 1990, followed by a marked privatization trend, which brings the index almost back to 1970 levels. In many countries the state is retreating from the provision of health-care services. Put differently, health-care service provision is being increasingly privatized. Considering the composite index of service provision, private provision prevails in social insurance and market-based health-care systems, while NHS systems rely on public service delivery. Owing to the lack of data, conclusions will have to be tentative. Nevertheless, it can be seen that public provision is most pronounced in Nordic countries, where not only the hospital sector is characterized by public service provision, but also outpatient care is delivered by public employees. On the other hand, in the market-based US health-care system, direct service delivery through public providers remains marginal.

The decrease of the public provision index in the US is influenced by a combined effect of shifts in the public–private mix *within* the inpatient sector and the decline of resource flows to inpatient care since the early 1980s. The same effect is true for Australia, England and Denmark where the change of the service provision index is not only due to an increase of private hospital beds, but related to the fact that private outpatient services are given more weight. By contrast, the change of the service provision index for

Table 8.1   The public service provision index (%)

	1970	1975	1980	1985	1990	1995	2000	2003	Trend 1990–2003
Denmark	–	–	65	64	57	57	–	52	Minus
Finland	76	76	79	83	84	79	78	77	Minus
Iceland	–	–	61	58	58	–	62	64	Plus
Norway	–	–	–	–	–	51	50	47	Minus
Australia	–	–	–	42	38	34	28	–	Minus
Austria	–	–	–	–	–	40	38	39	Minus
France	–	–	–	34	32	–	29	30	Minus
Germany	21	21	20	20	21	20	18	18	Minus
Japan	–	–	–	–	11	–	11	–	0
Netherlands	–	–	–	–	7	–	7	–	0
USA	–	14	14	12	10	9	7	6	Minus
England	–	–	–	–	81	78	75	–	Minus
New Zealand	–	–	–	–	–	34	27	26	Minus
Switzerland	–	–	–	–	–	43	40	41	Minus

Notes on the construction of the public service provision index: Generally, the public service provision index is constructed by multiplying the share of public inpatient beds with the share of resources devoted to the inpatient sector. Exceptions: In Iceland and Norway outpatient services are partly provided by public GPs. This has been considered by adding the public share of outpatient services as indicated by the share of employed GPs. In Finland outpatient services are primarily provided by municipal health centres and public employees. Therefore we classify the Finish outpatient sector as public.

Notes on cross-sectional comparability: The resource flows to the Dutch inpatient sector are distorted by a break in time series (OECD, 2006b). Considering this, we should rather observe a small increase of public service provision. For England we use different kinds of national data on resource flows, which are not directly comparable across countries. National data for resource flows in New Zealand are more similar to OECD definitions. The Swiss index is overestimated because public hospital beds include private non-profit hospitals which receive cantonal subsidies. It was not possible to adjust the Swiss data to the public–private definitions used for the other countries. Since the cross-sectional comparability of these countries is impaired we have listed them separately, while the other countries are listed according to health-care systems.

Sources: AIHW, various issues; Cacace, forthcoming; Department of Health, 2006; Henke and Schreyögg, 2005; Johnsen, 2006; Ministère de la Santé et des Solidarités, 2005; Ministry of Health New Zealand, 2004; OECD, 2006b; Österle, forthcoming; Øvretveit, 2003; Pedersen, 2005; Sigurgeirsdóttir, forthcoming; Statistik Norway, 2006; Statistics New Zealand, 2005; Statistisches Bundesamt, various issues; WHO, 2006.

Germany, New Zealand and Norway is mainly influenced by developments in the structure of inpatient and outpatient service provision. Especially during the last decade, public inpatient beds are declining at a fast pace, as concerns the German case, mainly to the benefit of private for-profit providers (Bruckenberger et al., 2005, p. 35). Hence, we can distinguish changes in the public–private mix which take place *within* health-care sectors from changes that occur as resources are shifted from sectors that are characterized by public provision to sectors dominated by private provision. In the latter case we can speak of *implicit privatization*.[11] In sum, the public service provision index tends downwards in most countries. A great deal of the trend towards private provision is caused by a shift of the sector weights, thus implicit privatization.

Changes in health-care regulation

The third and final dimension of health-care systems to be explored here is *regulation*. While there is no shortage of literature dedicated to the role and nature of regulation in numerous policy fields including health care, there is far less consensus as to its meaning. Indeed, regulation has been taken to refer to a wide variety of activities that are governmental in kind (but also open to third party actors working either in lieu or under the aegis of the state), and has been alternately distinguished in terms of a multiplicity of features ranging from the highly general to the highly specific (Lewis et al., 2006).

While various definitions of regulation will inform our evaluation, we mainly limit our focus to the more *structural* features of regulation. We also accept the view that regulation may be carried out by non-governmental bodies (Rothgang et al., 2005, forthcoming). More specifically, we examine the actors and the modes of interaction characterizing the mechanisms by which systems are coordinated (Rothgang, 2006). As concerns actors, we refer to three specific types that may come to predominate the health-care arena – namely, the state, corporate actors (e.g., associations of sickness funds or providers), and private market participants. In making this three-fold distinction, our definition of regulation goes beyond a strict interpretation resting on governmental activity alone, but rather encompasses all interactions that regulate the interrelationship of financing agencies, service providers and beneficiaries within the health-care system. With regard to the specific interactions taking place between actors, we identify three basic modes: (1) the exertion of *hierarchical control* typically on the part of the state; (2) the engagement in *collective bargaining* where contract partners interact on equal footing and are vertically aligned; and (3) the condition of *competition* which fosters rivalry between individuals or groups (Stigler, 1987).

The combination of actors and modes of interaction put forth here are taken to constitute *regulatory structures* which are expected to vary across divergent health-care systems and quite possibly over time. The purest types of regulatory structures can be said to result from combining actors and modes of interaction in a most intuitive way – that is, by linking state with hierarchy (as in NHS systems), collective actors with bargaining elements (as in social insurances schemes), and market actors with competition (as in private health-care systems) (Rothgang, 2006). However, in making these connections, it must be acknowledged that other groupings are also possible (cf. Cacace, forthcoming).

In the interest of representing most typical instances of relations between state and hierarchy, corporate actors and collective bargaining, and market

Table 8.2   Regulatory types

Mode of Interaction	Actors		
	State	*Corporate*	*Market*
Hierarchy	State-based hierarchical regulation (e.g. British NHS)		
Collective bargaining		Social self-regulation (e.g. German social insurance scheme)	
Competition			Private competition-based regulation (e.g. US private health-care system)

and competition, we turn to the cases of the British *National Health Service* (NHS), the German *social insurance scheme*, and the US *market system*, respectively. These countries are regularly referred to as the most ideal representations of their respective health-care systems (see e.g. Tuohy, 1999, Rothgang et al., 2005). From this, a heuristic model of regulatory types emerges that may guide our analysis of developments in health-care regulation in three national contexts, but also with far wider applications to cases not feasibly covered here (see e.g. Rothgang et al., 2006). By way of summary, this model is presented in Table 8.2.

As we proceed to apply this model of regulatory types to our three country cases, of particular significance will be the location of potential shifts within these health-care systems towards new system types. On the one hand, shifts might occur as a result of changing relations among key actors of the health-care system, such as between financing agencies, service providers, and beneficiaries (see Figure 8.1). On the other hand, systems might also see significant changes in the form of the *public–private mix*, which may, for example, lead systems away from market regulation towards more corporate or state-based systems. With these possible movements in mind, we will scrutinize changes in Britain, Germany and the US.

Beginning with the case of the British NHS, we find an example of a state-led health-care system that has actively shifted its centre and given way to greater localization in an effort to improve efficiency. Far from a mere restructuring, these changes have altered the nature of NHS regulation such that many essential health-care decisions are no longer made by central government but have been handed over to regional and local bodies (Lewis et al., 2006; Osborne and Gaebler, 1992). This is true for matters concerning services provided to patients, as well as primary and community care budgets, all of which are now left to Primary Care Trusts. With the establishment of hospital trusts, inpatient services have also seen greater autonomy in the direction of their financing and care. Beyond this, the creation and continued deepening of the internal market have opened the door to competition and a new treatment of the provider–purchaser relationship. Changes have been delivered in the way of groundbreaking reforms that mark critical junctures in the history of the British NHS (Baggot, 2004); however, these reforms have been followed by equally significant periods of incremental change, during which the necessary task of policy implementation has taken place and a new logic of action (i.e., managerialism and competition) institutionalized. Evidence of the latter can especially be seen in the continuity or coherence of British policy since 1974, made possible by the successive reinforcement and elaboration of policy ideas over time. As such, one may speak of a policy trajectory that culminates in transformation, but which can only unfold incrementally. This said, however, it would be misleading to suggest that the NHS has transformed itself into an altogether new type of health-care system as the system's fundamental mode of interaction continues to be that of hierarchy rather than cooperation or competition. As such, it may be concluded that the transformation of the NHS has remained limited to the intra-systemic level and that the public–private mix in regulation continues to be largely public in kind.

In the case of the German social insurance system, changes affecting the system's fundamental arrangement of mutual self-regulation have by and large transpired in a two-fold and competing manner: since the 1970s, reforms have been passed which either leave untouched or else reinforce the regulatory status quo, or, differently, challenge it with the introduction of novel elements of direct state intervention and market competition. As concerns the former, the establishment of cost-sharing measures starting in 1977, as well as the strengthening of the bargaining power of sickness funds in 1976 have largely preserved if not expanded mutual self-regulation between system actors (Alber, 1992; Döhler and Manow-Borgwardt, 1992). From the 1990s onwards, however, direct state intervention has become more and more important. With the introduction of budgets for inpatient services, outpatient services, drugs, and medical devices a major parameter of health policy was now controlled by the central government and no longer at the disposal of mutual self-regulation. Moreover, as part of the Health Insurance Contribution Rate Exoneration Act of 1996, all sickness funds were forced to cut their contribution rates by 0.4 percentage points, which corresponded with the aims for cost savings – although the fixing of contribution rates is formally one of the core competences of sickness funds. The Ministry also stepped in and took several decisions concerning the implementation of the DRG system; thus highlighting another feature of increasing direct state intervention – that is, the role of a referee if providers and funds cannot agree (cf. Rosenbrock and Gerlinger, 2006). At the same time, the infusion in 1992 of market competition among insurance funds and the granting of greater choice to blue collar insurants have presented further constraints on mutual self-regulation that usher in what appears to be a new logic of action resting on the principle of efficiency rather than mere cost-containment. Although there is a continued and preponderant reliance on mutual self-regulation, moves have been made upwards towards the state and downwards towards the market (Wendt et al., 2005b). Much like the case of the British NHS, this change has been realized through a series of critical junctures in which large-scale reforms have been passed, followed by essential periods of gradual transition during which policy implementation and the institutionalization of a new logic of action on the part of policy-makers have been given the necessary time to unfold. However, in this process, the German social insurance system has not entirely transformed itself into a new system. To speak in terms of the public–private mix, while Germany has made room for public (state) and private (market) actors in its health-care system, it is corporate actors that remain centre stage (cf. Rothgang et al., forthcoming).

Finally, with regard to the private health-care system of the US, policy developments can be said to have hit a turning point in 1965, after which state involvement in health care rose significantly as a result of the creation of the public programmes Medicare and Medicaid. In the years that followed, however, particularly since the 1970s, health-care regulation has proceeded on a far more incremental course of transformation, which has chiefly consisted in the gradual expansion of and control over the two federally funded programmes on the part of the state (Oberlander, 2003; Marmor, 2000). Beyond this, public funds are provided by the federal government to subsidize private insurance in the form of tax exemptions for employer-sponsored health-care programmes (Hacker, 2002). But, within the realm of private insurance, hierarchical state regulation remained weak, especially vis-à-vis service providers (Stone, 2000). At the same time, private insurance experienced the emergence of managed care proliferating quickly since the 1980s, which, although purely private by nature, has given way to a series of hierarchical arrangements that mimic state-based regulatory measures. Thus the most remarkable change in the regulation of the US health-care system is the emergence of new modes of governance, which remarkably do not come from the government but from private market actors, namely from managed care (Cacace, 2007, forthcoming). Taken in combination, the private market system of the US has undergone a series of discontinuities in its policy history that reflect an incremental yet transformative process of change that allows for a greater role for the state and for hierarchy in health care, thereby also indicating the adoption of a new logic of action on the part of system actors concerned with regulation. Thus the US stands alone among our three case studies, in so far as its transformation was not the result of critical junctures. Rather, policy changes in the US have been expressed by smaller scale (but by no means insignificant) developments. The public–private mix in regulation was altered by bringing in new modes governance into the health-care system; the system as such, however, inevitably retains its largely private character.

Conclusion

The basic goal of this chapter has been to examine whether there have been changes in the public–private mix in OECD health-care systems that indicate a 'hybridization' through the introduction of non-system specific elements in financing, service provision and regulation. With respect to *financing* we see that private health-care spending had been established or intensified as a mode of financing in many countries, but we find no absolute retreat of the state. On the contrary, on average, public health-care expenditure in the OECD world has been growing faster than the GDP since the 1970s. This process has particularly been fuelled by the catching up of formerly low-spending states. Since the turn of the tide in the mid-1970s, however, private health expenditure is growing even faster, leading to a relative retreat of the state, that is, a declining share of public health-care expenditure as part of total health-care expenditure. We therefore find that public and private sources of funding increasingly complement each other, leading to hybrid modes of health-care funding. In *service provision* we see privatization trends as the public service provision index, constructed to summarize developments in different health-care sectors, decreases in most countries. This process is not only driven by changes of the public–private mix within health-care sectors, but also by the expansion of health-care sectors which are characterized by private provision. Turning to *regulation* of health-care systems hybridization becomes most evident. Here we observe changes in the public–private mix in all three countries under scrutiny, which can best be characterized as movements towards more complex regulatory structures in which the dominant regulation mechanism, i.e. state hierarchy in Britain, mutual self-regulation in Germany and market competition in the US, is amended by those mechanisms originally lacking. In a nutshell, systems move towards hybrid forms of health-care systems when taking account for financing, service provision and regulation.

9
From Liberal Statism to Statist Liberalism: The Transformation of Unemployment Policies in Europe

Daniel Clegg

Introduction

Of all the welfare sectors to have come under pressure for reform in the contemporary context of fiscal austerity and economic liberalization, it is in unemployment policy that change has been most far-reaching. In some ways, the relationship between liberalization and unemployment policy reform seems straightforward. Even in the postwar decades of healthy economic growth, rising general prosperity and relative welfare state consensus, cash benefits for the unemployed were a *bête noire* for liberals everywhere, accused of obstructing the functioning of labour markets and of undermining the work ethic. Among citizen-voters more generally, unemployment benefits have long been perceived as the least legitimate form of welfare state provision (Coughlin, 1980). It is thus at first glance unsurprising, if not downright banal, that a period of widespread liberalization should have ushered in a wave of thoroughgoing reforms to these eternal 'benefits of doubt' (cf. Pennings, 1990).

This chapter argues that recent reforms of European unemployment policies nonetheless reveal an interesting and often-overlooked dimension of contemporary welfare state transformations, namely, the way in which much economic liberalization presupposes an *increase* in directive state activism. Certainly, the medium-term ambition of much contemporary unemployment policy reform is to reduce the scope for existence outside the market. Furthermore, in many countries public services that traditionally provided job-brokerage and other employment-related services are being opened up to competition from private, for-profit, providers (cf. Sol and Westerveld, 2006). But in a manner recalling Polanyi's seminal account of Poor Law reform in nineteenth-century England, these liberalizing processes rely not on a dismantling but instead on a streamlining and a re-aggregation of existing benefit systems, and in many respects an increase in public intervention, both in the operation of the unemployment policy sector and in shaping the choices and behaviour of (unemployed) citizens. Unemployment policy thus shows particularly clearly the statist dimension of some contemporary market liberalization,[1] and more broadly reveals how privatizing and collectivizing trends interact in complex ways across the different levels – discourse, institutions and outcomes – of welfare development.

Focused mainly on the institutional level, the principal concern of this chapter will be in mapping and explaining the differing degree to which unemployment policies have become more market-supporting in selected European countries over the last 10–15 years. Acknowledging the potential for arrangements at the institutional level to apparently contradict the broader thrust of policy development at the level of discourses and outcomes is important here for another, more explanatory, reason. As will be discussed, the unemployment benefit policies of the postwar 'golden age' of welfare statism were in many countries actually pursued through institutional arrangements in which the capacity of the state was strictly limited. Because contemporary market-supporting unemployment policies require enhanced state capacity, the degree of 'liberalism' in pre-existing policy arrangements and the solidity with which this was institutionalized is, I argue, a decisive factor in explaining the prospects for and limits on reform in different national contexts. In some countries, the principal challenge to making unemployment policies more market friendly is thus justifying more, not less, state intervention.

The chapter is organized in four main sections. The first expands on my overarching characterization of current trends in unemployment policy by contrasting, in ideal typical terms, the conception and organization of traditional and contemporary unemployment policies respectively. Section two examines the empirical cases of Denmark and the United Kingdom (UK), where notwithstanding the oft-remarked differences in the orientation of social and labour market policies recent governments have deployed the comparatively high leverage that the central state has always enjoyed over unemployment benefits to effect a decisive transition to a more market-supporting unemployment policy. This contrasts with the cases of Belgium, France and Germany, examined in section three. In each of these countries – largely, I suggest, as a result of the institutionalized influence of private actors in unemployment insurance policies – reforms have taken a different route. Though there have been considerable changes to unemployment policies in each of these countries, more wide-ranging and more market-conforming reforms of the kind seen in Denmark and the UK would arguably require a far more explicit coordinating role for the state. Underlining this point, section four briefly examines the case of the Netherlands, where the essential complementarity between *étatisation* and liberalization in contemporary unemployment policy reform is perhaps clearest. The chapter concludes by drawing out some implications of the argument for our understanding of contemporary welfare reform.

Liberal statism and statist liberalism

A characterization of the current wave of unemployment policy reforms as statist draws an implicit contrast with what they are today superseding, namely, the traditional unemployment policies of the 'golden age' of welfare state development. My contention is that compared to the recipes currently gaining ground, the unemployment policies deployed in the vast majority of European countries up to a fairly recent period were indeed quite liberal in some important respects. This is not to deny that the distributive implications of traditional unemployment policies were often bitterly combated by economic liberals and capital interests, for – as with the portrayal of current policies as statist – my argument refers more to institutions and procedures than to aims or outcomes. Nor is it to say that the state played no role in the institutionalization and operation of these policies; it certainly did, albeit – as we shall see below – with marked variations cross-nationally. But the conception of traditional unemployment policies was nonetheless everywhere premised on a relative restriction of the scope for 'political meddling' and bureaucratic judgementalism, and conversely on a respect for the consistency and transparency of entitlements and for the autonomy of the (unemployed) citizen. Such assumptions were furthermore institutionalized, in different ways and to differing degrees cross-nationally, in the organization of the unemployment policy sector.

The key institution in the traditional model of unemployment policy was social insurance. Though it was only through state intervention that the limits of mutual or private forms of insurance as a response to the problems thrown up by the development of industrial society could be overcome (Castel, 1995; De Swaan, 1988), social insurance was nonetheless built on the template of these pre-existing institutions. Social insurance was in many respects an outgrowth and a generalization of its mutual and commercial cousins, building as much on the contractual 'patterns of access' found in market relations and in civil society as it did on those habitually associated with the classic citizen–state relationship (Ferge, 2000). In the area of unemployment policy, social insurance, with its associated language of 'risk' and 'compensation', actually represented a liberal bulwark against the more 'transcendalist' policies of socio-economic regulation put forward by many socialists and conservatives alike (Walters, 2000, p. 59).

The institutionally liberal dimension of golden age unemployment insurance provisions can be seen in their *financing*, their *regulation* and their *content*.[2] Though they were obligatory and centrally set, unemployment (and other social) insurance contributions were traditionally quite differently conceived from regular taxation, and the individual rights to transfers they finance perceived as more inviolable than rights to access other collectively (tax-) financed goods and services. Unemployment insurance contributions were often equated with individual savings, and unemployment benefits seen as a 'deferred' part of an individual's duly earned salary (Palier, 1999). This special status was in many places institutionalized through the creation of discrete collection and distribution agencies, clearly separate from the national treasury, and not infrequently devolved to private or para-public institutions managed by non-state actors, such as trade unions and employers' associations. These same actors were, partly as a consequence, often also heavily involved in decision-making around unemployment insurance, diminishing the state's regulatory autonomy accordingly.

In contrast to the now-common characterization of all golden age social policies as standardized and homogenizing forms of provision, unemployment insurance benefits were – like other social insurances – also often distinctly differentiating, if not wholly individualized. Most basically, the contributory requirements for access to unemployment insurance benefits allowed the regularly employed worker to be distinguished from those more peripherally attached to the labour market, and to escape, when temporarily out of work, the collective condemnation that had traditionally fallen on the jobless as a whole. The introduction of social insurance thus allowed 'social risks' to be distinguished from 'social problems', however crudely (Topalov, 1994). Further, in the vast majority of unemployment insurance systems benefit levels were expressed as a percentage of individual salaries, ensuring that the individual risk resulting from the loss of employment was adequately compensated. Finally, the provision of untied cash benefits actually upheld and supported the capacity of the unemployed to make autonomous choices, both with respect to planning their professional reintegration and more broadly as normal consumer-citizens.

With respect to the last point, it might be objected that even for those with good contributory records unemployment benefits were never wholly unconditional; regulations always existed concerning periodic registration at employment offices, or obligations to accept work defined as 'suitable'. If deployed in moderation such regulations are however not antithetic to a liberal conception of insurance; they merely correspond to the protections against 'moral hazard' that are built into most standard forms of private insurance contract. It was with moderation – and many today would argue laxity – that such controls on the status and behaviour of benefit recipients were in fact deployed in the vast majority of golden age unemployment benefit systems. Only in those countries where policy-makers were already fixated with the impact of unemployment benefits on the operation of the labour market were regulatory and bureaucratic controls on the unemployed more intense and punitive, 'in the name of liberalism' (King, 1995, 1999).

The increasing emphasis across the developed world on activation and benefit conditionality (e.g. Barbier and Ludwig-Mayerhofer, 2004; Dufour et al., 2003; Lødemel and Trickey, 2001a) is perhaps the most obvious indicator of a more widespread shift to paternalistic unemployment policies in the contemporary period. Governments everywhere have come to see the liberty traditionally left to benefit recipients to organize their own labour market reintegration as problematic, encouraging insufficiently active or strategic job-search and leading to dangers of long-term labour market detachment and benefit dependency. In response, the emergent unemployment policy paradigm emphasizes the need for stricter behavioural controls and more directive interventions in the job-search (and eventually the job re-qualification) process, beyond the simple prevention of moral hazard. Though the shift is often characterized discursively as one of rebalancing individual rights with individual responsibilities, the new policies are just as much about an increase in collective, governmental enforcement and orientation capacities.

Beyond activation *per se*, it is a completely new conception of unemployment protection – and indeed unemployment – that is emerging. This can be seen in the challenge to the contribution principle that for so long underpinned the operation of unemployment insurance. In a labour market where more transitions and flexible employment trajectories are valorized, a contribution record – and more generally an individual's employment history and past status – is no longer considered a fair or useful basis for determining the access to and level of social support in unemployment, being seen to overcompensate some unemployed individuals at the expense of the financial penalization or even exclusion of others. The emergent trend is thus towards the levelling-out of eligibility and entitlements, whether this is achieved through an alignment on the situation of the traditionally least protected, on that of the traditionally most protected, or something in between. Related both to this and to the trend towards activation, a contribution history is also no longer seen as a meaningful proxy for 'autonomy' or 'proximity to the labour market', and thus as evidence that unemployment is the result of impersonal structural forces rather than personal deficiencies. The conventional distinction between the 'risk' of unemployment and the 'problem' of joblessness is collapsing (Walters, 1996). Though some gradations of benefit status among the jobless population persist, it is increasingly individual 'profiling' procedures that trigger additional interventions, a far cry from the old idea – implicit in the notion of the 'deferred salary' – that good contributors have some inalienable right to unconditional income support.

The emergent policy paradigm has implications not just for the content of unemployment benefit policies, but also for their financing and regulation. There are pressures, first of all, to ease the rigidity of the demarcation between the financial circuits of unemployment insurance and regular public taxation and expenditure. Unemployment policy is drawn ever closer to the field of fiscal policy, to facilitate both the fine-tuning of individual tax incentives and to make the financing of social protection more 'employment friendly', notably by shifting the financial burden from labour costs to general revenues (cf. Palier, 1999). The smooth integration of passive and active labour market policies also presupposes the ability to cross-finance initiatives that in the past were often funded out of social contributions and general taxation respectively. The dissolving barriers between active and passive labour market policies also challenge, secondly, an institutional separation between the public employment service and the unemployment benefit system. At the delivery level the emphasis is now placed on offering 'single gateways' to all employment-related services (Clasen et al., 2001), while at the policy level the need for co-regulation, as well as co-financing, of these two domains is ever more strongly affirmed. More generally, the demise of the distinction between the risk of unemployment and the problem of joblessness is undermining the notion that the treatment of the former can in some way be self-regulating, insulated from the more obviously politico-bureaucratic forms of regulation to which the latter has always been subjected.

Traditional unemployment policies are thus under increasing pressure for reform in Europe and beyond. But though the broader context for these calls for reform is one of economic liberalization, the thrust of institutional reform is in many ways statist, bringing statutory oversight and bureaucratic control back into a policy sector that had long operated more or less under its own steam. The 'more or less' of this last sentence is quite crucial, though, for as suggested in the country studies below it is largely by understanding the differing degrees of public influence over traditional unemployment policies that we can properly understand the varying ways in which the transformation of unemployment policy is actually advancing in the different welfare states of Europe.

Statist clean sweep: the British and Danish cases

The cases of Denmark and the United Kingdom (UK) are now well known in the international literature on unemployment policy reform, often held up as diametrically opposed models of contemporary, post-compensatory, unemployment policy (cf. Barbier, 2004; Torfing, 1999). Without necessarily contesting this portrayal, it can nonetheless be observed that from a more structural perspective reforms in the two countries also share a number of common features (Clasen and Clegg, 2006).

A first commonality between the two cases is to have effectively moved (further) towards a de-differentiated structure of benefit provision for the unemployed. In the UK this has essentially occurred through the progressive alignment of rights for all the unemployed on those conventionally reserved for workers without any contributory records, that is to say, unemployed recipients of social assistance. Conservative governments between 1979 and 1997 enacted the most significant reforms in this regard. After the modest earnings-related supplement paid to the unemployed with the longest contribution records was scrapped in 1982, reforms in 1988 tightened the contribution requirements for access to insurance-based unemployment benefit (UB). The duration of entitlement of these was then reduced from 1 year to 6 months with the introduction of Jobseekers Allowance (JSA) in 1996 and, tellingly, their monetary value aligned with means-tested benefits for the jobless (now called 'income-related JSA'). New Labour governments since 1997 have reversed none of these reforms, and the proportion of unemployed receiving insurance-based benefits, around 50 per cent in 1980, had fallen as a result to under 16 per cent in 2007 (DWP, 2008). Insurance-based benefits have been made so exclusive and modest that they are becoming increasingly irrelevant to the social protection of the jobless in Britain.

In Denmark unemployment benefit rights have actually long been relatively undifferentiated, a result first of the relatively open access to the insurance system and secondly of the comparatively low benefit ceiling, which limits the extent that insurance benefits can vary with earnings. Directly contrary to Britain, this is a system where the majority of the unemployed receive insurance benefits and only a very few social assistance. Recent reforms have mainly been concerned with safeguarding this historic 'levelling-up' approach to standardization in unemployment benefit provision. Thus, while some new differentiations in benefit rights were introduced in the 1980s – lower benefit rates for those with partial contribution records, for example – these were removed in subsequent reforms. Since the early 1990s cuts have instead largely been general ones, notably the progressive reduction in the maximum duration of insurance benefits from 7 to 4 years, irrespective of contribution record, between 1993 and 1998 (cf. Andersen, 2002a). These changes have allowed the Danish unemployment insurance system to remain economically viable even with a beneficiary rate[3] that, at around 80 per cent at the end of the 1990s, is the highest in Europe (Samek, 2001, p. 61).

Another similarity in recent unemployment policies enacted in the two cases is the embrace of generalized activation. Of course, there are significant differences in the content of activation, notably in the level of investment in training provision, far higher in the Danish than British case. We could with some justification contrast the 'positive' activation practised in Denmark and the 'negative' activation practised in the UK (Barbier, 2004; Torfing, 1999). In both countries activation has since the mid-1990s nonetheless become a core guiding principle in benefit provision for all the unemployed, and increasingly also for other inactive groups.

In both countries, finally, activation has also resulted in and been facilitated by significant changes to the organization of the policy sector. In the UK, UB and social assistance for the jobless were merged and harmonized with the creation of JSA. After the 'Restart' initiative launched in 1986 the administrations in charge of employment policy (the Employment Service) and benefit policy and administration (the Benefits Agency) were also ever more closely coordinated, culminating in their merger to create a 'Working Age Agency'. At the delivery level, finally, benefit and job search services are increasingly brought together in the so-called Jobcentre Plus, which is now the pivot of provision for all the registered unemployed as it is for other working age benefit claimants. This has institutionalized a shift away from the historic focus on unemployment and towards an emphasis on 'worklessness' in UK labour market policy (Clasen, 2004).

To date, institutional changes in Danish unemployment policy have been less radical. The pre-existing pillars of labour market policy – the trade union-run unemployment insurance system, the local authority-run social assistance, and the state-run public employment service – retain distinct institutional identities, though their activities and interventions have since the mid-1990s increasingly been channelled through and co-ordinated by tripartite labour market authorities which operate at the regional level (Ploug, 2004). From January 2007, though, the desire to provide a common gateway to all services for all of the unemployed has led to the creation of 90 new 'Jobcentres', fairly explicitly modelled on the integrated British system. In 10 pilot centres the administrative responsibility for the unemployed rests entirely with the local authorities. If this model is generalized, it will represent a considerable enhancement of the state's role in Danish labour market policy, essentially to the detriment of the trade union funds.

In sum, in Denmark and the UK major changes in the conception and the institutionalization of unemployment policy have taken place in recent years. More or less in parallel, these reforms have encouraged or consolidated a (more or less generous) standardized approach to unemployment benefit rights, have introduced broadly universal activation, and shaken up the organization of the policy sector to encourage coordination and single points of access to the system for all claimants; all characteristic reforms in the transition to an unemployment policy that is both more institutionally statist and explicitly market-supporting.

It is arguable that the relative ease with which British and Danish governments have been able to effect this transformation – a veritable 'clean sweep' across a number of interlocking policy dimensions – owes much to the fact that in both countries the state *always* retained considerable leverage over unemployment benefit policy, even when it operated on a more classic insurance basis. The broader context in which British unemployment policy operated was a welfare system characterized by Harris (1992, p. 116) as 'one of the most uniform, centralized and bureaucratic and "public" … in Europe, and indeed the modern world'. Though unemployment insurance benefits were financed from a national insurance fund, this fund always had limited independence from the Treasury. Furthermore, following Beveridge's principle of integrated administration, unemployment benefit was always controlled by a central government agency without social partner or other civil society involvement. Though the contribution principle may have been discursively important in postwar British unemployment policy, it was therefore never buffered by supportive institutional mechanisms, and was always vulnerable to being revoked by the state when conditions seemed to require this (Clasen, 2001).

The institutional set-up of the Danish unemployment policy sector was traditionally less unambiguously state-dominated than the British, and this no doubt helps to explain why institutional change has in recent years advanced somewhat less rapidly there than in the UK. Specifically, the important role accorded to trade unions in the management of the voluntary 'Ghent system' of unemployment insurance has complicated coordination efforts, the unions being highly resistant to any reforms that would undermine the perceived link between union membership and benefit rights that acts as a powerful recruiting agent for them (Lind, 2004). For a number of reasons this has not diverted the direction of reform too substantially, however. First, good relationships between the union movement and the social democratic party meant that the former could be encouraged to cooperate with many governmental reforms during the 1990s, when the social democrats were in office. More importantly, unemployment benefits in Denmark are around 80 per cent tax-financed and this, along with the broader context of a universalist welfare state tradition, gives the Danish state considerable legitimacy to steer unemployment policy reforms (Ploug, 2004). This emboldens governments less sympathetic to labour interests to advance reform agendas that the unions oppose, and diminishes the ability of the latter to mobilize support against such changes.

Embracing the more statist new unemployment policy paradigm has in short been relatively uncomplicated in Denmark and the UK because, in both these countries, state intervention was widely accepted and provided for in traditional unemployment benefit policy. The cases of Belgium, France and Germany remind us that this was not the case everywhere, and show that where the autonomy of unemployment insurance from the state was more strongly institutionalized the transition to a new unemployment policy paradigm has proved considerably more complicated.

Subsidiarity versus the market: the Belgian, French and German cases

Belgium, France and Germany are 'Bismarckian' or 'conservative' welfare states, and a guiding principle of such systems is subsidiarity (Van Kersbergen, 1995). In the realm of social insurance the practical implication of the subsidiarity principle has been the retention of significant managerial and sometimes also policy responsibilities by private corporate actors, notably the trade unions and/or employers associations. This can be seen in the Belgian, French and German unemployment insurance systems, albeit in different ways (cf. Clegg, 2007). In Belgium, unemployment benefits are formally a

Parliamentary prerogative, but they are administered largely by the trade unions in a compulsory variant of the Ghent system found in Denmark. In France trade unions and employers jointly regulate unemployment insurance through periodically renegotiated collective agreements, without there being any formal decision-making role for the state beyond validating (or otherwise) agreements reached by the social partners. In Germany, finally, unemployment benefits are a competence of the federal government, but managed through a tripartite institution in which the unions, employers and public authorities (Federal government, Länder and municipalities) are all represented. In each of these national cases the unwillingness or inability of successive governments to override the interests of private actors thus institutionalized in the governance of unemployment insurance has considerably complicated attempts to move resolutely towards a more market-conforming unemployment policy.

The social partners' influence over unemployment insurance legislation has, first of all, pushed against the adoption of reforms that fully decouple benefit rights from individual contributory records. As core workers with long work histories tend to be both unions' main constituency and the prime targets of employers' strategies to shed high cost–low productivity workers, both sides of industry have an interest in gearing social protection systems first and foremost to the needs of labour market 'insiders' (cf. Ebbinghaus, 2006). Furthermore, in a context where the legitimacy of the social partners' managerial role in social protection – which they value highly – derives essentially from the contributory nature of benefits, these actors have an obvious interest in reaffirming this, even if the price is a narrower definition of the risk that contributory benefits can cover.

In their role as joint decision-makers for the unemployment insurance system, the French social partners have thus in the main coped with a context of consistently high unemployment since the early 1980s by linking benefit rights more, not less, closely to contributions (cf. Daniel, 2001). 'Bad risks' were transferred to a tax-financed 'solidarity' system separate from unemployment insurance in reforms adopted in the early 1980s, and the dualism of the unemployment benefit system has since been reaffirmed and even reinforced. In Germany, reforms in the 1980s and 1990s also tended to reduce the generosity of unemployment protection mainly for job starters and those with repeated spells of unemployment while simultaneously extending entitlement for core workers. Though the Hartz IV reform of 2004 reversed the latter trend by limiting insurance-based support to a maximum of 12 months, it has if anything widened the rights gap between the (now smaller) core of claimants in receipt of wage-based support and a (growing) periphery of those who must rely on means-tested assistance (Clasen, 2005). While Hartz IV certainly represented a quite radical change to German unemployment protection (Seeleib-Kaiser and Fleckenstein, 2007), the calibration – if not the extent – of reform had closer parallels with the

French case (cf. Eichorst, 2007) than with the more homogenizing logic of British and Danish unemployment benefit reforms.

Unemployment benefit reform has followed a somewhat different path in Belgium. The system has certainly been instrumentalized in 'labour shedding' policies, thanks to the vast and to date difficult-to-reverse expansion of early retirement pensions financed out of unemployment insurance revenues (Kuipers, 2006). But normal benefits have otherwise become much less differentiated by contribution and employment history, as a result of maximum benefits being allowed to stagnate relative to minimum benefits and of benefit rates increasingly being adjusted to assumed household need (Marx, 2007). The Belgian trade unions have, it seems, implicitly accepted sacrificing the wage-protection function of unemployment insurance benefits to safeguard the traditional absence of any limits on the duration of payments. This unique historical feature of the Belgian system prevents the vast majority of the unemployed from falling into social assistance, but in so doing also safeguards the income that the union-run benefit payment agencies can claim from the federal government for each unemployed individual receiving insurance benefits from them. In other words, though benefit reforms in Belgium seem more in line with the new unemployment policy paradigm than those in France or Germany, this is less because Belgian governments have proved more adept at overriding the interests of institutionalized actors than because the actors in place and their interests differ somewhat.

The state's limited capacity for regulatory intervention has had more similar policy effects in the three countries with respect to the closely related areas of activation and the organizational reform of the unemployment policy sector. Regarding the former, the unions' desire to prevent downward pressure on wages coupled with employers' reticence about destabilizing existing complementarities between benefit regulations and collective bargaining arrangements has generally tended to act as a bulwark against the development of more negative activation policies. Positive forms of activation, such as greater short-term investment in training in search of (possible) longer-term savings, have for their part come up against the problem of the jealously guarded but always precarious fiscal autonomy of self-regulating unemployment insurance funds. More integrated financing and regulation of different labour market policies, meanwhile, has proved very difficult to reconcile with the institutionalized division of responsibilities between the state and private social actors. Indeed, to the extent that benefit reform has often involved drawing clearer distinctions between contributory (contribution-financed) and non-contributory (tax-financed) rights (see above), there are as many trends to further financial and managerial fragmentation as there are to integration (Clegg, 2007).

In France and Belgium governmental activation initiatives have accordingly largely concentrated on the assistance margins of the unemployment protection system, where the social partners have no institutionalized influence, and left the insurance core, where they do, relatively untouched. This is true in Belgium despite the fact that, due to the unlimited duration of unemployment benefits, most of the unemployed have been kept out of social assistance. The minimum income scheme (formerly Minimex, now *Revenu d'Integration Sociale*) has nonetheless been the site of most activation activity to date, and where explicit efforts to systematically link employment creation measures to benefit delivery have been most successful (Gilson and Glorieux, 2005). In France, too, the development of activation has followed a clearly selective path, with governmental employment measures being *de facto* targeted on groups excluded from unemployment insurance coverage (cf. Daniel and Tuchszirer, 1999), and contractual approaches to benefit policy being pioneered in schemes such as the *Revenu Minimum d'Insertion* social assistance. In both countries the activation logic has slowly 'worked up' to unemployment insurance since around the turn of the new millennium, but creating a coherent policy has to date been hampered by the difficulty of coordination problems between the unemployment insurance system and the state. The German situation is for its part a little different, given that the Federal Labour Office (BA) was always responsible for the financing of active as well as passive measures. The double effect of this situation was that measures were targeted on the insured unemployed, and tended to be strongly pro-cyclical (cf. Schmid et al., 1992). The recent Hartz reforms carry the promise of targeting measures on the basis of individual rather than budgetary considerations, but also the risk – given the substantial gulf in perceptions of the appropriate treatment of the new 'unemployment benefit I' and 'unemployment benefit II' claimants that the legislation manifests – of exacerbating rather than undermining status-based distinctions in the quality of social rights (Ludwig-Mayerhofer, 2005, p. 104).

In both France and Belgium the need for a more integrated approach to unemployment benefit and placement/employment policy has been recognized for a long time, but has yet to give rise to more than weak 'cooperation agreements' between the different institutional actors. This owes much to the perceived need not to encroach on the autonomy of the unemployment insurance institutions managed by the social partners (France) or the unions (Belgium), coupled with the unwillingness of governments to give these actors full control over the public employment service (De Lathouwer, 2004; Maire, 2005). That these actors may not operate fully in the public interest is thus recognized, but not sufficiently to justify their expulsion from their historic unemployment policy roles.[4] In Germany the situation is again somewhat different, given that the BA has long cumulated both placement and payment functions in unemployment policy. Recent reforms have however restructured the BA partly in an attempt to reduce the influence of the social partners, with at present uncertain success (Streeck and Trampusch, 2005, p. 186).

Differences between the cases notwithstanding, the important general point is that in all the participation of private actors in the regulation of unemployment insurance has acted as a brake on the smooth transition to a more market-supporting unemployment policy. By participating in its governance, private actors have developed a stake in classical insurance-based unemployment policy, and have been able to use their institutional position to defend it. This has not ruled out market-conforming reforms altogether, but ensured that they can develop only incrementally, in the gradually expanding interstices of pre-existing but increasingly stretched institutional arrangements (Clegg, 2007). A more coherent policy of recommodification, however, would seem to require the state assuming a far more central regulatory and steering role in unemployment protection than the subsidiarity principle has traditionally sanctioned.

A great transformation: the Dutch case

It is in this context that the Dutch case is particularly enlightening. On the one hand, the Netherlands is another welfare state that has conventionally been characterized as Bismarckian, at least with respect to the sectors like unemployment and disability that are covered by 'workers insurances' (cf. Kuipers, 2006). In the Netherlands, like in its three neighbours, the effective regulation of unemployment policy was accordingly long devolved in large part to the social partners, and the tradition of subsidiarity was very strong. And yet the Netherlands is, like Denmark and the UK, one of the European countries most often presented as having undergone a truly radical transformation in socio-economic policy generally, and unemployment policy specifically (e.g. Green-Pedersen et al., 2001). Understanding how this was possible should tell us something more about the conditions for fundamental liberalizing reforms in contemporary unemployment policy.

The Dutch reform trajectory in unemployment policy shows evidence of a marked change of direction in the early to mid-1990s (Clegg, 2007). Up to that point reform had followed a trajectory in which the institutionalized influence of the social partners was palpable. With respect to benefit reforms, this was clearest in the 1987 New Unemployment Insurance Act (NWW). Although the government had previously announced its intention to introduce a major 'system reform', NWW ultimately strongly reaffirmed the insurance character of unemployment benefits, notably by reducing the role of tax finance in unemployment insurance benefits and by linking benefit entitlement much more closely to employment record and particularly age. Following from and in part determining this, the reform also cemented the role of the social partners in the governance of the system (Boekraad, 1998, p. 735). Subsequent reforms, however, have been notably more nuanced in their distributive logic. With the 'Purple' Lib–Lab coalition led by Wim Kok now in power, a 1995 reform did further tighten contributory eligibility requirements, but also extended rights to prolonged benefits for younger claimants and introduced a new short-time, flat-rate benefit within the insurance system for those who did not meet the new eligibility requirements for full benefit. A 2005 reform made unemployment benefit rights less dependent on the so-called 'nominal' work record – in fact an indirect measure of age – and thereby corrected some of the age-bias of the system.

Again initially following a trajectory similar to Belgium, France and Germany, activation approaches in Dutch benefit policy were also developed largely at the assistance margins of the unemployment protection system. Faced with the growing number of unemployed people receiving social assistance, the late 1980s saw the introduction of 'reorientation interviews' for the long-term unemployed, organized around cooperation agreements between local social services departments and the placement offices of the national employment service (ibid, p. 756). The so-called 'stimulating function' of benefit administration was further reinforced by a new law on social assistance in 1989, and finally completed by the New National Assistance Act of 1996 which, in addition to simplifying and individualising benefit norms, imposed an explicitly contractual approach on assistance claimants directly inspired by the French RMI (Westerveld and Faber, 2005, p. 170). Finally, the Jobseekers Employment Act of 1997 created communal employment funds out of pre-existing special employment measures for the young and long-term unemployed, facilitating the more seamless and explicit linkage of the latter with the communally administered social assistance system.

If these activation initiatives were initially concentrated essentially on the assistance margins of the unemployment system, it was above all because the social partners used their governance role to prevent their developing at the system's insurance core. This was highlighted very explicitly by the report of a Parliamentary enquiry, under the chairmanship of the socialist Flip Buurmeijer, in 1993. The Buurmeijer Commission showed that, for all the talk of the need for activation or 'volume policy' since the mid- to late-1980s, the reality of the development of the workers' insurances had in fact been an 'inverted volume policy'. Regarding unemployment insurance, the commission highlighted that the bipartite industrial boards that managed the benefit had few contacts with the public employment service, and had done little to try to develop these. Although it emphasized the responsibility of legislation – and thus of state actors, the government and Parliament – for the passivity of the insurance system, it underlined that this was largely derivative of the considerable role in the shaping of social security policy that was exerted by the social partners, and the desire of successive governments not to encroach on the latters' terrain. While the responsible ministers had occasionally put out signals arguing the need for a more activating approach, the Commission demonstrated that these had gone essentially unheard by the industrial boards (cf. Boekraad, 1998, pp. 743–54).

The Commission would possibly never have been asked to report on the workers' insurances managed by the social partners had it not been for the swelling caseload of disability benefit recipients in the Netherlands, which pointed more clearly than elsewhere to dysfunctions in their operation. The parallel existence of a state-managed system of national insurances perhaps also made social partner involvement in social security regulation and administration appear less inevitable in the Netherlands than in other national contexts. For whatever reason, the 1990s saw a serious attack on the principle of subsidiarity in social policy affairs, of which the Buurmeijer Commission's report was just the first act. In the years following its publication, there were a succession of new 'laws on the organization of social insurances', in 1995, 1997 and 2000. The organizational reform path followed was complicated and in some ways confused (cf. Hemerijck, 2003, pp. 253–5; Wierink, 2000), but in general demonstrated a growing willingness no longer merely to adapt unemployment insurance policy according to the institutionalized logic, but instead to challenge institutional logics that do not fit with political and policy objectives. This has opened the way to a major restructuring of the work–welfare interface, and consequentially to a general activation approach that goes far beyond what was previously possible.

When in 1999 the social partners responded very critically to the government's proposal to try and further improve co-operations between the public Centres for Work and Income (CWI) and the workers' insurance institutions – which they saw as a menace to their managerial autonomy in social security – the government did indeed withdraw its policy proposal. But instead of then falling into line with the social partners' preferred option of a complete privatization of social security management, the government's new project in November 1999 opted 'for an integral return to public competence in the administration of benefits and a considerable reduction in the role of the social partners' (Wierink, 2000, p. 33). Although the government conceded the social partners a policy-advisory role in a new Council for Work and Income, it otherwise rode out their protests at being evicted from a sector that they esteemed to be their 'property'. The new organizational framework, with the public CWI at the centre as the point of access to all work and welfare services, was institutionalized in the 2001 law on 'implementation structures for work and income' (SUWI), which has effectively generalized the programmatic integration of employment policy and social security, and introduced the principle of obligatory profiling interviews for all of the unemployed (Hemerijck, 2003, p. 260).

It is probably fair to say that the Dutch welfare state reforms, including in the area of unemployment policy, remain open to a certain amount of misrepresentation in international debates. The theme of the consensual 'polder model' of revived corporatism and negotiated reform, with the 1982 Wassenaar agreement on wages and working hours as its epitome, came to dominate international debates, even though the works most often cited as supporting evidence (e.g. Visser and Hemerijck, 1997) tell at least a rather more complicated story across the Dutch political economy as a whole. Some have actually suggested that with respect to the reforms undertaken by the Kok governments in the mid-1990s, the emphasis on revived private interest government is just plain wrong; 'foreign observers celebrated the very characteristics of the Dutch system that the purple coalition had consigned to the dustbin of history' (Hendriks, 2001, p. 37). In unemployment policy, a good case can be made that the institutional reforms that unfolded in the years following the Burmeijer report were more a case of the state intervening decisively to make the fateful changes necessary for the market to develop, rather as Polanyi analysed in his account of 'the great transformation' in nineteenth-century England. In this respect the Dutch case also confirms better than perhaps any other the principal arguments of this chapter as a whole; current liberalizing reforms in unemployment policy require more not less state activism, and the ability to effectively deploy state power is one of the key predictors of whether liberalization will be fully and unequivocally embraced.

Conclusion

Uncomplicated narratives of welfare state transformation – such as the notion of a transition from welfare statism to liberalism – have unquestionable rhetorical appeal both for those who welcome contemporary changes and for those who deplore them. As this chapter has illustrated with reference to unemployment policies, however, such narratives often rely on a misremembering of the past and a misrepresentation of present trends. Close inspection reveals that in unemployment policy the heyday of welfare statism was in fact a time when the state often remained institutionally in the shadows, operating through the invisible hand of largely self-regulating social insurance arrangements. Inversely, although the public sector's share in the economy may today be shrinking, its retreat is in unemployment policy being marshalled and facilitated by far more explicit and obvious state interventionism than in the past. In unemployment policy the result is a certain dissonance in the logics of change at the level of institutions, on the one hand, and at the level of discourses and outcomes, on the other.

Recognition of this more complex reality, both historical and contemporary, has implications for how we explain the dynamics of ongoing welfare state transformations. For example, when Pierson (1994) argued that state capacity was 'hardly relevant' to the retrenchment dynamics of benefit programmes, he arguably had both an overly restrictive understanding of retrenchment and a limited view of state capacity. Many of the reforms promoted in the new unemployment policy paradigm can fairly easily be equated to retrenchment, and for many of them state capacity *qua* enforcement power is, as shown above, clearly relevant. Furthermore, state capacity should also be understood to mean rather more than simple bureaucratic probity or 'bricks and mortar' issues, and expanded to include the institutional arrangements underpinning specific policy areas that can determine the legitimacy of the state to intervene in and direct reform at all. As described above, variations in such capacities have been crucial in explaining the unemployment policy reform paths taken in different European countries in recent years.

Understanding the dissonance of current trends across different levels can also help us to more fully understand the challenges that contemporary welfare state reformers face. For the reasons described above, unemployment policy reform often requires the state doing more so that it can do less, wrestling responsibilities from private actors so that it can impose more responsibility on private individuals. Although this course of action makes perfect sense intellectually, it is difficult to package in a political world where uncomplicated narratives understandably hold sway. Between simple reform discourses and the complex nature of the welfare state transformations under way there is a gulf that can be exploited by opponents of change and where incomprehension and resentment can develop as reforms are forced through. Recognizing the complexity of contemporary welfare state transformations also helps us, therefore, tell richer stories about why these transformations are often difficult and usually politically risky.

10

The Transformation of Incapacity Benefits

Peter A. Kemp

This chapter explores the transformation of incapacity benefits in the advanced welfare states in recent decades. Protection against work incapacity has been a longstanding feature of many advanced welfare states. To that extent, it represents what Esping-Andersen (1999) and others (e.g. Taylor-Gooby, 2004b; Bonoli, 2006) have called an 'old social risk'. These authors have argued that the transition to a post-industrial society has resulted in the emergence of 'new social risks', such as population ageing and the work–life balance, that require corresponding changes in the welfare state. However, although new social risks may have emerged, that does not mean that old social risks have remained unchanged. This is because the economic and social conditions that create such risks have themselves changed in recent decades. Moreover, concepts such as work incapacity are not fixed or immutable. Rather, they are socially contingent, contestable and subject to change over time. Indeed, a central claim of this chapter is that both the social risk of incapacity to work, and the protection that the welfare state provides against it, have been transformed in the transition from industrial to post-industrial society.[1]

Incapacity as a social risk

The term 'incapacity benefits' is used here to refer to earnings replacement social security programmes for people who are unable to undertake paid employment because they are long-term sick or disabled. Depending on the country, these programmes are referred to as disability insurance, disability benefits, disability pensions, invalidity pensions or incapacity benefits. We prefer to use the term incapacity benefit in this chapter because, as the OECD (2003) report *Transforming Disability into Ability* pointed out, many recipients of these benefits are not disabled. Moreover, disability is not the same as incapacity to work. As Spicker (2003, p. 31) puts it, 'People can be disabled without being unable to work, and unable to work without being disabled.'

Neither 'disability' nor 'work incapacity' are fixed or immutable concepts. Rather, they are socially constructed and, as such, open to debate, contestation and change (cf. Clarke, 2004). Socially dominant norms about what conditions count as being disabled may vary from one society to another and over time. Likewise, people's willingness to define themselves as disabled – and hence to submit a claim for incapacity benefits – may also vary (Piachaud, 1986). And while some impairments are easy to identify, many others are less readily apparent. Indeed, Marin (2003, p. 23) has argued that disability is an 'inherently subjective' concept and de Jong (de Jong, 2003, p. 96) has called it 'elusive'. Likewise, incapacity to work is also, to some extent, a subjective concept and in practice it is often difficult to determine who is incapable of work and who is not (Burkhauser and Daly, 2002). Again, changing expectations may affect how work incapacity is perceived. Marin (2003) argues that the types of condition that are recognized as constituting work incapacity have tended to widen over time.

The fact that incapacity to work is to some extent subjective and not easy to determine in practice may account for the moral hazard concerns that often surround it (Kemp, 2006). Two common features of incapacity benefit programmes exacerbate such concerns. The first is that the level of incapacity benefits is often higher than unemployment benefits or social assistance. In theory, this difference in benefit levels gives non-employed people with health problems a financial incentive to claim incapacity benefits rather than unemployment benefits (Bound and Burkhauser, 1999).

The second is that incapacity benefits are generally subject to less stringent work search requirements than unemployment benefit. Thus, in theory, people who have health problems and cannot find a job have an incentive to claim disability rather than unemployment benefits.[2] In reality, the factors affecting decisions about whether to claim incapacity benefits are likely to be more complex than this. Nevertheless, it is because of these moral hazard concerns that applicants are often required to undergo more or less strict medical testing in order to ensure that they 'really' are incapable of work as defined by the incapacity benefit programme in their country. These medical tests may be made more or less strict over time, thereby shifting the boundary between capacity and incapacity.

The qualifying criterion for incapacity benefit programmes in countries that recognize only total incapacity – such as the liberal welfare states of Australia, Britain, Canada and the US – is typically whether an applicant's health or impairments render them incapable of work. But, to an extent, whether or not someone is incapable of work must depend upon the nature of the work. A long-term limiting condition may prevent someone from doing some types of work but not others. For example, visual impairment may make it difficult for someone to work on a building site but not in an office.

In countries that recognize partial as well as full disability – such as the conservative welfare regimes of Germany and the Netherlands and social democratic Denmark and Sweden – the qualifying criterion for incapacity benefit is the degree to which the applicant suffers from reduced working capacity. This is often expressed in terms of reduced earnings capacity, a definition that requires some benchmark against which to assess full earnings capacity. The latter may be defined in terms of average earnings in the applicant's previous occupation or much more broadly to include any suitable occupation. Whatever definition is used, it may affect the applicant's assessed degree of incapacity, the size of the award that is granted or even whether the application is successful at all. This further underlines the socially constructed nature of 'incapacity to work'.

Moreover, the types of work that someone can do may also be affected, not just by their health, but also by their education, skills and experience. These human capital factors may also influence whether or not people with limiting health conditions are able to successfully compete for jobs in the labour market, quite apart from whether or not they are capable of doing them. Indeed, Graetz and Mashaw (1999) have argued that it is conceptually impossible to distinguish between anything less than a total incapacity to undertake gainful employment and the human capital and attitudinal factors that make people less successful in the labour market.

Employer attitudes to people with limiting health conditions or disabilities are also important. If employers discriminate against them, or are unwilling to make work-place adaptations that may enable someone with an impairment to do a particular job, that can make it more difficult for disabled people to find work. This may be especially the case when the economy is in recession and jobs are scarce. More generally, as the nature of work changes over time, it is possible that conditions that are not incapacitating in one period become so in another, and vice versa.

The difficulty of determining whether applicants for disability benefits are incapable of work has arguably become more difficult with the rise of what some commentators refer to as the 'new disabilities'. Thus, Overbye (2005) has argued that, in the past, disability tended to refer to relatively easily observable, functional impairments such as being deaf, blind or needing to use a wheelchair. These were impairments that limited people's ability to work in a largely industrial (or agricultural) economy, where manual jobs were predominant, especially for people with relatively low educational attainment and few skills. However, the main problem today, Overbye (2005) argues, is with less readily observable disabilities such as chronic muscular pain, stress and depression. Because these conditions are less easy to recognize, it is arguably more difficult to determine whether they affect work capacity. And because they are less visible they may raise doubts about whether, and to what extent, they really exist or are just imagined. Hence the 'new' disabilities are much more likely than the 'old' ones to generate concerns about malingering (Kemp, 2006).

Changing risks

Along with pensions and unemployment, incapacity to work was one of the first contingencies to be protected by social insurance schemes; to that extent, it can be regarded as an 'old social risk' associated with industrial capitalism (Bonoli, 2006). However, a key argument of this chapter is that the dichotomy between old and new social risks is to some extent a false one. As noted above, work incapacity is not a fixed or immutable concept, but rather a socially contingent one. The nature and perception of work incapacity as a social risk have in fact been transformed since the 'golden age' of the welfare state. The conditions that give rise – and the way in which the welfare state defines and responds – to this social risk in post-industrial society are, to an important extent, different from those that were predominant under industrial capitalism. Likewise, there have been important changes in the types of people claiming incapacity benefits, which also mirror the shift to post-industrial society.

In general, insurance against incapacity to work has been provided separately from benefits covering accidents at work.[3] Protection against the risk of long-term work incapacity has largely been provided by the state rather than the private sector.[4] Because of adverse selection, moral hazard and covariance between the risks of work incapacity and unemployment, it is difficult for the private market to provide actuarially sound and affordable disability insurance for the working-age population as a whole (Aarts et al., 1996; de Jong, 2003). Even in the US, where private insurance is probably the most extensive among the advanced welfare states, only a minority of employees is enrolled in insurance programmes that cover long-term disability (Graetz and Mashaw, 1999).[5]

The earliest incapacity programmes tended to be for industrial injuries and war veterans. But Germany introduced an invalidity pension in 1889 for adult workers who had lost at least two-thirds of earnings capacity. Gordon (1988) reports that, by the early 1930s, 16 of the countries included in her study of social security programmes in the industrialized countries had introduced what she tellingly referred to as 'invalidity' schemes. However, it was not until the 1950s and 1960s that more general programmes for work incapacity began to be introduced more widely, entitlement to which was usually based on social insurance contributions. During the full employment years of the 'golden age' of the welfare state (Esping-Andersen, 1996a), incapacity benefit caseloads were generally low. However, the coverage of such schemes tended to widen over time, with corresponding increases in the number of recipients and in programme costs. This expansion was part of the growth of the welfare state more generally in the immediate postwar decades.

In the 1950s and 1960s, recipients of incapacity insurance tended to be regarded as among the 'deserving poor'. Their impairments were frequently

Table 10.1   Incapacity benefit recipiency rate*

	%		%
Liberal		*Conservative*	
Australia	5.2	Austria	4.6
Canada	3.9	Belgium	5.9
UK	6.7	France	4.6
USA	4.7	Germany	4.2
Social democratic		Italy	5.5
Denmark	7.7	Netherlands	9.0
Norway	9.2		
Sweden	8.2		

* Incapacity benefit recipients as % of the working age population.

Source: OECD (2007) Social Expenditure Database.

products of industrial capitalism, usually physical, often visible, and generally had to be permanent – hence the typical description of them as 'disability' insurance or benefits. Thus workers who were granted incapacity benefits were not usually expected to find work again, a status that in some countries was implicitly recognized in the inclusion of words like 'invalidity' or 'pensions' in the names used to describe these benefits. It was also reflected in the fact that, in some countries, such as Germany and Sweden, they were formally part of the pension system even though the recipients were below official pension age. Not surprisingly, therefore, incapacity benefit recipients – 'invalids' – were not expected to be available for work or meet work search requirements, unlike unemployment insurance recipients. Benefit levels were usually earnings related and sometimes more generous than unemployment insurance. Thus, incapacity benefit programmes entailed a relatively high degree of decommodification, especially when compared with unemployment insurance.

In the 1970s and 1980s the number of incapacity benefit recipients in many advanced welfare states increased substantially, in some cases quite sharply (Gordon, 1988). Although rates of growth have since tailed off and in some countries – such as Denmark and the Netherlands – have fallen, they remain at high levels. Thus, by the late 1990s, incapacity benefit recipients typically accounted for around 5 to 7 per cent of the working age population (OECD, 2003).

However, the incapacity benefit recipiency rate varies between countries. Table 10.1 presents figures for selected OECD countries grouped into Esping-Andersen's welfare regimes (Esping-Andersen, 1999). Although the average for these 13 countries is 6.1 per cent of the working age population, the recipiency rate for the social democratic welfare regimes (8.4 per cent) is noticeably higher than for the liberal (5.1 per cent) and conservative (5.6 per cent) welfare regimes. At 9.0 per cent, the recipiency rate for the Netherlands is more akin to the levels in the social democratic than the conservative welfare states.

One reason why the social democratic welfare states have such high levels of incapacity benefit receipt may be that they have made less use of early retirement schemes than the conservative welfare regimes (Ebbinghaus, 2006) as a means of labour shedding in the face of deindustrialization (see below). A second factor is likely to be the very high rate of female labour force participation in the social democratic countries.

It is important to note that incapacity benefit caseloads have not just grown; they have also changed in composition (Kemp, 2006). Three main changes have taken place. First, people claiming incapacity benefits are no longer overwhelmingly men. In many countries there has been a growth in the relative importance of female recipients. Indeed, in the social democratic welfare states of Denmark, Norway and Sweden women now outnumber men in the incapacity benefit caseload. Second, in recent years many countries have witnessed relative growth in middle-aged (and to a lesser extent, younger) beneficiaries, though rates are still highest for people age 50 to 64.[6] Third, there has been a decline in the relative importance of physical conditions such as cardiovascular conditions and a marked shift towards mental disorders, particularly stress and depression as the medical condition for which incapacity benefit is granted. Mental illness now typically accounts for about a third of incapacity benefit recipients (OECD, 2003).

The transition to post-industrial society

The growth in incapacity benefit caseloads has reflected a range of demand and supply side factors (see Kemp, 2006). The importance of these drivers has varied between countries and over time, as has the timing of the growth in caseloads. Notwithstanding these variations in the pattern and timing of change, however, many of the drivers are associated with the economic restructuring that took place from approximately the mid-1970s.

This economic restructuring involved a secular decline in manufacturing industry (and in agricultural employment) and growth in service sector employment (Glyn, 2006). Deindustrialization was accompanied by a shake-out of workers, especially those who were older or deemed less productive, such as some people with limiting health problems and impairments. The very high levels of unemployment that characterized many economies in the 1980s and 1990s made it more difficult for older, less educated and sick or disabled people to find work. Hence, the growth in incapacity benefit caseloads was associated especially with older men, often with musculoskeletal complaints, who previously might have been able to find new work but were unable to do so in the new post-industrial economy.

Meanwhile, the demand for unskilled work declined across the developed world (Nickell and Bell, 1995). The consequent decline in relative earnings for unskilled labour helped to make incapacity benefits a more attractive option for people with health problems. This was especially true for blue collar workers with highly specific skills that were no longer required, particularly in areas of high unemployment (Alcock et al., 2003), for whom incapacity benefits became a de facto early retirement programme. More generally, as Iversen (2005) has argued, there is a major skill boundary between manufacturing (and agriculture) and services, such that skills transfer poorly between them. Hence, 'even low-skilled blue-collar workers, almost all males, find it exceedingly hard to adjust to similarly low-skilled service sector jobs because they lack something that, for want of a better word, may be thought of as a form of social skills' (Iversen, 2005, p. 187).

On the supply side, in the 1970s and 1980s when unemployment was at relatively high levels, governments, unions and employers acquiesced in the use of incapacity benefits as an early retirement mechanism (van Oorschot and Boos, 2000). The aim here was to mitigate the worst effects of this industrial restructuring and to shift the supply of older workers out of the labour market to make way for younger and more productive workers (see Ebbinghaus, 2006).[7] In many welfare states – such as Denmark, the Netherlands and Sweden – it became possible for older workers to receive incapacity benefits for labour market reasons in the absence of a health diagnosis. Thus, in the era of mass unemployment it was no longer necessary even to have a serious medical condition in order to qualify. To become an incapacity benefit recipient, as Hvinden (2004) has remarked, was seen as a socially acceptable (and in some countries an officially sanctioned) way for older workers to take an early exit from the labour market.

In the Netherlands, this 'labour market diagnosis' qualification for incapacity benefit even included workers aged under 45 (Aarts et al., 1996). This reflected the fact incapacity benefits in that country were being used, not only as an early retirement pathway, but also as a way of keeping a lid on the politically sensitive problem of mass unemployment resulting from deindustrialization. In Britain, although not formal policy, in practice unemployment offices were encouraged to steer older workers in poor health towards invalidity benefit as a way of keeping down the number of people on the unemployment register (Walker and Howard, 2000). This provided a more attractive option than unemployment benefit for people who would have preferred a job but could not find one (Alcock et al., 2003). Hence in the 1980s and 1990s incapacity benefits were being used as a means of disguising high levels of unemployment (Beatty and Fothergill, 1996).

Thus, incapacity benefit was no longer simply the institution for providing insurance against medical incapacity to work that it had been under industrial capitalism. Instead, deindustrialization had prompted many of the advanced welfare states implicitly or explicitly to use incapacity benefits for two additional roles, namely both early retirement and 'hidden unemployment' purposes. This transformation in the role of incapacity benefits represents a form of partial institutional 'conversion' (Thelen, 2003) in which old institutions are given new purposes.

The surge in incapacity benefit receipt associated with deindustrialization in the 20 years from approximately the 1970s and 1980s may be a cohort effect (Kemp, 2006). The demand for incapacity benefit from that source is likely to decline as deindustrialization peters out. But that does not mean that incapacity benefit caseloads will therefore go back to pre-1970s levels once this wave of older men has worked its way through the system. This is because the transformation of work in the post-industrial economy is creating new health risks of its own (Esping-Andersen, 2002; Gallie, 2002) which is fuelling the current inflow into incapacity benefits. These new health risks do not just affect older men. As we have seen, in recent years the biggest growth in incapacity benefit recipiency has been among women and middle aged (and in the Netherlands, younger) people. Meanwhile, the share of recipients with cardiovascular and (to a lesser extent) musculoskeletal complaints has decreased and the share with mental disorders – particularly depression and complaints associated with stress – has increased.

The growth in female beneficiaries has been associated with the rise in labour force participation among women. Much of this female employment has been in the distributive and personal services sectors, in which the labour process is characterized by low control, low social support and high levels of psychological demands. Associated with the growth of service sector employment has been an increase in non-traditional jobs including ones that are precarious or low paid. Moreover, increased work intensity and organizational restructuring (such as downsizing) are common features of the post-industrial economy. Although the exact pathways and causal mechanisms are yet to be firmly established, there is growing evidence that these structural changes in the labour market have a negative impact upon health (Mustard et al., no date; Quinlan et al., 2001) and are associated with an increased risk of claiming incapacity benefits (Vahtera et al., 2005).

Some authors have explained this growth in female incapacity benefit recipients by the so-called 'double burden' hypothesis. Hvinden (2004, p. 176), for example, has argued that many women in the Nordic countries were 'simply exhausted from the double burden of being at the same time worker and main homemaker/care provider for their families'. The argument is that many women now have to cope with the dual burden of motherhood and paid employment, whereas previously they had only to deal with motherhood, while men did the breadwinning. In fact, since women are still responsible for the largest share of both domestic labour *and* child-care, those who are also in work face a triple burden rather than a double one. Coping with the varying demands of these tasks may create role conflict and overload, thereby leading to high levels of stress (Bratberg et al., 2002). To some extent, therefore, the growth in female claims for incapacity benefit may reflect a 'new social risk' of difficulty in reconciling the work–life balance (on which see Bonoli, 2006). However, the research evidence on the double burden is mixed, with some studies showing that working mothers are in better health than those who are not, while other studies have found the opposite. In any event, although difficulty in reconciling work–life balance may be one factor, it is unlikely to be the main driver behind the rise in incapacity benefit receipt among women.

Overbye (2005, p. 167) has suggested that 'The old disability stereotype of an industrial or agricultural male with a worn-out back is in the process of being replaced by another kind: A woman from a mixed social and occupational background with psychological or psychosomatic problems.' This is inevitably an over-simplification of a more complex process, not least because the growth in mental disorders has occurred among men as well as women. Nevertheless, it is apparent that the shift from an industrial (and in some countries such as Denmark, an agricultural) to a post-industrial society has brought with it a change in the nature of the health conditions and impairments associated with incapacity benefit and in the gender and age composition of those who receive it. This reflects the transformation in the social risk of work incapacity rather than a switch from 'old' to 'new' social risks.

Restructuring incapacity benefits

The OECD (2003) report on disability benefits noted that member countries typically spend much more on such schemes than they do on unemployment programmes. Table 10.2 shows expenditure on incapacity-related benefits as a percentage of Gross Domestic Product in 2003 for 15 countries. On average, these countries spend 2.9 per cent of GDP on these schemes, though the figures range from 1.0 per cent in Canada to 6.0 per cent in Sweden. The social democratic welfare states spend an average of 4.8 per cent, compared with 2.4 per cent among conservative and 2.0 per cent among liberal welfare states. Once again, spending levels in the Netherlands are closer to those in Scandinavia than to the other conservative welfare states.

Not surprisingly, the high level of expenditure on incapacity benefits has not gone unnoticed among policy-makers. Indeed, it has caused alarm in many countries (Hvinden, 2004; van Oorschot and Boos, 2000), especially perhaps those that have experienced falling unemployment, since this has not generally been matched by declining incapacity benefit caseloads. Hence, incapacity benefits have not been immune to the retrenchment pressures that have affected the welfare state more generally in recent decades.

According to Pierson (2001b), the advanced welfare states are facing an era of permanent fiscal austerity that is forcing retrenchment and restructuring onto the agenda of the advanced welfare states. He argues that, although the

Table 10.2 Expenditure on incapacity benefits 2003*

	%		%
Liberal		*Conservative*	
Australia	2.5	Austria	2.6
Canada	1.0	Belgium	2.3
NZ	2.9	France	1.7
UK	2.5	Germany	2.0
USA	1.3	Italy	1.8
Social democratic		Netherlands	3.9
Denmark	4.2		
Finland	3.5		
Norway	5.4		
Sweden	6.0		

* Incapacity benefit-related social expenditure as % of GDP.
Source: OECD (2007) Social Expenditure Database.

welfare state is subject to considerable 'institutional stickiness', change can be identified along three key dimensions: cost containment, recommodification and recalibration. This section shows that incapacity benefit programmes have been subject to reforms in all three dimensions.

Cost containment

Concerns about rising incapacity benefit caseloads and costs have prompted periodic attempts by governments to curb programme growth. Indeed, in some cases these cost containment measures were taken in response to increases in caseloads prompted by previous reforms that widened the coverage or increased the generosity of incapacity benefits. For example, in the US amendments passed in 1972 acted to increase the availability and the generosity of disability insurance, and were followed by a rapid increase in the number of recipients. Then in 1980 legislation was passed to tighten up administrative controls over the disability determination process, including the introduction of periodic 'continuing disability reviews', which helped to reduce the number of new awards and increase the number of terminations. However, in 1984 the disability determination process was liberalized again (Autor and Duggan, 2003; Bound and Burkhauser, 1999). This further highlights the fact that work incapacity is to some extent an unstable and contested concept, as is true of the welfare state more generally (Clarke, 2004).

In Sweden, there have been numerous changes to the rules governing disability benefit. In the 1970s and 1980s these changes tended to increase eligibility, but in the 1990s they were more restrictive (Kruse, 2003). Dutch attempts to curb the very high number of disability benefit recipients have been described as the 'battle against the numbers' (Oorschot and Boos, 2000).

This battle has included both actions to reduce the inflow to incapacity benefits and measures towards reintegrating disabled people into the labour market in order to increase the outflow.

Retrenchment measures to cut the *inflow* to incapacity benefits include tightening the definition of incapacity, making the medical test more stringent, and increasing the responsibility of employers to address long-term sickness. Measures to increase the *outflow* include introducing claim reviews and medical re-testing (or making them more regular or more stringent), new financial incentives to encourage recipients to return to work, enhancing measures for rehabilitation of disabled people and improving re-integration initiatives.

Attempts to reduce the generosity of incapacity benefits aim not only to reduce the cost of payments to existing or (more typically) new claimants. They also seek to both decrease the inflow to, and increase the outflow from, such schemes. However, few countries have actually reduced benefit levels (OECD, 2003), at least for existing claimants. The resilience of incapacity benefits to cuts in generosity probably reflects the fact that disabled people are often seen as relatively 'deserving' and therefore have broad public support. Unlike the unemployed, disabled people are typically viewed as not having a hand in their fate, which makes benefit cuts unpopular (Kuipers, 2006). In addition, in many countries disabled people are represented by vociferous lobby groups, the existence of which makes it more difficult politically to cut disability benefits.

Cuts in benefit levels have been introduced in Britain and the Netherlands. In Britain, a major reform introduced by the Conservative government in 1995 abolished the earnings-related element of incapacity benefit and made it taxable. The medical test that acts as the gateway to incapacity benefit was also tightened up. The main aim of this reform was to cut the rapidly rising number of people claiming this benefit (Walker and Howard, 2000). The rate of growth in the caseload did slow down after this reform, though other factors, such as the sustained growth in employment from 1993, may also have been important (Kemp and Thornton, 2006). In 2000, the Labour government implemented a further cutback by introducing a 50 per cent income taper for recipients with occupational or private pension income in excess of £85 per week.

In the Netherlands, the replacement rate for incapacity benefit was cut in 1987 from 80 per cent to 70 per cent of former earnings (when fully disabled). However, according to Kuipers (2006, p. 186) this cut 'barely affected the vast majority of Dutch employees' because the social partners (employers' organizations and trade unions) agreed to privately insure the gap between 80 per cent and 70 per cent in the replacement rate. These collective agreements covered about 80 per cent of the workforce. This supplement represented a partial privatization of the financing of incapacity benefit payments. Other measures aimed at cutting benefit levels included reduction of the earnings base from which benefits were calculated, changes to benefit indexation, and the introduction of social insurance contributions on benefit income. The net result was a substantial reduction in the average level of compensation for income loss due to disability during the 1990s (Kuipers, 2006; de Vos, 2006).

The evidence suggests that outflows into paid work are more difficult to influence than inflows. Once on the incapacity benefit rolls, relatively few people leave to return to work, though return-to-work rates vary significantly from one country to another (Bloch and Prins, 2001). However, while it appears to be easier to reduce inflows, measures having that goal may divert claimants onto other income support programmes such as unemployment benefits or social assistance. In other words, there may be substantial substitution effects arising from measures that seek to restrict the inflows to incapacity benefit programmes (Rasmussen et al., 2006). Some measures aimed at reducing outflows, such as medical re-testing, may also have substitution effects. This is because some people who lose entitlement to benefit following a review of their case may move onto other social security benefits rather than into paid employment. Hence, measures that reduce incapacity benefit caseloads may result in increases in the numbers of people claiming other benefits.

Recommodification

While many of the early retrenchment initiatives focused on cost-containment – such as attempts to restrict benefits to those 'genuinely' in need of them – over the last decade they have been broadened to include elements of recommodification. In particular, in some countries there has been a shift away from passive to more active, work-focused approaches (OECD, 2003), though much less so than is true of unemployment benefit regimes.

For example, three liberal welfare regimes – Australia, Britain and New Zealand – have introduced work-focused or employment preparation interviews for people on incapacity benefits. In addition, voluntary schemes such as the New Deal for Disabled People in Britain seek to encourage people on incapacity benefits to try out paid work or engage in activities that help move them closer to the labour market. Meanwhile, the Pathways to Work pilot scheme includes a financial incentive to encourage incapacity benefit recipients to find employment by giving them £40 per week on top of their weekly earnings for the first year of paid employment.

Some countries have made benefits conditional on participation in rehabilitation measures (OECD, 2006c). In Austria and Germany, for example, the policy is 'rehabilitation before disability'. Likewise, in the Netherlands and Sweden long-term sickness benefit claimants are expected to engage in rehabilitation or reintegration activities before they can claim incapacity benefit. In Denmark, people assessed as having partial disability are no longer eligible for incapacity benefit unless there is not a suitable 'flex-job' available to them. Flex-jobs provide full-time employment for an indefinite duration and are targeted at people with a permanent, partial reduction in working capacity who are not able to obtain or sustain employment under 'normal' working conditions. In return, employers are provided with a permanent subsidy (Rae, 2005; Rasmussen, 2006).

Thus welfare states are moving toward partial recommodification of incapacity and other non-employment benefits (see OECD, 2006c). To some extent, this trend reflects concerns about population ageing. On the one hand, there is concern that unless employment rates increase the proportion of the population dependent on benefits 'may rise to unsustainable levels' (Carcillo and Grubb, 2006, p. 8). On the other hand, in so far as people on incapacity benefits are able to do some paid work, they represent a potential reserve army of labour in the context of a shrinking working age population (Grover and Piggott, 2005). However, labour shortage is of less concern in countries such as Germany that continue to have high rates of unemployment.

Meanwhile, there is concern that measures taken to tighten eligibility for unemployment benefits and active labour market programmes may encourage some unemployed people with health problems to claim incapacity benefits instead, thereby boosting the rolls with people who are in fact capable of doing paid work. This potential for displacement between incapacity benefit and unemployment insurance reflects the fuzzy boundary between unemployment and incapacity to work (Marin, 2003).

Recalibration

As well as explicit recommodification initiatives, what Pierson (2001b) calls recalibration can also be detected. In the case of incapacity benefits, this involves attempts to change the 'culture of disability' (Rae, 2005) from one that sees people as incapable of all work to one that focuses on what work people might still be able to do. For example, the OECD (2006c) has criticized the all or nothing criteria that are often employed in medical tests for incapacity, which rest on the assumption that applicants either can or cannot work, when in fact some may face partial rather than complete barriers to work.

Meanwhile, lobby groups representing disabled people have campaigned against the 'medical model' – on which, incidentally, incapacity benefits under industrial capitalism was implicitly based – that sees disability as inherent in people's impairments. They have instead promoted the 'social model', which sees disability as a result of the failure by society to provide an environment in which people with impairments can, for example, obtain suitable employment. This new perspective shifts the focus onto employers and their willingness to employ people with impairments and to make necessary work accommodations. The switch to a more enabling perspective on disability and employment also legitimates a shift away from seeing incapacity benefit recipients as 'invalids' who are permanently incapable of all work, to one in which some could do certain kinds of work in the right circumstances.[8] Thus recalibration in this context reinforces efforts at recommodification.

Moves towards recalibration of incapacity benefits can be seen in reforms introduced or planned in Britain, the Netherlands and Sweden. In the latter country, reforms introduced in 2003 aimed to discursively reposition incapacity benefit, shifting it away from being an invalidity pension to one that was more in tune with the Swedish 'work line' welfare model. Incapacity benefit was removed from the pension system and integrated with the sickness insurance system (Rae, 2005). It was also renamed: the term 'disability pension' was replaced by 'activity compensation' for recipients aged from 19 to 29 and 'sickness compensation' for those aged between 30 and 64. Activity compensation can only be granted for a maximum of three years at a time, thereby emphasizing that it is seen as a temporary benefit, not a permanent pension. The social insurance offices are required to examine whether recipients are capable of participating in activities that could help improve their health or capacity to work. The aim is 'to diminish as far as possible any passive dependence on benefits and to increase the individual's own ability to provide for himself or herself' (Swedish Social Insurance Agency, 2002, p. 49). The new system did not involve significant change to the basic grounds for entitlement to benefit. This minimized potential opposition to the reform and reinforced the perception that the aim of the policy was to change the culture of claiming rather than to cut the cost of incapacity benefit.

In the Netherlands, efforts at recalibration have been more than simply discursive. The Employment and Income (Capacity for Work) Act, which was implemented in 2006, aimed to encourage partially incapacitated people to return to work. As with reform of incapacity benefit under New Labour in Britain, the government wished to shift the focus away from what people could not do and onto what work people could still do. An important principle of the new system is therefore that recipients of partial incapacity benefits have a duty to seek reintegration into paid work (de Vos, 2006). Both partially disabled workers and their employers have to demonstrate to the Social Security Institute that they have made adequate efforts at reintegration.

In Britain, reforms to be introduced in October 2008 replace the incapacity benefit with a new 'employment and support allowance' (ESA). As in Sweden, the name change is significant and involves an attempt to discursively reposition this benefit towards the work that people can do rather than that which they cannot. It reflects a belief that 'labelling people on incapacity benefits as "incapable of work" is wrong and damaging' (DWP, 2006, p. 41). Hence, the new ESA seeks to make a distinction between claimants who potentially could undertake full-time or part-time employment in the future and the more severely impaired for whom that prospect is unlikely. The new payment involves a new element of 'benefit conditionality' for those judged to be capable of doing some work in the future.

New ESA claimants will initially be awarded a holding benefit that is paid at the same rate as unemployment benefit, until their ability to work has been assessed. Claimants who are judged to be likely to be able to return to full- or part-time work in the short to medium term will be paid the 'employment support' component of the new allowance, which will be more generous than unemployment benefit. But entitlement to this more generous payment will be conditional on claimants agreeing to an action plan focused on rehabilitation and ultimately on work-focused activity. Meanwhile, claimants who are assessed as having the most serious health conditions or disabilities will be exempt from the rehabilitation and work-focused requirements but may take part on a voluntary basis. They will be paid the 'support' component of the new ESA, which will be more generous than the 'employment support' component (DWP, 2006). This distinction between the recipients of these two components of the ESA bears some resemblance to that between temporary/partial and full/permanent benefit recipients introduced in the 2006 Dutch reform.

Institutional resettlement

In addition to these dimensions of welfare state change identified by Pierson (2001b) – that is, cost containment, recommodification and recalibration – several countries have engaged in what Trampusch (2005) has described as 'institutional resettlement'. An alternative term might be institutional 'replacement' or 'reconfiguration'. The disability insurance programme in Netherlands is perhaps the most marked example of institutional reconfiguration.

In the Netherlands, incapacity benefits were for many years administered by a bilateral organization controlled by employers' organizations and trade union federations. Both social partners had an interest in the use of incapacity benefits to facilitate labour exit and provide a more attractive alternative to unemployment (Kuipers, 2006). In the 1990s debates about the high proportion of working age people receiving incapacity benefit shifted from the programme (benefit levels, medical assessment, etc.) to the organizations responsible for delivering it (de Vos, 2006). In 1993, a committee of inquiry concluded that there had been widespread abuse of the system and recommended that the social partners should no longer be involved in the administration of benefits, which should instead be privatized (Kuipers, 2006).

In 1996 sickness benefits were privatized, with responsibility for finance and administration handed over to employers. Two years later the Dutch government introduced 'experience rating' for incapacity benefit in which the premiums paid by firms increase if one of their employees is awarded benefit and fall if they employ a recipient (Aarts and de Jong, 2003). The aim of this measure was to provide employers with an incentive to avoid laying off workers who were on long-term sick leave and to encourage them to recruit sick or disabled incapacity benefit recipients who could do some work. Experience rating was, in effect, a form of partial privatization of the risk pooling associated with incapacity benefits.

Meanwhile, in 1997 the public insurance agencies operated by the social partners were grouped into five organizations and privatized in the hope that this would stimulate a competitive market for contracts to administer unemployment and disability (i.e. incapacity) insurance. The contracts were to be commissioned by a new public agency and another new public agency would supervise and inspect administration. However, in the face of political opposition, the government halted these plans in 1999 (Kuipers, 2006; de Vos, 2006). In 2002 the government did manage to curtail the involvement of the social partners in incapacity benefit administration. In its place, the government created a public agency (the Social Insurance Institute) to run incapacity and unemployment insurance under contract to the Ministry of Social Affairs and Employment. Meanwhile, the delivery of reintegration programmes was privatized (de Vos, 2006), echoing a process that has also been taking place in Australia and Britain.

Thus although the Dutch government had hoped to privatize incapacity benefit administration, it was forced to backtrack and nationalize it instead. Nevertheless, its broader aim of curtailing the involvement of the social partners was achieved. The latter was partially reversed in 2006 when the Employment and Income (Capacity for Work) Act (discussed above) was introduced (see de Vos, 2006). Under this Act, incapacity benefit was separated into two schemes. The first comprises a publicly-funded insurance-based benefit for people whose incapacity is full and permanent. The second is a private insurance scheme financed by the social partners for people whose impairments are judged to be partial or temporary. Thus the 2006 reform involved a partial privatization of incapacity benefit, with the aim of shifting the cost, and the incentive to contain the cost, of partial incapacity benefit onto the social partners.

Institutional reconfiguration also took place in Sweden when the 'Ghent' model of social insurance administration was abolished in 2005. A government agency called the Swedish Social Insurance Agency was created to replace the federation of social insurance organizations (FKF). The 21 regional offices were merged and became government agencies staffed by civil servants. Thus, as in the Netherlands, institutional resettlement involved the nationalization of administration. An important aim of this reconfiguration in Sweden was to give the government stronger control over, and to make more uniform, the implementation of social insurance policy, especially incapacity benefit (Rae, 2005).

Conclusions

This chapter has argued that the nature of incapacity to work as a social risk has changed in recent decades and that this transformation is associated with the shift to a post-industrial society. Incapacity benefit caseloads not only increased, they also changed significantly in composition. In general, the share of incapacity benefit recipients that are female or young has grown while the shares accounted for by males and older recipients have fallen. Incapacity benefit recipients are also much more likely now to be diagnosed with mental health problems, which are often more subjective, and often less visible, than physical impairments; and as such, are more likely to generate concerns about malingering and 'inappropriate' claims for incapacity benefits.

These trends in the size and composition of the disability benefit rolls are associated with the transition to post-industrial society. Many of the people laid off as a result of deindustrialization – especially older, male, low-skilled workers with health problems – have had difficulty competing for jobs in the post-industrial service-based economy. Some of the people with health problems or impairments were unable to find work and ended up claiming disability benefits instead of unemployment benefit. Moreover, the experience of unemployment is known to cause or exacerbate health problems, which in turn can lead to a claim for disability benefits. Meanwhile, the widening disparity in wages and the progressivity of benefit computations have increased the replacement rate for low wage workers in countries such as the US, thereby increasing the financial incentive for people with few or no skills to claim disability benefits rather than seek work.

Those who do have the requisite levels of education and skills to obtain work in the new post-industrial economy are also exposed to health risks. As Esping-Andersen (2002) noted, the transformation of work has affected the health risks associated with employment, from dangers to physical health in the old economy to stress-related health risk in the new economy. This may be one of the factors behind the increase in mental ill-health including depression, anxiety and nerves. Certainly, there is growing evidence to suggest that stressful working conditions and organizational downsizing are associated with an increased risk of claiming disability benefits (Vahtera et al., 2005).

For the time being governments are likely to continue seeking ways to reduce or at least contain the growth in their disability benefit caseload and its associated costs. This pressure arises both from the perceived need to keep social security expenditures under control and to augment the labour supply as a result of population ageing (although the importance of the latter imperative varies from country to country). For reasons explored in the chapter, many welfare states are now seeking to shift the focus and culture of benefit recipients towards a more temporary and increasingly work-focused outlook; and that of employers towards an enabling rather than a disabling approach to people with health problems and impairments.

This emerging approach to incapacity benefit includes the restructuring processes of cost containment, recommodification and recalibration identified by Pierson (2001b). In addition, some welfare states with high incapacity benefit caseloads have also engaged in examples of institutional resettlement. The latter has involved reconfiguration of the public–private mix in incapacity benefits, though not in a simple, linear direction of 'more private and less public'. In some cases, this process has involved increased private sector involvement (e.g. in reintegration and activation service delivery, as in Australia, Britain and the Netherlands), while in others it has involved a greater role for the state in administration at the expense of the social partners (as in the Netherlands and Sweden). The underlying aim of institutional resettlement, however, has been to provide additional or more effective mechanisms to promote the processes of cost containment, recommodification and recalibration. How successful such measures will be in substantially cutting programme costs, in activating claimants and encouraging them to return to work, and in reducing employer incentives to offload workers with health problems or disabilities onto incapacity benefits, remains to be seen.

11
The 'Public' and 'Private' of Work–Family Reconciliation: Unsettling Gendered Notions and Assumptions

Dalia Ben-Galim and Richenda Gambles[1]

In a context of population ageing, changing labour markets, growing recognition of a variety of family formations and concerns about child poverty, 'traditional' male breadwinner approaches to welfare have lost much of their saliency in recent years. Instead, there has been a notable shift towards adult worker approaches in which women as well as men are increasingly expected to be fully active in paid work (Lewis, 2001, 2002). Work–family reconciliation policies – including various paid and unpaid leaves, opportunities for more flexible working arrangements and development of child and other care services – are seen as an important way of enabling this. In this chapter we explore the 'public' and 'private' of work–family reconciliation using a gendered perspective and aim to *further* contest and unsettle notions of 'public' and 'private'. Issues of work–family reconciliation are centrally concerned with the roles of men and women and so policy discourses and initiatives have to negotiate gendered assumptions about what is considered 'public' or 'private'.

We explore work–family reconciliation policies and their gendered 'public–private' dynamics focusing on the UK in the wider European context. The UK has been chosen as a particularly interesting case for our purposes. In the early 1990s it was identified as displaying strong male breadwinner policy logic (Lewis, 1992) and compared with many other European countries has had to cover much ground in recent years in terms of supporting women – particularly mothers – as adult workers. This raises questions about the work–family reconciliation discourses that have been drawn upon, as well as the adequacy of initiatives designed to adapt to these changes. We begin by briefly discussing policy approaches at the EU level before proceeding to explore recent UK policy. The focus of this chapter is on parents with dependent children – as work–family reconciliation policies have been targeted towards and so prioritize this 'group'. We discuss the ways in which New Labour has navigated particular gendered assumptions about what is seen as 'public' and what is seen as 'private' by focusing on its policy discourses and positioning as well as policy initiatives relating to supporting parents combine paid work with informal family care. We end this chapter by reflecting on the ways in which 'public' and 'private' have been used within policy. We argue that the ways in which 'public' and 'private' are understood are themselves gendered, which conceals and perpetuates gendered dynamics and inequalities. If employment targets associated with the adult worker ideal are to be achieved, gendered notions of 'public' and 'private' need to be understood in more nuanced and multi-dimensional ways.

Policy discourses and initiatives at the European Union level

There has been a noticeable shift in policy rhetoric and direction, at EU and member state level, towards an adult worker model in which men and women are increasingly assumed to be active in paid work. Traditional assumptions associated with male breadwinning have been criticized on a number of grounds including institutionalizing gendered inequalities, failing to keep pace with men and women's changing experiences and expectations, and failing to utilize the labour market potential and skills of many women (OECD, 2001; Esping-Andersen et al. 2002; Daly and Rake, 2003). Responding to some of these concerns as well as global economic pressures, the European Employment Strategy (EES) was formulated identifying (among other things) the need to increase women's labour market participation with work–family reconciliation policies considered necessary to achieve this. The EES is part of the Lisbon Strategy established in 2000 and includes employment targets to increase the number of women in employment to over 60 per cent by 2010. Interim 2005 targets of 57 per cent were also set (European Union, 2005).[2] With these targets in mind, work–family reconciliation policies – including paid and unpaid leaves, flexible working rights and other child-care supports – have been considered necessary, promoted through EU Directives and implemented in various ways by member states.

Indicative of a shift towards an adult worker model, targets associated with the EES reflect an emphasis on paid workers: work–family reconciliation is seen as a mechanism primarily to facilitate women's labour market participation, despite it often being presented as a way to share informal family care responsibilities between women and men (Employment and Social Affairs, 2006). This ties in with criticisms of an adult worker model that looks only at mechanisms to increase women's labour market participation without considering tensions and complexities surrounding gender relations and issues of *who* takes responsibility for informal family care (Lewis, 2002; Gambles et al., 2007). The emphasis on targets relating to women's employment encourages member states to develop policies to support employment for women and employment for mothers in particular. Indeed, Jane Lewis (2006) notes that there has been a re-emphasis on policies that facilitate women's employment – and in the context of facilitating mothers' employment, it could be argued that child-care targets were added to the EES[3] as a way of removing disincentives to female labour market participation (European Commission 2005). But no targets or incentives have been set to encourage men, or fathers, to share family care responsibilities and make use of paternity or parental leave. Without these incentives, and with policies that focus mainly on getting mothers into paid work, many mothers across Europe, albeit to different extents and different degrees, continue to struggle in combining paid work alongside various care activities, responsibilities and relationships, while men continue to be excluded – and/or exclude themselves – from extensive involvement in the daily activities associated with family care (Daly and Rake, 2003; Crompton et al., 2007). This means gendered inequalities in the 'private' domain of the home continue, with women taking on the majority of domestic and unpaid care work in the home (Gershuny, 2000; Lader et al., 2006). And this, in turn, interacts with and impacts on gendered inequalities in the 'public' labour market (Daly and Rake, 2003; Crompton et al., 2007).

It has been argued that the priority of increasing women's labour market participation has occurred at the same time as issues of gender equality have been demoted or side-lined within the European Union (Rubery et al., 2003). The perennial criticisms towards the EU are maintained: it focuses on the economy and employment (Stratigaki, 2004), prioritizes the supply side of the labour market, and places less emphasis on the role of men or fathers in caring for children and/or other dependants than it does on directly encouraging women's labour market participation (Rubery, 2002). Another way of interpreting this is that the EU maintains a perennial focus on areas considered as 'public' sites of intervention – that of paid employment – while leaving aside issues typically considered as 'private' and beyond the scope of intervention – issues of who takes responsibility for various paid and unpaid activities and gender relations and identities that are produced through this. Consequently the strategy fails to enhance women's labour market participation in ways that also promote gender equality.

To achieve women's labour market participation in ways that also promote gender equality, many feminists argue that it is necessary to work with the assumption that both men as well as women have responsibilities and opportunities in paid work *and* informal care activities and relationships (Pateman, 1989; Fraser, 1997; Gornick and Meyers, 2003). The idea is that those with informal care responsibilities are not seen as 'unusual' but rather the norm. Such an approach focuses attention on gender identities and relations and requires changes at multiple interacting levels of society including (but not exclusive to) government policies; workplace structures, cultures and practices; and within family relationships. But what is seen as 'public' areas for policy intervention and what is seen as 'private' and beyond the scope of policy intervention? In many senses gendered identities, family relationships and informal family care are deemed to be 'private' and so beyond the scope of legitimate intervention from governments or workplaces. But gendered identities, family relationships and informal family care activities are shaped, in part, through government and workplace assumptions and interventions. Workplace organizations can also be seen as 'private' yet they are public (gendered) spaces that are shaped, in part, through government interventions and family experiences. Discussing public–private dynamics from a gendered perspective, and drawing on Nancy Fraser's work, Borchorst argues,

> A central issue for determining specific policies of parenting and gender equality is what is framed as a public concern, and what is defined as private, which the state should not interfere in. The outcome of discursive battles on this distinction mirrors patterns of gendered power and dominance relations. (Borchorst, 2006, p. 104)

If EES targets are to be reached, and if there is to be a real transformation in terms of women's participation in paid work, what is perceived as 'public' (as in something states can or should intervene in) and what is seen as 'private' (as in beyond the scope of 'public' intervention) matters. We now turn to the UK to offer a more situated illustrative case study.

Work–family reconciliation and the UK government's position

In many senses Conservative governments in the 1980s and early 1990s took the view that it was inappropriate and beyond the scope of governments to 'intervene' in the 'private' world of gendered identities and relationships within family settings (Fox Harding, 1996; Muncie and Wetherell, 1995).[4] At the same time, economic reforms had increased male unemployment and depressed the wages of many, leading to rising levels of inequality (Hills, 2004) and encouraging many women to seek paid employment. But while many mothers with professional qualifications were becoming increasingly active in paid work, albeit struggling to combine this alongside caring for children, many mothers with few or no qualifications found it particularly hard to find employment or employment that paid sufficient wages to adequately fund child-care arrangements (Hewitt, 1993; Brannen and Moss, 1998). Also, while female labour market participation rates were increasing, the prominence of 'flexible working' (which throughout the 1980s and 1990s was broadly used by employers as a way to regulate work flow and reduce costs) had significant and often negative implications, such as low pay and lack of job security for women as well as men (McRae, 1989). New Labour before, and shortly after, being elected into government argued that Conservative approaches had left many parents to struggle with the challenges of combining paid work with caring for their young children and left many parents facing extreme time and/or economic poverty (Coote et al., 1990; Hewitt,

1993; Home Office, 1998). New Labour sought to demonstrate, instead, that it was a 'modern' party capable of being a 'modern' government able to respond to and support 'modern' needs with issues of supporting families – including issues of work–family reconciliation – as central to this 'modern' self-positioning (see Clarke and Newman, 2004).

Shortly after its election to government in 1997, New Labour published a Green Paper titled, *Supporting Families* (Home Office, 1998). Emphasizing its new 'modern' approach, the then Home Secretary Jack Straw declared in the foreword that this was 'the first time any Government [in the UK] has published a consultation document on the family' (Home Office, 1998, p. 2). This document outlined changes in the tax-benefit system to support parental participation in paid work alongside plans to extend amounts of maternity pay, introduce parental leave and develop affordable child-care facilities to make it easier for parents to combine paid work with caring for their children. Through its publication, New Labour was making a clear statement that it recognized that policy should actively involve itself in family matters, and that it understood that parents of dependent children needed more support than they had been receiving under previous governments. In the *Supporting Families* Green Paper, the government argued that Conservative policy approaches had failed to keep pace with changing family experiences. In essence, New Labour was indicating that it recognized that much of what had been seen as 'private' struggles should and would now be seen as struggles that needed 'public' support. The government drew attention to the fact that while many more women, and mothers in particular, were active in paid work, parental leave schemes or publicly-funded child care had been left off or dismissed from the agenda by the Conservatives.

New Labour opted back in to the EU's Social Chapter and began updating its legislative and policy frameworks in light of recommendations and directives. A National Childcare Strategy was developed in 1998 aiming to provide more extensive and good quality child care; and a range of policies connected with parental leaves and working times were introduced (discussed below in more detail). Reflecting more generically on New Labour's modernization project Clarke and Newman (2004, p. 54) argue that it is articulated around major fault lines. In particular,

> These fault lines have formed around New Labour's ideal of building a consensual, inclusive society (addressing the divisions, conflicts and inequalities produced and deepened by the policies of Conservative governments) and its determination to continue the agenda of neo-liberal economic reform based on the presumed requirements of a global economy. (Clarke and Newman, 2004, p. 54)

New Labour sought to make 'public' much of what Conservative governments saw as 'private' through policies and initiatives on parental leaves, working hours and child-care provisions as a way of addressing conflicts and inequalities experienced by parents. *But* the broader pressures of economic success and competition were also drivers. Policies and initiatives to better support all parents to combine paid work with caring for their children were (and continue to be) positioned not only as socially 'progressive' but also economically necessary for competing within the 'modern' global economy. The framing of many of New Labour's policy developments, particularly those promoting a better 'work–life balance', has seen much emphasis given to the 'business case' for change: New Labour's 'work–life balance' campaign launched in 2000 emphasized to employers that provisions supporting parents to combine 'paid work' and 'family life' will result in more productive and motivated staff who are, in the case of mothers in particular, more likely to return to paid work after periods of parental leave (see for example DfES, 2000; HM Treasury and DTI, 2003). Case studies of 'win–win' examples in which leaves and flexible working practices help parents manage their paid work alongside their child-care activities as well as helping employers to operate a more dynamic and responsive business were presented to employers.[5]

The term 'work–life balance' is now commonly used in the UK, though there is no universally accepted definition of work–life balance. The UK government through the then named Department of Trade and Industry (DTI) have in the past described work–life balance as being 'about adjusting working patterns. Regardless of age, race or gender, everyone can find a rhythm to help them combine work with their other responsibilities or aspirations' (DTI, 2004).

The DTI further categorizes work–life balance provisions into categories of: 1) when staff work through schemes such as job sharing, term-time working, time off in lieu, flexi-time, compressed or annualized working; 2) where staff work such as home-working or tele-working; or 3) giving staff a break such as maternity, paternity and adoption leave, parental leave, sabbatical or career breaks, or study leave (DTI, 2004). Other services and benefits, such as child-care assistance through nursery vouchers or subsidies, tax credits particularly child-care credits, or elderly care assistance, are also considered to be part of work–life balance policies.

This conceptualization presents the universality of work–life balance policies, but this has been widely criticized. First, while presented as a gender-neutral term, 'work–life balance' conceals many gendered assumptions (Smithson and Stokoe, 2005) particularly given the gender disparities in paid and unpaid work. It has been argued that the term 'work–life balance' offers an oversimplistic conceptualization of 'work' and 'life' as distinct activities, ignores distinctions between paid and unpaid work and undervalues unpaid care-work (Gambles et al., 2006). 'Work–life balance' also rests on gendered notions and assumptions about the separation between the 'public' sphere of paid work and the 'private' sphere of family life, in which the former is often associated with socially constructed notions of competence and commitment produced through and producing of male dominance in paid work (see Rapoport et al., 2002). Secondly, work–life balance policy discourse and initiatives overwhelmingly prioritize parents with young children where both parents are active in the labour market. This means many people who have other care commitments or parents who are not active in the labour market can be overlooked and specific challenges facing them can be concealed. Yet the language of *parenting* in work–life balance discourses is significant from a gendered perspective. Day Sclater et al. (1999, p. 4) argue that in the context of postwar constructions and assumptions of 'traditional' male breadwinner families 'the gender-neutral term "parent" could hardly have emerged, let alone carried the range of meanings that it does today'. So why the current use of 'parent' in work–life balance policy discourses and initiatives and what are the links here with a shift to adult worker assumptions? On the one hand, the term 'parent' in policy discourses and initiatives can be seen as indicative of supporting *both* parents to be active in paid work and to care for their children in gender-neutral ways. On the other hand, while the language of parenting is increasingly used, mothers continue to be the primary carer of children and it has been suggested that the gender-neutral term 'parent' conceals many ongoing gendered dimensions and inequalities (see Williams, 2005; Featherstone, 2004). We now explore (gendered) 'work–life balance' policy initiatives and (gendered) outcomes for parents, reflecting on the ways in which these are produced through and producing of particular gendered notions and assumptions about what is 'public' and what is 'private'.

'Work–life balance' initiatives and outcomes

In focusing on work–life balance policy initiatives that aim at supporting parents, we draw on leave and workplace flexibility policies. This is because while Pfau-Effinger (2006) argues that 'the time that parents can spend with their children is regarded not so much as a duty but as an important part of self-fulfilment' (2006, p. 142), time for parents to care can be particularly gendered. It is useful to explore how gendered assumptions impact what is considered 'public' and 'private' in relation to time-orientated work–life balance initiatives. We now explore policy approaches and gendered outcomes in relation to 1) maternity, paternity and transferable parental leaves and 2) flexible working.

Maternity, paternity and transferable parental leaves

Statutory maternity leave has recently been extended from 26 to 39 weeks and the rate of maternity pay has increased: since 1997, New Labour has nearly doubled statutory maternity pay (paid at £117.18 per week since 6 April 2008). Data from 2005 illustrate that the take up of maternity leave is high. In 2005 the number of women who took 26 weeks maternity leave was about half those eligible, with an additional 14 per cent taking additional maternity leave (another 26 weeks in which mothers are not entitled to statutory maternity pay) (Smeaton and Marsh, 2006). Of mothers who were employed during pregnancy, 80 per cent returned to paid work (with 88 per cent of those making changes to their work arrangements if they had one child and 68 per cent if they had more than one child). It has further been noted that 'mothers in higher-level jobs providing flexible opportunities, often in unionized workplaces, and treated well by their employers, were the most likely to return to work after maternity leave' (Smeaton and Marsh, 2006, p. 3). One-fifth of mothers changed employers after maternity leave – a figure that had almost halved since 2001 (Smeaton and Marsh, 2006). The availability of a right to request flexible working has been cited as a reason contributing to this decrease (see below) and taken together these figures indicate that 'public' provision by government and 'private' provision via employers significantly impact on decisions that parents take. Although there are many women returning to work following maternity leave, it is notable that many women – such as those on low pay or self-employed – don't take their full maternity entitlement as the low rates of maternity pay and high costs of child-care often mean that it is unaffordable.

Paternity leave in the UK was also introduced in 2003 giving fathers the opportunity to take up to two weeks statutory paid leave. Evaluation on take up thus far has been mixed. Evidence suggests that more fathers want to play a greater role in being involved in their children's lives (Equal Opportunities Commission, 2003; O'Brien, 2005). This suggests that they want more involvement in activities often seen as 'private'. Yet many fathers find that there is a conflict between this and 'public' expectations about their roles and responsibilities: indeed for many fathers a conflict of responsibilities emerges between 'providing' and 'being involved' (Warin et al., 1999, p. 41). Fathers are taking more leave around the time of their child's birth (Smeaton and Marsh, 2006) but many rely on annual leave or contractual terms and conditions rather than statutory provision (Carvel, 2006). This can be linked to the low rate of pay associated with paternity leave (currently paid at £117.18 per week, the same as statutory paid maternity leave), which demonstrates that this is a significant obstacle to many new fathers who cannot afford the loss of income (or who do not want to lose their higher income) at such a crucial time in their lives (O'Brien, 2005; Kilkey, 2006).

While maternity leave has already been extended to nine months, there are proposals intending to extend it to a full 12 months, as well as offering a period of transferability in which the leave can be transferred from mother to father. Yet allowing mothers to transfer leave to the father if *she* so wishes, can be seen as reflecting strong assumptions about maternal needs and responsibilities: that it is her leave to give in the first place. Moreover it has been argued that 'provisions fall far short of what might be needed to optimize the opportunity for fathers to re-balance work and care' (Kilkey, 2006, p. 173).

Discussing the extent to which fathers are included or excluded by recent and proposed legislative changes, Kilkey (2006) argues that significant obstacles to fathers sharing care have been glossed over: additional paternity pay will not be earnings related, which may dissuade fathers from being the ones to take this time out of paid work if their earnings are higher than that of their female partners; and there is no flexibility as to when and how many times the transfer between couples from maternity to paternity leave can happen. Under this scheme, she suggests that it is likely that couples will 'play it safe' and use the 12 months as *maternity leave.*

The introduction of transferability brings UK policy initiatives more in line with more progressive approaches: in Nordic and a number of Continental European countries parents make choices about how they divide an extended transferable parental leave (after a shorter statutory maternity leave period). However, evidence from Nordic experiences suggests that choices are constrained and that only a minority of fathers take transferable parental leaves (Lammi-Taskula, 2006). Indeed, Lammi-Taskula argues that while well-educated parents employed in the public sector make up the majority of couples sharing parental leave,

> for large numbers of Nordic parents, unverified assumptions – for example, about economic consequences of equal sharing of parental leave as well as cultural conceptions of gender and parenthood, especially motherhood – hamper negotiations both in the family and in the workplace. Unreflected unequal gender assumptions are naturalized and remain unchallenged. (Lammi-Taskula, 2006, p. 95)

Nordic countries also have a 'daddy quota'. This is a month or two of paid leave that is reserved exclusively for fathers, which are lost if not taken. Consequently, take-up rates are high – up to 90 per cent in Norway and 80 per cent in Iceland, for example (Lammi-Taskula, 2006, p. 83).[6] These findings relating to differential take-up by fathers of transferable and father-only non-transferable leaves has interesting implications: 'public' rules of non-transferability give fathers more ability to negotiate this with their employers as well as with their female partners (cf. Brandth and Kvande, 2001, 2002). Yet while there has been increased attention focused on fathers in the UK (Kilkey, 2006), a daddy quota of leave is not currently in place in the UK context. It seems that *who* takes the leave – in terms of mothers or fathers – remains a 'private' matter or 'choice' between parents seen as being beyond the scope of 'public' intervention.

Flexible working

The right to request flexible working was introduced in 2003.[7] This provides parents with children under 6 (or children under 18 if their children are in receipt of the Disability Living Allowance) the opportunity to request to work flexibly and obliges employers to consider it. While the government initially intended this to be a *right* to flexible working, as it is the case in a number of Continental European countries, this was watered down in response to business concerns to a *right to request* (Kilkey, 2006). Nevertheless, according to recent DTI research, flexible working 'is now the norm rather than the exception' (Fitzner and Grainger 2007, p. ii) with over 90 per cent of employees reporting that flexible work options are available to them and 56 per cent reporting that they are either currently using a flexible work option, or have used one in the past year (cf. Hooker et al., 2007). Flexible working in this sense often relates to anything that deviates from standard working hours and usually refers to part-time work. However, a note of caution must be added: despite the high rates of availability of flexible working, the high frequency of part-time working is of concern as it is associated with the most significant gender pay gap, workplace vulnerability and downward trajectory. Moreover, it is mostly women in the UK who work part-time, with a significant proportion of part-time workers being mothers with young children.

In terms of exploring specific take-up of the right to request, available evidence is inconclusive. This is because available data do not indicate whether or not requests for flexible working are made by mothers or fathers under the 'right to request' or by employees more generally. Nevertheless, from what is available the most recent reported data outline that 17 per cent of employees had made a request to reduce their working hours and that women (22 per cent) were more likely than men (14 per cent) to request to work flexibly. Employers rejected 23 per cent of requests made by men and 13 per cent made by women (Hooker et al., 2007), with men in the private sector least likely to have their requests accepted (Fitzner and Grainger, 2007). This suggests that mothers are making more requests than fathers and having more of their requests accepted – a claim that is certainly substantiated in research on fathers in the UK (see O'Brien, 2005).

Fathers are increasingly taking more time out of paid work for caring for their children through flexi-time and working from home. However, these changes usually do not incur financial penalties or contractual changes: notably only four per cent of fathers reported changing their hours to part-time which does impact pay (Smeaton and Marsh, 2006). The current gender pay gap encourages more fathers to stay in paid employment and mothers to work part-time because of financial penalties. It also reproduces gendered assumptions that fathers will be more active in the 'public' sphere of paid work while mothers will 'choose' to be more active in the 'private' sphere of family care. Indeed a key feature of the UK labour market is that men with partners and dependant/s are more likely to work long hours with their partners employed part-time (Hogarth et al., 2001; Houston and Waumsley, 2003). According to *Out of time: Why Britain needs a new approach to work-time flexibility*, a report published by the TUC, removing the 'opt-out' clause of the European Working Time Directive and broadening the legislative framework for flexible working would contribute to reducing the impact of these constraints (Fagan et al., 2006). However, the UK maintains its commitment to retaining the 'opt-out' clause.

Through 'work–life balance' policy discourses and initiatives – including maternity, paternity and parental leaves, as well as flexible working opportunities – *it is now somewhat assumed that parents can negotiate their working lives in ways of their choosing* (Mooney, 2004). New Labour has sought to make 'public' much of what previous Conservative governments saw as 'private', and policy discourses and initiatives imply that parents now have more supports and options from which to choose. The message seems to be that 'public' policies have now made possible multiple kinds of 'private' choices for parents. Yet Mooney (2004) stresses that ways of parents choosing are *deeply* constrained. Indeed, in a recent government commissioned Equalities Review it was found that mothers with young children face more discrimination, as a group, than any other group (Equalities Review, 2007). And within this 'group' Perrons (2006) notes that many low-skilled and migrant mothers are particularly vulnerable in the UK's low pay economy. Additionally, it has been noted that while 'Black' women are more likely to remain in full-time employment, 'White' and 'Indian' women tend to work part-time (Lindley et al., 2004). Fiona Williams (2005) finds little acknowledgement of intersecting issues of gender, class and ethnicity within policies and initiatives to 'support' parents to participate in paid work. This suggests that notions of 'public' and 'private' are not only gendered but also classed and racialized in profoundly complex ways.

Proposed changes of further extending maternity (and adoption leave) to twelve months, introducing transferable parental leave that could be taken by a mother or father and a widening of access to the right to request, all point towards a more comprehensive 'work–life balance' agenda for fathers as well as mothers. However, without significant increases in pay for maternity leave and without a right for fathers to take leave as their own named-paternal right, messages about gendered stereotypes – linked to 'public' and 'private' gendered spheres and assumptions – are further reinforced through 'public' provisions. Opportunities provided by employers to 'balance' work and life are also distributed disproportionately through the job hierarchy (Lambert and Waxman, 2005) creating different 'choices' for many men and women depending on their socio-economic locations.

Towards multi-dimensional conceptualization of 'public' and 'private'

There have been normative shifts towards adult worker expectations, greater recognition of the ideal of gender equality and many policy changes that reflect transformation – or a blurring of boundaries – of 'public' and 'private' provisions with public understood as government activity and private understood as market activity. Yet we have sought to demonstrate what is more significant here are gendered assumptions and articulations of 'public' and 'private' in terms of what is understood as legitimate or beyond the scope of government intervention.

While New Labour's approach to supporting parents combine paid work with caring for children has involved a re-articulation of what is seen as 'public' and what is seen as 'private', 'outcomes' remain deeply gendered. As Hilary Graham (1983, p. 18) noted 25 years ago, 'caring is "given" to women: it becomes the defining characteristic of their self-identity and their life's work. At the same time, caring is taken away from men: not caring becomes a defining characteristic of manhood'. And despite policy enabling more 'choice' for parents, a giving of care to women and a taking away of care from men, continues to be perpetuated, in part, through policy. While policy discourse emphasizes supporting parents to combine paid work with caring for their children, policy initiatives within the EES and policy initiatives developed in the UK place more emphasis on supporting mothers to be active in paid work than on supporting fathers to become more involved with the care of their children. Significantly the 'ideal' adult worker imagined in policy discourses and initiatives – as well as in many workplace environments – continues to be imagined as a (gendered) adult worker who does not have other responsibilities, relationships or interests in life. Indeed workplace culture and structures continue to act as a barrier for many fathers to become actively involved in caring for their children (O'Brien, 2005). Not surprisingly, then, the outcomes of this are that many mothers are less involved in paid work and many fathers are less involved in caring for children.

Questions remain as to the causes of these gendered differences and inequalities. Is it the consequence of 'public' policy structures that fail to give due support for women to participate in paid work and men to be more active in caring for their children? Is it the consequence of 'private' workplace structures and cultures that continue to assume that an ideal worker is someone without pressing informal care responsibilities? Or is it the result of men and women who are 'privately' resistant to making particular changes in their family arrangements? Fathers may be resistant to making such a change which feels alien to their (socially constructed) self identity as financial provider; similarly, while the numbers of mothers in paid work have increased, many mothers may be reluctant to be more active in paid work because of concerns that they will be neglecting family care activities for which they have been made to feel 'personally' responsible for through social constructions of femininity (Duncan et al., 2003; Williams, 2004). Gendered identities, family relationships and informal family care are often seen as 'private' as in beyond the scope of intervention from governments or workplaces, but gendered identities, family relationships and informal family care arrangements are shaped, in part, through government and workplace assumptions and interventions. Workplace organizations can also be seen as 'private' yet they are public gendered spaces that are shaped, in part, through government interventions as well as family experiences. What is considered 'public' and what is considered 'private' is 'the outcome of discursive battles' relating to 'patterns of gendered power and dominance relations' (Borchorst, 2006, p. 104). These discursive battles occur through gendered assumptions and the outcomes of these discursive battles shape policy initiatives and policy outcomes in profoundly gendered ways.

A combination of policies utilizing 'public' as state and 'private' as market mechanisms for supporting the adult worker to combine paid work with family care ignores gendered notions of 'public' and 'private'. Policies have also largely ignored dynamics of class and ethnicity that interact with gender to create multiple forms of disadvantage and a failure to appreciate the significance and invasiveness of gendered notions of 'public' and 'private' perpetuates a range of interacting inequalities. A failure to recognize the ways that policy contributes to the shaping of gendered relationships and identities means that ongoing gendered inequalities can be dismissed as 'natural', so beyond the scope of 'public' government intervention. Thus a failure to interrogate gendered assumptions of 'public' and 'private' within work–life balance discourses and initiatives itself *further* produces assumptions that gendered behaviours and responses from mothers and fathers are 'natural' *rather than* socially constructed and socially constrained. Gender neutral language – and conceptualizations – within work–life balance discourses and initiatives, including the emphasis on and use of the gender-neutral term parent, works to conceal and perpetuate ongoing gendered dynamics and inequalities. Unless more nuanced and multi-dimensional notions of 'public' and 'private' are teased out, acknowledged and acted upon, adult worker approaches and attempts to meet EES targets will fail. More significantly, as long as adult worker approaches prioritize getting mothers into paid work without corresponding efforts to get fathers more involved in family care activities, a number of gendered inequalities will continue. More gender sensitive and multi-dimensional conceptualizations of socially constructed and mutually constituting 'publics' and 'privates' are thus urgently needed.

Part III
Conclusions

12
Reconstructing Nation, State and Welfare: The Transformation of Welfare States

John Clarke

The transformation of welfare states has been the subject of diverse disputes – centred around the depth or scale of transformation; around the causes of transformation; around the direction of transformation; and around the degree of convergence or difference between welfare states. Such intensive debates have tended to assume the existence of a specific object of analysis – the welfare state, or sometimes its plural companion, welfare states. This assumption has some troubling consequences. On the one hand, it means that conceptual difficulties about the character of welfare states are avoided – displaced by a presumption that authors and readers will share a common, or taken-for-granted, conception of welfare state-ness. As usual, in the social sciences, taken-for-granted assumptions or forms of knowledge should be marked 'handle with care'. On the other hand, the lack of conceptual attention leads directly into a casual empiricism – in which more specific objects of inquiry are allowed to stand for welfare states. Typically, these are spending programmes or patterns of social expenditure. For example, recent books take major social programmes (unemployment/labour market policies, pensions programmes) or larger scale patterns of social expenditure as proxies through which to examine the changing fortunes of welfare states/the welfare state (see, for example, Castles, 2004; Ellison, 2006).

The problems of selecting specific indicators as proxies for welfare states are extensively discussed (see, *inter alia*, Castles, 2004; Daly, 2000; Sykes, 1998), but these tend to centre on the contested principles of selection – of adequacy, of focus (the relative visibilities and invisibilities that are created), or of comparability. They rarely extend to the conceptual problem of the relationship between the proxy and the object being discussed. For example, Castles sets up his use of the OECD Social Expenditure Database by noting that: 'In respect of the majority of chapters focusing on social expenditure trends, an important preliminary point to recognize is that spending is not the be-all and end-all of the welfare state' (2004, p. 14). But the other things that might make up the welfare state remain resolutely invisible, obscured by the might (and availability) of the expenditure data. This oscillation between taken-for-granted abstraction and casual empiricism leaves untouched a number of major issues about welfare states. In this context I intend to raise some questions about how we understand the 'welfare state' as a concept and link these to recent developments in studying states as compound entities. Terms such as assemblages, constellations, and articulated formations point to new possibilities that might, and perhaps ought to, be extended to thinking about welfare state-ness. I then suggest that thinking about welfare states as formations that articulate welfare, state and nation can illuminate the issue of 'transformation'. In particular, such a view makes visible the different, and potentially divergent, dynamics of transformation that are at stake in the reconstruction of welfare states.

What's a welfare state?

In some senses, the foundational problem for studies of welfare states is the elusiveness of the term itself. As Raymond Williams's *Keywords* (1976) indicated, the term 'welfare' had a history that linked generalized sense of well-being (as an inversion of the injunction to 'fare well') to a public or collective sense of doing things to support such well-being. We might stop and contemplate the significance of the more recent revival of 'well-being' in policy circles, carrying a different set of meanings to welfare. Alternatively we could return to Williams's view of how the term 'welfare' came to be used – not least in its connection to 'state' – to express an alternative to nineteenth-century British ideas and practices of Charity and Philanthropy. In political and popular usage, then, the idea of the 'welfare state' combined two positive orientations – a disposition to promoting collective well-being and an opposition to the socially narrow and prejudiced world of philanthropy.

However, these popular usages do not point to any degree of conceptual rigour. Rather they point to the ways in which ideas of welfare and the welfare state are potently located in popular discourses (and the political antagonisms they express). In more academic settings, 'welfare state' has been consistently elusive in conceptual terms. The state-ness of welfare, for example, may refer to very different types of state and very different forms of state activity. In relation to welfare, we might distinguish different roles played by states – funding, the direct provision of services, the coordinator of 'mixed economies of provision', regulation and arm's length governance, guarantor of rights, and so on. Which of these defines the 'state-ness' of welfare states? Equally, there are questions about how to identify the 'welfare' aspects of states. As I noted earlier, the tendency in studies of welfare states is to identify what might be called 'core' activities or programmes: welfare states appear to involve unemployment/labour market related policies (though we might return to the question of whether it matters if they are directed to unemployment or labour markets). They appear to involve policies addressed to old age (at least pensions, but possibly policies of social care as well). In British social policy, the welfare state used to be construed as the institutions involving public policies towards income maintenance, health, education and housing.

Such programmatic specifications leave open two questions. The first is about those other state policies and practices that might promote well-being, but are rarely counted as part of the domain of the welfare state. The existence of state funded, promoted or regulated 'leisure' institutions and activities might be seen as attempts by the state to promote a healthy, balanced and happy population. Are these objectives different from 'welfare'? Equally, questions of transport (infrastructure, provision, regulation) might also be thought of as 'welfare' questions, since they impact in multiple ways on individual and collective health, well-being and social participation. A third, and perhaps more troubling, set of policies and practices involves the policies and apparatuses of policing, criminalization and the law which, many scholars have argued, have come to take on an increasing part of what used to be 'welfare' parts of the state's role (see, for example, Garland, 2001; Stenson, 2000). Such a view suggests a shift in analytic focus from the 'welfare' activities of states to a concern with shifting combinations of policies and practices directed at 'governing the social' (Clarke, forthcoming a).

The second set of questions implied by programmatic conceptions of the 'welfare' character of states concerns their relationship to social relations. Many studies of welfare states have an implicit normative character that presumes 'welfare' is both benevolent and progressive. In many ways, this implicit normative orientation to welfare has been deepened by the anti-welfarist and anti-statist politics of neo-liberal and neo-conservative political movements. With such enemies, how could we entertain doubts about welfare states (except in instrumental terms about improving their efficiency and effectiveness, perhaps)? Nevertheless, there are reasons for making the 'social' character of welfare states more visible than is conventionally the case. It might enable us to think about the structured patterns of inclusion and exclusion in relation to the resources of welfare. We might also see more of the conditions of inclusion: the forms of subordinated or dependent inclusions where access to welfare is not an individual or unconditional status. Such issues link welfare states to questions of citizenship and its formation in relations of class, gender, sexuality, age, nationality/ethnicity, and able-bodiedness. Each of these forms of differentiation has provided constitutive dynamics shaping citizen status and access to the welfare provision of states.

More challengingly, such issues might point us to the role of welfare in producing social divisions and differences. Most studies of welfare states see them as 'secondary' social institutions, acting upon the social relations of the societies of which they are part. In those terms we can assess their impact or effects: have they reinforced or remedied structured forms of social inequality? Have they reduced class differentials? Have they narrowed the gender gap, and so on? But welfare states are also formative institutions: they establish the categories through which services and benefits are organized and distributed. They determine and act upon points of difference (think, for example, about how many of our age categories are inscribed in welfare policies and practices). They sort, categorize and allocate positions to people; they issue incentives and rewards for certain classes of people and certain types of behaviour, and dole out constraints and punishments for others. It is in such terms that the Foucauldian concern with 'governing populations' offers a distinctive and potent vantage point on welfare and welfare states (see, for example, Marston and McDonald, 2006). Welfare states, in this light, work on populations – organizing, categorizing, improving, regulating and directing them.

Taking these detours in response to the banal question 'what's a welfare state?' may appear both unnecessary and frustrating. But I want to insist that both of the terms 'welfare' and 'state' are difficult and elusive, and that bringing them together as an object of inquiry is a fraught enterprise. In what follows I want to offer an approach to studying welfare states that treats this conceptual difficulty as an inherent part of welfare state-ness, rather than being something that can be resolved either by theoretical fiat ('a welfare state is the sum of pensions, health care, labour market and education policies') or by empirical convenience ('we have comparative data for these three programmes'). Instead, I want to start from the view that the phrase 'welfare state' is, above all, a *practical* concept – one that is deeply rooted in popular and political discourse. Its practicality, then, leads to a concern with its use – how it is made to mean; how its meanings are mobilized, challenged, changed, valued and devalued. From this starting point, welfare states are fundamentally ideas or images that come to be realized in complicated combinations of institutions, policies and practices.

Assembling welfare states

We might engage with this question of 'complicated combinations' by reflecting on how the term welfare state incorporates divergent understandings of 'welfare' (from its American usage to mean supplementary, or non-social insurance programmes, such as Aid to Families with Dependent Children, abolished in the 'end of welfare' in 1996, to the array of benefits and services linked together in the Nordic 'welfare model'). These are linked with very different models of how states do welfare: direct provision to the regulation and funding of diverse non-state agencies. Dismantling the concept of the welfare state in such ways enables us to see how different national welfare states have involved particular combinations of welfare and state, in which both differences of the substance and meaning of welfare, and differences in the role played by the state, are central to the form of 'welfare state'.

This interest in combinations coincides with developments elsewhere in the social sciences, particularly, but not only, in approaches to the state. Combination has echoes of 'assemblages' (Latour, 2005), 'ensembles' (Sharma and Gupta, 2006), 'constellations' (Leibfried and Zürn, 2005b) and 'articulated formations' (Clarke, 2004). Each of these terms speaks to a sense of construction and combination – the building of elements into a temporary unity. For Latour, assemblage is a concept that re-opens the question of how the social is constituted:

> When social scientists add the adjective 'social' to some phenomenon, they designate a stabilized state of affairs, a bundle of ties that, later, may be mobilized to account for some other phenomenon. There is nothing wrong with this use of the word as long as it designates what is *already* assembled together, without making any superfluous assumption about the *nature* of what is assembled. (Latour, 2005, p. 1; emphasis in original).

For Latour, this idea of assemblage as a 'stabilized state of affairs' foregrounds the analytical challenge of tracing *associations* – the production of the network of connections between people and things that create an assemblage. Latour provides us with two important insights in this brief comment. The first is the idea of assembling as a process (with assemblages as its result). The second is the insistence on temporality – 'what is already assembled'; a 'stabilized state of affairs'. This inserts questions of time into our view of institutions, systems and structures – they are assembled, or constructed, and stabilized – for a determinate period of time. They are vulnerable to destabilization, deconstruction and projects of reassembling.

In their Introduction to a recent collection on *The Anthropology of the State*, Sharma and Gupta argue that the 'conditions for studying the state have shifted', requiring 'new ways of thinking' (2006, p. 27):

> Thinking about how states are culturally constituted, how they are substantiated in people's lives, and about the socio-political and everyday consequences of these constructions, involves moving beyond macro-level institutional analyses of 'the state' to looking at social and bureaucratic practices and encounters and at public cultural texts. (2006, p. 27)

For Sharma and Gupta, states are ensembles – assemblages of ideas (imaginaries of states and state-ness), policies, practices, people and objects (in which state-ness is embodied). Such conceptions of the state are liberating for a field of study that has been dominated by institutionalist understandings of states that treat them as integral and coherent objects of analysis. Sharma and Gupta's second analytic move is to consider states in a 'transnational frame', arguing that 'the current regime of globalization necessitates that we unhinge the study of the state from the frame of the nation-state' (2006, p. 28). I will return to some of the implications of this unhinging later, but here its importance is the coincidence of this concern with the framing of states as nation-states and the reflections by Stephan Leibfried and Michael Zürn on nation-states as 'constellations'. More specifically, they argue that the 'golden age' nation-states can best be understood as a constellation of four key elements – resources, law, legitimacy and welfare – assembled together in congruent social and political space. This assemblage they name TRUDI, designating the form of nation-state that 'had evolved four dimensions and fashioned them into a tightly woven fabric – a multi-functional state that combines the Territorial State, the state that secures the Rule of Law, the Democratic State, and the Intervention State' (2005b, p. 3).

While it is true that Leibfried and Zürn's conception of the multi-functional state comes out of a more conventionally political institutionalist view of states, the metaphors of 'constellation' and 'fabric' point to a more constructed (if not constructivist) understanding of the formation and transformation of states. So, for example, when they explore the 'reconfiguring' of the national constellation, their metaphors emphasize the complexity of assemblages and their dis-assembling. For example, talking about possible current and future trajectory, the 'fabric' metaphor takes a dominant role in the hypothesis that:

> the changes over the past 40 years are not merely creases in the fabric of the nation-state, but rather an unravelling of the finely woven national constellation of its Golden Age. Nor does there appear to be any standard, interwoven development of its four dimensions on the horizon. However, although an era of structural uncertainty awaits us, it is not uniformly chaotic. Rather, we see structured, but asymmetric change in the make-up of the state, with divergent transformations in each of its four dimensions. (2005b, p. 1).

And, later they explore TRUDI in similar terms:

> Is TRUDI worn out, is it unravelling? Can, and will, it be mended or rewoven – perhaps transformed into one gigantic world state with a uniform pattern, or re-styled into semi-sovereign, sub-national, regional governments? Or will the threads of TRUDI simply separate and follow individual fates in post-modern fashion, with the rule of law moving into the international arena while the nation-state clings to the resources of the territorial state, and the intervention state comes unspun and goes every which way? (2005b, p. 3)

It might be argued that such terms are merely metaphorical, rather than strictly conceptual. But they do point to the analytic problems of conceptualizing states and their transformations and, for me, have the important value of identifying two dynamics at the same time – both the woven-ness (what Latour might prefer to call a 'stabilized state of affairs') of elements into a form of state and the possibility that different elements (the 'threads') might be subject to different pressures and trajectories of change (rather than the singular transformation of the state). For me, their reflections also make more visible the contingent and constructed national character of the nation-state; important given the 'methodological nationalism' that has been an organizing principle of welfare state studies. Welfare states are – more or less implicitly – understood as nation-states (Clarke, 2005).

In my own work, I have become increasingly interested in treating welfare states (and their shadow couplet nation-states) as specific articulated formations in which ideas and institutionalized practices of welfare, state and nation are assembled together (e.g., Clarke, 2004; Clarke and Fink, forthcoming). As with the 'Golden Age' of nation-states identified by Leibfried and Zürn, so the 'Golden Age' welfare states (Huber and Stephens, 2001) involved assemblages of elements – expansive conceptions of welfare; enlarged state scope for social intervention, in specific nation building/rebuilding projects – that were solidified or stabilized into the formations we came to call 'welfare states'. Such stabilizations of assemblages tend to conceal the conditions of their own assembly – they come to look like, and be addressed as coherent, singular entities. Only as the threads become unwoven, as the carefully articulated joints become unglued, does it become possible to see the 'traces of association' through which they were constructed. And, at such points, it becomes more possible to see how the different elements might be the subject of different, divergent, or even contradictory, forces, pressures and political-cultural projects seeking new directions and new assemblages.

These were, of course, national formations in at least two senses. They took place in that (apparently) stable territorial political and social space that nation-states claimed to both occupy and represent. But they were also nation-states in the sense that they were part of the field of agencies, policies and practices through which nations were being constructed, invented and improved. Nations – the unique combinations of people, place and politics – were always in process of being brought into being, although this is rarely the focus of welfare state studies (for some different exceptions see Castells and Hineman, 2002; Hughes and Lewis, 1998; and Lewis, 1998). Treating welfare states as articulated formations of welfare, state and nation makes visible three key things: first, the different elements that have been articulated; second, the specific significance of the nation for thinking about welfare states; and third, the possibility of dis-articulation of the different elements. Let me make one further point about the question of disarticulation in the context of debates about welfare state transformation or welfare reform. As I will argue in the final section, it becomes important for assessing whether what is being 'reformed' or 'transformed' is welfare, the state or the nation. The temptation is always to confuse and conflate these. Instead, just as Leibfried and Zürn suggest with their 'threads', we may be better advised to disentangle the different elements and their trajectories.

Welfare states as nation states: producing peoples and populations

In this section I want to look a little more at the question of welfare states as nation-states. The methodological nationalism of welfare state studies means that the 'national' character of welfare states has been treated banally: how do we assess and explain the difference between different national welfare states or systems? This takes the 'national' as a matter of the place where welfare states happen: it uses a 'container' model of the national space. Sometimes, the nation is a more active element in such analyses – as a politics or a culture that is distinctively different from other nations which is reflected or reproduced in welfare policies. But such approaches to the nation never pose it as an object of construction, as something to be worked on, assembled, produced by social practices (nation-building is thought to be the business of developing or emergent nations and their states, not relevant to the study of 'mature' societies).

Sharma and Gupta are surely right that the 'current regime of globalization' has made more visible the constructed character of the nation (and its articulation with states). Various processes have contributed to 'unsettling' the apparent stability of the nation – both in practice and in academic work. Questions of globalization, international or supra-national institutions, the flows of finance, commodities and people across national borders, and the increasingly contested and mobile spaces of nations (from the unification of Germany to the end of the Soviet bloc) have all posed problems about the nation-state as a stable and unified entity (and for sovereignty). It may be important to note that the new visibility of these issues should not allow us to think that no such flux, uncertainty or unsettling existed in the past. The 'stabilized state of affairs' that we call the nation-state concealed the conditions of its own construction (particularly its intimate entanglement with – and dependency on – other places, especially its colonial others). In the current regime of globalization, it is easier to see the transnational conditions of formations of the national. But earlier regimes of globalization – especially that of European colonialism – underpinned the rise of the (apparently) territorially closed nation-state which rested on economic, political and cultural relations with 'elsewhere'.

Nation-making can be viewed as a continuous process rather than a specific phase of national development. States have been a crucial engine for such processes, installing and disseminating national histories, projected futures and conceptions of the national character or culture that needs to be protected or projected. Welfare policies and practices have been one of the assemblages through which states do such work – ranging from specifying and monitoring 'national membership' (and thus 'eligibility') through 'improving' the population to current concerns to make policy personal and ensure that citizens are active. I will return to some of these issues in the following section, but it is important to think about how welfare is engaged in the process of nation-making. I think that these nation-welfare articulations have two aspects: making peoples and making populations, identified in recent work by Partha Chatterjee (2003). Chatterjee argues that citizenship is bracketed by a double logic – the homogeneous conception of the nation, and the heterogeneous conception of the objects of governing:

> In short, the classical idea of popular sovereignty, expressed in the legal-political facts of equal citizenship, produced in the homogeneous construct of the nation, whereas the activities of governmentality required multiple, cross-cutting and shifting classifications of the population as the targets of multiple policies. Here, then, we have the antinomy between the lofty political imaginary of popular sovereignty and the mundane administrative reality of governmentality: it is the antinomy between the homogeneous national and the heterogeneous social. (2003, p. 36)

I find this an immensely suggestive distinction. Welfare states have been one of the critical sites for homogeneous constructs of the nation – particularly the promulgation (and contestation, we might add) of the 'legal-political facts of equal citizenship'. The Marshallian view of citizenship rests on these developments and their institutionalization in the apparatuses of the state, with 'social' citizenship being represented in the welfare policies and practices of states. But welfare also articulates the more specifically national character of particular places, valorizing and enforcing specific conceptions of national character, values, culture and ways of life.

Welfare is also a key site for the construction and management of populations: the 'mundane reality of governmentality'. It involves the labour of classification (what sorts of people are there?). It requires the production of knowledge about the composition of the population (its shifting and always problematic demography), about its actual and desired levels of development (health, education, etc.), about its 'needs', and about its disorders (dysfunctional families; the socially excluded; the delinquent; the passive-dependent individuals, and so on). Studies of governmentality, deriving from Foucault's work, have made a major impact on our understanding of welfare and its importance as a site for defining and governing populations (e.g., Marston and McDonald, 2006). 'Governing the social' frames the welfare work of states in a different way and, in doing so, makes us think about the 'social facts' (or what Poovey, 1995, calls 'political arithmetic') that have been a core concern of social policy studies since the nineteenth century.

Transforming welfare states: deconstruction and reconstruction?

In this final section, I return to the possibilities created by thinking of welfare states as articulated formations, assemblages, ensembles or constellations. Earlier, I indicated that such concepts might allow us to think of how the different elements articulated in welfare state formations have been differently contested and subject to potentially divergent political projects for their 'reform'. To put it crudely, some political projects have had 'welfare reform' as their focus; some have had 'state reform' as their objective; and others have certainly been about the remaking of the nation. These may all contribute to the 'transformation of welfare state' but we should be wary of thinking that they all fit together and share a coherent and singular direction. Indeed, both within specific national welfare states and in contrasts between them, it might be better to argue that contemporary processes of transformation are incoherent, multiple and possibly contradictory (Clarke, 2006 and forthcoming b).

Each of the terms here – welfare, state and nation – has been the focus of multiple challenges (Clarke, 2004). 'Anti-welfarism', for example, combines and condenses social movement critiques of welfare's inadequacy, inaccessibility, and demeaning conditionality, welfare providers' anxieties and frustrations about the problems of managing relations with 'client groups', and neo-conservative as well as neo-liberal critiques of 'welfare dependency'. That such neo-liberal and neo-conservative challenges have become the dominant position in the reform of some national welfare provision (most notably in the US, of course) should not disguise the multiple and contradictory orientations that are condensed in anti-welfarism and the drive to 'welfare reform'. Active subjects are not only the fantasy of neo-liberals. Similarly, 'anti-statism' condenses many different doubts about, and challenges to, the authoritative position of the state as a 'power' in, and over, society. Even those who have viewed the state as the best available 'engine' for social improvement have doubts about both its effectiveness and about its 'dark side': the exercise of power and authority without adequate controls ('social control' in the older socialist sense). Social movements in both the North and the South have both looked to states to underwrite rights, justice and equality, while at the same time looking to an active and powerful civil society as a means of both challenging and making demands on the state. Such ambivalence about the state needs to be kept in view even as we take note of the dominance of neo-liberal 'market liberating' discourses of anti-statism – both in some national settings and in international organizational settings of 'global governmentality' (Larner and Walters, 2004).

Projects of state reform are rarely singular and coherent (Clarke et al., 2007). The remaking of the apparatuses, practices and personnel through which the social is governed has been shaped by different forces – and has taken different forms. We might also want to consider how state reform projects have typically been about much more than the 'welfare state', but about remaking the whole architecture of governance and the relationships between state and society, state and economy, as well as inter-state relations. Questions posed in debates about governance and governmentality, arguments about states becoming 'disaggregated', or the shifting relationships between different modes of authority have had little impact on the discussion of welfare states (as though welfare states were somehow separate from states: see, *inter alia*, Newman, 2005; Slaughter, 2004; Hansen and Salskov-Iversen, forthcoming; van Berkel, 2007).

Such state reforms have often been co-terminous with the contested reinvention of 'nations'. Here, too, we can see the tense and strained intersection of different forces, interests and projects – ranging from the pressures to 'open' the nation to the flows of a globalizing world to the attempts to restore the 'traditional' unity of people, place and race in the face of movements of people (or, at least, the wrong sorts of people). Europe has become increasingly susceptible to such restorationist projects – versions of ethnic-cultural 'protectionism' (in the context of economic liberalization). For example, Kalb argues that one effect of 'globalizing' neo-liberal market reforms has been 'an upsurge of counter-narratives of nationalism, localism, religion and tradition, often of a male chauvinist and paternalist persuasion' (Kalb, 2005, p. 187). Such divergent contestations of the nation have powerful implications for both welfare and state, since managing to construct a unifying conception of the people fits uncomfortably with the challenge of governing a multi-ethnic population.

For studies of welfare states and their transformation, distinguishing these three elements opens up new analytic possibilities. Many of the debates of the last 20 years have been about conceptions of transformation that are uniform and unilinear (the end of/survival of the welfare state; globalization and convergence versus national difference; the rise of neo-liberalism and the end of the 'social'). By looking at these three elements and the forms in which they are articulated, we might see more uneven and differentiated dynamics of change. In Clarke (2004), I used a triangle to make visible the multiple and divergent contestations of welfare, state and nation that had unsettled taken-for-granted articulations (which we had talked of as welfare states). Here, I want address the third axis between welfare and state and pose the question of what sorts of governance arrangements of welfare are being put into place? The elementary forms of this discussion tend to be phrased in terms of distinctions between state and market forms (or between hierarchy, markets and networks). Alternatively, the concept of mixed economies of welfare has been used to address the shifting alignments and roles of multiple 'sectors' (public, private, not-for-profit/third sector) in the delivery of welfare – though, as Seeleib-Kaiser in Chapter 1 to this volume reminds us, such governance arrangements need to address processes of provision, funding and regulation. In such roles, states may continue to act as agents of what

Jessop calls 'meta-governance', organizing the architecture of governance and its internal relationships:

> Within the complex of new governance mechanisms, the state 'reserves to itself the right to open, close, juggle and re-articulate governance arrangements, not only terms of particular functions, but also from the viewpoint of partisan and overall political advantage'. (Jessop, 2000, p.19)

While the typologies of governance systems and sectors point to some of the contemporary dynamics of change in the governance of welfare, they seem a little too inflexible to cope with emergent and hybrid forms of organization involved in the production and distribution of welfare (Clarke, forthcoming b). Cross-sectoral forms of working (in the UK such forms as Trusts, Partnerships and social enterprises) pose novel problems of analysis and evaluation. Janine Wedel's thoughtful and suggestive work on 'flex organizations', that function on and across sectoral boundaries between public and private, points to one way of engaging with such developments (Wedel, 2000). Such governance arrangements cannot be grasped in purely sectoral terms, nor in simple models of privatization or marketization. Instead, we need to examine how resources, authority, expertise and (occasionally) accountability are being reconstructed in hybridized architectures of welfare governance. Such innovations also affect the spatial and scalar organization of welfare as 'new spaces of welfare' are brought into being (Cochrane, 2006). Forms of decentralization and devolution coincide, sometimes, with changes in the welfare mix. For example, Aldred's study of public–private partnership in health reveals both innovative organizational forms engaged in the invention, and bringing into being, of 'local health economies' (Aldred, 2007); while van Berkel points to how labour market activation policies in the Netherlands have combined 'personalization' in policy and practice with privatization and decentralization of the activation service itself (van Berkel, 2007).

In short, treating welfare states as assemblages or articulated formations makes these processes more visible and, perhaps, explains some of the frustrations of contemporary debates about the transformation of welfare states. If welfare states are not coherent and singular objects of analysis, then tracking change is likely to demand more than a singular indicator (or even a singular set of indicators). In the end this is an argument for a more fine-grained approach to the study of welfare states (singly or comparatively). It requires attention to social objects as assemblages, ensembles, constellations or formations and thus to the possibility of multiple, rather than singular, processes of transformation.

It also implies escaping from the methodological nationalism that has dominated studies of welfare states. This is not a return to the unproductive debate about the global versus the national. Rather it is a claim that all national formations are produced in and through transnational relations, processes and practices (and that such transnational conditions vary in place and time). National welfare systems certainly persist, and national political and institutional formations remain important locations for political and governmental projects and conflicts. Nevertheless, conceptions of welfare, nation and state (and how they might be best assembled) are themselves subject to transnational flows of ideas, policies, comparative-competitive evaluation, models of 'best practice' and relations of learning and mimicry (see, *inter alia*, Djelic and Sahlin-Andersson, 2006; Hansen and Salskov-Iversen, forthcoming; Larner and Walters, 2004; Lendvai and Stubbs, 2006; Newman, 2006). Each 'national' project of welfare reform is articulated with such transnational flows, borrowing, rejecting and indigenizing different elements. While such flows and institutionalizations of 'global governmentality' carry certain dominant messages, models and discourses (not least circulating the whole battery of neo-liberal conceptions of the need for both welfare and state reform), they form a field of exchange in which specific national projects are engaged. Those engagements are multiple (rather than a singular relation or mode of transmission) and allow spaces of possibility for 'national' calculation and manoeuvre – albeit, such spaces are differently distributed between nations. Here, too then, we ought to avoid singular conceptions of our objects of study (and the binary distinctions that they bring in their wake): not pure nations (and the global/national distinction) but national formations lodged in transnational fields of connection. Did anyone say that studying welfare states should be easy?

13
Multiple and Multi-Dimensional Welfare State Transformations

Martin Seeleib-Kaiser

The analyses in this book have shown that we are not witnessing a one-dimensional welfare state transformation that could be easily characterized as a silent surrender or withering away of *public* responsibility and the triumph of 'neo-liberalism'. Neither are we witnessing 'frozen welfare state landscapes' allowing only minor changes. Moreover, welfare state transformations are very complex processes that cannot be captured and expressed in a simple way; in reality we find multiple and multi-dimensional welfare state transformations. For instance, 'privatization' in one policy domain may go along with increased government intervention in another policy domain or 'privatization' in one or two modes of *public* intervention within one policy domain, for instance financing and provision, might be accompanied by an expansion of government intervention in the third mode (regulation). In addition, while some states have clearly expanded overall *public* financing, as already shown by the aggregate spending data in Chapter 1, other countries have reduced the overall *public* spending levels, while at the same time allocated more public financial resources to specific policy areas such as social services. Thus the findings of our project are in accordance with the argument put forward by Levy (2006b, p. 27) stating that 'instead of just expanding or contracting, the state should be understood as evolving, as shifting in its purposes and modes of intervention.'

By analysing the various modes of intervention, that is, financing, provision and regulation, our research shows that the three dimensions of change identified in previous research, that is, retrenchment, recommodification and recalibration, often cannot fully capture the dynamics of change. Furthermore, it has to be stressed that the modes of governance have changed in a number of countries and policy areas in such ways that would not have been expected based on the assumptions of the regime literature. All chapters clearly demonstrate that significant social policy changes have taken place during the recent decade and some of these can indeed be characterized as processes of transformations that have 'unsettled' previous social policy arrangements with regard to the public–private mix, as theorized in

Chapter 12 by Clarke. Thus, we find more significant changes than would have been expected based on much of the previous research focusing on path dependence (cf. Pierson, 2001a), especially as incremental changes can cumulate and over time lead to significant change or even policy transformations (cf. Seeleib-Kaiser, 2002; Bleses and Seeleib-Kaiser, 2004; Streeck and Thelen, 2005b). In a nutshell: we are witnesses of significant and complex policy changes that cannot be subsumed under the general heading of withdrawing public responsibility or 'privatization', but that are characterized by a refocusing of state interventions and redefinitions of the mixed economy of welfare (cf. Siegel and Jochem, 2003; Levy, 2006b). As van Kersbergen (2000, p. 30) has stated: 'There may be far more radical or fundamental changes than we expected or have so far observed. Still, not every radical reform of the welfare state necessarily leads to the collapse of the welfare state.' It is far from clear, however, whether these processes of transformations have led to new institutional *settlements*. Although we have not explicitly focused on mature Conservative welfare states in Part I of our book, our findings are also largely mirrored by recent analyses of change in these countries (cf. Palier and Claude, 2007; Seeleib-Kaiser et al., 2008).

Summarizing the results

The analysis of the British case by Powell (Chapter 2) clearly demonstrates that a variety of dynamics are under way. At the level of political discourse, the promotion of private social policy is no longer a sole domain of the Conservative Party; after years of fierce opposition more private engagement in the social policy domain is also supported and promoted by New Labour, using choice and diversity as key concepts. At the institutional level we have witnessed significant changes. In some areas, such as social housing, the state clearly withdrew from its previous role of providing a service without significantly expanding its regulatory reach in parallel, while in some other areas, such as health care and education, increased private provision was accompanied or even accomplished by more government spending and stricter regulatory guidelines. Using Public–Private Partnerships the New Labour government has overseen the largest hospital building programme in the history of the NHS. With regards to traditional income security programmes, such as unemployment compensation and pensions, policy changes have led to a further recommodification of workers, while tax credits have been expanded to support those with the lowest incomes. At the same time the regulatory framework for occupational pensions has been strengthened. Based on the available empirical data, an overall categorization of welfare state changes in Britain seems not to be possible; it can be stated, however, that an increased *private* involvement, especially in regards to provision, has not been synonymous with an overall decline in *public* responsibility.

Goul Andersen (Chapter 3) emphasizes that the concepts of retrenchment and recommodification are insufficient to understand and characterize the recent welfare state developments in Denmark. Furthermore, he stresses that services have indeed been expanded. From an institutional perspective the changes in the social security programmes could lead observers to characterize them to follow a path of retrenchment or recommodification, but if *outcomes* are taken into account, the conclusions differ. For instance, although replacement rates for the unemployed average production worker (APW) have been curtailed and conditionality strengthened, Goul Andersen maintains that it is usually not the APW that becomes unemployed, but those earning less. For the lowest income groups Denmark still provides very generous unemployment benefits. The changes in the pension system have been significant and to some extent achieved without major legislative changes. There has clearly been a shift towards formally 'private' pensions (called labour market pensions), which are governed by collective bargaining agreements that cover nearly all employees. Within social services Denmark has introduced market principles with regard to provision; however, the primary aim has not been to retrench, but to provide better quality services, freedom of choice and an empowerment of users, largely within the state system. With regards to child-care, Goul Andersen concludes that 'the entire policy field has been one of expansion, not retrenchment'. According to him, the transformed Danish welfare state has 'the net effect of maintaining or even ensuring the status quo with regards to outcomes'. Yet, the crucial question remains, whether these outcomes can be achieved in the future, especially should economic conditions deteriorate.

As Guillén and Petmesidou point out in Chapter 4, Southern European countries have witnessed an expansion of *public* responsibilities in some important domains of social policy, which were driven by catch-up processes and strong pressures for public intervention to address extensive unmet needs. In this context the introduction of *public* National Health Systems in all four Southern European countries studied, that is, Greece, Italy, Portugal and Spain, needs to be emphasized. Nevertheless, health-care provision in Greece continues to rely heavily on out-of-pocket expenditures and social insurance contributions. Public social care has also seen expansions; however, as Guillén and Petmesidou stress 'universally available provision of first-stop systematic services has scarcely developed'. With regard to pension policies, the Southern European countries continue to rely mainly on the public pillar, which for many retirees, especially in Greece and Portugal, only provides very inadequate pension benefits. Although Spain has witnessed retrenchment in pension entitlements for core workers, improvements of the protection for workers in non-standard employment were implemented. Occupational pensions are not very highly developed in the Southern European countries; however, among the four countries, Italy seems to be a leader in this domain. Personal private pensions also do not play a large role, with the exception of Spain, where approximately 22 per cent of the working population contributes to such schemes, which have been publicly promoted through the expansion of fiscal exemptions. Within the domains of labour market and employment policy there has been a clear trend towards liberalization and flexibilization, although in some instances these processes were embedded in a policy approach of flexicurity. Many of the welfare state reforms in Spain, Italy and to a lesser extent in Portugal were achieved through negotiated agreements between the state and the social partners and can be characterized as transformations. However, in Greece changes have been more of an incremental nature and do not add up to substantially changing the rules of the game.

Without question the most far-reaching social policy transformations have occurred in the Central and Eastern European transition countries (Chapter 5). Although all countries have witnessed significant privatizations and processes of recommodification, public provision and financing of social policy still play a significant role. The processes of recommodification have been especially severe in the domain of employment and unemployment policies. With the exception of the Czech Republic, all countries have introduced mandatory second tier old-age pension schemes run by private enterprises. Despite a number of similarities, Potůček argues that those eight post-communist countries that have joined the EU in 2004 developed quite different policy trajectories, leading to a variety of public–private mixes. According to his estimation, the Baltic countries more or less fall into the category of a residual liberal welfare state, while Slovakia is moving towards such a model. Slovenia on the other hand resembles most closely the Continental European welfare state model, while the picture for Hungary and Poland is less clear, as they are said to grapple with major difficulties.

According to Potůček, the Czech Republic, which he analyses in greater detail, went through various stages of reform, while the general trajectory was anchored in a Bismarckian concept of welfare. Overall, the level of public social policy expenditure has remained quite stable, despite the fact that liberal-conservative governments were in charge for the period from 1992 to 1997, followed by governments led by Social Democrats from 1998 to 2006. Although the latter brought about some expansions in ALMP, unemployment insurance benefits continue to be very low and the duration of benefit receipt rather short, contributing to a significant number of unemployed workers having to rely on social assistance. While the replacement ratio of the *public* pension scheme has been reduced significantly and in the future might drop below the subsistence level, the government supports the option of voluntary private pension contracts through state subsidies and income tax allowances since 1994. These contracts cover close to 40 per cent of the population above the age of 18. In health care, provision was almost completely privatized, but financing continues to be largely a state responsibility. Finally, public family policies, including parental leave arrangements and child-care provision, have recently been significantly expanded. The Czech case as well as the comparative analysis of CEE countries clearly shows a variety of dynamics within the different social policy domains that in their sum warrant to speak of social policy transformations that, however, have not yet led to new policy equilibria.

For a long time Japan was either not considered within comparative welfare state analyses or characterized as a unique case. In Chapter 6, Goodman traces various social policy reforms of the 1990s and early 2000s, taking the 'Japanese model' of social welfare as a reference point. The 'Japanese model' relied on comparatively low state spending, with a focus of resources on social investment in health and education, and a high reliance on families, corporations and communities as providers of welfare. These 'private' providers have come under 'attack' through various socio-economic challenges and have triggered some significant policy changes. Focusing on family policy and social care, Goodman can convincingly show that the state has expanded a number of programmes that shifted the responsibility from families to the state in the fields of child and elderly care. With regard to the provision of institutional care, the state has on the one hand emphasized market principles such as competition, while at the same time demanded more transparency and accountability from institutions receiving government subsidies. Employment programmes were more clearly focused towards investment for those unemployed workers with special needs, instead of providing subsidies to companies for employment maintenance. At the same time, however, the state continued to indirectly stabilize employment through various macro-economic Keynesian measures. The government's approach to employment is rooted in the conception that the opportunity for work continues to be considered a basic right in Japan.

In accordance with the focus on work, unemployment programmes, which have never been very comprehensive, have been retrenched. Public pension programmes saw a number of curtailments, including the reduction of benefits and increases in the retirement age to be phased in over a number of years. In health-care co-payments, which are capped and do not apply to the poor, were increased. Accordingly these changes could be characterized as steps towards privatization in terms of financing, which, however, run counter to social policy developments in other realms. Thus, similar to developments in the other welfare states analysed, we are witnesses of a number of dynamics that have unsettled the previous public–private mix, which, however, as they point into different directions, cannot easily be subsumed under one concept or heading.

In Part II of the book, we took a closer look at social policy developments from a cross-sectional perspective. In pension policies we have seen probably the most far-reaching changes in those countries that have shifted from public systems, leaving only little room for private provision, to multipillar pension systems. In a novel and original approach, Bridgen and Meyer, modelled the effects these shifts will have for future retirees, that is, those retiring in the year 2050, belonging to various income groups and occupations in six countries (Britain, Germany, Italy, the Netherlands, Poland and Switzerland) from the perspective of a *welfare system*, introduced in Chapter 1. Although they show that in principle private provision can complement public provision and provide a level of income that ensures social inclusion, only the combined public and private pension systems of the Netherlands and Switzerland come close to fulfilling the conditions of a welfare system, in such a way as providing an income for the various groups close to the defined social inclusion level. Both countries offer the strongest public provision and the most encompassing coverage with regards to private occupational pension plans. However, even in these countries the role of public and private pensions are said to be only similar and not functionally equivalent, since the private schemes provide a weaker protection for labour market detachment, are less redistributive and less certain with regards to future benefit levels. Bridgen and Meyer are somewhat sceptical about the future of these arrangements as they have come under pressure and have experienced some retrenchment.

In Chapter 8, Rothgang et al. examine health-care systems in OECD countries, clearly showing that there has not been a one-dimensional process towards privatization, as the mean public expenditures in per cent of GDP have indeed continued to grow. This increase is primarily driven by catch-up processes in countries previously considered low spenders on public health. However, on average private spending has grown faster, leading to a *relative* decline of public efforts, measured as the mean share of public spending in per cent of total health-care expenditure in 23 OECD countries. With regard to provision they identify a process towards more private provision. More importantly, however, they show that the three countries they have studied in greater detail with regards to regulation, that is, Britain, Germany and the US, have each lost some of their previous characteristics. Overall, they diagnose processes towards hybridization of health-care systems, driven by shifts along the various modes of intervention in the mixed economies of health.

Although most likely not only to be the case with regard to employment and unemployment policies, Clegg in Chapter 9 clearly demonstrates that liberalization policies can presuppose an *increase* in state activism. First, Clegg reminds us that in the heyday of the 'golden' welfare state era, insurance against the risk of unemployment was in many instances governed through systems of self-governance run by social partners in the shadow of the state. Second, he shows that the major reforms of the British and Danish unemployment systems owed much to the considerable leverage the state has had in governing unemployment benefits, whereas change was less far-reaching and much more difficult to achieve in Belgium, France and Germany, countries in which the social partners had a greater stake in the governance of the systems. Thus, Clegg argues that the participation of 'private' actors in the governance and regulation of unemployment benefits has functioned as a 'brake' in the transition to more market-supporting and more strongly recommodifying policies. According to him, the Netherlands were able to enact more far-reaching reforms, compared with the other Conservative welfare states, as a consequence of a reasserted state role within the institutional arrangements governing unemployment benefits.

Also, within the realm of incapacity benefits, we have seen the state in the Netherlands and Sweden increase its involvement in the administration of benefits at the expense of the social partners, as pointed out by Kemp in Chapter 10. The underlying aim of many reforms in the two countries mentioned, but also in a number of other OECD countries, has been to shift the focus and culture of the incapacity programmes from a compensatory approach towards enabling people to reintegrate into the labour market. Kemp emphasizes that the concept of incapacity to work is not stable across countries and over time. Although he points to the transition of industrial societies towards post-industrial societies as a main driver for the overall increase of incapacity benefit recipients, mature welfare states have used incapacity or disability programmes to differing degrees. The Scandinavian welfare states have the highest incapacity benefit recipiency rates among OECD countries. Within the world of Conservative welfare states the Netherlands stand out, with recipiency rates higher than in some Scandinavian countries. And among the Liberal welfare states, it is the UK that has a comparatively high rate of incapacity benefit recipients. After the percentage of workers on incapacity benefits and spending for these programmes in a number of countries had significantly risen (in some countries to levels higher than those for unemployment programmes) and as the overall focus had shifted towards increasing employment rates, states also began to reform and indeed transform incapacity policies.

While many states have increased conditionality for unemployment compensation payments starting in the 1980s and 1990s, some, at least for some time, have implicitly or even explicitly used incapacity programmes to protect certain (vulnerable) groups, thereby 'compensating' the reduced *public* responsibility in providing benefits to 'unemployed' workers. It is interesting to see that this strategy was applied in Britain, resulting in about a quarter of the workforce in some former industrial regions of the north relying on incapacity benefits, whereas virtually no workers were in receipt of incapacity benefits in some of the most prosperous post-industrial regions of the south (cf. Toynbee and Walker, 2005, p. 68).

As Ben-Galim and Gambles show in Chapter 11, New Labour in Britain has promoted a policy transforming the formerly perceived policy of work–life balance as belonging to the 'private' domain towards the 'public' domain of state intervention. Subsequently, public family policies, and more widely work–life balance policies, have indeed been significantly expanded and are now much more in tune with policies in other European countries. However, they emphasize that the approach was gendered in many respects, mainly resulting from its focus on prioritizing mothers' employment and not correspondingly addressing the issue of involving fathers more in family care. Furthermore, they highlight that outcomes remain deeply gendered, partly because of the way the adult worker is imagined in the political discourse and in workplace practices. Their chapter clearly shows how far concepts of *public* and *private* are socially constructed. Implicitly they point to the fact that the role played by *private* firms can be crucial for the success of *public* policies (cf. Crompton, 2006).

Comparing social policy transformations

Despite the variety of countries and policies studied and the emphasis given in the chapters on the multiple directions and extent of social policy reforms with regard to the public–private mix, a number of similarities can be discerned. Most countries have increased their reliance on *private* provision and financing with regard to pension policies, either implicitly by reducing benefits or explicitly by actively encouraging private or occupational pension plans through various regulatory measures or by expanding tax incentives. Changes with regard to unemployment compensation have usually strengthened measures to activate and recommodify unemployed workers, albeit in some countries these policies were embedded in a concept of flexicurity. Japan was the only country that implemented a strategy of Keynesian deficit spending to keep unemployment low.

In parallel, most countries have expanded public responsibility through increased public financing and provision for certain services with regards to child and elderly care, while at the same time allowing or encouraging elements of market competition within public service provision and more outright private provision. Although public provision of health-care services has declined in all OECD countries with the exception of Iceland, the Netherlands and Japan, as pointed out by Rothgang et al. in Chapter 8, public financing has increased in a number of countries. Among the welfare states examined in greater detail in this volume Britain and Denmark increasingly use certain market mechanisms as well as private provision and the Czech Republic has almost completely privatized provision. In contrast the Mediterranean countries have established National Health Systems and subsequently increased public funding for health care. The English NHS has also witnessed significantly increased funding since the late 1990s. Nevertheless, it should be noted that the consumption of ever increasing economic resources for health care in the rich OECD countries has on average led to a relative decline of public funding and an expansion of private financing in these countries (cf. Chapter 8). Finally, many countries have witnessed an increase in regulation, be it with regards to (health) care provision, work–life balance and family policies or private and occupational pensions. Changed regulatory frameworks improving access to social security for non-standard employees also fall into this often overlooked, but increasingly ever more important category.

Although the country case studies and comparisons as well as the cross-sectional analyses in this volume demonstrate that significant differences continue to persist, common development trends point to a convergence at the level of institutional design, in the sense that the distinctiveness of national approaches to social policies, welfare states or even regimes has declined in significance – elsewhere I have characterized this phenomenon as a process of 'divergent convergence' (Seeleib-Kaiser, 2001). The finding of convergence is not mainly based on the quantitative data presented in Chapter 1, but primarily by comparing the results of the nuanced analyses in the subsequent chapters focusing on financing, provision and regulation. The analysis of Denmark demonstrates most clearly that compared with the heyday of the state-centric Social-Democratic approach many reforms have significantly changed the institutional design, which now includes more private arrangements and the use of market mechanisms. Also Britain seems to have moved away from its 'etatiste' version of the welfare state towards a more mixed approach of welfare pluralism. In the Mediterranean countries studied, we witness processes of rationalization of the once highly fragmented welfare states as well as the introduction and expansion of new public social policies, perhaps least prominent in Greece, while for instance in Japan we are witnessing clear expansions of *public* intervention through increased financial resources and higher accountability standards within the domain of care. The previous Communist welfare states of CEE have moved towards Liberal or Conservative welfare state models. As already indicated above, health-care policies in OECD countries have undergone a process of convergence, most countries now rely on multi-pillar pension systems and have moved towards activation of the workless. The introduction and expansion of *public* work–life balance polices in Britain, for a long time a laggard within the EU, have moved the country closer to policies pursued in other European countries.

From welfare states to welfare systems: the outcome perspective

Based on the concept of *welfare systems* introduced in Chapter 1, the jury is still out on whether and in how far increased private provision and financing in certain sectors can indeed produce similar outcomes as would be the case in a public system. However, in this context it should be emphasized that not all *public* social policies ensure fair and equitable outcomes. With regards to services it must be highlighted that despite the increased use of market mechanisms (within the public sector) and private providers in Denmark, universalism and state responsibility are not questioned. Within the English NHS waiting times have been reduced, partially through more private provision available to NHS patients (King's Fund, 2007). Although

Southern European countries have seen some expansions of *public* service provision, the family continues to be the main provider of care, while at the same time we witness the emergence of an 'informal privatization' of care arrangements, i.e. families continue to coordinate care, but the care itself is provided by mostly female migrant workers. And in CEE countries, the poor quality of the *public* health-care systems has led to the parallel establishment of 'informal' or 'private' care systems, financed through out-of-pocket payments. Unfortunately, data limitations do not allow for a quantification of these developments. Thus, despite convergence at the institutional level, we witness continued significant differences among countries at the outcome level.

If we look at income poverty as a measure to assess the overall effectiveness of welfare arrangements, differences continue to persist. Overall, the risk of poverty has stayed more or less stable in the EU and the differences among countries have changed only very little over the past decade (see Table 13.1).[1] It seems plausible that the shifts within the public–private mix have not (at least not yet) had a significant impact on the aggregate levels of the risk of poverty.

However, in order to answer the question about the distributional impact of more private provision and financing in a more nuanced way we need more detailed analyses, taking into account the specific regulatory frameworks and governance structures. In some cases the changes will only materialize some time in the future, especially in the case of pensions. Indeed Bridgen and Meyer emphasize in Chapter 7 that the combination of *private* and *public* pensions in a number of countries will be insufficient to insure against the risk of old age in such a way as to provide benefits above a social inclusion threshold for those retiring in 2050. Although in some countries that rely on voluntarism such as Britain, even low income earners can avoid poverty, however, according to Bridgen and Meyer's analysis 'the main determinant of who escapes among this group [of low income earners] and who does not is largely arbitrary: it is the result of accidents of opportunities rather than planning or intention'. In order to overcome such 'accidents of opportunities' a *collective* framework governing these arrangements, making the provision of occupational pensions more or less obligatory for every employer to provide or every employee to enrol in, would be necessary. Basically this can be achieved either through statutory regulations or the practice of collective bargaining, as is the case in Switzerland and the Netherlands. However, in how far such a mandatory approach constitutes a real political possibility will depend on the power resources of unions and/or supporters of encompassing private or occupational arrangements in parliaments.

As pointed out by Goul Andersen, the Danish pension system is becoming 'one of the most "privatized" systems in the world'. Nevertheless, through the broad coverage of employees and the governance by the social partners the 'private' labour market pensions can be characterized as being more or less

Table 13.1 Population at risk of poverty* after social transfers in per cent

	1995	1996	1997	1998	1999	2000	2001	2002	2003	2004	2005
EU (25 countries)	:	:	:	15[s]	16[s]	16[s]	16[s]	:	15[s]	16[s]	16[s]
EU (15 countries)	17[s]	16[s]	16[s]	15[s]	16[s]	15[s]	15[s]	:	15[s]	17[s]	16[s]
Czech Republic	:	:	:	:	:	:	8	:	:	:	10[b]
Denmark	10	:	10	:	10	:	10	:	12[b]	11	12
Estonia	:	:	:	:	:	18	18	18	18	20[b]	18
Greece	22	21	21	21	21	20	20	:	21[b]	20	20
Spain	19	18	20	18	19	18	19	19[b]	19	20[b]	20
Italy	20	20	19	18	18	18	19	:	:	19[b]	19
Latvia	:	:	:	:	:	16	:	:	:	:	19[b]
Lithuania	:	:	:	:	:	17	17	:	:	:	21[b]
Hungary	:	:	:	:	:	11	11	10	12	:	13[b]
Poland	:	:	:	:	:	16	16	:	:	:	21[b]
Portugal	23	21	22	21	21	21	20	20[p]	19[p]	20[b]	19
Slovenia	:	:	:	:	:	11	11	10	10	:	12[b]
Slovakia	:	:	:	:	:	:	:	:	:	:	13[b]
United Kingdom	20	18	18	19	19	19[b]	18	18	18	:	18[b]

*The share of persons with an equivalised disposable income below the risk-of-poverty threshold, which is set at 60% of the national median equivalized disposable income (after social transfers).
(:) Not available.
(s) Eurostat estimate.
(b) Break in series.
(p) Provisional value.
Source: Eurostat; downloaded from http://epp.eurostat.ec.europa.eu/, 21 November, 2007.

functionally equivalent to state pensions, based on defined contributions. One could argue that these pension arrangements, although formally *private*, constitute a good example for what has been defined as private social policies within the *public* domain in Chapter 1. Similar to the Swiss and Dutch cases, the Danish case demonstrates that an approach increasingly relying on private arrangements does not necessarily have to be identical with a withdrawal of public responsibility. The public social policy arrangements for low-income pensioners and the subsequently low poverty rates for these groups symbolize this continued public responsibility in Denmark. Within the domain of services there has indeed been outsourcing, that is, private provision, and marketization in Denmark; however, generally the aim was to improve and not to retrench services. Overall, the Danish example shows quite well that countries can remain inclusive *welfare systems*, even if the overriding principle of recent welfare state transformations has been for the welfare state to act more in conformity with the market, including a higher reliance on private provision and financing.

Finally, as pointed out by Clarke in Chapter 12, comparative welfare state research needs to take into account the more complex formations or assemblages of welfare as well as pay more attention to the specific governance structures. The chapters in this volume have aimed at addressing the shifts in the public–private mix and the interrelationships of the various actors along three modes of policy intervention, that is, financing, provision and regulation. Although offering first insights into multiple and multi-dimensional welfare state transformations, more systematic and in-depth data needs to be collected and analysed. Especially with regards to the distributional effects of *private* provision and regulation the available data is still quite limited. Finally, we need to move governance structures and the different forms of accountability involved to the centre stage of our research, because it is very likely that they will determine the inclusiveness of welfare systems relying to a greater extent on private provision and financing.

Notes

1 Welfare State Transformations in Comparative Perspective: Shifting Boundaries of 'Public' and 'Private' Social Policy?

1. Studies emphasizing little change in the public social policy effort in countries of Northern and Western Europe predominantly rely on such quantitative indicators (cf. Taylor-Gooby, 2002).
2. There is one caveat in that only Italy within the group of Southern European countries and no country from Central and Eastern Europe is included in this dataset. Furthermore, these findings are in contrast to Korpi and Palme (2003) who argue that, although we have seen retrenchment throughout most countries, liberal welfare states have witnessed the largest retrenchment. According to them 'the British welfare state has been rolled back to a pre-Beveridge level, at or below that of the 1930s' (Korpi and Palme, 2003, p. 433 f.).
3. Countries have used various pathways to 'reduce' unemployment through other welfare state programmes. Especially the Nordic countries and the Netherlands seem to have comparatively high levels of the working age population receiving incapacity/disability benefits. In the UK the caseload of incapacity beneficiaries has increased substantially in the 1990s and has surpassed the caseload of unemployment beneficiaries as this was declining (Carcillo and Grubb, 2006, pp. 55–60). In other countries, especially in 'conservative welfare states' such as Germany, early retirement was a preferred pathway to 'reduce' unemployment since the mid-1980s (Ebbinghaus, 2006).
4. However, it has to be acknowledged that this is a very rough picture (e.g. tax benefits for private pension schemes are still not included in this data) and systematic comparative work seems to be still widely lacking. The above disclaimer in regards to public social expenditure data should obviously also apply to this dataset.
5. Burchardt (1997) and Smithies (2005) have systematically scrutinized the shifting balance within the British welfare state from 1979 until 1999, however without sufficiently analysing tax expenditures and regulation. For a critical assessment of the mixed economy in Britain, see Powell (2007).
6. See however the work by Shalev (1996) and Rein and Schmähl (2004).
7. For a discussion of various accountability mechanisms see Grant and Keohane (2005).
8. Within the Ghent system financing and the provision of benefits is dependent on union membership, while the unions are also responsible for administering the scheme. For a discussion of the erosion of the Ghent System in Finland see Böckerman and Uusitalo (2006).
9. In this I differ somewhat from Marquand's definitions, who differentiates between the private and market domains. It needs to be acknowledged, however, that in developed nation states even the private domain is not fully independent of the state; moreover, the state determines the legal framework within which actors can become active (Polanyi, 2001); e.g., what constitutes a family or philanthropic institution is largely determined by the state.
10. This can easily be demonstrated in the field of education by the example of private/independent universities, which are usually categorized as part of the third

sector. Obviously, these institutions of higher education primarily rely on their academic reputation. However, those institutions without large endowments especially, are increasingly governed by a market logic, having to attract students (customers) in the global market place as well as outside research funding, based on 'full economic costs', in order to finance themselves (for a critical assessment of the university sector see Slaughter and Rhoades, 2004).

11. Depending on the policy area communication might turn out to be a preferred mode of government intervention. In this respect the most obvious might be educational policies aimed at the public to improve health, for instance, campaigns to change behavioural habits to minimize lung cancer or sexually transmitted diseases.

12. Based on a replication and re-analysis of the de-commodification variable recent research has questioned the overall regime approach more fundamentally (Scruggs and Allan, 2006).

2   Welfare State Reforms in the United Kingdom

1. This section gives a brief overview of the major changes in the UK welfare state under Conservative and New Labour governments from an institutional perspective. It draws on general (Powell, 1999, 2002; Powell and Hewitt, 2002; Timmins, 2001; Toynbee and Walker, 2005) and service sources (Klein, 2005; Mullins and Murie, 2006; Powell, 1997), and focuses on England as there are some differences in the devolved administrations, such as student finance and long-term care in Scotland (Stewart, 2004).

2. Robert Maxwell was a leading industrialist who took large sums of money from his companies' pension funds.

3. For a comparative perspective see Clegg in this volume.

4. For a comparative perspective on occupational pensions cf. Bridgen and Meyer in this volume.

3   Welfare State Transformations in an Affluent Scandinavian State: The Case of Denmark

1. Actually the decline is even larger as the figures are not corrected for a technical increase of 1.6 per cent of GDP in 1993 when a number of social security payments were changed from net payments to taxable income and raised accordingly.

2. Own calculations, based on public consumption expenditures in current prices and deflator for public consumption derived from national account information on public services in basic prices, in current and fixed prices (Statistics Denmark, 2003). The Ministry of Finance (2003, p. 35) reports a figure of 'almost 25 per cent' for the same period.

3. Due to space limitations, we have not been able to include taxation in the account. There have been three major tax reforms in 1985, 1993 and 1998. All have widened the tax base and lowered tax rates. Highest marginal income tax rates have been reduced from 73 per cent to 62–63 per cent. The only genuine tax relief adopted in 2003 was targeted at lower- and middle incomes for people in employment.

4. Besides, wage earners' pension improvements are not counted in. For instance, GNP in current prices increased by 44 per cent 1994–2003, personal incomes

increased by 39 per cent, but pensions and unemployment benefits only increased by 22 per cent (source: Statistics Denmark).

5. Calculations by the Ministry of Labour in 2001 on request by a MP (http://www.folketinget.dk/Samling/20001/spor_sv/S3584.htm).

6. Statistical yearbook, various issues, and www.statistikbanken.dk (table AB61107). When unemployment went significantly below 150 000, however, the proportion declined. By mid-2007, 78 per cent received unemployment benefits. In addition to 21 000 unemployed without unemployment insurance (normally receiving social assistance), there are some 70 000 persons receiving social assistance who are not registered as unemployed as they have 'other problems than unemployment'. The total number of persons receiving social assistance was fairly stable until 2006 when it began to decline.

7. Basically, this was a misinterpretation: the wage increases in 1987 were *politically* determined by the mobilization of the unions in the collective negotiations and the willingness of the government to provide public employees with high wage increases. There was little underlying wage drift (Ibsen, 1992; Andersen, 1993, pp. 297–300).

8. A third large package, the *welfare reform* in 2006, based on a broad compromise including the Social Democrats, strengthened the works test even further by assessment of availability for a job every third month, and by requiring those unemployed to look for a job on the internet each week.

9. This also includes Danish citizens returning from these countries.

10. In the mid-2000s, there was a sudden increase in private unemployment insurance, and some insurance companies believed in a great market here. This runs contrary to theories of the near-impossibility of private unemployment insurance (Barr, 2001). Because of the fear of competition, trade unions went into the business and thereby developed a model which *may* be sustainable as they could avoid the separation of risk groups that normally makes private unemployment insurance infeasible. Sweden has similar arrangements for supplementary insurance by unions (for an overview of private welfare in Sweden, see Lindqvist and Wadensjö, 2005, 2006).

11. The bourgeois government elected in 2006 promised to replace the Ghent model by mandatory unemployment insurance (this system is also found in Norway). In the mandate for the commission, however, is a premise that the unemployment insurance funds should be maintained (Andersen and Kongshøj, 2007).

12. It should be underlined that policies in Denmark are nearly always highly pragmatic and seldom *directly* related to theory.

13. Unlike in many continental European countries, there is little debate about new combinations of work and family care. But there are a few instances, characterized by strong rationing and high compensation, e.g. improved maternity/parental leave, care for seriously ill family members, etc. (Andersen and Johansen, 2006). There has been a debate about family provision of home help care but, in general, the dual earner model and the strong need for labour power tend to exclude such solutions in a Nordic context. Finally, the Conservatives and Liberals were once very favourable to giving families opportunity to care for their own children, and this possibility actually exists. But as take-up of such possibilities would be far higher among immigrants, and as the government wants immigrants to be integrated in the labour market, while the children should indeed attend kindergartens, this issue is rarely discussed anymore.

14. In a municipal reform (called 'structure reform'), counties were merged into five regions with health care as their main task. Unlike the counties, the regions have no right to collect taxes. Other things being equal, this will transform regional politicians into 'expenditure advocats'. In the 1990s, Denmark, Norway, Sweden and Finland were the only countries that did not experience increasing health-care expenditures as per cent of GDP – and at that time they were all managed and financed by the counties.

4   The Public–Private Mix in Southern Europe: What Changed in the Last Decade?

1. Cf. Ferrera and Gualmini, 2000, 2004; Graziano, 2003; Guillén, Álvarez, and Adào e Silva, 2003.
2. Cf. the contributions in Petmesidou and Mossialos, 2006.
3. The replacement rate would decrease to 60 per cent for main pensions and would refer to the gross earnings of the last five years (this condition was ameliorated some years later).
4. Of which there are about 30 today.
5. These were kept very low by the socialist governments over the 1980s, so as to discourage private investment in secondary health care. The sudden increase of per diem hospital reimbursement rates led to soaring deficits of health insurance funds. But the 1992 law hardly touched the need for rationalizing funding and tackling perverse distribution of resources.
6. Which, however, still remains comparatively high (accounting for roughly about 30 per cent of GDP in the early 2000s (Schneider, 2002)).
7. With this Act, minimum pensions will converge for all funds to 70 per cent of pensionable income by 2017.
8. A provision in line with directive 2003/41 of the EU for the functioning and regulation of occupational pension benefits.
9. The scenario of pension costs explosion in 2050 becomes even more alarming if we take into account the comparatively low overall employment rate in Greece (60 per cent).
10. Presently the minimum pension benefit is at the level of the minimum wage.
11. Pereira da Silva et al. (2006) estimate that the 2002 reform together with the stabilization fund (amounting to 4.3 per cent of GDP at the moment) would ensure the balance of the social security budget until 2020.
12. The poverty line is defined as 60 per cent of the country's median equivalent household income; cf. Papatheodorou and Petmesidou (2006) p. 65.
13. Taking into account internal dynamics and external pressures in the run-up to the EMU, Ferrera and Gualmini (2004) explain the changes as an occasion for Italy 'to be rescued by Europe'.
14. For instance, according to legislation passed in the early 2000s, region-specific supplementary pension funds can be established.
15. On the basis of data offered by the Association of Employees in Social Protection Services, in 2005 roughly about two-thirds of pensioners (excluding peasants) received a pension equal to 500€ or less, to which a social assistance benefit of up to 149€ was added (http://www.popokp.gr/deltia_typou/syntakseis2005.html); the latter increased to 195 € in 2007.
16. A major reform of occupational pensions took place in 1993 in Italy, while in 2004 further tax incentives were provided particularly in the case where employees

transfer their annual contribution from the state severance pay fund (TRF) to an occupational pension fund.

17. Contributions Tax-Exempt (E), Investment Growth Tax-Exempt (E), Taxation of benefits (T).
18. In this section we refer to OECD data electronically accessed at http://www.oecd.org/statsportal/.
19. This share increased from 70 per cent in the late 1990s to 79 per cent in the early 2000s.
20. Namely, we observe very low activity rates, particularly for women and people aged between 55 and 64, comparatively high unemployment, mostly for women and the young, and alarmingly high long-term unemployment.
21. A National Evaluation Agency was created in Spain in 2007.
22. Non-contributory disability and retirement pensions are the responsibility of regional governments.
23. Also private insurance has grown from 3 per cent of total health expenditure in 1993 to 4.3 per cent in 2004 (OECD, 2006).
24. Similar trends characterize Italy as well (see Bifulco and Vitale, 2006 for significant differences in the regulatory mix concerning social care services in a northern and southern region of Italy).
25. For Greece we should also add the ethnic-Greek repatriates from the former Soviet Union and Albania.
26. In 2006 over 80 per cent of temporaries 'leased' by companies were young unemployed between 19 and 35 years of age, and over 50 per cent of such temporary recruitments were of one-month duration (data obtained by the Ministry of Labour).
27. The establishment of the National Council for Linking Vocational Education and Training to Employment, in 2005, is expected to contribute to this direction in the future.

5   Metamorphoses of Welfare States in Central and Eastern Europe

1. I would like to thank my colleague Magdalena Mouralová for her assistance in providing relevant information.
2. The only exception to this rule is the stagnation of this indicator for the male population in the Baltic States.
3. Corresponding figures are less than 2 per cent for the rest of the group.
4. In Slovakia the government decided to reduce the minimal provisions considerably at the beginning of 2003.
5. One has to bear in mind that the Czech state does not define social and health benefits as a taxable income. This fact complicates the comparison with other states.
6. The Czech Social Democratic Party was founded as early as 1878 and was able to survive in exile, during the period of Communist rule.
7. As my late colleague, the distinguished Czech sociologist Miroslav Purkrábek put it once: 'Czechs like to be liberals: with a state wind supporting their backs.'
8. Cerami (2005) suggests the emergence of a peculiar Eastern European model of solidarity coming from the fusion of pre-communist (Bismarck social insurance), communist (universalism, corporatism and egalitarianism) and post-communist (market-based schemes) characteristics. Aidukaite (2004) sees strong evidence in

favour of identifying a post-socialist regime type stemming from the territorial and political area of the Baltic States. However, most authors oppose this view. Rys (2001) believes that there is not a common tendency to converge welfare systems as they differ significantly according to the 'national' conditions. Ferge (2001) assures that there is no unique ideal-typical label to describe these countries. Sengoku (2006) has difficulties in classifying the welfare system of the CEEs as a single variant of the European welfare model. For Horibayashi (2006) and Keune (2006), the welfare system in Central Europe is still in the formation process and is too early to define its type.

6   The State of Japanese Welfare, Welfare and the Japanese State

1. This chapter is written from the background of a social anthropologist who stumbled into the study of social policy and social welfare.
2. See Korobtseva (2006) for a full account as to why this is so when so many other features of family life, especially divorce rates, have changed so dramatically in recent decades.
3. For a good description of the underlying logic behind the approval and introduction of for-profit players in the provision of welfare services as a means of increasing competition, efficiency and quality, see Izuhara (2003, p. 83).
4. There are many comparative accounts of welfare between Japan and Scandinavian countries in Japanese (for an overview of this literature, see Toivonen, 2007). For an account in English from the 1980s that represents the tone of this literature particularly well, see Gould (1993).

7   Politically Dominant but Socially Flawed: Projected Pension Levels for Citizens at Risk in Six European Multi-pillar Pension Systems

1. Up to an upper earnings limit of 2520 € in 2006; for occupational schemes a further lump sum of 1800 € has been added for 2007 (Bundesministerium für Arbeit und Soziales, 2007).
2. This was meant to be a temporary expedient up to 2008 but was extended by the Pensions minister Franz Müntefering in July 2007 in light of fears that the removal of this incentive would halt the development of occupational schemes.
3. Cf. Bridgen and Meyer, 2007a for a detailed discussion of this methodology.
4. A plausible level of wages for each biography was agreed between the research partners. They are illustrative rather than representative of actual wage levels in the six countries.
5. The Swiss second pillar has been calculated at the level guaranteed by the *Obligatorium* to reflect a general levelling down of occupational provision in Switzerland in recent years (Bertozzi and Bonoli, 2007).

8   The Changing Public–Private Mix in OECD Health-care Systems

1. Due to space limitations, the normative base of Figure 8.1 will not be explored.
2. Except for the financing dimension where the entire UK is implied, all developments referring to Great Britain (service provision and regulation) principally refer to England.

3. For a greater discussion of these ideal types and the selection of our empirical cases, see Rothgang (2006), Rothgang et al. (2006), and Wendt et al. (forthcoming).
4. We consider those 23 OECD countries that can be regarded as democracies with respect for the rule of law for the entire period between 1970 and 2004: Australia (AUS), Austria (AUT), Belgium (BEL), Germany (GER), Denmark (DEN), Finland (FIN), France (FRA), Greece (GRC), Ireland (IRL), Iceland (ICE), Italy (ITA), Japan (JAP), Canada (CAN), Luxembourg (LUX), the Netherlands (NLD), Norway (NOR), New Zealand (NZL), Portugal (POR), Sweden (SWE), Switzerland (CHE), Spain (ESP), United States (USA), United Kingdom (UK).
5. We cannot report all the graphs here. To give a brief overview, the public share continuously increases from 70 per cent to about 82 per cent in Japan, from 37 per cent to 45 per cent in the US and from 47 per cent to 59 per cent in Switzerland. Portugal's public financing share is volatile until the mid-1980s and then rises from roughly 50 per cent to 73 per cent. In the UK the state reduced its financing share from 92 per cent in 1975 to 80 per cent in 1996. By 2003 public health-care financing was back to 85 per cent of total spending. Ireland provides a similar picture with a reduction to about 70 per cent and an increase to almost 78 per cent by 2003 (Source: OECD, 2006b).
6. The classification of health care sectors can either follow functional rules or institutional rules. A functional classification highlights the kind of services that are provided. The institutional classification uses the unit and location of service provision as a means to distinguish health sectors. Since we are interested in the nature of service providers, we would prefer an institutional classification. However, comparable data over adequate time series is only available for the US. Therefore we chose a functional classification, which differentiates inpatient care, outpatient physician services, dental services and pharmaceuticals, as a substitute (OECD, 2006b). E.g., we estimate the size of the hospital sector using monetary resource flows to inpatient care. This method tends to underestimate the size of the hospital sector.
7. Since OECD (2002) data is inconsistent with respect to the classification of non-profit hospitals into the dichotomous public–private category, we use national data sources, WHO data (WHO, 2006) and will have to rely on secondary literature in order to assure that the share of public inpatient beds is by and large consistent across countries.
8. Hence, we focus on material changes as opposed to formal or functional categories. Here, formal change would refer to the legal form of hospital management. According to our classification, publicly-owned hospitals that have adopted private management structures are still considered public. Functional change covers the out-sourcing of functions which used to be met by public hospitals to the private sector (cf. Strehl, 2003).
9. However, the public–private classification of GPs is debatable, since GPs can only contract with the NHS and there is often little opportunity to choose private alternatives, which makes GPs under NHS conditions in a way similar to public employees.
10. The non-varying index of service provision in the Netherlands is mainly caused by a break in time series, which has led to a decrease of the inpatient financing share. There is no valid information on the 'true' changes of the weight of the inpatient sector. The share of public beds has increased from 11 per cent to 14 per cent in the years 1990 to 2001 (Henke and Schreyögg, 2005).
11. A similar observation has been termed *passive privatization* by Tuohy (2004, p. 367) referring to a shift towards more private financing as health-care sectors that are

predominantly financed privately grow faster than sectors dominated by public money. The term *implicit privatization* has also been used by Maarse (Maarse, 2004, p. 26) to describe the side-effects of policy decisions or effects of non-decisions, i.e. the incapacity or reluctance to react to health-care problems which triggers the emergence or expansion of private alternatives.

9   From Liberal Statism to Statish Liberalism: The Transformation of Unemployment Policies in Europe

1. Authors such as King (1999) and Standing (2001) have already highlighted the illiberal face of liberalization in unemployment policy. For a similar argument applied to public policy more broadly, see the collection edited by Levy (2006a).
2. This triad of financing, regulation and content is intended as a synthesis between the 'mixed economy of welfare' framework (financing, regulation and provision) used elsewhere in this volume and the four institutional variables (mode of access, benefit structure, financing and governance) commonly referred to in the cross-national analysis of income maintenance programmes (cf. Ferrera, 1996; Bonoli and Palier, 1998).
3. Proportion of unemployed individuals receiving unemployment benefits.
4. In January 2008 the French government however passed a law merging the public employment service and the unemployment insurance system at delivery level. At the time of writing (May 2008), the extent to which this reform will undermine the autonomy of the social partners in unemployment insurance policy is unclear.

10   The Transformation of Incapacity Benefits

1. Parts of this chapter draw on my contributions to Kemp et al. (2006). I would like to thank Daniel Clegg and Martin Seeleib-Kaiser for very helpful comments on the first draft.
2. An additional incentive to claim incapacity benefit may be that it is often paid indefinitely whereas unemployment insurance is generally time-limited.
3. The Netherlands has been an important exception since 1967 when industrial injury and incapacity benefits were combined (de Vos, 2007).
4. This contrasts with short-term sickness benefits, which in some welfare states – including Britain, the Netherlands and the US – are provided as sick pay by employers.
5. However, as discussed later in the chapter, incapacity benefits were partially privatized in the Netherlands in 2006 as part of an attempt to tackle moral hazard problems that were thought to account for the high rate of claims in that country.
6. Given the very low exit rates from incapacity benefits (OECD, 2003) the increase in younger claimants may be one of the reasons why benefit durations have risen in many countries; and this in turn may be one of the factors behind the growth in caseloads.
7. This reinforces the argument made by Iversen (2005) that welfare states can help to improve the operation of markets and not just undermine them.
8. The desire among a growing number of advanced welfare states for a work-focused cultural shift in incapacity benefits involves an implicit acceptance of the social model of disability.

11 The 'Public' and 'Private' of Work–Family Reconciliation: Unsettling Gendered Notions and Assumptions

1. We are grateful to Adam Whitworth for contributions to earlier drafts.
2. These interim targets were not reached in some EU member states, nor in the EU as a whole (Eurostat 2005).
3. Child-care targets set at the Barcelona summit (2002) aim to provide by 2010 child-care to at least 90 per cent of children between three and mandatory school age and at least 33 per cent of children under three.
4. In a rather tense set of contradictions, New Right policies also promoted a specific imagery of 'the family' as consisting of a married, heterosexual couple with dependent children who were able to operate as a self-supporting and self-sufficient unit. See Abbott and Wallace (1992) or George and Wilding (1994) for discussions of these contradictions.
5. See for example www.employersforwork–lifebalance.org.uk; www.dti.gov.uk (or the new Department of Business, Enterprise and Regulatory Reform, which has now replaced this at www.berr.gov.uk).
6. Germany has recently introduced new regulations in terms of parental leave pay. Under these regulations parental pay is paid to mothers or fathers for a maximum of 14 months with a maximum of 12 months for one parent unless they are a lone parent. This, in effect, results in a proportion of paid parental leave and pay that is reserved for the father for couples living in a heterosexual relationship. But as these new regulations only came into force in 2007 levels of take up among such fathers are currently unknown.
7. The right to request was extended in April 2007 to allow carers of adults the right to request flexible working. There are increasing calls to extend the right to request further; for example, the Children's Minister, Beverley Hughes MP, has called for the right to be extended to all employees (Hughes and Cooke, 2007).

13 Multiple and Multi-Dimensional Welfare State Transformations

1. Exceptions are Portugal, which has seen a significant decline by four percentage points, and Poland, which has witnessed an increase of five percentage points during the past decade.

Bibliography

Aarts, L.J.M., Burkhauser, R.V. and de Jong, P.R. (eds) (1996) *Curing the Dutch Disease: An International Perspective on Disability Policy Reform* (Aldershot: Avebury).

Aarts, L.J.M. and de Jong, P.R. (2003) 'The Dutch Disability Experience' In C. Prinz (ed.) *European Disability Pension Policies* (Aldershot: Ashgate), pp. 253–76.

Abbott, P. and Wallace, C. (1992) *Family and the New Right* (London: Pluto).

Adema, W. (2001) 'Net Social Expenditure. 2nd Edition', *OECD Labour Market and Social Policy Occasional Papers*, No. 52 (Paris: OECD).

Adema, W. and Ladaique, M. (2005) 'Net Social Expenditure. 2005 Edition. More Comprehensive Measures of Social Support', *OECD Social, Employment and Migration Working Papers*, No. 29 (Paris: OECD).

Adào e Silva, P. (2003) 'Putting the Portuguese Welfare System in Context' In F. Monteiro, J. Tavares, M. Glatzer and A. Cardoso (eds) *Portugal: Strategic Options in a European Context* (Boston, MA: Lexington Books).

Aidukaite, J. (2004) *The Emergence of the Post-Socialist Welfare State* (Stockholm: Södertörns Högskola).

AIHW (various issues) *Australia's Health* (Canberra: Australian Institute of Health and Welfare).

Alber, J. (1992) *Das Gesundheitswesen der Bundesrepublik Deutschland. Entwicklung, Struktur und Funktionsweise* (Frankfurt a. M.: Campus).

Alber, J. (2003) 'Health, Care, and Access to Services', First Draft of a Report. (Berlin: Wissenschaftszentrum für Sozialforschung).

Alcock, P., Beatty, C., Fothergill, S., Macmillan, R. and Yeandle, S. (2003) *Work to Welfare: How Men Become Detached from the Labour Market* (Cambridge: Cambridge University Press).

Aldred, R. (2007) *Governing 'local health economies': The case of NHS Local Improvement Finance Trust (LIFT)*. PhD thesis (London: Goldmsiths College, University of London).

Andersen, J.G. (1993) *Politik og samfund i forandring* (Copenhagen: Columbus).

Andersen, J.G. (1996) 'Marginalisation, Citizenship and the Economy: The Capacity of the Universalist Welfare State in Denmark' In E.O. Eriksen and J. Loftager (eds), *The Rationality of the Welfare State* (Oslo: Scandinavian University Press), pp.155–202.

Andersen, J.G. (1997) 'Beyond Retrenchment: Welfare Policies in Denmark in the 1990s', Paper prepared for the ECPR Round Table on 'The Survival of the Welfare State'. Bergen, Sept.18–21, 1997. *Working Paper* (Aalborg: Department of Economics, Politics and Public Administration, Aalborg University).

Andersen, J.G. (2000) 'Welfare Crisis and Beyond' In S. Kuhnle (ed.), *Survival of the European Welfare State* (London: Routledge), pp. 69–87.

Andersen, J.G. (2002a) 'Work and Citizenship: Unemployment and Unemployment Policies in Denmark, 1980–2000' In J.G. Andersen and P.H. Jensen (eds), *Changing Labour Markets, Welfare Policies and Citizenship* (Bristol: Policy Press), pp. 59–84.

Andersen, J.G. (2002b) 'Denmark: From the Edge of the Abyss to a Sustainable Welfare State' In J.G. Andersen, J. Clasen, W. van Oorschot and K. Halvorsen, *Europe's New State of Welfare. Unemployment, Employment Policies and Citizenship* (Bristol: Policy Press), pp. 143–62.

Andersen, J.G. (2002c) 'De-standardisation of the Life Course in the Context of a Scandinavian Welfare Model: The Case of Denmark', Paper Presented at the

International Seminar: Recomposing the Stages in the Life Course. Paris, Maison des Sciences de l'Homme, 5–6 June, 2002.

Andersen, J.G. (2002d) 'Velfærd uden skatter. Det danske velfærdsmirakel i 1990'erne', *Politica*, 34(1), 5–23.

Andersen, J.G. (2003) 'Farligt farvand: Vælgernes holdninger til velfærdspolitik og skatter' In J.G. Andersen and O. Borre (eds), *Politisk forandring. Værdipolitik og nye skillelinjer ved folketingsvalget 2001* (Aarhus: Systime), pp. 293–314.

Andersen, J.G. (2004) 'Pensionsbomber og pensionsreformer. Danmark som rolle-model', *Social Kritik*, 94, 24–45.

Andersen, J.G. (2005) 'Ambiguity of Welfare State Change. Discourse, Institutions, Output and Outcomes', Paper prepared for ESPAnet Conference, Fribourg, 22–24 Sept., 2005.

Andersen, J.G. (2007a). 'Conceptualizing Welfare State Change', Paper prepared for the ECPR Conference, Pisa, 6–8 Sept., 2007.

Andersen, J.G. (2007b) 'Public Support for the Danish Welfare State. Interests and Values, Institutions and Performance' In E. Albæk, L. Eliason, A.S. Nørgaard and H. Schwartz (eds), *Crisis, Miracles and Beyond: Negotiated Adaptation of the Danish Welfare State* (Aarhus: Aarhus University Press).

Andersen, J.G. (2007c) *Ældrepolitikken og velfærdsstatens økonomiske udfordringer. Tilbagetrækning, pension og ældreservice i Danmark.* CCWS Working Paper No. 47.

Andersen, J.G. (2007d) 'Restricting Access to Social Protection for Immigrants in the Danish Welfare State', *Benefits*, 15(3), 257–70.

Andersen, J.G. and Borre, O. (eds) (2003) *Politisk forandring. Værdipolitik og nye skillelinjer ved folketingsvalget 2001* (Aarhus: Systime).

Andersen, J.G. and Christiansen, P.M. (1991) *Skatter uden velfærd* (Copenhagen: DJØF Forlag).

Andersen, J.G. and Hoff, J. (2001) *Democracy and Citizenship in Scandinavia* (Basingstoke: Palgrave).

Andersen, J.G. and Johansen, B.H. (2006) 'Welfare Regimes and De-standardisation of the Life Course: The Case of Denmark'. Paper presented at international conference on *Welfare State Change: Conceptualisation, Measurement and Interpretation*, St. Restrup, Denmark, 13–15 January, 2006.

Andersen, J.G. and Kongshøj, K. (2007) 'Privatisation of Social Risk: From State Financing to Member Financing of Unemployment Benefits in Denmark and Sweden', CCWS Working Paper (in press).

Andersen, J.G. and Larsen, C.A. (2002) 'Pension Politics and Policy in Denmark and Sweden: Path Dependencies, Policy Style, and Political Outcome'. Paper Presented at XV World Congress of Sociology, Brisbane, 7–13 July, 2002.

Andersen, J.G. and Pedersen, J.J. (2007) 'Continuity and Change in Danish Active Labour Market Policy: 1990–2006. The Battlefield between Activation and Workfare', CCWS Working Paper.

Andersen, J.G. and Rossteutscher, S. (2007) 'Small-scale Democracy. Citizen Power in the Domains of Everyday Life' In J.W. van Deth, J.R. Montero and A. Westholm (eds), *Citizenship and Involvement in European Democracies: A Comparative Analysis* (London: Routledge), pp. 221–54.

Andersen, J.G., Halvorsen, K. and Ervasti, H. (eds) (2007) Unemployment and Citizenship in the Nordic Countries. Unpublished book manuscript.

Anderson, K.M. (2004) 'Pension Politics in Three Small States: Denmark, Sweden and the Netherlands', *Canadian Journal of Sociology*, 29(2), 289–312.

Anderson, K.M. (2007) 'The Netherlands: Political Competition in Proportional System' In K. Anderson, E. Immergut and I. Schulze (eds), *The Handbook of West European Pension Politics* (Oxford: Oxford University Press), pp. 713–57.

Anessi-Pessina, E., Cantu, E. and Jommi, C. (2004) 'Phasing Out Market Mechanisms in the Italian National Health System', *Public Money & Management*, 24(5), 309–16.

Arber, S. (1989) 'Class and the Elderly', *Social Studies Review*, 4(3), 90–5.

Ascoli, U. and Ranci, C. (2002) *Dilemmas of the Welfare Mix. The New Structure of Welfare in an Era of Privatization* (New York: Kluwer).

Association of British Insurers (2004) *European Pension Reform and Private Pensions* (London: ABI).

Association of Greek Insurance Companies (2006) *Private Insurance in Greece. 2005 Report.* (AGIC: Athens) (in Greek).

Atkinson, A.B., Cantillon, B., Marlier, E. and Nolan, B. (2005) *Taking Forward the EU Social Inclusion Process.* An Independent Report commissioned by the Luxemburg Presidency of the Council of the European Union. (Luxembourg. Available at: http://www.ceps.lu/eu2005_lu/report/final_report.pdf).

Autor, D.H. and Duggan, M.G. (2003) 'The Rise in the Disability Rolls and the Decline in Unemployment', *Quarterly Journal of Economics*, 118(1), 157–205.

Baggott, R. (2004) *Health and Health Care in Britain* (Basingstroke: Palgrave Macmillan).

Baldwin, P. (1990) *The Politics of Social Solidarity. Class Bases of the European Welfare State 1875–1975* (Cambridge: Cambridge University Press).

Bannink, D. and de Vroom, B. (2007) 'The Dutch Pension System and Social Inclusion' In T. Meyer, P. Bridgen and B. Riedmüller (eds), *Private Pensions versus Social Inclusion? Non-state Provision for Citizens at Risk in Europe* (Cheltenham, UK and Northampton, US: Edward Elgar).

Barbier, J.-C. (2004) 'Systems of Social Protection in Europe: Two Contrasted Paths to Activation, and Maybe a Third' In J. Lind, H. Knudsen and H. Jørgensen (eds), *Labour and Employment Regulation in Europe* (Brussels: Peter Lang), pp. 233–54.

Barbier, J.-C. and Ludwig-Mayerhofer W. (2004) 'Introduction: The Many Worlds of Activation', *European Societies*, 6(4), 423–36.

Barr, N. (1998) *The Economics of the Welfare State,* 3rd edition (Oxford: Oxford University Press).

Barr, N. (2001) *The Welfare State as Piggy Bank. Information, Risk, Uncertainty, and the Role of the State* (Oxford: Oxford University Press).

Beatty, C. and Fothergill, S. (1996) 'Labour Market Adjustment in Areas of Chronic Industrial Decline: the Case of the UK Coalfields', *Regional Studies*, 34(7), 627–40.

Ben-Ari, E. (1991) *Changing Japanese Suburbia: A Study of Two Present-Day Localities* (London: Kegan Paul International).

Benio, M. and Ratajczak-Tuchołka, J. (2007) 'The Polish Pension System and Social Inclusion' In T. Meyer, P. Bridgen and B. Riedmüller (eds), *Private Pensions versus Social Inclusion? Non-state Provision for Citizens at Risk in Europe* (Cheltenham, UK and Northampton, US: Edward Elgar).

Bentzon, K.-H. (ed.) (1988) *Fra vækst til omstilling – moderniseringen af den offentlige sektor* (Copenhagen: Nyt fra Samfundsvidenskaberne).

Bertozzi, F. and Bonoli, G. (2007) 'The Swiss Pension System and Social Inclusion' In T. Meyer, P. Bridgen and B. Riedmüller (eds), *Private Pensions versus Social Inclusion? Non-state Provision for Citizens at Risk in Europe* (Cheltenham, UK and Northampton, US: Edward Elgar).

Bestor, V.L. (2002) 'Toward a Cultural Biography of Civil Society in Japan' In R. Goodman (ed.), *Family and Social Policy in Japan: Anthropological Approaches* (Cambridge: Cambridge University Press).

Bettio, F., Simonazzi, A. and Villa, P. (2006) 'Change in Care Regimes and Female Migration: the "Care Drain" in the Mediterranean', *Journal of European Social Policy*, 16(3), 271–85.

Bifulco, L. and Vitale, T. (2006) 'Contracting for Welfare Services in Italy', *Journal of Social Policy*, 35(3), 495–513.

Bleses, P. and Seeleib-Kaiser, M. (2004) *The Dual Transformation of the German Welfare State* (Basingstoke and New York: Palgrave Macmillan).

Bloch, F. S. and Prins, R. (eds) (2001) *Who Returns to Work and Why? A Six-country Study on Work Incapacity and Reintegration* (Somerset, US: Transaction Publishers).

Blomqvist, P. (2004) 'The Choice Revolution: Privatization of Swedish Welfare Services in the 1990s', *Social Policy & Administration*, 38(2), 139–55.

Blomqvist, P. and Rothstein, B. (2000) *Välfärdsstaten nya ansikte. Demokrati och marknadsreformer inom den offentliga sektorn* (Stockholm: Agora).

Böckerman, P. and Uusitalo, R. (2006) 'Erosion of the Ghent System and Union Membership Decline: Lessons from Finland', *British Journal of Industrial Relations*, 44(2), 283–303.

Bode, I. (2006) 'Disorganized Welfare Mixes: Voluntary Agencies and New Governance Regimes in Western Europe', *Journal of European Social Policy*, 16(4), 346–59.

Bode, I. (2005) 'Einbettung und Kontingenz. Wohlfahrtsmärkte und ihre Effekte im Spiegel der neueren Wirtschaftssoziologie', *Zeitschrift fur Soziologie*, 34, 250–269.

Boekraad, B. (1998) 'Un modèle de polder en pleine evolution: histoire recente et reorganisation de la sécurité sociale aux Pays-bas', *Revue Belge de Sécurité Sociale*, 40(4), 723–67.

Bolanowski, W. (2007) 'Organizational Attachment of Interns in Poland to Healthcare System', *International Journal of Occupational Medicine and Environmental Health*, 20(3), 281–5.

Bolderson, H. (1986) 'The State at One Remove: Examples of Agency Arrangements and Regulatory Powers in Social Policy', *Policy and Politics*, 13(1), 17–36.

Boling, P. (1998) 'Family Policy in Japan', *Journal of Social Policy*, 27(2), 173–90.

Bonoli, G. (2003) 'Two Worlds of Pension Reform in Western Europe', *Comparative Politics*, 35(4), 399–416.

Bonoli, G. (2006) 'New Social Risks and the Politics of Post-industrial Social Policies' In K. Armingeon and G. Bonoli (eds), *The Politics of Post-Industrial Welfare States* (London: Routledge).

Bonoli, G. and Palier, B. (1998) 'Changing the Politics of Social Programmes: Innovative Change in British and French Welfare Reforms', *Journal of European Social Policy*, 8(4), 317–30.

Borchorst, A. (2006) 'The Public–Private Split Rearticulated: Abolishment of the Danish Daddy Leave' In A.L. Ellingsaeter and A. Leira (eds), *Politicising Parenthood in Scandinavia: Gender Relations in Welfare States* (Bristol: Policy Press), pp. 101–20.

Borghi, V. and van Berkel, R. (2007) 'New Modes of Governance in Italy and the Netherlands: the Case of Activation Policies', *Public Administration*, 85(1), 83–101.

Bound, J. and Burkhauser, R.V. (1999) 'Economic Analysis of Transfer Programs Targeted on People with Disabilities' In O. Ashenfelter and D. Card (eds), *Handbook of Labor Economics*. Volume 3C (Amsterdam: Elsevier).

Brady, D., Beckfield, J. and Seeleib-Kaiser, M. (2005) 'Economic Globalization and the Welfare State in Affluent Democracies, 1975–2001', *American Sociological Review*, 70, 921–48.

Brandth, B. and Kvande, E. (2001) 'Flexible Work and Flexible Fathers', *Work, Employment and Society*, 15(2), 251–67.

Brandth, B. and Kvande, E. (2002) 'Reflexive Fathers: Negotiating Parental Leave and Working Life', *Gender, Work and Organization*, 9(2), 186–203.

Brannen, J. and Moss, P. (1998) 'The Polarisations and Intensifications of Parental Employment: Consequences for Children, Families and the Community', *Community, Work and Family*, 1(3), 229–47.

Bratberg, E., Dahld, S.-A. and Risa, A.E. (2002) 'The Double Burden: Do Combinations of Career and Family Obligations Increase Sickness Absence among Women?', *European Sociological Review*, 18, 233–49.

Bredgaard, T., Larsen, F. and Møller, L.R. (2005) 'Contracting out the Public Employment Service in Denmark: A Quasi-market Analysis' In T. Bredgaard and F. Larsen (eds), *Employment Policy from Different Angles* (Copenhagen: DJØF Forlag), pp. 211–33.

Bredgaard, T. and Larsen, F. (2006) *Udliciteringen af beskæftigelsespolitikken — Australien, Holland og Danmark* (Copenhagen: DJØF Forlag).

Bredgaard, T. and Larsen, F. (2007) 'Implementing Public Employment Policy: What Happens when Non-public Agencies Take Over?' *International Journal of Sociology and Social Policy*, 27(7/8), 287–300.

Bridgen, P. and Meyer, T. (2007a) 'The British Pension System and Social Inclusion' In T. Meyer, P. Bridgen and B. Riedmüller (eds), *Private Pensions versus Social Inclusion? Non-state Provision for Citizens at Risk in Europe* (Cheltenham, UK and Northampton, US: Edward Elgar).

Bridgen, P. and Meyer, T. (2007b) 'Private Pensions versus Social Inclusion? Three Patterns of Provision and their Impact on Citizens at Risk' In T. Meyer, P. Bridgen and B. Riedmüller (eds), *Private Pensions versus Social Inclusion? Non-state Provision for Citizens at Risk in Europe* (Cheltenham, UK and Northampton, US: Edward Elgar).

Bruckenberger, E., Klaue, S. and Schwintowski H.-P. (2006) *Krankenhausmärkte zwischen Regulierung und Wettbewerb* (Berlin: Springer-Verlag).

Brunsdon, E. and May, M. (2007) 'Occupational Welfare' In M. Powell (ed.), *Understanding the Mixed Economy of Welfare* (Bristol: Policy Press), pp. 149–76.

Brunsson, N. and Olsen, J.P. (1993) *The Reforming Organization* (London: Routledge).

Bundesen, P. and Henriksen, L.S. (2001) *Filantropi, selvhjælp og interesseorganisering: Frivillige organisationer i dansk socialpolitik 1849–1990'erne* (Odense: Odense Universitetsforlag).

Bundesamt für Statistik (2001) *Rechtlich-wirtschaftlicher Status der Betriebe. Statistik der stationären Betriebe des Gesundheitswesens* (Neuchâtel: Bundesamt für Statistik der Schweiz).

Bundesministerium für Arbeit und Soziales (2007) 'Rente – Zusätzliche Altersvorsorge – Staatliche Förderung der betrieblichen Altersversorgung', http://www.bmas.bund. de/BMAS/Navigation/Rente/Zusaetzliche-Altersvorsorge/Betriebliche-Altersvorsorge/ staatliche-foerderung.html; accessed 4 April 2007.

Bundesministerium für Wirtschaft und Arbeit (2007) 'Tarifvertragliche Arbeitsbedingungen im Jahr 2004', http://www.bmas.bund.de/BMAS/Redaktion/ Pdf/tarifvertragliche-arbeitsbedingungen-2004; accessed 4 April 2007.

Burchardt, T. (1997) 'Boundaries between Public and Private Welfare: A Typology and Map of Services', *CASEpaper* 2, (London: LSE).

Burchardt, T. and Hills, J. (1999) 'Public Expenditure and the Public/Private Mix' In M. Powell (ed.), *New Labour, New Welfare State?* (Bristol: Policy Press), pp. 29–49.

Burke, T.F. (1997) 'On the Rights Track: The Americans with Disabilities Act' In P.S. Nivola (ed.), *Comparative Disadvantages? Social Regulations and the Global Economy* (Washington, D.C.: Brookings Institution), pp. 242–318.

Burkhauser, R.V. and Daly, M.C. (2002) 'Policy Watch: U.S. Disability Policy in a Changing Environment', *Journal of Economic Perspectives*, 16(1), 213–24.

Cabiedes, L. and Guillén, A. (2001) 'Adopting and Adapting Managed Competition: Health Care Reform in Southern Europe', *Social Science & Medicine*, 52, 1205–17.

Cacace, M. (2007) 'The Changing Public/Private Mix in the American Health Care System', *TranState Working Paper*, No. 58, (Bremen: TranState Research Center).

Cacace, M. (forthcoming) 'The Coexistence of Market and Hierarchy in the US Health-care System' In H. Rothgang, M. Cacace, S. Grimmeisen, U. Helmert and C. Wendt *The Changing Role of the State in OECD Health Care Systems. From Heterogeneity to Homogeneity?* (Basingstoke: Palgrave Macmillan).

Campbell, J.C. (2002) 'Japanese Social Policy in Comparative Perspective', *World Bank Institute Working Papers*.

Campbell, J.C. and Ikegami, N. (2003) 'Japan's Radical Reform of Long-Term Care', *Social Policy and Administration*, 37(1), 21–34.

CANSTAT (2004) *Statistical Bulletin 2003/4* (Praha: Český statistický úřad).

Capano, G. (2003) 'Administrative Traditions and Policy Change: When Policy Paradigms Matter. The Case of Italian Administrative Reform during the 1990s', *Public Administration*, 81(4), 781–801.

Carcillo, S. and Grubb, D. (2006) 'From Inactivity to Work: The Role of Active Labour Market Policies', *OECD Social, Employment and Migration Working Papers*, No. 36 (Paris: OECD).

Carvel, J. (2006) 'Fathers fail to make full use of paternity leave, survey finds' *The Guardian*, 1.8.06, www.guardian.co.uk.

Castel, R. (1995) *Les métamorphoses de la question sociale: une chronique du salariat* (Paris: Fayard).

Castellino, O. and Fornero, E. (2000) 'Il TFR: una coperta troppo stretta', *Rivista di Politica Economica*, 90(9).

Castells, M. and Himenan, P. (2002) *The Information Society and the Welfare State: The Finnish Model* (Oxford: Oxford University Press).

Castles, F. (2004) *The Future of the Welfare State* (Oxford: Oxford University Press).

Castles, F.G. and Obinger, H. (2006) 'Towards More Comprehensive Measures of Social Support: Adding in the Impact of Taxes and Private Spending or Netting Out the Impact of Politics on Redistribution?', *ZeS-Arbeitspapier*, Nr. 04/2006 (Bremen: Centre for Social Policy Research, University of Bremen).

Cavounidis, J. (2006) 'Migration and Policy Trends' In M. Petmesidou and E. Mossialos (eds), *Social Policy Developments in Greece* (Aldershot: Ashgate).

CBI (2006) *CBI Submission to the Department of Work and Pensions. Responding to the Pensions Commission Final Report* (London: Confederation of British Industry).

Cerami, A. (2005) Social Policy in Central and Eastern Europe. Emergence of a New European Model of Solidarity?. PhD Dissertation, (Erfurt: Universität Erfurt).

CES, Consejo Económico y social, 1994–2006, yearly publication: *España 1993–2005. Economía, trabajo y sociedad. Memoria sobre la situación socioeconómica y laboral.* (Madrid: CES).

CES (May 2005) 'Una década de Empresas de Trabajo Temporal', *Observatorio de Relaciones Industriales*, no. 81 (Madrid: Consejo Económico y Social).

CES (June–July 2006) 'Acuerdo para la mejor del crecimiento y del empleo', *Observatorio de Relaciones Industriales*, No. 92 (Madrid: Consejo Económico y Social).

CES (2006) 'Acuerdo sobre medidas en materia de Seguridad Social', *Observatorio de Relaciones Industriales*, no. 93, August–September (Madrid: Consejo Económico y Social).

Chatterjee, P. (2003) *The Politics of the Governed* (New York: Columbia University Press).

Chorney, H. (1996) 'Debits, Deficits and Full Employment' In R. Boyer and D. Drache (eds) *States Against Markets – The Limits of Globalization* (London and New York: Routledge), pp. 357–79.

Christensen, J.G. (1991) *Den usynlige stat* (Copenhagen: Gyldendal).

Christensen, A.M. (2007) '300 timers reglen – hvordan virker den? Effekter af stærke økonomiske incitamenter på de ledige – og på systemet', CCWS Working Paper no. 52, 2007.

Christiansen, P.M. (1998) 'A Prescription Rejected: Market Solutions to Problems of Public Sector Governance', *Governance*, 11(2), 179–202.

Chulià, E. (2006) 'Spain: Incremental Changes in the Public Pension System and Reinforcement of Supplementary Private Pensions' In K.M. Anderson, E. Immergut and I. Schulze (eds), *Oxford Handbook of West European Pension Policies* (Oxford: Oxford University Press).

Clark, G. (2003a) *European Pensions and Global Finance* (Oxford: Oxford University Press).

Clark, G. (2003b) 'Twenty-first Century Pension (In-)security' In G. Clark and N. Whiteside (eds), *Pension Security in the 21st Century* (Oxford: Oxford University Press), pp. 225–49.

Clark, G. (2006) 'The UK Occupational Pension System in Crisis' In H. Pemberton, P. Thane and N. Whiteside (eds), *Britain's Pension Crisis: History and Policy* (Oxford: Oxford University Press), pp. 145–68.

Clark, G., Munnell, A. and Orszag, M. (2007) 'Pensions and Retirement Income in a Global Environment' In G. Clark, A. Munnell and M. Orszag (eds), *The Oxford Handbook of Pensions and Retirement Income* (Oxford: Oxford University Press), pp. 10–28.

Clarke, J. (2004) *Changing Welfare, Changing States: New Directions in Social Policy* (London: Sage).

Clarke, J. (2005) 'Welfare States as Nation States: Some Conceptual Reflections', *Social Policy and Society*, 4(4), 407–15.

Clarke, J. (2006) 'Disorganizzare Il Publicco?', *La Rivista delle Politiche Sociali*, no. 2 (April–June).

Clarke, J. (forthcoming a) 'Introduction: Governing the Social', *Cultural Studies* (special issue on Governing the Social).

Clarke, J. (forthcoming b) 'Governance Puzzles' In L. Budd and L. Harris (eds), *eGovernance: Managing or Governing?* (London: Routledge).

Clarke, J. and Fink, J. (forthcoming) 'Unsettled Attachments: National Identity, Citizenship and Welfare' In M. Opielka, B. Pfau-Effinger and W. van Oorschot (eds), *Culture and Welfare State* (Cheltenham: Edward Elgar).

Clarke, J. and Newman, J. (2004) 'Governing in the Modern World?' In D.L. Steinberg and R. Johnson (eds), *Blairism and the War of Persuasion: Labour's Passive Revolution* (London: Lawrence and Wishart), 53–65.

Clarke, J., Newman, J., Smith, N., Vidler, E. and Westmarland, L. (2007) *Creating Citizen-Consumers: Changing Publics and Changing Public Services* (London: Sage).

Clasen, J. (2001) 'Social Insurance and the Contributory Principle: a Paradox in Contemporary British Social Policy', *Social Policy and Administration*, 35(6), 641–57.

Clasen, J. (2004) 'From Unemployment to Worklessness; The Transformation of British Unemployment Policy', Unpublished manuscript.

Clasen, J. (2005) *Reforming European Welfare States: Germany and the United Kingdom Compared* (Oxford: Oxford University Press).

Clasen, J. and Clegg, D. (2006) 'Beyond Activation: Reforming European Unemployment Protection Systems in Post-industrial Labour Markets', *European Societies*, 8(4), 527–53.

Clasen, J. and Siegel, N. (2007) *Exploring the Dynamics of Reform. The Dependent Variable Problem in Comparative Welfare State Analysis* (Cheltenham: Edward Elgar).

Clasen, J., Duncan, G., Eardley, T., Evans, M., Ughetto, P., van Oorschot, W. and Wright, S. (2001) 'Towards "Single Gateways"? A Cross-national Review of the Changing Roles of Employment Offices in Seven Countries', *Zeitschrift für ausländisches und internationales Sozialrecht*, 15(1), 43–63.

Clayton, R. and Pontusson, J. (1998) 'Welfare-State Retrenchment Revisited: Entitlement Cuts, Public Sector Restructuring, and Inegalitarian Trends in Advanced Capitalist Societies', *World Politics*, 51(1), 67–98.

Clegg, D. (2007) 'Continental Drift: On Unemployment Policy Change in Bismarckian Welfare States', *Social Policy and Administration*, 41(6), 597–617.

Cochrane, A. (2006) *Understanding Urban Policy* (Oxford: Blackwell).

Colombo, F. and Tapay, N. (2004) *Private Health Insurance in OECD Countries: The Benefits and Costs for Individuals and Health Systems* (Paris: OECD).

Coote, A., Harman, H. and Hewitt, P. (1990) *The Family Way: A New Approach to Policy Making* (London, IPPR).

Coughlin, R. (1980) *Ideology, Public Opinion and Welfare Policy: Attitudes Towards Taxes and Spending in Industrialised Countries* (Berkeley: University of California Press).

Crompton, R. (2006) *Employment and the Family. The Reconfiguration of Work and Family Life in Contemporary Societies* (Cambridge: Cambridge University Press).

Crompton, R., Lewis, S. and Lyonette, C. (2007) *Women, Men, Work and Family in Europe* (Basingstoke: Palgrave Macmillan).

Cutler, T. and Waine, B. (2001) 'Social Insecurity and the Retreat from Social Democracy: Occupational Welfare in the Long Boom and Financialisation', *Review of International Political Economy*, 18(1), 96–118.

Dahlberg, L. (2005) 'Interaction between Voluntary and Statutory Social Service Provision in Sweden: A Matter of Welfare Pluralism, Substitution or Complementarity?', *Social Policy & Administration*, 39(7), 740–63.

Daly, M. (2000) *The Gender Division of Welfare* (Cambridge: Cambridge University Press).

Daly M. and Rake K. (2003) *Gender and the Welfare State: Care, Work and Welfare in Europe and the USA* (Cambridge: Polity Press).

Daniel, C. (2001) 'Les politiques sociales françaises face au chômage' In C. Daniel and B. Palier (eds), *La protection sociale en Europe: le temps des réformes* (Paris: La Documentation Française), pp. 141–9.

Daniel C. and Tuchszirer C. (1999) *L'État face aux chômeurs. L'indemnisation du chômage de 1884 à nos jours* (Paris: Flammarion).

Davaki, K. and Mossialos, E. (2006) 'Financing and Delivering Health Care' In M. Petmesidou and E. Mossialos (eds), *Social Policy Developments in Greece* (Aldershot: Ashgate).

Day Sclater, S., Bainham, A. and Richards, M. (1999) 'Introduction' In A. Bainham, S. Day Sclater and M. Richards (eds), *What is a Parent? A Socio-Legal Analysis* (Oxford: Hart Publishing), pp. 1–22.

Deacon, B. (1993) 'Developments in East European Social Policy' In C. Jones (ed.), *New Perspectives on the Welfare State in Europe* (London and New York: Routledge), pp. 177–97.

De Jong, P.R. (2003) 'Disability and Disability Insurance' In C. Prinz (ed.) *European Disability Pension Policies* (Aldershot: Ashgate), pp. 77–106.

De Lathouwer, L. (2004) 'Reforming Policies and Institutions in Unemployment Protection in Belgium', Unpublished manuscript.

Department of Health (2006) 'Expenditure on In-patient and Out-patient Services by NHS Organisations in England', e-mail correspondence, 13 October.

De Swaan, A. (1988) *In Care of the State: Health Care, Education and Welfare in Europe and the USA in the Modern Era* (Cambridge: Polity).

De Vos, E.L. (2006) 'New Initiatives to Privatise Social Security in the Netherlands' In H. Emanuel (ed.), *Ageing and the Labour Market: Issues and Solutions* (Antwerp: Intersentia).

DfES (2000) *Creating a Work–Life Balance: A Good Practice Guide for Employers* (DfES: London).

DH (1988) *Community Care: An Agenda for Action.* Griffiths Two (London: HMSO).

DH (2000) *The NHS Plan* (London: HMSO).

DHSS (1981) *Growing Older* (London: HMSO).

Djelic, M.-L. and Sahlin-Andersson, K. (eds) (2006) *Transnational Governance: Institutional Dynamics of Regulation* (Cambridge: Cambridge University Press).

DoE (1987) *Housing: The Government's Proposals* (London: HMSO), Cm 214.

Döhler, M. and Manow-Borgwardt, P. (1992) 'Korporatisierung als gesundheitspolitische Strategie', *Staatswissenschaften und Staatspraxis*, 3, 64–106.

Drakeford, M. (2000) *Privatisation and Social Policy* (Harlow: Pearson).

DSS (1998) *New Ambitions for Our Country* (London: HMSO).

DTI (2004) *What is Work–Life Balance?*, DTI, www.dti.gov.uk (accessed March 2005).

Dufour, P., Boismenu, G. and Noel, A. (2003) *L'aide au conditionnel: La contrepartie dans les mesures envers les personnes sans emploi en Europe et en Amérique du Nord* (Brussels: P.I.E.-Peter Lang).

Duncan, S., Edwards, R., et al. (2003) 'Motherhood, Paid Work and Partnering', *Work, Employment and Society*, 17(2), 309–30.

DWP (2004) *Income Related Benefits Estimates of Take-up in 2000/2001* (London: Department for Work and Pensions).

DWP (2006) *A New Deal for Welfare: Empowering People to Work* (London: The Stationery Office).

DWP (2008) 'Job Seekers' Allowance Claimants: Time Series by Type of JSA', http://83.244.183.180/5pc/jsa_prim/ccdate/ccstatu/a_stock_r_ccdate_c_ccstatu.html, consulted 30 April 2008.

Ebbinghaus, B. (2006) *Reforming Early Retirement in Europe, Japan and the USA* (Oxford: Oxford University Press).

Eichorst, W. (2007) 'The Gradual Transformation of Continental European Labour Markets: France and Germany Compared', *IZA Working Paper,* No. 2675.

Ejersbo, N. and Greve, C. (2005) 'Public Management Policymaking in Denmark, 1983–2005'. Paper for IIM/LSE Workshop on Theory and Methods for Studying Organizational Processes: Institutional, Narrative and Related Approaches, LSE 17–18 Feb. 2005.

Ellison, N. (2006) *The Transformation of Welfare States?* (London: Routledge).

Elmeskov, J. and MacFarland, M. (1993) 'Unemployment Persistence', *OECD Economic Studies*, 21, (Paris: OECD), pp. 59–88.

Employment and Social Affairs (2006) *Equality between Women and Men in the European Union 2006* (Luxembourg: Office for Official Publications of the European Communities).

Equal Opportunities Commission (2003) 'Fathers: Balancing Work and Family' Research findings (Manchester, Equal Opportunities Commission: 7).

Equalities Review (2007) *Fairness and Freedom: The Final Report of the Equalities Review* (London: HMSO).

Esping-Andersen, G. (1990) *The Three Worlds of Welfare Capitalism* (Cambridge: Polity Press).

Esping-Andersen, G. (ed.) (1996a) *Welfare States in Transition: National Adaptations in Global Economics* (London: Sage).

Esping-Andersen, G. (1996b) 'After the Golden Age? Welfare State Dilemmas in a Global Economy' In G. Esping-Andersen (ed.), *Welfare States in Transition. National Adaptations in Global Economies* (London: Sage), pp. 1–31.

Esping-Andersen, G. (1997) 'Hybrid or Unique? The Japanese Welfare State between America and Europe', *Journal of European Social Policy*, 7(3), 179–89.

Esping-Andersen, G. (1999) *Social Foundations of Postindustrial Economies.* (Oxford: Oxford University Press).

Esping-Andersen, G., Gallie, D., Hemerijck, A. and Myles, J. (2002) *Why We Need a New Welfare State* (Oxford: Oxford University Press).

Etzioni, A. (1993) *The Spirit of Community. Rights, Responsibilities, and the Communitarian Agenda* (New York: Crown Publishers).

European Central Bank (2004) *Statistics Pocket Book* (Frankfurt/M.: European Central Bank), December 2004, http://ecb.eu/pub/pdf/stapobo/spb200412en.pdf.

European Commission (2005) *Reconciliation of Work and Private Life. A Comparative Review of Thirty European Countries.* Directorate-General for Employment, Social Affairs and Equal Opportunities (Luxembourg: Office for Official Publications of the European Communities).

European Commission (2007) *European Social Statistics. Social Protection, Expenditure and Receipts. Data 1996–2004* (Luxembourg: Office for Official Publications of the European Communities).

European Insurance and Reinsurance Federation (2006) 'European Insurance in Figures in 2005', *CEA Statistics*, No. 24 (CEA: Brussels).

European Observatory on Health Systems and Policies (1999) *Health Care Systems in Transition: United Kingdom* (Copenhagen: WHO Regional Office for Europe on behalf of the European Observatory on Health Systems and Policies).

European Observatory on Health Systems and Policies (2000) *Health Care Systems in Transition: Norway* (Copenhagen: WHO Regional Office for Europe on behalf of the European Observatory on Health Systems and Policies).

European Union (2005) *The EES: A Key Component of the Lisbon Strategy.* European Commission, http://ec.europa.eu/employment_social/employment_strategy/index_en.htm (accessed August 2007).

Eurostat (2005) *Structural Indicators.* European Commission. Eurostat, http://epp.eurostat.ec.europa.eu/ (accessed August 2007).

Eurostat (2006) Various data found on: http://epp.eurostat.ec.europa.eu.

Evandrou, M. and Falkingham, J. (2005) 'A Secure Retirement for All? Older People and New Labour' In J. Hills and K. Stewart (eds), *A More Equal Society? New Labour, Poverty, Inequality and Exclusion* (Bristol: Policy Press).

Fagan, C., Hegewisch, A. and Pillinger, J. (2006) *Out of Time: Why Britain Needs a New Approach to Work-time Flexibility* (London: Trades Union Congress).

Featherstone, B. (2004) *Family Life and Family Support: A Feminist Analysis* (Basingstoke: Palgrave Macmillan).

Ferge, Z. (2000) 'In Defence of Messy or Multi-Principle Contracts', *European Journal of Social Security*, 2(1), 7–33.

Ferge, Z. (2001) 'Welfare and "ill-fare" Systems in Central-Eastern Europe' In R. Sykes, B. Palier and P. Prior (eds), *Globalization and European Welfare States. Challenges and Change* (Basingstoke: Palgrave Macmillan), pp. 127–52.

Ferrera, M. (1996) 'Modèles de solidarité, divergences, convergences: perspectives pour l'Europe', *Swiss Political Science Review*, 2(1), 55–72.

Ferrera, M. (2003) 'European Integration and National Social Citizenship. Changing Boundaries, New Structuring', *Comparative Political Studies*, 36(6), 611–52.

Ferrera, M. and Gualmini, E. (2000) 'Reforms Guided by Consensus: the Welfare State in the Italian Transition' In M. Ferrera and M. Rhodes (eds), *Recasting European Welfare States* (London: Frank Cass).

Ferrera, M. and Gualmini, E. (2004) *Rescued by Europe. Social and Labour Market Reforms in Italy from Maastricht to Berlusconi* (Amsterdam: Amsterdam University Press).

Ferrera, M. and Jessoula, M. (2007) 'Italy: a Narrow Gate for Path-shift' In K. Anderson, E. Immergut and I. Schulze (eds), *The Handbook of West European Pension Politics* (Oxford: Oxford University Press), pp. 396–498.

Filippini, M. and Farsi, M. (2004) *An Analysis of Efficiency and Productivity in Swiss Hospitals*. Final Report to the Swiss Federal Statistical Office and Swiss Federal Office for Social Security, June.

Finlayson, G. (1994) *Citizen, State and Social Welfare in Britain 1830–1990* (Oxford: Clarendon Press).

Fitzner, G. and Grainger, H. (2007) 'The Right to Request Flexible Working: A Review of the Evidence. Executive Summary', *Employment Relations Research Series*, no. 59 (Department for Trade and Industry).

Flora, P. (ed.) (1986) *Growth to Limits: The Western European Welfare States since World War II*. (Berlin: de Gruyter).

Fox Harding, L. (1996) *Family, State and Social Policy* (Basingstoke: Macmillan).

Fraser, N. (1997) 'After the Family Wage: A Postindustrial Thought Experiment' In N. Fraser, *Justice Interruptus: Critical Reflections on the 'Postsocialist' Condition* (New York and London: Routledge), pp. 41–66.

Freedland, J. (1998) *Bring Home the Revolution* (London: Fourth Estate).

Freeman, R. and Schmid, A. (forthcoming) 'Health Systems, Western Europe' In K. Heggenhougen (ed.), *International Encyclopedia of Public Health* (Amsterdam: Elsevier).

Frericks, P., Maier, R. and de Graaf, W. (2005) 'Shifting the Pension Mix: Consequences for Dutch and Danish Women', *Social Policy & Administration*, 40(5), 475–92.

Gallie, D. (2002) 'The Quality of Working Life in Welfare Strategy' In G. Esping-Andersen (ed.), *Why We Need a New Welfare State* (Oxford: Oxford University Press).

Gambles, R., Lewis, S. and Rapoport, R. (2006) *The Myth of Work–Life Balance: The Challenge of Our Time for Men, Women and Societies* (London: John Wiley and Sons).

Gambles, R., Lewis, S., et al. (2007) 'Evolutions and Approaches to Equitable Divisions of Paid Work and Care in Three European Countries: A Multi-level Challenge' In R. Crompton, S. Lewis and C. Lyonette (eds), *Women, Men, Work and Family in Europe* (Basingstoke: Palgrave Macmillan), pp. 17–34.

Garland, D. (2001) *The Culture of Control: Crime and Social Order in Contemporary Society* (Chicago: University of Chicago Press).

Gazeta Wyborcza (2005) 'Konkurs na najlepszy fundusz emerytalny rozstrzygnięty'.

George, V. and Wilding, P. (1994) *Welfare and Ideology* (London: Prentice Hall).

Gershuny, J. (2000) *Changing Times: Work and Leisure in Postindustrial Society* (Oxford: Oxford University Press).

Giddens, A. (1998) *The Third Way. The Renewal of Social Democracy.* (Cambridge: Polity Press).

Giddens, A. (2002) *Where Now for New Labour?* (Cambridge: Polity Press).

Gilbert, N. (2002) *Transformation of the Welfare State. The Silent Surrender of Public Responsibility* (Oxford: Oxford University Press).

Gilbert, N. (2005) 'The "Enabling State?" From Public to Private Responsibility for Social Protection: Pathways and Pitfalls', *OECD Social, Employment and Migration Working Papers*, No. 26 (Paris: OECD).

Gilson, S. and Glorieux, M. (2005) 'Le droit à l'intégration sociale comme première emblématique de l'Etat social actif: Quelques commentaires de la loi du 26 mai 2002' In P. Vielle, P. Pochet and I. Cassiers (eds), *L'Etat social actif: vers un changement de paradigme?* (Brussels: P.I.E-Peter Lang), pp. 233–55.

Ginn, J. and Arber, S. (1991) 'Gender, Class and Income Inequalities in Later Life', *British Journal of Sociology*, 42(3), 369–93.

Ginn, J. and Arber, S. (1993) 'Pension Penalties: The Gendered Division of Occupational Welfare', *Work, Employment and Society*, 7(1), 47–70.

Glasby, J. and Littlechild, R. (2002) *Social Work and Direct Payments* (Bristol: Policy Press).

Glyn, A. (2006) *Capitalism Unleashed: Finance, Globalization and Welfare* (Oxford: Oxford University Press).

Goodman, R. (1996) 'On Introducing the UN Convention of the Rights of the Child into Japan' In R. Goodman and I. Neary (eds), *Case Studies on Human Rights in Japan*, (Japan Library, Curzon Press).

Goodman, R. (1998) 'The Delivery of Personal Social Services and the "Japanese-Style Welfare State"' In R. Goodman, G. White and H.-J. Kwon (eds), *The East Asian Welfare Model: Welfare Orientalism and the State* (London and New York: Routledge).

Goodman, R. (2000) *Children of the Japanese State: The Changing Role of Child Protection Institutions in Contemporary Japan* (Oxford: Oxford University Press).

Goodman, R. (2001) 'Images of the Japanese Welfare State' In H. Befu and S. Guichard-Anguis (eds) *Globalizing Japan: Ethnography of the Japanese Presence in Asia, Europe and America* (London and New York: Routledge).

Goodman, R. (2002) 'Child Abuse in Japan: 'Discovery' and the Development of Policy' In R. Goodman (ed.) *Family and Social Policy in Japan: Anthropological Approaches* (Cambridge: Cambridge University Press).

Goodman, R. (2003) 'Can Welfare Systems Be Evaluated Outside their Cultural and Historical Context? A Case Study of Children's Homes in Contemporary Japan' In M. Blecher, B. Benewick and S. Cook (eds), *Asian Politics in Development* (London: Frank Cass).

Goodman, R. (2006) 'Policing the Japanese Family' In M. Rebick and A. Takenaka (eds), *The Japanese Family* (London: RoutledgeCurzon Press).

Goodman, R. and White, G. (1998) 'Welfare Orientalism and the Search for an East Asian Welfare Model' In R. Goodman, G. White and H.-J. Kwon (eds), *The East Asian Welfare Model: Welfare Orientalism and the State* (London and New York: Routledge), pp. 3–24.

Gordon, M. (1988) *Social Security Policies in Industrial Countries* (Cambridge: Cambridge University Press).

Gornick, J.C. and Meyers, M. (2003) *Families that Work: Policies for Reconciling Parenthood and Employment* (New York: Russell Sage Foundation).

Gould, A. (1993) *Capitalist Welfare Systems – A Comparison of Japan, Britain and Sweden* (London, New York: Longman).

Graetz, M.J. and Mashaw, J.L. (1999) *True Security: Rethinking American Social Insurance* (New Haven: Yale University Press).

Graham, H. (1983) 'Caring: A Labour of Love' In J. Finch and D. Groves (eds), *A Labour of Love: Women, Work, and Caring* (London and Boston: Routledge & K. Paul), pp. 12–30.

Grant, R.W. and Keohane, R.O. (2005) 'Accountability and Abuses of Power in World Politics', *American Political Science Review*, 99(1), 29–43.

Graziano, P. (2003) 'Europeanization or Globalization? A Framework for Empirical Research (with some evidence from the Italian case)', *Global Social Policy*, 3(3), 173–94.

Green-Pedersen, C. (2002a) *The Politics of Justification. Party Competition and Welfare-State Retrenchment in Denmark and the Netherlands from 1982 to 1998* (Amsterdam: Amsterdam University Press).

Green-Pedersen, C. (2002b) 'New Public Management Reforms of the Danish and Swedish Welfare States: The Role of Different Social Democratic Responses', *Governance*, 15(2), 271–94.

Green-Pedersen, C. (2004) 'The Dependent Variable Problem within the Study of Welfare-State Retrenchment: Defining the Problem and Looking for Solutions', *Journal of Comparative Policy Analysis*, 6(1), 3–14.

Green-Pedersen, C. (2007) 'Denmark: a "World Bank" Pension System' In E.M. Immergut, K.M. Anderson and I. Schulze (eds), *The Handbook of West European Pension Politics* (Oxford: Oxford University Press), pp. 454–95.

Green-Pedersen, C., Hemerijck, A. and Van Keesbergen, K. (2001) 'Neo-liberalism, Third Way or What?', *Journal of European Public Policy*, 8(2), 307–25.

Greve, C. (2007) 'Kvalitetsreformen og moderninseringen af den offentlige sektor', *Samfundsøkonomen*, no. 3, pp. 4–8.

Greve, C. and Ejersbo, N. (2005) *Moderniseringen af den offentlige sektor* (Copenhagen: Børsens Forlag).

Grimmeisen, S. (forthcoming) 'The Role of the State in the British Health Care System – Between Marketization and Statism' In H. Rothgang, M. Cacace, S. Grimmeisen, U. Helmert and C. Wendt, *The Changing Role of the State in OECD Health Care Systems. From Heterogeneity to Homogeneity?* (Basingstoke: Palgrave Macmillan).

Grover, C. and Piggott, L. (2005) 'Disabled People, the Reserve Army of Labour and Welfare Reform', *Disability and Society*, 20(7), 705–17.

Guillén, A. (2002) 'The Politics of Universalization: Establishing National Health Services in Southern Europe', *West European Politics*, 25(4), 49–68.

Guillén, A., Álvarez, S. and Adào e Silva, P. (2003) 'Redesigning the Spanish and Portuguese Welfare States: The Impact of Accession into the European Union', *South European Society and Politics*, 8(1), 231–69.

Gutiérrez, R. and Guillén, A. (2000) 'Protecting the Long-Term Unemployed. The Impact of Targeting Policies in Spain', *European Societies*, 2(2), 195–216.

GVG (2002) *Study on the Social Protection Systems in the 13 Applicant Countries*. Study carried out for the Commission by Gesellschaft für Versicherungswissenschaft und–gestaltung. November. Second Draft (Brussels: Commission of the European Communities).

Hacker, J.S. (2002) *The Divided Welfare State: The Battle over Public and Private Social Benefits in the United States* (Cambridge MA: Cambridge University Press).

Hall, P.A. (1993) 'Policy Paradigms, Social Learning and the State', *Comparative Politics*, 25(3), 275–96.

Hansen, H. (2002) *Elements of Social Security*. 9th ed. Report 2002:05. (Copenhagen: Danish National Institute of Social Research).

Hansen, H. (2006) *From Asylum Seeker to Refugee to Family Reunification. Welfare Payments in These Situations in Various Western Countries* (Copenhagen: The Rockwool Foundation Research Unit).

Hansen, H.K. and Salskov-Iversen, D. (eds) (forthcoming) *Critical Perspectives on Private Authority in Global Politics* (Basingstoke: Palgrave Macmillan).

Harada, S. (1998) 'The Ageing Society, the Family, and Social Policy' In J. Banno (ed.), *The Political Economy of Japanese Society*. Vol. 2, (Oxford: Oxford University Press), pp. 175–228.

Harris, J. (1992) 'Political Thought and the Welfare State 1870–1940: An Intellectual Framework for British Social Policy', *Past and Present*, no. 135, 116–41.

Hemerijck, A. (2003) 'A Paradoxical Miracle: The Politics of Coalition Government and Social Concertation in Dutch Welfare Reform' In S. Jochen and N. Siegel (eds), *Konzertierung, Verhandlungsdemokratie und Reformpolitik im Wohlfahrstaat* (Opladen: Leske & Budrich), pp. 232–70.

Hendriks, F. (2001) 'Polder Politics in the Netherlands: the Viscous State Revisited' In F. Hendriks and A. Toonen (eds), *Polder Politics: The Reinvention of Consensus Democracy in the Netherlands* (Aldershot: Ashgate), pp. 21–40.

Henke, K.-D., Schreyögg, J. (2005) *Towards Sustainable Health Care Systems* (Geneva: ISSA).

Henriksen, L.S. and Bundesen, P. (2004) 'The Moving Frontier in Denmark: Voluntary-State Relationships since 1850', *Journal of Social Policy*, 33(4), 605–25.

Hernes, H. (1988) 'Scandinavian Citizenship', *Acta Sociologia*, 31(3), 199–215.

Hewitt, P. (1993) *About Time: The Revolution in Work and Family Life* (London: IPPR).

Hill, M. (2007) 'The Mixed Economy of Welfare: A Comparative Perspective' In M. Powell (ed.), *Understanding the Mixed Economy of Welfare* (Bristol: Policy Press), pp. 177–98.

Hills, J. (2004) *Inequality and the State* (Oxford: Oxford University Press).

Hiraoka, K. (2001) 'Long-Term Care Insurance and Welfare Mix in Japan', *Ochanomizu University Studies in Arts and Culture*, vol. 54, 133–47.

Hiršl, M. (2003) *V jaké míře přispívá český stát na náklady spojené s výchovou dětí*. Prague. Unpublished manuscript.

HM Treasury and Department of Trade and Industry (2003) *Balancing Work and Family Life: Enhancing Choice and Support for Parents* (Norwich: HSMO).

Hogarth, T., Hasluck, C. and Pierre, G. (2001) *Work–Life Balance 2000: Results from the Baseline Study* (Nottingham: DfEE).

Home Office (1998) *Supporting Families: A Consultation Document* (London: HMSO).

Hood, C. (1991) 'A Public Management for all Seasons?', *Public Administration*, 69(1), 3–19.

Hood, C., Scott, C., James, O., Jones, G. and Travers, T. (1999) *Regulation Inside Government. Waste-watchers, Quality Police and Sleaze-Busters* (Oxford: Oxford University Press).

Hooker, H., Neathey, F., Casebourne, J. and Munro, M. (2007) 'The Third Work–Life Balance Employees' Survey: Main Findings', *Employment Relations Research Series*, no. 58 (London: Department of Trade and Industry), p. 9.

Horibayashi, T. (2006) 'Central European Welfare System: The Present Characteristics'. (Available at http://project.iss.u-tokyo.ac.jp/nakagawa/members/papers/ 4(4) Horibayashi.final.pdf).

Houston, D.M. and Waumsley, J.A. (2003) *Attitudes to Flexible Working and Family Life* (Bristol: Published for the Joseph Rowntree Foundation by The Policy Press).

Howard, C. (1997) *The Hidden Welfare State. Tax Expenditures and Social Policy in the United States* (Princeton: Princeton University Press).

Huber, E. and Stephens, J.D. (2001) *Development and Crisis of the Welfare State. Parties and Policies in Global Markets* (Chicago: University of Chicago Press).

Hughes, B. and Cooke, G. (2007) 'Children, Parenting and Families: Renewing the Progressive Story' In N. Pearce and J. Margo (eds), *Politics for a New Generation* (Basingstoke: Palgrave Macmillan), pp. 235–55.

Hughes, G. and Lewis, G. (eds) (1998) *Unsettling Welfare: The Reconstruction of Social Policy* (London: Routledge/The Open University).

Hvinden, B. (2004) 'Nordic Disability Policies in a Changing Europe: Is There Still a Distinct Nordic Model?', *Social Policy & Administration*, 38(2), 170–89.

Ibsen, F. (1992) 'Efter Zeuthen-rapporten', *Samfundsøkonomen*, vol. 10, pp. 37–45.

IEA (1967) *Towards a Welfare Society* (London: IEA).

Immergut, E. (2001) 'Health Policy' In N.J. Smelser and B.P. Baltes (eds), *International Encyclopedia of the Social Behavioral Science* (Cambridge MA: Elsevier Science Ltd.), pp. 6586–91.

Institute of Health Information and Statistics of the Czech Republic (2006) Czech Health Statistics 2005 (Prague: ÚZIS ČR) Available at: http://www.uzis.cz/ download.php?ctg=10&search_name=ro%E8enka®ion=100&mnu_id=5300.

IPPR Commission on Public Private Partnerships (2001) *Building Better Partnerships* (London: IPPR).

Ito, Y. (1995) 'Social Work Development in Japan', *Social Policy and Administration*, 29(5), 258–68.

Iversen, T. (2005) *Capitalism, Democracy, and Welfare* (Cambridge: Cambridge University Press).

Izuhara, M. (2003) 'Ageing and Intergenerational Relations in Japan' In M. Izuhara (ed.), *Comparing Social Policies: Exploring New Perspectives in Britain and Japan* (Bristol: Policy Press), pp. 73–94.

Jessop, B. (2000) 'Governance Failure' In G. Stoker (ed.), *The New Politics of British Local Governance* (Basingstoke: Macmillan).

Johnsen, J.R. (2006) *Health Care Systems in Transition: Norway* (Copenhagen: WHO Regional Office for Europe on behalf of the European Observatory on Health Systems and Policies).

Jordan, B. (2006) *Social Policy for the Twenty-First Century* (Cambridge: Polity Press).

Jørgensen, H. (2000) 'Danish Labour Market Policy Since 1994: The New Columbus Egg of Labour Market Regulation' In P. Klemmer and R. Wink (eds), *Preventing Unemployment in Euope: A New Framework for Labour Market Policy* (Cheltenham: Edward Elgar), pp. 108–36.

Jørgensen, H. (2006) *Arbejdsmarkedspolitikkens fornyelse – innovation eller trussel mod dansk 'flexicurity'?* (Aalborg: LO & FTF).

Jørgensen, H. (2007) Frit valg og sociale skillelinjer. MSc Thesis (Aalborg: Department of Economics, Politics and Public Administration, Aalborg University).

Kaelble, H. (2004) 'Das europäische Sozialmodell – eine historische Perspektive' In H. Kaelble and G. Schmid (eds), *Das europäische Sozialmodell. Auf dem Weg zum transnationalen Sozialstaat*. WZB-Jahrbuch 2004 (Berlin: Edition Sigma), pp. 31–50.

Kalb, D. (2005) 'From Flows to Violence: Politics and Knowledge in the Debates on Globalization and Empire', *Anthropological Theory*, 5(2), 176–204.

Kasza, G.J. (2002) 'The Illusion of Welfare Regimes', *Journal of Social Policy*, 31(2), 271–87.

Kasza, G.J. (2006) *One World of Welfare. Japan in Comparative Perspective* (Ithaca and London: Cornell University Press).

Kaufmann, F.-X. (1994) 'Staat und Wohlfahrtsproduktion' In H.-U. Derlien, U. Gerhardt and F.W. Scharpf (eds), *Systemrationalität und Partialinteresse*. Festschrift für Renate Mayntz (Baden-Baden: Nomos), pp. 357–80.

Kemp, P.A. (2006) 'Comparing Trends in Disability Benefit Receipt' In P.A. Kemp, A. Sundén and B. Bakker Tauritz (eds) *Sick Societies? Trends in Disability Benefits in Post-industrial Welfare States* (Geneva: International Social Security Association).

Kemp, P.A. and Thornton, P. (2006) 'Disguised Unemployment? The Growth of Incapacity Benefit Claims in Great Britain' In P.A. Kemp, A. Sundén and B. Bakker Tauritz (eds) *Sick Societies? Trends in Disability Benefits in Post-industrial Welfare States* (Geneva: International Social Security Association).

Kemp, P.A., Sunden, A. and Bakker Tauritz, B. (eds) (2006) *Sick Societies? Trends in Disability Benefits in Post-industrial Welfare States* (Geneva: International Social Security Association).

Kendall, J., Anheier, H. and Potůček, M. (2000) 'Ten Years After: The Third Sector and Civil Society in Central and Eastern Europe', *Voluntas*, 11(2), 103–6.

Keune, M. (2006) 'The European Social Model and Enlargement' In M. Jepsen and A. Serrano (eds), *Unwrapping the European social model* (Bristol: Policy Press), pp. 167–88.

Kilkey, M. (2006) 'New Labour and Reconciling Work and Family Life: Making it Fathers' Business', *Social Policy and Society*, 5(2), 167–75.

King, D. (1995) *Actively Seeking Work: The Politics of Unemployment and Welfare Policy in the United States and Great Britain* (Chicago: Chicago University Press).

King, D. (1999) *In the Name of Liberalism: Illiberal Social Policy in the United States and Great Britain* (Oxford: Oxford University Press).

Kingo, T. (2003) 'Development of Social Policy in Japan' In M. Izuhara (ed.), *Comparing Social Policies: Exploring New Perspectives in Britain and Japan* (Bristol: Policy Press), pp. 35–47.

King's Fund (2007) '18-week Waiting Times Target – An Update'. Briefing August 2007. Retrieved from http://www.kingsfund.org.uk/publications/briefings/18week_waiting.html; 22 November.

Kittel, B. and Obinger, H. (2003) 'Political Parties, Institutions, and the Dynamics of Social Expenditure in Times of Austerity', *Journal of European Public Policy*, 10(1), 20–45.

Klein, R. (2005) *The New Politics of the National Health Service* (Oxford: Pitman Medical).

Kono, M. (2005) 'The Welfare Regime in Japan' In A. Walker and C.-K. Wong (eds), *East Asian Welfare Regimes in Transition: From Confucianism to Globalisation* (London: Polity Press).

Korobtseva, E. (2006), Making the Choice to Become an Unwed Mother in Contemporary Japan. Unpublished DPhil Thesis (Oxford: Department of Sociology, University of Oxford).

Korpi, W. (2002) *Velfærdsstat og socialt medborgerskab. Danmark i et komparativt perspektiv, 1930–1995* (Aarhus: Magtudredningen).

Korpi, W. (2003) 'Welfare-State Regress in Western Europe: Politics, Institutions, Globalization, and Europeanization', *Annual Review of Sociology*, 29, 589–609.

Korpi, W. and Palme, J. (1998) 'The Paradox of Redistribution and Strategies of Equality: Welfare State Institutions, Inequality, and Poverty in Western Countries', *American Sociological Review*, 63(5), 661–87.

Korpi, W. and Palme, J. (2003) 'New Politics and Class Politics in the Context of Austerity and Globalization: Welfare State Regress in 18 Countries 1975–1995', *American Political Science Review*, 97(3), 425–46.

Kruse, A. (2003) 'Social Security and Disability in Sweden' In C. Prinz (ed.), *European Disability Pension Policies* (Aldershot: Ashgate).

Kuipers, S. (2006) *The Crisis Imperative: Crisis Rhetoric and the Reform of Social Security in Belgium and the Netherlands* (Amsterdam: Amsterdam University Press).

Lader, D., Short, S. and Gershuny, J. (2006) *The Time Use Survey, 2005: How We Spend Our Time*. A report on research using the ONS Omnibus Survey produced on behalf of the Economic and Social Research Council (ESRC), Department of Culture, Media and Sport (DCMS), Department for Education and Skills (DfES), Department of Health (DH), Office for National Statistics (ONS) (London: ONS).

Lambert, S.J. and Waxman, E. (2005) 'Organizational Stratification: Distributing Opportunities for Balancing Work and Personal Life' In E.E. Kossek and S.J. Lambert (eds) *Work and Life Integration: Organizational, Cultural, and Individual Perspectives* (Mahwah, N.J.: Lawrence Erlbaum Associates Publishers), pp. 103–26.

Lammi-Taskula, J. (2006) 'Nordic Men on Parental Leave: Can the Welfare State Change Gender Relations?' In A.L. Ellingsaeter and A. Leira (eds), *Politicising Parenthood in Scandinavia: Gender Relations in Welfare States* (Bristol: Policy Press), pp. 79–100.

Larner, W. and Walters, W. (eds) (2004) *Global Governmentality* (London: Routledge).

Latour, B. (2005) *Reassembling the Social: An Introduction to Actor-Network-Theory* (Oxford: Oxford University Press).

Le Grand, J. (2005) 'Inequality, Choice and Public Services' In A. Giddens and P. Diamond (eds), *The New Egalitarianism* (Cambridge: Polity), pp. 200–10.

Leibfried, S. and Zürn, M. (eds) (2005a) *Transformations of the State?* (Cambridge: Cambridge University Press).

Leibfried, S. and Zürn, M. (2005b) 'Reconfiguring the National Constellation' In S. Leibfried and M. Zürn (eds), *Transformations of the State* (Cambridge: Cambridge University Press), pp. 1–36.

Leisering, L. (2003) 'From Redistribution to Regulation. Regulating Private Pension Provision for Old Age as a New Challenge for the Welfare State in Ageing Societies', Paper presented at the 4th International Research Conference on Social Security, Antwerp, 5–7 May 2003. *Regina Working Paper*, No. 3 (Bielefeld: University of Bielefeld).

Leisering, L. (2007). 'The Social Regulation of Welfare Markets. Chances and Limits of Social Policy beyond the Post-war Welfare State' *ESPAnet Conference 2007*. Vienna.

Lendvai, N. and Stubbs, P. (2006) 'Translation, Intermediaries and Welfare Reforms in South Eastern Europe', Paper presented at the 4th ESPAnet Conference, Bremen, September 2006.

Leven, B. (2005) 'Corruption and Reforms: A Case of Poland's Medical Sector', *Communist and Post-Communist Studies*, 38(4), 447–55.

Levy, J. (ed.) (2006a) *The State after Statism: New State Activities in an Age of Liberalization* (Cambridge: Harvard University Press).

Levy, J.D. (2006b) 'The State Also Rises. The Roots of Contemporary State Activism' In J.D. Levy (ed.), *The State after Statism. New Activities in the Age of Liberalization* (Cambridge: Harvard University Press), pp. 1–28.

Lewis, G. (1998) *Forming Nation, Framing Welfare* (London: Sage).

Lewis, J. (1992) 'Gender and the Development of Welfare Regimes', *Journal of European Social Policy*, 2(3), 159–73.

Lewis, J. (2001) 'The Decline of the Male Breadwinner Model: Implications for Work and Care', *Social Politics*, 8(2), 152–69.

Lewis, J. (2002) 'Gender and Welfare State Change', *European Societies*, 4(4), 331–57.

Lewis, J. (2006) 'Work/family Reconciliation, Equal Opportunities, and Social Policies: The Interpretation of Policy Trajectories at the EU Level and the Meaning of Gender Equality', *Journal of European Public Policy*, 13(3), 420–37.

Lewis, J. and Campbell, M. (2007) 'Work/Family Balance Policies in the UK since 1997: A New Departure?', *Journal of Social Policy*, 36(3), 365–81.

Lewis, J. and Giullari, S. (2004) 'The Adult Worker Model Family, Gender Equality and Care: The Search for New Policy Principles and the Possibilities and Problems of a Capabilities Approach', *Economy and Society*, 34, 76–104.

Lewis, R., Alvarez Rosete, A. and Mays, N. (2006) *How to Regulate Health Care in England? An International Perspective* (London: Kings Fund).

Leys, C. (2001) *Market-driven Politics* (London: Verso).

Lind, J. (2004) 'The Restructuring of the Ghent Model in Denmark and Consequences for the Trade Unions', *Transfer*, 10(4), 621–5.

Lindley, J., Dale, A. and Dex, S. (2004) 'Ethnic Differences in Women's Demographic, Family Characteristics and Economic Activity Profiles, 1992–2002', *Labour Market Trends*, 112(4), 153–65.

Lødemel, I. and Trickey, H. (eds) (2001a) *An Offer You Can't Refuse. Workfare in International Perspective* (Bristol: Policy Press).

Lødemel, I. and Trickey, H. (2001b) 'A New Contract for Social Assistance' In I. Lødemel and H. Trickey (eds) *An Offer You Can't Refuse. Workfare in International Perspective* (Bristol: Policy Press), pp. 1–40.

Lowe, R. (2004) 'Modernizing Britain's Welfare State: The Influence of Affluence, 1957–64' In L. Black and H. Pemberton (eds), *An Affluent Society?* (Aldershot: Ashgate), pp. 35–51.

Ludwig-Mayerhofer, W. (2005) 'Activating Germany' In T. Bredgard and F. Larsen (eds), *Employment Policy from Different Angles* (Copenhagen: DJOF Publishing), pp. 95–112.

Maarse, H. (ed.) (2004), *Privatisation in European Health Care. A Comparative Analysis in Eight Countries* (Maarsen, Elsevier).

Maarse, H. and Okma, K. (2004) 'The Privatisation Paradox in Dutch Health Care' In H. Maarse (ed.), *Privatisation in European Health Care. A Comparative Analysis in Eight Countries* (Maarsen, Elsevier), pp. 97–116.

Madsen, P.K. (2002) 'The Danish Model of Flexicurity: A Paradise – With Some Snakes' In H. Sarfati and G. Bonoli (eds), *Labour Market and Social Protection Reforms in International Perspective: Parallel or Converging Tracks?* (London: Ashgate), pp. 243–65.

Madsen, P.K. (2006) 'Strukturreformen og beskæftigelsespolitikken', *Samfund-søkonomen*, no. 6, pp. 26–30.

Madsen, P.K. (2007): Distribution of Responsibility for Social Security and Labour Market Policy. Country Report: Denmark. Amsterdam: Amsterdam Institute for Advanced Labour Studies, University of Amsterdam. AIAS working paper.

Mairé, J. (2005) *Service(s) public(s) de l'emploi? 40 années de rapports et de demi-mesures à mmoitié appliqués,* note prepared for UNSA colloquium 'Pour un service public de l'emploi rénové au service des chômeurs', Paris, 21 November.

Mares, I. (2001). 'Firms and the Welfare State: When, Why, and How Does Social Policy Matter to Employers?' In P. Hall and D. Soskice (eds), *Varieties of Capitalism* (Oxford: Oxford University Press).

Marin, B. (2003) 'Transforming Disability Welfare Policy. Completing a Paradigm Shift' In C. Prinz (ed.) *European Disability Pension Policies: 11 Country Trends 1970–2002* (Aldershot: Ashgate).

Marmor, T. (2000) *The Politics of Medicare.* 2nd Edition (New York: De Gruyter).

Marquand, D. (2004) *Decline of the Public* (Cambridge: Polity Press).

Marshall, T.H. (1950) *Citizenship and Social Class and Other Essays* (Cambridge: Cambridge University Press).

Marshall, T.H. (1975) *Social Policy in the Twentieth Century* (London: Hutchinson).

Marshall, T.H. (1992) *Bürgerrechte und soziale Klassen. Zur Soziologie des Wohlfahrtsstaates* (Frankfurt/M.: Campus).

Marston, G. and McDonald, C. (eds) (2006) *Analysing Social Policy: A Governmental Approach* (Cheltenham: Edward Elgar).

Martin, C.J. (2004) 'Reinventing Welfare Regimes. Employers and the Implementation of Active Social Policy', *World Politics,* 57(1), 39–69.

Marx, I. (2007) *A New Social Question? On Minimum Income Protection in the Postindustrial Era* (Amsterdam: Amsterdam University Press).

McRae, S. (1989) *Flexible Working Time and Family Life: A Review of Changes* (London: Policy Studies Institute).

Meyer, T. and Bridgen, P. (2008) 'Class, Gender and Chance. The Social Division of Welfare and British Occupational Pensions', *Ageing and Society,* 28(3), 353–81.

Meyer, T., Bridgen, P. and Riedmüller, B. (eds) (2007) *Private Pensions versus Social Inclusion? Non-state Provision for Citizens at Risk in Europe* (Cheltenham, UK and Northampton, US: Edward Elgar).

Ministère de la Santé et des Solidarités (2005) *Les Etablissements de Santé* (Paris: DREES).

Ministerio de Trabajo y Asuntos Sociales (1996) *Anuario de Estadísticas Laborales y de Asuntos Sociales 1995* (Madrid: Ministerio de Trabajo y Asuntos Sociales).

Ministry of Employment (2005) *Flexicurity. Udfordringer for den danske model* (Copenhagen: Ministry of Employment).

Ministry of Employment (2006) *Kulegravning af kontanthjælpsområdet* (Copenhagen: Ministry of Employment).

Ministry of Finance (2003) *Budgetredegørelse 2003* (Copenhagen: Ministry of Finance).

Ministry of Finance (2007a) *Økonomisk redegørelse.* May 2007. (Copenhagen: Ministry of Finance).

Ministry of Finance (2007b) *Budgetredegørelse 2007* (Copenhagen: Ministry of Finance).

Ministry of Health, New Zealand (2004) *Health Expenditure Trends in New Zealand 1990–2002* (Wellington: Ministry of Health).

Ministry of Labour (2000) *Effekter af Aktiveringsindsatsen* (Copenhagen: Ministry of Labour).

Ministry of Labour and Social Affairs (2004a) *National Employment Action Plan 2004–2006* (Prague: Ministry of Labour and Social Affairs).

Ministry of Labour and Social Affairs (2004b) *Joint Inclusion Memorandum* (Prague: Ministry of Labour and Social Affairs).

Ministry of Labour and Social Affairs (2005a) *National Action Plan on Social Inclusion 2004–2006* (Prague: Ministry of Labour and Social Affairs).

Ministry of Labour and Social Affairs (2005b) *Koncepce rodinné politiky* (Praha: Ministerstvo práce a sociální politiky).

Ministry of Labour and Social Affairs (2006) Various data found on: http://www.mpsv.cz.

Mooney, G. (2004) 'The Shifting Relations of Work, Welfare and Personal Lives' In G. Mooney (ed.), *Work: Personal Lives and Social Policy* (Bristol: Policy Press), pp. 145–60.

Morissens, A. and Sainsbury, D. (2005) 'Migrants' Social Rights, Ethnicity and Welfare Regimes', *Journal of Social Policy*, 34(4), 637–60.

Moran, M. (2003) *The British Regulatory State* (Oxford: Oxford University Press).

Mullins, D. and Murie, A. (2006) *Housing Policy in the UK* (Basingstoke: Palgrave Macmillan).

Muncie, J. and Wetherell, M. (1995) 'Family Policy and Political Discourse' In J. Muncie, M. Wetherell, R. Dallos and A. Cochrane (eds), *Understanding the Family* (London: Sage).

Mustard, C., Lavis, J. and Ostry, A. (no date) 'Labour Market Experiences and Health', mimeo.

Myles, J. and Pierson, P. (2001) 'The Comparative Political Economy of Pension Reform' In P. Pierson (ed.), *The New Politics of the Welfare State* (Oxford: Oxford University Press), pp. 305–33.

Naegele, G., Barkholdt, C., de Vroom, B., Andersen, J.G. and Krämer, K. (2003) *A New Organisation of Time over Working Life* (Dublin: European Foundation for the Improvement of Living and Working Conditions).

Natali, D. (2006) 'From Italy to Europe: A Review of Recent Italian Literature on Social Policy', *Journal of European Social Policy*, 16(3), 287–92.

Newman, J. (ed.) (2005) *Remaking Governance: Peoples, Politics and the Public Sphere* (Bristol: Policy Press).

Newman, J. (2006) 'Constituting Trans-national Governance: Spaces, Actors and Vocabularies of Power', Paper presented to 4th ESPANET conference, Bremen, September, 2006.

Neyer, J. and Seeleib-Kaiser, M. (1995) 'Bringing the Economy Back In: Economic Globalization and the Re-commodification of the Workforce', *ZeS-Arbeitspapier*, Nr 16/95 (Bremen: Bremen University).

Nickell, S. and Bell, B. (1995) 'The Collapse in Demand for the Unskilled and Unemployment across the OECD', *Oxford Review of Economic Policy*, 11(1), 40–62.

Nielsen, J.A. and Andersen, J.G. (2006) *Hjemmehjælp mellem myter og virkelighed* (Odense: University Press of Southern Denmark).

Nivola, P.S. (ed.) (1997) *Comparative Disadvantages? Social Regulations and the Global Economy* (Washington, D.C.: Brookings Institution).

Nullmeier, F. (2001) 'Sozialpolitik als marktregulative Politik', *Zeitschrift für Sozialreform*, 42, 645–67.

Oberlander, J. (2003) *The Political Life of Medicare* (Chicago: University of Chicago Press).

Obinger, H. and Starke, P. (2007) 'Are Welfare States Converging?' In I. Dingeldey, H. Rothgang (eds), *Governance of Welfare State Reform. A Cross National and Cross Sectoral Comparison of Policy and Politics* (Cheltenham: Edward Elgar).

O'Brien, M. (2005) 'Shared Caring: Bringing Fathers into the Frame', *EOC Working paper series*, No. 18 (Manchester: EOC).

OECD (1994) *The Reform of Health Care Systems. A Review of Seventeen OECD Countries* (Paris: OECD).

OECD (1999) *Historical Statistics* (Paris: OECD).

OECD (2001) *Balancing Work and Family Life: Helping Parents into Paid Employment* (Paris: OECD).

OECD (2002) *OECD Health Data 2002* (Paris: OECD).

OECD (2003) *Transforming Disability into Ability: Policies to Promote Work and Income Security for Disabled People* (Paris: OECD).

OECD (2004a) 'Special Session of the Education Committee: Pilot Review of the Quality and Equity of Schooling Outcomes in Denmark'. Examiner's report. EDU/EC(2004)4. (Paris: OECD). Also available at http://pub.uvm.dk/2004/oecd/final.pdf.

OECD (2004b) *Proposals for a Taxonomy of Health Insurance* (Paris: OECD).

OECD (2005a) *Extending Opportunities. How Active Social Policy Can Benefit Us All* (Paris: OECD).

OECD (2005b) *Pensions at a Glance, Public Policies across OECD Countries*. 2005 Edition (OECD: Paris).

OECD (2005c) *OECD Reviews of Health Systems: Finland* (Paris: OECD).

OECD (2006a) *Economic Outlook*, no. 79 (Paris: OECD).

OECD (2006b) *OECD Health Data 2006* (Paris: OECD).

OECD (2006c) *Employment Outlook: Boosting Jobs and Incomes* (Paris: OECD).

OECD (2007a) *Economic Outlook*, no. 81 (Paris: OECD).

OECD (2007b) *OECD Social Expenditure Database, 1980–2003* (Paris: OECD).

Offe, C. (1984 [1993]) *Contradictions of the Welfare State*. Edited by John Keane. 5th printing. (Cambridge: MIT Press).

Oliveira, M.D., Magone, J.M. and Pereira, J.A. (2005) 'Nondecision Making and Inertia in Portuguese Health Policy', *Journal of Health Politics, Policy and Law*, 30(1–2), 211–30.

Ongaro, E. (2006) 'The Dynamics of Devolution Processes in Legalistic Countries: Organizational Change in the Italian Public Sector', *Public Administration*, 84(3), 737–70.

Orenstein, M.A. and Haas, M.R. (2003) 'Globalization and the Development of Welfare States in Postcommunist Europe' (Cambridge, MA: Belfer Center for Science and International Affairs, J.F. Kennedy School of Government, Harvard University).

Osawa, M. (2005) 'Comparative Social Policy Systems from a Gender Perspective', *Social Science Japan*, no. 31, March, pp. 9–13.

Osborne, D. and Gaebler, T. (1992) *Reinventing Government. How the Entrepreneurial Spirit is Transforming the Public Sector* (Reading MA: Addison-Wesley).

Österle, A. (forthcoming) 'Austria' In H. Rothgang, M. Cacace, S. Grimmeisen, U. Helmert and C. Wendt (eds), *Financing, Providing, and Regulating Health Care. The Role of the State in Twelve OECD Health Care Systems from 1970 till Today* (Buckingham: Open University Press).

Overbye, E. (2005) 'Dilemmas in Disability Activation and How Scandinavians Try to Live with them' In P. Saunders (ed.), *Welfare to Work in Practice* (Aldershot: Ashgate).

Øvretveit, J. (2003) 'Nordic Privatization and Private Health Care', *International Journal of Health Planning and Management*, 18, 233–46.

Palier, B. (1999) 'Du salaire différé aux charges sociales: les avatars du mode de financement du système français de Sécurité sociale', *EUI Working Paper, EUF 99/11*, (Florence: European University Institute).

Palier, B. and Martin C. (2007) 'From "a Frozen Landscape" to Structural Reforms: The Sequential Transformation of Bismarckian Welfare Systems', *Social Policy and Administration*, 41(6), pp. 535–54.

Papatheodorou, C. and Petmesidou, M. (2006) 'Poverty Profiles and Trends. How do Southern European Countries Compare with Each Other?' In M. Petmesidou and C. Papatheodorou (eds), *Poverty and Social Deprivation in the Mediterranean. Trends, Policies and Welfare Prospects in the New Millennium* (London: Zed Books).

Pateman, C. (1989) 'The Patriarchal Welfare State' In C. Pateman, *The Disorder of Women: Democracy, Deminism and Political Theory* (Cambridge: Polity Press), pp. 179–209.

Pearson, M. and Martin, J.P. (2005) 'Should We Extend the Role of Private Social Expenditure?', *OECD Social, Employment and Migration Working Papers*, No. 23 (Paris: OECD).

Pedersen, K.M. (2005) 'The Public–Private Mix in Scandinavia' In A. Maynard (ed.) *The Public–Private Mix for Health* (Oxford: Radcliffe Publishing), pp. 161–90.

Peng, I. (2002) 'Gender and Welfare State Restructuring in Japan' In C. Aspalter (ed.), *Discovering the Welfare State in East Asia* (Westport, Connecticut and London: Praeger).

Peng, I. (2005) 'The New Politics of the Welfare State in a Developmental Context: Explaining the 1990s Social Care Expansion in Japan' In H.-J. Kwon (ed.), *Transforming the Developmental Welfare State in East Asia* (Basingstoke: Palgrave/UNRISD).

Pennings, F. (1990) *Benefits of Doubt: A Comparative Study of the Unemployment Benefits and Reintegration Opportunities of Great Britain, France, the Federal Republic of Germany and the Netherlands* (The Hague: Springer).

Pensions Commission (2004) *Pensions: Challenges and Choices. The First Report of the Pensions Commission* (London: HMSO).

Pereira da Silva, C.M., Vaz-Paralta, S.S. and Marcos, S. (2006) 'Presentation of the Recent Retirement Reforms in Portugal', *Revue Française des Affaires Sociales*, no. 1, 253–70.

Perrons, D. (2006) 'Squeezed Between Two Agendas: Work and Childcare in the Flexible UK' In J. Lewis (ed.) *Children, Changing Families and Welfare States* (Cheltenham: Edward Elgar), pp. 243–66.

Peters, B.G. (2005) 'I'm OK, You're (Not) OK: The Private Welfare State in the United States', *Social Policy and Administration*, 39(2), 166–80.

Petmesidou, M. (2006a) 'Tracking Social Protection: Origins, Path Peculiarity, Impasses and Prospects' In M. Petmesidou and E. Mossialos (eds), *Social Policy Developments in Greece* (Aldershot: Ashgate).

Petmesidou, M. (2006b) 'Social Care Services: "Catching up" amidst High Fragmentation and Poor Initiatives for Change' In M. Petmesidou and E. Mossialos (eds), *Social Policy Developments in Greece* (Aldershot: Ashgate).

Petmesidou, M. and Mossialos, E. (eds) (2006) *Social Policy Developments in Greece* (Aldershot: Ashgate).

Pfau-Effinger, B. (2006) 'Cultures of Childhood and the Relationship of Care and Employment in European Welfare States' In J. Lewis (ed.) *Children, Changing Families and Welfare States* (Cheltenham: Edward Elgar), pp. 137–53.

Piachaud, D. (1986) 'Disability, Retirement and the Unemployment of Older Men', *Journal of Social Policy*, 15(2), 145–62.

Pierson, P. (1994) *Dismantling the Welfare State* (Cambridge: Cambridge University Press).

Pierson, P. (1996) 'The New Politics of the Welfare State', *World Politics*, 48(2), 143–79.

Pierson, P. (ed.) (2001a) *The New Politics of the Welfare State* (Oxford: Oxford University Press).

Pierson, P. (2001b) 'Coping with Permanent Austerity: Welfare State Restructuring in Affluent Democracies' In P. Pierson (ed.), *The New Politics of the Welfare State* (Oxford: Oxford University Press), pp. 410–56.

Pierson, P. (2004) *Politics in Time. History, Institutions, and Social Analysis* (Princeton: Princeton University Press).

Ploug, N. (2001) 'Det danska ålderspensionssystemet – ful ankung eller vacker svan?' In J. Palme (ed.), *Privata och offentlige pensionsreformer i Norden – slut på folkpensionsmodellen?* (Stockholm: Pensionsforum), pp. 10–32.

Ploug, N. (2004) 'The Danish Employment Miracle: Contents and Impact of Institutional Reform of Labour Market Policies in Denmark in the 1990s', Unpublished manuscript.

Polanyi, K. (2001 [1944]) *The Great Transformation. The Political and Economic Origins of Our Time.* 2nd paperback edition (Boston: Beacon Press).

Pollock, A. (2004) *NHS PLC: The Privatisation of Our Health Care* (London: Verso).

Poovey, M. (1995) *Making a Social Body: British Cultural Formation 1830–1864* (Chicago: University of Chicago Press).

Potůček, M. (1999) *Not Only the Market. The Role of the Market, Government and Civic Sector in the Development of Postcommunist Societies* (Budapest: CEU Press).

Potůček, M. (2004) 'Accession and Social Policy: The Case of the Czech Republic', *Journal of European Social Policy*, 14(3), 253–66.

Potůček, M. (2007) 'Czech National Action Plan on Social Inclusion 2004–2006: Did it Matter?', *Prague Social Science Studies, PPF-024*, (Prague: Faculty of Social Sciences, Charles University).

Powell, M. (1996) 'Granny's Footsteps, Fractures and the Principles of the NHS', *Critical Social Policy*, 16(2), 27–44.

Powell, M. (1997) *Evaluating the National Health Service* (Buckingham: Open University Press).

Powell, M. (1999) *New Labour, New Welfare State?* (Bristol: Policy Press).

Powell, M. (2002) *Evaluating New Labour's Welfare Reforms* (Bristol: Policy Press).

Powell, M. (2003) 'Quasi-markets in British Health Policy: A *longue duree* Perspective', *Social Policy and Administration*, 37(7), 725–41.

Powell, M. (ed.) (2007) *Understanding the Mixed Economy of Welfare* (Bristol: Policy Press).

Powell, M. and Hewitt, M. (2002) *Welfare State and Welfare Change* (Buckingham: Open University Press).

Power, M. (1997) *The Audit Society* (Oxford: Clarendon Press).

PPI (2006) *An Evaluation of the White Paper State Pension Reform Proposals* (London: Pensions Policy Institute), Available online at http://www.pensionspolicyinstitute.org.uk/uploadeddocuments/Nuffield/PPI_evaluation_of_WP_state_pension_reforms_20_July_2006.pdf (accessed October).

Propper, C., Wilson, D. and Burgess, S. (2006) 'Extending Choice in English Health Care: The Implications of the Economic Evidence', *Journal of Social Policy*, 35(4), 537–57.

Quinlan, M., Mayhew, C. and Bohle, P. (2001) 'The Global Expansion of Precarious Employment, Work Disorganization, and the Consequences for Occupational Health', *International Journal of Health Services*, 31(2), 335–414.

Rae, D. (2005) 'How to Reduce Sickness Absences in Sweden: Lessons from International Experience', *OECD Economics Department Working Papers*, No. 442 (Paris: OECD).

Raitano, M. (2007) 'The Italian Pension System and Social Inclusion' In T. Meyer, P. Bridgen and B. Riedmüller (eds), *Private Pensions versus Social Inclusion? Non-state Provision for Citizens at Risk in Europe* (Cheltenham, UK and Northampton, US: Edward Elgar).

Rapoport, R., Bailyn, L., Fletcher, J.K. and Pruitt, B.H. (2002) *Beyond Work–Family Balance: Advancing Gender Equity and Workplace Performance* (Chicester: Wiley).

Rasmussen, M. (2006) 'Work First: Explaining the Drop in Disability Claims in Denmark' In P.A. Kemp, A. Sundén and B. Bakker Tauritz (eds) *Sick Societies? Trends in Disability Benefits in Post-industrial Welfare States* (Geneva: International Social Security Association).

Rasmussen, M., Balkus, R., Wiseman, M., Sunden, A. and Svensson, I. (2006) 'The Disability Benefit Programme and its Alternatives' In P.A. Kemp, A. Sundén and B. Bakker Tauritz (eds) *Sick Societies? Trends in Disability Benefits in Post-industrial Welfare States* (Geneva: International Social Security Association).

Rebick, M. (2005) *The Japanese Employment System: Adapting to a New Economic Environment* (Oxford: Oxford University Press).

Rein, M. and Schmähl, W. (eds) (2004) *Rethinking the Welfare State. The Political Economy of Pension Reform* (Cheltenham: Edward Elgar).

Research Institute for Labour and Social Affairs (2007) *Main Economic and Social Indicators of the Czech Republic 1990–2006* (Prague: Vydal Výzkumný ústav práce a sociálních věcí, v.v.i.). Available at http://www.vupsv.cz/fulltext/BullNo22.pdf

Riedmüller, B. and Willert, M. (2007) 'The German Pension System and Social Inclusion' In T. Meyer, P. Bridgen and B. Riedmüller (eds), *Private Pensions versus Social Inclusion? Non-state Provision for Citizens at Risk in Europe* (Cheltenham, UK and Northampton, US: Edward Elgar).

Roberts, G. (2002) 'Pinning Hopes on Angels: Reflections from an Ageing Japan's Urban Landscape' In R. Goodman (ed.) *Family and Social Policy in Japan: Anthropological Approaches* (Cambridge: Cambridge University Press).

Rodríguez Cabrero, G. (2004) *El Estado del Bienestar en España: debates, desarrollo y retos* (Madrid: Editorial Fundamentos).

Rosenbrock, R. and Gerlinger, T. (2006) *Gesundheitspolitik. Eine systematische Einführung.* 2nd Edition (Bern: Verlag Hans Huber).

Rostgaard, T. (2006) 'Constructing the Care Consumer: Free Choice of Home Care for the Elderly in Denmark', *European Societies*, 8(3), 443–63.

Rothgang, H. (2006) 'Die Regulierung von Gesundheitssystemen in vergleichender Perspektive: Auf dem Weg zur Konvergenz?' In C. Wolf and C. Wendt (eds) *Soziologie der Gesundheit.* Special issue (46/2006) of the *Kölner Zeitschrift für Soziologie und Sozialpsychologie* (Wiesbaden: VS Verlag für Sozialwissenschaften), pp. 298–319.

Rothgang, H., Cacace, M. and Schmid, A. (2006) 'Blurring Regimes' In *Healthcare: Convergence in Financing, Service Provision and Regulation of Healthcare?* Paper presented at the 4th ESPAnet Conference at the University of Bremen, 21–23 September. Stream No. 10: Health Market and Social Policy.

Rothgang, H., Schmid, A. and Wendt, C. (forthcoming) 'The Self-Regulatory German Health Care System Between Growing Competition and State Hierarchy' In H. Rothgang, M. Cacace, S. Grimmeisen, U. Helmert and C. Wendt, *The Changing Role of the State in OECD Health Care Systems. From Heterogeneity to Homogeneity?* (Basingstoke: Palgrave Macmillan).

Rothgang, H., Cacace, M., Grimmeisen, S. and Wendt, C. (2005) 'The Changing Role of the State in Health Care Systems' In S. Leibfried and M. Zürn (eds), *Transformations of the State?* (Cambridge: Cambridge University Press).

Rothstein, B. (1992) 'Labor Market Institutions and Working-Class Strength' In S. Steinmo, K. Thelen and F. Longstreth (eds), *Structuring Politics: Historical Institutionalism in a Comparative Perspective* (Cambridge: Cambridge University Press), pp. 33–56.

Ruane, S. (1997) 'Public–Private Boundaries and the Transformation of the NHS', *Critical Social Policy*, 17(2), 53–78.

Rubery, J. (2002) 'Gender Mainstreaming and Gender Equality in the EU: The Impact of the EU Employment Strategy', *Industrial Relations Journal*, 33(5), 500–22.

Rubery, J., Grimshaw, D., et al. (2003) 'Gender Equality Still on the European Agenda – But for How Long?', *Industrial Relations Journal*, 34(5), pp. 477–97.

Russell, H. and Whelan, C.T. (2003) *Income, Deprivation, Economic Strain and Multiple Disadvantage in the Candidate Countries* (Dublin: Economic and Social Research Institute).

Rys, V. (2001) 'Transition Countries of Central Europe Entering the European Union: Some Social Protection Issues', *International Social Security Review*, 52(2–3), 177–89.

Rzeczpospolita (2005) 'Moje Pieniądze. *Różnice są dość duże'*, Suplement.

Samek, M. (2000) 'The Dynamics of Labour Market Reform in Europe' In G. Esping-Andersen and M. Regini (eds), *Why Deregulate Labour Markets?* (Oxford: Oxford University Press), pp. 35–60.

Saraceno, C. (ed.) (2002) *Social Assistance Dynamics in Europe* (Bristol: Policy Press).

Sass, S. (1997) *The Promise of Private Pensions. The First Hundred Years* (Cambridge, MA: Harvard University Press).

Sass, S. (2006) 'Anglo-Saxon Occupational Pensions in International Perspective' In H. Pemberton, P. Thane and N. Whiteside (eds), *Britain's Pension Crisis: History and Policy* (Oxford: Oxford University Press), pp. 191–207.

Schlüter, P. (1982) Inaugural Speech, Danish Parliament, Oct. 5. www.dansketaler.dk

Schmid, A., Cacace, M. and Rothgang, H. (forthcoming) 'Convergence in Health Care Systems: Blurring of Regimes in Germany, Britain, and the United States', *TranState Working Paper*, (Bremen: TranState Research Center).

Schmid, G., Reisset, B. and Bruche, G. (1992) *Unemployment Insurance and Active Labour Market Policy: An International Comparison of Financing Systems* (Detroit: Wayne State University Press).

Schmidt, V.A. (2002) *The Futures of European Capitalism* (Oxford: Oxford University Press).

Schneider, F. (2002) 'The Size and Development of the Shadow Economies of 22 Transition and 21 OECD Countries', *Discussion Paper*, No. 514 (Bonn: Institute of Labour Studies).

Scruggs, L. (2004) 'Generosity Index'. Welfare State Entitlements Data Set: A Comparative Institutional Analysis of Eighteen Welfare States, Version 1.2., updated 4/2/06.

Scruggs, L. and Allan, J. (2006) 'Welfare-state Decommodification in 18 OECD Countries: a Replication and Revision', *Journal of European Social Policy*, 16(1), 55–72.

Seeleib-Kaiser, M. (1995) 'The Development of Social Assistance and Unemployment Insurance in Germany and Japan', *Social Policy and Administration*, 29(3), 269–93.

Seeleib-Kaiser, M. (2001) *Globalisierung und Sozialpolitik* (Frankfurt/M.: Campus).

Seeleib-Kaiser, M. (2002) 'A Dual Transformation of the German Welfare State?', *West European Politics*, 25(4), 25–48.

Seeleib-Kaiser, M. (2006) 'Japan' In T. Fitzpatrick, H.-ju Kwon, N. Manning, J. Midgley and G. Pascall (eds), *International Encyclopedia of Social Policy*. Vol. 2 (London: Routledge).

Seeleib-Kaiser, M. and Fleckenstein, T. (2007) 'Discourse, Learning and Welfare State Change: The Case of German Labour Market Reforms', *Social Policy and Administration*, 41(5), 427–48.

Seeleib-Kaiser, M., van Dyk, S., and Roggenkamp, M. (2008) *Party Politics and Social Welfare: Comparing Christian and Social Democracy in Austria, Germany and the Netherlands* (Cheltenham: Edward Elgar).

Sengoku, M. (2006) *Emerging Eastern European Welfare States: A Variant of the 'European' Welfare Model?* (Available at http://src-h.slav.hokudai.ac.jp/coe21/publish/no2_ses/3–2_Sengoku.pdf).

Shalev, M. (ed.) (1996) *The Privatization of Social Policy. Occupational Welfare and the Welfare State in America, Scandinavia and Japan* (Basingstoke: Macmillan).

Sharma, A. and Gupta, A. (2006) 'Rethinking Theories of the State in an Age of Globalization' In A. Sharma and A. Gupta (eds), *The Anthropology of the State: A Reader* (Oxford: Blackwell Publishing).

Shonfield, A. (1965) *Modern Capitalism: The Changing Balance of Public and Private Power* (Oxford: Oxford University Press).

Siegel, N. (2002) *Baustelle Sozialpolitik.* (Frankfurt/M.: Campus).

Siegel, N. and Jochem, S. (2003) 'Staat und Markt im internationalen Vergleich – Empirische Mosaiksteine einer facettenreichen Arbeitsverschränkung' In R. Czada and R. Zintl (eds) *Politik und Markt.* Sonderheft der PVS 34/2003. (Wiesbaden: Verlag für Sozialwissenschaften), pp. 351–88.

Sigurgeirsdóttir, S. (forthcoming) 'The Icelandic National Health Service: The Trend Towards State Centralisation and Private Provision' In H. Rothgang, M. Cacace, S. Grimmeisen, U. Helmert and C. Wendt (eds) *Financing, Providing, and Regulating Health Care. The Role of the State in Twelve OECD Health Care Systems from 1970 till Today* (Buckingham: Open University Press).

Sinfield, A. (1978) 'Analyses in the Social Division of Welfare', *Journal of Social Policy*, 7(2), 129–56.

Sinfield, A. (2007) 'Tax welfare' In M. Powell (ed.) *Understanding the Mixed Economy of Welfare* (Bristol: Policy Press), pp. 129–48.

Sirovátka, T. (2007a) Efektivita opatření aktivní politiky zaměstnanosti a její podmínky. Unpublished manuscript, (Brno: Masaryk University).

Sirovátka, T. (2007b) 'The Work and Social Assistance Act (WWB) in the Netherlands'. Peer Review, 4–5 June.

Skocpol, T. (1994) 'Is the Time Finally Ripe? Health Insurance Reforms in the 1990s' In J.A. Morone and G.S. Belkin (eds) *The Politics of Health Care Reform – Lessons from the Past, Prospects for the Future* (Durham, NC and London: Duke University Press), pp. 57–76.

Slaughter, A.-M. (2004) *A New World Order* (Princeton, NJ: Princeton University Press).

Slaughter, S. and Rhoades, G. (2004) *Academic Capitalism and the New Economy. Markets, State, and Higher Education* (Baltimore: Johns Hopkins University Press).

Smeaton, D. and Marsh, A. (2006) 'Maternity and Paternity Rights and Benefits: Survey of Parents 2005', *Employment Relations Research Series*, No. 50 (London: Department of Trade and Industry).

Smithies, R. (2005) 'Public and Private Welfare Activity in the United Kingdom, 1979 to 1999', *CASEpaper* 93 (London: LSE).

Smithson, J. and Stokoe, E.H. (2005) 'Discourses of Work–Life Balance: Negotiating "Genderblind" Terms in Organizations', *Gender, Work and Organization*, 12(2), 147–68.

Social Protection Committee (2006) 'Current and Prospective Theoretical Pension Replacement Rates, Report by the Indicators Sub-Group (ISG) of the (SPC) – 19th May 2006'.

Sol, E. and Westerveld, M. (eds) (2005) *Contractualism in Employment Services: A New Form of Welfare Governance* (The Hague: Kluwer).

Spicker, P. (2003) 'Distinguishing Disability and Incapacity', *International Social Security Review*, 56(2), 31–43.

Standing, G. (2001) *Beyond the New Paternalism: Basic Security as Equality* (London: Verso).

Statistics Denmark (2006). *Statistik Tiårsoversigt 2003* (Copenhagen: Statistics Denmark).

Statistics New Zealand (2005) *New Zealand Long Term Data Series*. Health, Table C5.5 (Wellington: Statistics New Zealand).

Statistik Norway (2006) *Spesialisthelsetjenesten. Aktivitet og senger/døgnplasser, etter landsdel og tjenesteområde*. Tabell:04434. Retrieved from: http://statbank.ssb.no.

Statistisches Bundesamt (various issues) *Gesundheitswesen. Grunddaten der Krankenhäuser und Vorsorge- oder Rehabilitationseinrichtungen*. Fachserie 12/ Reihe 6.1. (Wiesbaden: Statistisches Bundesamt).

Stenson, K. (2000) 'Crime Control, Social Policy and Liberalism' In G. Lewis, S. Gewirtz and J. Clarke (eds), *Rethinking Social Policy* (London: Sage/The Open University).

Stepan, A. and Sommersguter-Reichmann, M. (2005) 'Monitoring Political Decision-Making and its Impact in Austria', *Health Economics*, 14, 7–23.

Stewart, J. (2004) *Taking Stock: Scottish Social Welfare after Devolution* (Bristol: Policy Press).

Stewart, J. (2007) 'The Mixed Economy of Welfare in Historical Context' In M. Powell (ed.) *Understanding the Mixed Economy of Welfare* (Bristol: Policy Press), pp. 23–40.

Stigler, G.J. (1987) 'Competition' In J. Eatwell, M. Milgate, and P. Newman (eds), *The New Palgrave: A Dictionary of Economics*. Vol. I (New York: Norton), pp. 531–46.

Stone, D. (2000) 'United States', *Journal of Health Politics, Policy and Law*, 25(5), 953–8.

Stratigaki, M. (2004). 'The Cooption of Gender Concepts in EU Policies: The Case of "Reconciliation of Work and Family"', *Social Politics*, 11(1), 30–56.

Streeck, W. and Thelen, K. (eds) (2005a) *Beyond Continuity. Institutional Change in Advanced Political Economies* (Oxford: Oxford University Press).

Streeck, W. and Thelen, K. (2005b) 'Introduction: Institutional Change in Advanced Political Economies' In W. Streeck and K. Thelen (eds), *Beyond Continuity. Institutional Change in Advanced Political Economies* (Oxford: Oxford University Press), pp. 1–39.

Streeck, W. and Trampusch, C. (2005) 'Economic Reform and the Political Economy of the German Welfare State', *German Politics*, 14(2), 174–95.

Strehl, R. (2003) 'Privatisierungswelle im deutschen Krankenhauswesen?' In M. Arnold, J. Klauber and H. Schellschmidt (eds), *Krankenhaus-Report 2002. Schwerpunkt: Krankenhaus im Wettbewerb* (Stuttgart and New York: Schattauer-Verlag), 113–29.

Swedish Social Insurance Agency (2002) *Social Insurance in Sweden 2002* (Stockholm: Swedish Social Insurance Agency).

Sykes, R. (1998) 'Studying European Social Policy – Issues and Perspectives' In R. Sykes and P. Alcock (eds), *Developments in European Social Policy: Convergence and Diversity* (Bristol: Policy Press).

Szebehely, M. (ed.) (2005) *Äldreomsorgsforsknin i Norden. En kunnskapsöversikt* (Copenhagen: Nordisk Ministerråd).

Tachibanaki, T. (2005) 'Jakusha no Hinkonka ga Kakusa wo Jochō' ('The Rising Tide of Poverty in Japan'), *Ronza*, June, 102–7.

Tavares, L. and Alves, A. (2007) 'The Future of Portuguese Public Administration and a New Agenda for Public Administration Sciences in the 21st Century', *Public Administration*, 84(2), 389–406.

Taylor-Gooby, P. (2002) 'The Silver Age of the Welfare State: Perspectives on Resilience', *Journal of Social Policy*, 31(4), 597–621.

Taylor-Gooby, P. (2004a) *New Risks, New Welfare. The Transformation of the European Welfare State* (Oxford: Oxford University Press).

Taylor-Gooby, P. (2004b) 'New Risks and Social Change' In P. Taylor-Gooby (ed.), *New Risks, New Welfare: The Transformation of the European Welfare State* (Oxford: Oxford University Press).

Taylor-Gooby, P., Larsen, T. and Kananen, J. (2004) 'Market Means and Welfare Ends: The UK Welfare State Experiment', *Journal of Social Policy*, 33(4), 573–92.

Thatcher, M. (1993) *The Downing Street Years* (London: Harper Collins).

Thelen, K. (2003) 'How Institutions Evolve: Insights from Comparative Historical Analysis' In J. Mahoney and D. Rueschemeyer (eds), *Comparative Historical Analysis in the Social Sciences* (Cambridge: Cambridge University Press).

Timmins, N. (2001) *The Five Giants*. 2nd Edition (London: HarperCollins).

Titmuss, R. (1958) 'The Social Division of Welfare: Some Reflections on the Search for Equity' In R. Titmuss *Essays on The Welfare State* (London: George Allen and Unwin), pp. 34–55.

Titmuss, R. (1976) *Essays on the Welfare State*. 3rd Edition (London: George Allen and Unwin).

tns Infratest (2005). Situation und Entwicklung der betrieblichen Altersversorgung in Privatwirtschaft und öffentlichem Dienst 2001 – 2004. Endbericht. München.

Toivonen, T. (2007) 'Is Japanese Family Policy Turning Nordic?' *Barnett Paper in Social Research*, 2007/1. (Oxford: Department of Social Policy and Social Work, University of Oxford).

Topalov, C. (1994) *La naissance du chômeur: 1880–1910* (Paris: Albin Michel).

Torfing, J. (1999) 'Workfare with Welfare: Recent Reforms of the Danish Welfare State', *Journal of European Social Policy*, 9(1), 5–28.

Torfing, J. (2004) *Det stille sporskifte i velfærdsstaten. En diskursteoretisk beslutningsprocesanalyse* (Aarhus: Aarhus University Press).

Torres L. and Pina, V. (2004) 'Reshaping Public Administration: The Spanish Experience Compared to the UK', *Public Administration*, 82(2), 445–64.

Townsend, P. (1979) *Poverty in the United Kingdom. A Survey of Household Resources and Standards of Living* (Harmondsworth: Penguin).

Toynbee, P. and Walker, D. (2005) *Better or Worse? Has Labour Delivered?* (London: Bloomsbury).

Trampusch, C. (2005) 'Institutional Resettlement: The Case of Early Retirement in Germany' In W. Streeck and K. Thelen (eds), *Beyond Continuity: Institutional Change in Advanced Political Economies* (Oxford: Oxford University Press).

Tranæs, T., Jensen, B. and Gervasini Nielsen, M. (2006) *A Comparison of Welfare Payments to Asylum Seekers, Refugees, and Reunified Families in Selected European Countries and in Canada* (Copenhagen: The Rockwool Foundation Research Unit).

Tuohy, C.H. (1999) *Accidental Logics* (New York: Oxford University Press).

Tuohy, C.H., Colleen, M.F. and Stabile, M. (2004) 'How Does Private Finance Affect Public Health Care Systems? Marshalling the Evidence from OECD Nations', *Journal of Health Politics, Policy and Law*, 29(3), 359–96.

Udliciteringsraadet (2004) *Konkurrenceudsættelse af velfærdsydelser i Sverige* (Copenhagen: Udliciteringsraadet).

Udliciteringsraadet (2005) *Gennemgang af kommunale opgavers udbudshyppighed* (Copenhagen: Udliciteringsraadet).

Udredningsudvalget (1992) *Udredningsudvalget vedr. arbejdsmarkedets strukturproblemer; Rapport om arbejdsmarkedets strukturproblemer.* Del I (Copenhagen: Udredningsudvalget).

UNICEF (2001), 'A Decade of Transition', *Regional Monitoring Report*, No. 8, (Florence: UNICEF Innocenti Research Centre).

Úřad státního dozoru v pojišt'ovnictví a penzijním připojištění (2005) *Výroční zpráva za rok 2004* (Prague: Ministerstvo financí ČR).

US OMB (2006) *Analytical Perspectives, Budget of the United States Government, Fiscal Year 2007* (Washington, DC: GPO).

Vahtera, J., Kivimaki, M., Forma, P., Wikström, J., Halmeenmäki, J., Linna, A. and Pentti, J. (2005) 'Organisational Downsizing as a Predictor of Disability Pension: the 10-town Prospective Cohort Study', *Journal of Epidemiology and Community Health*, vol. 59, 238–42.

Van Berkel, R. (2007) *Making it Personal* (Bristol: Policy Press).

Van de Ven, W.P.M.M. (1996) 'Market-oriented Health Care Reforms: Trends and Future Options', *Social Science & Medicine*, 43(5), 655–66.

Van Kersbergen, K. (1995) *Social Capitalism: A Study of Christian Democracy and the Welfare State* (London: Routledge).

Van Kersbergen, K. (2000) 'The Declining Resistance of Welfare States to Change?' In S. Kuhnle (ed.), *Survival of the European Welfare State* (London: Routledge), pp. 19–36.

Van Oorschot, W. and Boos, K. (2000) 'The Battle against the Numbers: Disability Policies in the Netherlands', *European Journal of Social Security*, 2(4), 343–61.

Van Riel, B., Hemerijck, A. and Visser, J. (2003) 'Is there a Dutch Way to Pension Reform?' In G. Clark and N. Whiteside (eds), *Pension Security in the 21st Century* (Oxford: Oxford University Press), pp. 64–91.

Večerník, J. (2005) 'Proměny a problémy české sociální politiky', *Sociologický časopis/Czech Sociological Review*, 41(5), 863–80.

Visser, J. and Hemerijck, A. (1997) *A Dutch Miracle: Job Growth, Welfare Reform and Corporatism in the Netherlands* (Amsterdam: Amsterdam University Press).

Vogel, E.F. (1980) *Japan as Number One: Lessons for America* (Tokyo: Tuttle).

Walker, R. and Howard, M. (2000) *The Making of a Welfare Class? Benefits Receipt in Britain* (Bristol: Policy Press).

Walters, W. (1996) 'The Demise of Unemployment?', *Politics and Society*, 24(3), 197–219.

Walters, W. (2000) *Unemployment and Government: Genealogies of the Social* (Cambridge: Cambridge University Press).

Warin, J., Joseph Rowntree Foundation., et al. (1999) *Fathers, Work and Family Life* (London: Family Policy Studies Centre for the Joseph Rowntree Foundation).

Watanuki, J. (1986) 'Is there a "Japanese-Type Welfare Society"?', *International Sociology*, 1(3), 259–69.

Webb, P. (2002) 'Time to Share the Burden: Long Term Care Insurance and the Japanese Family', *Japanese Studies*, 22(2), 113–29.

Wedel, J. (2000) *Collision and Collusion: The Strange Case of Western Aid to Eastern Europe* (New York: Palgrave).

Wendt, C., Frisina, L. and Rothgang, H. (forthcoming 2008) 'Healthcare System Types – A Conceptual Framework for Comparison', *TranState Working Paper* (Bremen: TranState Research Center).

Wendt, C., Grimmeisen, S. and Rothgang, H. (2005a) 'Convergence or Divergence of OECD Health Care Systems' In I. Marx (ed.), *International Cooperation in Social Security, How to Cope With Globalisation?* (Antwerpen: Intersentia), pp. 15–45.

Wendt, C., Rothgang, H. and Helmert, U. (2005b) 'The Self-regulatory German Health Care System Between Growing Competition and State Hierarchy', *TranState Working Paper* No. 32 (Bremen: TranState Research Center).

Westerveld, M. and Faber, K. (2005) 'Client Contracting in Social Security in the Netherlands' In E. Sol and M. Westerveld (eds), *Contractualism in Employment Services: A New Form of Welfare Governance* (The Hague: Kluwer).

Whelan, C. and McGinnity, F. (2000) 'Unemployment and Satisfaction: A European Analysis' In D. Gallie and S. Paugam (eds), *Welfare Regimes and the Experience of Unemployment in Europe* (Oxford: Oxford University Press), pp. 286–306.

White, S. (2003) *The Civic Minimum* (Oxford: Oxford University Press).

Whiteside, N. (2003) 'Historical Perspectives and the Politics of Pension Reform' In G. Clark and N. Whiteside (eds), *Pension Security in the 21st Century* (Oxford: Oxford University Press), pp. 21–43.

Whiteside, N. (2006) 'Adapting Private Pensions to Public Purposes: Historical Perspectives on the Politics of Reform', *Journal of European Social Policy* 16(1), 43–54.

WHO (2006) *European Health-for-all Database.* Available at: www.euro.who.int/hfadb

Wierink, M. (2000) 'Pays-Bas: Réforme des structures de la protection sociale et révision de la place des partenaires sociaux', *Chronique Internationale de l'IRES*, no. 64, 26–38.

Wilensky, H.L. (2002) *Rich Democracies. Political Economy, Public Policy, and Performance* (Berkeley: University of California Press).

Williams, F. (2004) *Rethinking Families* (London: Calouste Gulbenkian Foundation).

Williams, F. (2005) 'New Labour's Family Policy' In M. Powell, L. Bauld and K. Clarke (eds) *Analysis and Debate in Social Policy, 2005* (Bristol: Policy Press), pp. 289–302.

Williams, R. (1976) *Keywords: A Vocabulary of Culture and Society* (London: Fontana).

Wilthagen, T., Tros, F. and van Lieshout, H. (2004) 'Towards 'flexicurity'? Balancing Flexibility and Security in EU Member States', *European Journal of Social Security*, 6(2), 113–36.

World Bank (1994) *Averting the Old Age Crisis: Policies to Protect the Old and Promote Growth* (Oxford University Press: Oxford).

Zaidi, A., Marin, B. and Fuchs, M. (2006) *Pension Policy in EU25 and its Possible Impact on Elderly Poverty* (Vienna: European Centre for Social Welfare Policy and Research).

Zweifel, P. (2000) 'Switzerland', *Journal of Health Politics, Policy and Law*, 25(5), 937–44.

Index